A History *of* Chicago *in* Ten Stories

〔 RICHARD B. FIZDALE 〕

AMP&RSAND, INC.

Chicago · New Orleans

ISBN 978-1-4675-4528-0

Design
David Robson, Robson Design

Published by
AMPERSAND, INC.
1050 North State Street
Chicago, Illinois 60610

———

203 Finland Place
New Orleans, Louisiana 70131

———

www.ampersandworks.com

Published and Produced in the United States of America.
Printed in China.

ENDSHEET PHOTOGRAPHY: BART HARRIS, CHICAGO

To Suzanne, you encouraged me to write, assured me that I could write and when I wanted to give up, you prodded me with equal measures of prickliness and love to get back to it. Without you there would be no book, confirming what I've known for a long time—you are the enduring love of my life.

A letter to the *Chicago Tribune* and the response
from their OUR TOWN column, April 12, 1964:

I have an address WHICH CANNOT EXIST!
It's 999 N. Lake Shore dr. and it's all wrong.
The building is on the wrong side of the street,
where even numbers are assigned, but it has an
odd number. Also, the number is out of sequence.
Am I wrong? Or how come?

DISGUSTED R. L. R.

It's all wrong according to the bureau of maps. The building, with a long frontage on Lake Shore drive and a corner entrance where the drive turns east and west in the vicinity of Oak street, never was assigned such a number, said W. R. Anthon, superintendent of maps. In addition the last number going north before the drive turns east and west should be 954, he said. Apparently 999 has been there for years. OUR TOWN left Mr. Anthon shaking his head and muttering "999...999..."

CONTENTS

FOREWORD 9

INTRODUCTION
On the Shores of *Mishigami* 19

THE PREHISTORY OF 999

CHAPTER ONE	The Disappearance of the North Side.............................	25
CHAPTER TWO	The Meandering Shore..	29
CHAPTER THREE	A Prescient Plan...	34
CHAPTER FOUR	The Visionary..	37
CHAPTER FIVE	The Con Man Cometh...	45
CHAPTER SIX	Stop and Go and Stop...	50
CHAPTER SEVEN	Senator Bartling and Attorney General Moloney Go to War	54
CHAPTER EIGHT	Streeter Redux	63
CHAPTER NINE	The Millionaires' Colony	72
CHAPTER TEN	Who Were Those Guys?	75

HISTORY

CHAPTER ELEVEN	The Address	86
CHAPTER TWELVE	A Rental Building to a Co-operative to Rental to Co-op.................	89

THEY LIVED AT 999

	Sidebar: A Guide to Reading the Residents' Entries	94
CHAPTER THIRTEEN	1912–19: The Originals	95
CHAPTER FOURTEEN	1920–29: Settling In..	115
	Sidebar: The Heiress Who Married a Ghost......................................	121
	Sidebar: The Flying Squadron Led by a Cadillac..............................	145
CHAPTER FIFTEEN	1930–46: The Difficult Years	148
	Sidebar: The Birds and Beasts Were There..	161
CHAPTER SIXTEEN	1947–2013: The New Status Quo...................................	166
	"A" Units..	167
	Sidebar: The Car of Tomorrow, Today...	184
	"B" Units and Penthouse	188
	"C" Units	200

CHAPTER SEVENTEEN	FOREVER RELEVANT	214

AFTERWORD 225

ACKNOWLEDGEMENTS 229

SELECTED REFERENCES.. 232

INDEX 252

ABOUT THE AUTHOR 259

At the beginning of this project, before I had written a word about 999 Lake Shore Drive, I mentioned the possibility of the book to someone familiar with East Lake Shore Drive. "Why bother?" she asked. "Your building has no pedigree."

I inscribed her snide remark on the blackboard of my mind. "Well, we shall see."

When I started 999, I possessed a few grains of factual information about the building and, perhaps a wheelbarrow full of misconceptions. This is what I thought I knew: 999 sits on landfill, when and how it got there were mysteries; the architect was the esteemed Benjamin H. Marshall, a Chicago genius worthy of a place in the same architectural pantheon as Louis Sullivan, Dankmar Adler and Frank Lloyd Wright; Marshall's mother lived in the building, although no one remembered her name; 999 was always a co-op, a construct where the tenants own shares in the building and lease their apartments; the original address was 666, the devil's number. Some long-ago resident turned the dreaded 666 welcome-mat upside down, making it read 999 and the residents were saved. Or so the story goes. ☞

The legend of how the 666 was
transformed into 999 may be the stuff
of hushed tones around a campfire,
but it is 100% untrue.

I wanted to create a historically accurate narrative for the building. Unfortunately, between 1912, universally accepted as the year when 999 was completed, and 1991 when I purchased my shares, I knew nothing for certain. If I were going to write something longer than a couple of paragraphs, I needed to work my way up a steep learning curve, having no idea what that entailed or how long it would take. Three years were spent in the tedious pursuit of facts. I lived for the eureka moments when I would shout to my wife, "THE DUNCAN YO-YO MAN LIVED HERE!"

Eventually my notes contained thousands of randomly discovered, unordered factoids, waiting to be arranged into coherent history. A bit of everything I thought I knew was wrong and belonged in the wheelbarrow. For example Benjamin Marshall was a risky choice for an architect. He was a playboy, who wore all white suits, drove hot cars, dated showgirls and never spent one minute formally studying architecture. He wanted to be a tailor. In 1906 he co-founded the architectural firm of Marshall and Fox with Charles Eli Fox, a specialist in steel construction and project management. Marshall, who had an innate sense of design, was an excellent businessman who assembled a brilliant team of architects, designers, drafters, estimators and managers.

They formed the nuts and bolts of the Benjamin Marshall brand. A natural salesman, he worked his high society connections to secure some of Chicago's best projects during the late nineteenth and early twentieth centuries. He does not rank with Sullivan, Adler and Wright. What Marshall did better than anyone else was redefine the way wealthy people lived in an urban setting. When he built 999, he helped end a 40-year building drought, during which nothing went up between Pearson and Oak Streets.

Not a hiccup of evidence could be found supporting the presence of his mother, Celia F. Le Baillie Marshall, living in the building. 999 was not always a co-op. It was a rental building first and then a co-op; the cycle repeated itself: a rental building again in 1937 and ten years later a co-op for the last time. When and how the landfill was created turned out to be a power struggle between some of the most well-known families in the city and a rag-tag parade of ne'er-do-wells. That story occupies the first 83 pages of the book.

The legend of how the 666 was transformed into 999 may be the stuff of hushed tones around a campfire, but it is 100% untrue. The address was 999 before anybody lived there. It never was 666. Even if somebody turned a welcome mat around, it still would have read 666 from the other direction. Nevertheless the choice of 999 is confounding. It is

The address was 999 before anybody
lived there. It never was 666. Even
if somebody turned a welcome mat
around, it still would have read 666
from the other direction.

too large a number to stand next door to 229 East Lake Shore Drive and it's an odd number, which means it does not belong on the same side of the street as 990. Two published accounts, which don't happen to agree, explain the impossible address. Both explanations are in the book. For what it's worth, I favor the lucky number scenario over the world's fastest locomotive theory.

On March 17, 1913, the city building inspector approved 999 for occupancy. On that date in 2013, I sent a note to the building's residents declaring it our 100th anniversary. Subsequently I learned that at least two families—the Dickasons and the Baldwins—moved in during the fall of 1912. Occupancy rules must have been mushier in those days. Exact move-in dates proved impossible to ascertain. March 17th appears to be the day we were officially open for business. Meanwhile our actual 100th anniversary came and went on an unknown day in 2012.

999, the book, is divided into five sections. The *Introduction* is a salute to the most beautiful vintage building in Chicago. Described from many vantage points, its exterior architectural details are linked to the subjective effects they achieve.

The *Prehistory* of 999 details the story of a section of Lake Shore Drive from Lincoln Park to Grand Avenue and the influence it had on the landfill. I had assumed debris from the Chicago

Fire of October 8–10, 1871 was plowed into Lake Michigan north of the River, the way Lake Park was enlarged into Grant Park. But that's not what happened. The Fire did play a pivotal role. The wall of flames destroyed almost every building on the north side of Chicago, which, at the time, ended at Fullerton, ironically, exactly where the Fire also stopped. Before the Fire, the north side near the lake was the location of industries like breweries that needed access to water and a large number of men willing to work for low wages. Fortuitously an immigrant labor force lived between the Chicago River and Fullerton. Since the Streeterville land mass did not yet exist, the actual dimensions of the near north side were smaller than they are today. The water's edge meandered between Sand Street and Pine Street. Today we call them St. Clair and Michigan Avenue.

A battle over the best way to reinvent the north side began almost immediately. Eleven months after the Fire, an idea was presented to a group of millionaires that gradually gained traction over four decades. It called for the building of Lake Shore Drive in Lake Michigan beginning at Oak Street and ending at Indiana Street (Grand Avenue to us). That part of the plan was actually a subtle misdirection. Newspapers would report the pros and cons of a roadway in the lake

McClurg comes across as a fusion
of Indiana Jones, Random House,
Thomas Lipton and, whenever
he had a chance, as much Lothario
as he could muster.

and dazzle their readers with the wonders of pylons and esplanades.

The real game, however, had to do with submerged land. The construction of Lake Shore Drive would dredge up sand and clay, which would fill in the shallow water between the new location of the Drive and the old shore. The question of who owned this new above-water land became a mammoth legal confrontation, which occasionally turned violent. It pitted a consortium of millionaires against a host of wannabes—a folkloric figure, who lent his name to the neighborhood; a native American tribe that had converted to Catholicism; a couple of squatters, who acted as if they knew the law; the Federal Land Office whose top dog was a crook; a couple of swindlers and their lawyers working for a percentage of the take; and a crusading attorney general of Illinois, who believed the State owned it. All of them believed they had a legitimate claim to the land.

I left the Illinois Central Railroad out of the narrative. Their attempt to "own" the submerged land began before the Fire. The tail end of their court case ran concurrently with some of the significant events in the *Prehistory*. Their inclusion seemed like one ingredient too many in an already complex stew. The entire story is the stuff of cinema. It should have been filmed decades ago in the style of *Gangs of New York*.

But what does any of that have to do with 999?

During those years (1871–1910), gun battles took place all over Streeterville. There was one fatality. The intended victim murdered the hit man hired to kill him on the very land where 999's courtyard would one day be built. But the deepest connection between 999 and the battle for Streeterville is that its construction ended the war.

The *Prehistory* section concludes with biographical sketches of the three men who built 999—Ogden Trevor McClurg, who owned 75% of it, Stuart Gore Shepard, his 25% partner, and Benjamin Marshall.

McClurg comes across as a fusion of Indiana Jones, Random House, Thomas Lipton and, whenever he had a chance, as much Lothario as he could muster. To be sure, he was a lesser version of each, but that was enough to make him one of the most interesting people ever to live at 999. If the memory of Thomas Lipton has faded, it should not detract from the tea-maker's skill as a yachtsman. McClurg shared Lipton's passion for sailing races, but not his habit of losing.

By comparison, Stewart Gore Shepard seemed too straight-laced to pal around with McClurg. But he made a more lasting contribution. He co-founded a powerhouse law firm that still exists.

*Never having researched or written
a book, I stumbled forward like an
inexperienced archeologist, somehow
finding places to dig.*

Benjamin Marshall was so much a man of his time that the Roaring Twenties seem like they were created for him.

The *History* section is very brief and covers the genesis of 999's address, which officially is not 999, as well as the building's transitions back and forth from a rental building to a co-op.

They Lived at 999 is the centerpiece of the book. The initial concept was to list the names and apartments of *everybody* who ever lived in the building accompanied by brief biographies, which could be as short as a sentence, or as long as a few pages. Sadly, that mountain of good intentions could not be scaled. I could not identify every 999er, and, since I don't know exactly how many people lived here between opening day and this minute, I could not even calculate by how much I missed the mark. Nevertheless I am delighted with how many long lost residents were rediscovered—in total we identified 230 families and 677 people.

Never having researched or written a book, I stumbled forward like an inexperienced archeologist, somehow finding places to dig. Slowly, the names of people who lived at 999 were teased out of hiding. A favorite place to explore was the society pages in daily newspapers, which spewed forth trivialities about weddings, cotillions, charity balls, vacations, bridge tournaments, lectures, tea parties, grand openings, luncheons, college graduations, new dresses, new hats, new wallpaper— anything really, no matter how mundane. Its equivalent does not exist today. Society pages began a slow fade to black in the 1950s. The writers and editors of these upper crust comings and goings were not discreet. They printed names and addresses without regard to privacy, as in "*Mrs. John Winterbotham of 999 Lake Shore Drive wore a chic little dress embroidered in silver....*"

Perusing through *Who's Who in America*, social registers, cross-telephone directories, club memberships and lists of college graduates was dull sledding but almost always produced another name or two. *R. L. Polk's Directory*, a direct marketing tool started in the 1870s, contained the last name and first initial of additional 999 residents. Long form obituaries often mentioned industries worked in, jobs held, titles earned, hobbies practiced and the occasional home address. Old books, aging newspapers and vintage magazines coughed up details that imbued raw data with human dimension.

One of the best sources of information was the U.S. Census from 1920, 1930 and 1940. Every ten years the census bureau releases another decade's worth of data. For example, 1950 will be published in 2021. One of my happiest moments working on the book occurred on the day in

One of my happiest moments
working on the book occurred on the
day in 2011 that the 1940 census
became available online.

2011 that 1940 became available online.

The census is more than a list of people. The U.S. population is organized first by state, and then town, ward, street, address and individual name. So finding out who was living at 999 in 1920 was dumbbell simple. The head of household is listed first, followed by spouse, children, boarders and servants. Sex, age, citizenship, father's and mother's names, places of birth and occupations also were included on the census form. Taking a name in the census and typing it and other key words (banker, Chicago, 1920) into a sophisticated search engine often yielded pages of downloadable information and proved decisive in building biographies for most residents.

When it came to reading census data, handwriting was the hair in the butter. The census taker (the official job title is enumerator) sat across a table in the apartment of her subjects and interviewed them according to a written protocol she carried with her. The interviewees answered her questions and she wrote in longhand whatever she thought she heard. Decades later, her handwriting, such as it was, often led to long bouts of confusion. With too many examples to recount, one will suffice. In 1920, a man named William M. Birton lived at 999, although it might have been Biston. Ancestry.com offered both spellings as possibilities. When I searched for either

version, I learned that nobody with those names lived in Chicago or even the United States in 1910, 1920 or 1930. Months flew by. I gave up.

In a completely different context an acquaintance asked me what jobs I had had as a youngster. "Delivery boy, mostly," I said. And then, without thinking about it, I dragged a forgotten image up from my deep past. "I was a census taker," I blurted out, "for a few weeks in 1959." Instantly I knew what happened to the lost Mr. Birton. William said his last name was Burton. B-U-R-T-O-N. Only he didn't spell it out and the enumerator didn't ask. I looked *him* up. Sure enough, William M. Burton lived at 999. He also had led a team of researchers to the discovery of a breakthrough in fuel technology. Later he ran Standard Oil of Indiana.

A few other drawbacks rendered census data less than ideal. If people weren't home when the enumerator came calling, they were not recorded and not included in the United States population. They became the bookkeeping equivalent of Soviet-style non-persons. Anybody who moved into 999 in, say, 1923 and left by 1928 would not have popped up in either the 1920 or 1930 census. Only a fortuitous appearance in something like the society pages would have coughed up their existence.

In 1920, the census did not capture apartment

numbers. In 1930, it did, as well as the apartment's perceived market value. At the time, the most valuable domicile was 9B with an estimated worth of $75,000. The 1940 census ignored the value but listed its kissing cousin, the monthly rent. Depending on your floor and tier, you could have lived at 999 for anywhere between $115 and $295 a month.

The best source for identifying residents and their apartments turned out to be the files at Wolin-Levin, Inc. (now FirstService Residential), 999's management company. Since 1947, when the building became a co-op for the second time, every outgoing tenant signed and dated the proprietary lease transferring his shares and leasehold to the incoming tenant, who also signed the serial lease, and so on and on and on. One document, one unit and every shareholder, a windfall of information, except nothing is ever perfect. The proprietary leases don't list children, long-term houseguests or servants. The practice of live-in servants has been disappearing since the end of World War II. But we probably missed many children. Their importance to the chronicle of 999 will become vivid when you get to John Mahin and John, Jr.

There is no established rhythm for how long tenants lived in the building. Some people bought shares and never moved in. Others stayed and stayed and stayed. Seventeen families lived at 999 for over 30 years. The longest tenured were Elizabeth Paepcke—64 years, the Stuarts—62, James Wilson Reilly—56, Eloise ReQua—50, and Florence Willett—46. The hold 999 has on its residents testifies to its enduring greatness.

Sometimes it was impossible to construct even a stub of a biography for a tenant. When there was nothing to say, nothing was written. Some residents received a sentence, e.g., "Mary Hempstead grew up in Evanston and was a Daughter of the American Revolution." Others left behind the equivalent of a résumé. Sometimes the family history was more interesting or easier to obtain than a specific resident's life and that is what you get—a brief family bio. A handful of 999 citizens made headlines and touched history. Others lived exemplary lives or excessively sloppy ones. These larger than life characters demanded more space and received a page or more for the telling of their stories. Sometimes, a sidebar was required to capture their weirdest moment—wait until you get to Muriel Rockefeller McCormick—or their grandest gesture, Colonel Langhorne and his Cadillac Touring Car.

From the beginning, I had hoped that 999 had tenants who mirrored the prototypes in Carl Sandburg's poem, "Chicago." "Hog Butcher for the World, Tool Maker, Stacker of Wheat, Player

To maintain privacy and keep
peace in the family, nothing was
written about current tenants.
On some level, I will always
regret that decision.

with Railroads and the Nation's Freight Handler."

We did have a Swift and a Pullman, relatives of Gustavus and George, who also worked in the family businesses of meat packing and railroading. David Sciaky invented and manufactured a tool that gave the Allies a competitive edge in World War II. Walt Willett and Jack Snead handled the nation's freight, and William Requa most definitely stacked wheat. I do not know if we had any "painted women under the gas lamps luring the farm boys." But history never yields all of its secrets.

To maintain privacy and keep peace in the family, nothing was written about current tenants. On some level, I will always regret that decision. Great individual stories ride up and down 999's elevators every day.

Namedropping is a measure of nothing consequential. But that didn't stop me from searching for famous people who had a drink or a meal or a meeting at 999. Julia Child was here and Bing Crosby and B. J. Armstrong, who played for the Bulls, and Mayor Rahm Emmanuel, Illinois Governor Jim Thompson and President Barack Obama, the junior Senator from Illinois at the time. Except for Crosby, you won't read another word about the others because they were visiting current residents. I'm certain there were many, many other celebrities who crossed our doorstep.

But the effort to locate them vastly exceeded the value of their inclusion. So I called off the hunt. Nonetheless, Tarzan, Pancho Villa, the Wizard of Oz, Douglas MacArthur, Albert Schweitzer, Thomas Edison, Margaret Thatcher, Charles de Gaulle and Mary, Queen of Scots, make guest appearances in the book.

The final section, *Forever Relevant*, was to be a thumbnail history of every construction project undertaken since 1947. This cratered when the information proved too difficult to obtain, sparing the reader a litany of bent nails. Now it details some of the improvements made to 999 in the last decade and features four-color photographs of contemporary apartments.

The title of the book—999—was the title from beginning. But the subtitle *The History of Chicago in Ten Stories* popped into my wife's head while she was exercising and was a last minute addition. We both liked it, even though we abhor puns. Even more icky than a pun is a pun you have to explain. Nevertheless, *Ten Stories* does not mean that *The History* unfolds in ten separate stories, but that 999 the building, is ten stories tall. I decided to incorporate it and have nobody to blame but myself.

The biggest surprise I received during the life of this project happened while I was sitting in a training room at Wolin-Levin looking through

*The biggest surprise I received during
the life of this project happened while I
was sitting in a training room at Wolin-
Levin looking through the file folder
for apartment 2C.*

the file folder for apartment 2C. In 1977 Melvyn Kushner lived there with his wife Barbara and her daughter. I yelled to my younger daughter who was helping me: "MELVYN! MELVYN KUSH-NER!" She stared at me like I was crazy.

I went to high school with him. Even though he was a year younger, we were friends. He competed with another guy I also knew to see who would finish last in their graduating class. In early June 1958, Melvyn's senior year, I had to drive to Houston to rejoin my parents who had moved there. In need of a companion to help idle away the miles, I went to Senn High School, found the classroom where Melvyn sat look-ing anaesthetized and asked him, "Wanna go to Texas?" Without saying a word, he left the room—and the city—before taking a single final exam, thereby solidifying his class ranking.

We stopped in Little Rock, Arkansas and asked a traffic cop for directions to Central High School. A year earlier Central had dominated the national news. A showdown between Arkansas Governor Orville Faubus and President Dwight Eisenhower was resolved when nine black stu-dents, escorted by police officers, walked through the doors of their new school. The traffic cop took one look at my Chicago city sticker and drawled, "If you Yankee boys like living, y'all leave this state. Now."

In Texarkana, my stick shift 1951 Plymouth broke down. The first night it was being serviced, a two-day affair, we went to the movies and were appalled by separate White and Colored ticket offices and water fountains. I deliberately drank out of the wrong fountain. Across the street, good ol' boys began wrapping belts around their fists. Melvyn and I ran back to our cheap motel room, pushed some of the furniture against the door and the rest in front of the lone window, and waited to be lynched.

The next morning, Melvyn decided to take a bus home. I was told later that he got on the first bus he saw at the station, fell asleep and woke up in Memphis. After that I lost track of him.

I called a mutual friend from the old days, who told me that Melvyn had had a successful career in real estate, changed his name to Nicoli and dropped out of sight. In lieu of a biography, I leave you with Melvyn getting off the bus in Memphis, hair a jumble, shirt half tucked into his pants, looking puzzled.

Richard B. Fizdale
Chicago, Illinois
2014

On the Shores
of MISHIGAMI

I f you lived in Chicago any time after 1912 and drove a car along the lakefront on the near north side, chances are you marveled at the red brick building, ten stories high, sitting like a contented cat on the corner of the city's most desirable residential street. If a poll had been taken 100 years ago or 50 or even yesterday asking Chicagoans to pick their favorite apartment building based solely on looks, this one would have been a frequent winner. Zipping past it with your foot on the accelerator and your eyes on the road ahead is not the ideal way to appreciate 999 Lake Shore Drive. That's a bit like guzzling Lafite Rothschild from the bottle.

To begin to savor 999's many facets, you need to take a leisurely stroll on the doublewide sidewalks of East Lake Shore Drive. Start at the Drake Hotel, an homage to the Renaissance palaces of sixteenth century Rome and Florence. Over the years the Drake has hosted Queen Elizabeth II, Winston Churchill, Jawaharlal Nehru of India, King Hussein of Jordan, Charles Lindbergh and every American President from Herbert Hoover to Barack Obama. Walk east past the other great properties, all completed between 1913 and 1929, past the dazzling rows of flowers kneeling at the bases of the buildings they adorn, past the watchful eyes of uniformed doormen, past the clean, manicured lawns and the parade of trees, past the small park across the street and beyond it the Outer Drive and the blue-gray waves of Lake Michigan, until you get to the far end of the block and 999 Lake Shore Drive, gracefully sweeping around its corner, exposing its broad face to the world.

Enter the recently restored *porte-cochere* highlighted

Zipping past it with your foot on the accelerator and your eyes on the road ahead is not the ideal way to appreciate 999 Lake Shore Drive. That's a bit like guzzling Lafite Rothschild from the bottle.

by its limestone frame and you can't help but wonder why Benjamin Marshall conceived a covered driveway only slightly wider than a car. Motoring was one of Marshall's passions, so he knew that automobiles already came in a variety of shapes and sizes. But as he made his first rough sketches of 999, only 500 motorized vehicles, trucks included, were operating on Chicago's streets. He could stare at a 1911 topless Aero Four Passenger Speedster all day and not foresee the length of a stretch limo or the height and width of a luxury SUV. Despite Marshall's momentary lapse in clairvoyance, any competent driver can navigate 999's driveway with ease, even while wishing for an extra inch of leeway.

Strikingly beautiful up close, 999 Lake Shore Drive does not reveal all its charms in a single glance. Standing on the corner, you can crank your neck as far back as it will go and not be able to take it all in. The best place to see it in the context of the entire street is from a blanket on Oak Street Beach. From that vantage point you can see that the eight buildings on East Lake Shore share a similarity of scale and rhythm, a compatibility of color and texture, and a moment in history when old world elegance reigned supreme. They appear to have been cultivated to be seen together, like a garden in the Gilded Age. Not surprisingly, Marshall and his colleagues were the creative force behind five of them: the Drake Hotel, Drake Tower, 199, 209 and 999. The firm of Fugard and Knapp did the others, instilling in them the same harmonic order. In the presence of such continuous beauty 999 stands out, the most vibrant and spirited of the lot. Its steep-sided, double-pitched mansard roof with projecting sheet metal dormers, nearly invisible up close, confirms the building's pedigree as

The eight buildings of the East Lake Shore Drive Landmark District offer front row seats on the lakefront.

Second Empire; the architectural movement in vogue during Baron Georges-Eugene Haussmann's renovation of Paris in the 1850s. In 1985, East Lake Shore Drive was designated a landmark district, and all eight of those wonderments were granted Chicago landmark status *en masse*. No changes to the exteriors can be made without the approval of the appropriately stingy Commission on Chicago Landmarks.

Seen from another angle, say through the viewfinder of a camera from the lakefront promenade between East Lake Shore and Walton, 999's facade fills the frame with a waltz of terra cotta; grace notes of red brick and white limestone; a dance of swells and recesses; and the metered cadence of wood framed windows, some elongated, others bayed in counterpoint. It is as if Marshall were listening to Chopin when he approved this look.

From the deck of a boat you can observe the sun's love affair with 999. One moment it is blushing pink, in the next a lusty red-violet. The building's colors vary with the action of the waves, the passage of the sun and the serendipitous stirrings of the clouds.

If you look northwest from inside 999, your view takes in Oak Street Beach and the stylistic hodgepodge of high-rises on North Lake Shore Drive, which ultimately dissolve into the lush greenery of Lincoln Park. They occupy ground where once stood 32 mansions belonging to the likes of Rockefellers; McCormicks; Palmers; Robert Todd Lincoln, Abe and Mary's sole surviving son; and other A-listers who pioneered elegant living on the near north side.

The windows of 999 that face east look at the old Municipal Pier No. 16, one of the city's top tourist attractions, now known as Navy Pier. Fireworks shows from its deck illuminate summer skies on Wednesday and Saturday nights.

The communal bond of those lucky enough to live at 999 is Lake Michigan. The Ojibwa called it *Mishigami*, meaning "great water," which it certainly is—1,640 miles of shoreline, 1,180 cubic miles of water, the fifth largest lake in the world and the largest within a single country. 999ers can see, admire and contemplate it from almost every window in their apartments.

Stand near any window in 999.
Look out and you will never see
the same lake twice.

On November 10, 1913, the earliest residents of 999 had ringside seats for one of those storms of the century. Hurricane-force winds whipped a blizzard into a horrifying whiteout. Thirty-five foot waves sent 19 ships to the bottom and stranded another 19. After 16 hours of hell, 328 were dead and 68,300 tons of coal, iron ore and grain were lost. "The Big Blow," as it was called, is happily long forgotten.

There may no better venue to contemplate the changing of the seasons than the windows of 999. In the fall, as days grow shorter, the sky turns gloomy by degrees. The wind flexes its muscles, shakes dead leaves from sleeping trees and, with gathering menace, ushers in the white wolf of winter. Waves rise up like scepters and, on extremely bitter nights, freeze in midair, curled like claws, within striking distance of an unreachable shore. When the long barren lull of winter is broken, the signal comes from the fulgurating brilliance of lightning bolts accompanied by the growl of thunder. Soon, all is quiet. The lake is as serene as a haiku. Sailboats appear like quarks out of nothingness. On the shore where drifts of snow and patches of ice reclined come nannies navigating strollers, joggers, fishermen, cyclists, sun worshipers, skateboarders, roller skaters, dog walkers and the occasional businessman on a midday hiatus, feeling strangely young again, a limp suit jacket draped over his arm—all of them drawn to the water like ten thousand Ishmaels.

Stand near any window in 999, look out and you will never see the same lake twice. Close your eyes and listen to what used to be—back when men wore checkered suits and strolled down Pine Street with women holding parasols; when horses clomped across badly paved streets drawing wagons filled with beer, coal or ice; when large sections of the lake shore north of the river were a low water, insect infested, goo laden marsh and you might hear the hiccupping engine of George Wellington Streeter's boat coming to claim the submerged land under *Mishigami,* the land on which 999 would later be built.

The
PREHISTORY
of 999

TOP: *Lithograph by Currier and Ives titled* Chicago in Flames, *a scene from the Chicago Fire of 1871. (Chicago History Museum ICHi-23436. Image cropped.)*

BOTTOM: *Chicago Fire Cyclorama. Scene the First:* Ruins of the Business Center looking southwest from the site of old Fort Dearborn. *It presaged images of Hiroshima. (Chicago History Museum ICHi-63836. Image cropped.)*

CHAPTER ONE

The DISAPPEARANCE
of the NORTH SIDE

The prehistory of 999 began in terror, as the Great Chicago Fire of 1871 rose like a starving beast from a barn near Canal and Taylor Streets. It descended on a city that was bone dry after months of drought. Gale force winds molded it into a wall of flames ten stories high and a mile wide. It dined on a city made of wood. When the Fire reached the downtown business district, it consumed everything in its path—everything—and belched out towering clouds of black smoke. And then it did the impossible and jumped the Chicago River. As the first sparks danced in midair, like a Fourth of July celebration run amuck, rows and rows of neatly stacked two-by-fours, dry as dust, waited on the far bank to be devoured. Invigorated by this new source of fuel, the Fire now raged on the other side of the river, where it did its greatest damage.

The neighborhood north of Chicago Avenue between Lake Michigan and the North Branch of the Chicago River was thickly blanketed with the pine cottages of the poor—the homes of tens of thousands of German and Scandinavian immigrants. Here they lived, worked, prayed and, on this night, fled for their lives, as the night sky turned apocalyptic orange.

Three escape routes were shouted out in the languages of Northern Europe. Those who crossed the North Branch of the river (about where Kingsbury is today) found safety on the west side. Other refugees headed north toward Fullerton. The going was frightful. As they ran for their lives, flames lapped at their heels. The noise was everywhere, the loudest, most horrible sounds they had ever heard—the crash and crunch of falling buildings, the thunderous drumbeats of barrels of oil and cans of paint exploding, and the unrelenting screams of the nearly dead and those unwilling to die.

A great many people alive today owe a debt of thanks

View of the corner of State and Madison Streets after the Chicago Fire of 1871. (Chicago History Museum ICHi-02811)

to ancestors who outran the Chicago Fire. Some escapees fled to the beaches and parks on the lakefront. They suffered the most. As the inferno engulfed trees, bushes, park benches and picnic tables, there was nowhere to hide but in the cold lake water for teeth-chattering hours.

Two days later, a providential rainstorm stopped the Fire at Fullerton Avenue, the city's northernmost boundary. The north side was no more. What little remained presaged images of Hiroshima in the next century.

Across the city, the conflagration destroyed approximately $200 million worth of real estate—one-third of the city's valuation. An equal amount of personal property—Sunday dresses, scuffed shoes, loaves of bread, bed-bugged mattresses, moth-eaten blankets, family Bibles, letters from the old country, unfinished homework, torn rag dolls, unspent paper money and everything else—had been incinerated, the ashes scattered every which way by super-hot thermal updrafts. Gone were 73 miles of roads,

The day after the Fire, Schock, Bigford and Company was the first business to reopen. They sold tobacco, fruit and cider in the middle of the rubble. (Chicago History Museum ICHi-02773)

120 miles of wooden sidewalks and 17,500 buildings. Also lost were two to three million books. Over four square miles were left smoldering. Three hundred people died, most of them burned beyond recognition. Grieving relatives looking for missing loved ones could only shrug when shown the charred bodies.

On the north side, 13,800 structures existed before the Fire; only 500 remained after it died down. The only home that wasn't incinerated was a full-scale mansion on Walton Street between Dearborn and Clark, the present day site of the Newberry Library. An abrupt shift in the wind saved the residence of one of Chicago's leading citizens, Mahlon D. Ogden, the brother of William B. Ogden, Chicago's first mayor, the founder of the city's first railroad, and one of the largest property owners in the history of the city.

Seventy-four-thousand, four-hundred-fifty people—mostly from the German and Scandinavian immigrant community—were left homeless. A few found shelter with friends and relatives on the west side. But the majority of the survivors huddled together in makeshift encampments north of Fullerton. They faced a bleak, uncertain future. Would the city fathers rebuild their neighborhood, their homes, their places of work and worship? Surely they did not have the resources to do it themselves.

The day after the fire, with smoke and red hot embers still rising from the ruins of downtown, an enterprising Chicagoan opened a tobacco, fruit and cider stand in the midst of the rubble. That small gesture was photographed. The image circled the globe, and was characterized as a symbol of determination: Chicago was on its way back.

Architects and draftsmen dashed off plans for replacement structures downtown that could resist or, at worst, retard future calamities. The fire code was rewritten and the fire department upgraded. In the first week 5,497 temporary structures were built and 200 permanent buildings were underway. Men with strong backs boarded trains all over the country to help clean up and rebuild the city. Debris was plowed into the lake, expanding Lake Park into the renamed Grant Park. Donations poured in from the around the world. A. H. Burgess, a Londoner, proposed the "English Book Donation" and challenged his countrymen to present a Free Public Library to Chicago. Most Chicagoans are unaware that private donors like Alfred Lord Tennyson, John Stuart Mill, Benjamin Disraeli and Her Majesty, Queen Victoria helped start the Chicago Public Library. Within a year, at least one new building opened every day, many of them five and six story skyscrapers. Within a decade 120 square miles had been added to the city and the population had doubled.

The new Chicago didn't rise from the ashes without controversy. The proposed passage of a new law regulating building materials pitted rich against poor, nativists versus the foreign born. The Republicans under Joseph Medill, the former publisher of the *Chicago Tribune* and the newly elected mayor of Chicago, wanted to rebuild a fireproof Chicago out of brick, stone, marble and iron.

The poor on the north side could not afford building materials more expensive than wood. Their ranks were composed of immigrants. They had no natural leader. They found their strength in numbers, and they were opposed to any laws that would interfere with rebuilding their

Map of the Chicago Fire of 1871. Published for the benefit of the
Relief Fund by the R. P. Studley Company, St. Louis, Missouri,
3rd Edition. (Chicago History Museum ICHi-02870)

Carte-de-visite featuring Kerfoot's Block after the Chicago Fire
of 1871. (Chicago History Museum ICHi-02859)

After the Fire, donations of books from Queen Victoria and other prominent British citizens helped start the new Chicago Public Library. (Photos.com)

devastated neighborhoods. The fire had wiped them out. Even their workplaces were gone, leaving them without jobs. Insurance companies had not covered their losses. Of the $88 million in claims, only half were ever collected.

Medill's allies—many with ancestries traceable to colonial America—countered with what seemed like the backs of their hands. Getting their way was their birthright and they had decided: there shall be no wooden buildings in Chicago. The rights of small, private property owners had to be abridged in favor of public safety. Making Chicago fireproof was a civic duty. The City Council was crafting a new code. When it passed, every property owner would be obliged to obey it.

To sidestep the upcoming vote in the Council, the immigrants rushed to build homes made of wood. They also launched a rhetorical campaign designed to win the sympathy of the city's entire underclass. Suddenly the new building code had become a tug-of-war over who had political authority in Chicago.

"The preservation of Chicago as a city where the German element has the same power and social standing as one of native birth depends on the reconstitution of the north side." The displaced German community hoped

the Irish, Italian, Jews and African Americans would see themselves in that statement.

"We can't have a Yankee nest where"...the rest of us... "form a contemptible subordinate class."

The nativists are trying to "drive a stake into the heart of the working class."

The day of the vote arrived. Council members were ensconced in their meeting room in City Hall, which ironically had been rebuilt out of wood. Celebratory cigars were stuffed in their breast pockets awaiting the final tally. Out the windows the councilmen could see a mob of poor people assembling. The throng marched toward City Hall. Peacefully. But the councilmen panicked. There was a motion to adjourn. It was seconded. All hands signified aye, and they were gone.

In the next few weeks, the council sought a compromise. But bricks of clay and knotty pine have difference essences. Yet, something subtle emerged from their last minute deliberations. Fireproofing was mandated for the central business district and the upscale residential neighborhoods to the south and west of downtown. Strict controls were imposed over the location of businesses that specialized in flammable products, such as paint or lumber. Poorer communities north of the river became islands of democracy. The property owners on a block would vote: brick or wood? The majority ruled. The immigrants had won their right to tinderboxes.

True to the nature of Chicago politics, the bill came with an escape hatch. There was no enforcement clause. None. After the most devastating fire in modern history, *laissez-faire* remained the order of the day.

The Great Rebuilding of the Central Business District was completed with an obedient adherence to the new rules. Even City Hall was remade of sterner stuff. Downtown remained functionally the same, home to the courthouse, banks, law offices, corporate headquarters, financial management firms, commodities trading, railway terminals, retailing, quality restaurants and legitimate theater.

The near north side didn't exactly return to its former state. The breweries and small manufactories that employed cheap local labor either weren't rebuilt or were relocated to different neighborhoods. The immigrants themselves moved both slightly north and west of their old haunts. The grocers, butchers, barbershops and saloons that depended on their loyalty followed suit. The first modern apartment building in the city—a three-story walk-up—was built on Erie between State and Dearborn. It contained small suites that were nicknamed "flats."

Meanwhile, a few men of means wanted to change the character of the devastated neighborhood by making it bigger and more residential. They had a problem. Other influential men had a different plan.

CHAPTER TWO

The Meandering Shore

CHICAGO.(in1862)

Lith by Ed. Mendel, 162 Lake St Chicago

Prior to the Fire, the mouth of the Chicago River was the
location of a major port. (Courtesy of University of Illinois
at Urbana-Champaign Library)

Friday, October 6, 1871, two days before the Fire, the future site of 999 was under water. Nobody stood on the shore at Oak Street and fantasized about an apartment building 1,000 feet out in the lake. To the south, the junction of the Chicago River and Lake Michigan was a swirl of piers, docked ships, stacks of wooden crates, barrels bound by metal hoops, grappling hooks, coils of thick rope, and sweating men hard at work. Looking east, schooners and steamships filled every lane in the lake, bringing lumber from Wisconsin and iron ore from Minnesota, and returning with commodities like bread and cured ham in their over-stuffed holds.

Chicago was already the nation's largest inland port and its transportation hub, an outgrowth of 1848, when the new Illinois-Michigan Canal linked Lake Michigan to the Mississippi River, and the city's first railroad was completed.

Most of the hustle and bustle from shipping took place south of the river. Despite the presence of a few warehouses and a handful of workers, the north bank—a parcel of land called Kinzie's Addition to Chicago—was largely vacant. It stretched from the river to Chicago Avenue. In 1831, Robert Kinzie, the son of John Kinzie, Chicago's first permanent settler, registered it with the U.S. Government. In 1837, he was granted the equivalent of a deed.

Twenty years later, William Butler Ogden and Cyrus Hall McCormick, the heads of two of Chicago's most established families, bought a portion of Kinzie's Addition, roughly from Indiana Street to the river. Ogden had built the city's first railroad—the Galena and Chicago Union—and he was the city's first mayor. McCormick perfected the mechanical reaper based on breakthrough designs developed by other men. He created a company that became International Harvester to market and sell his machine.

The Meandering Shore 29

This image of William Ogden, first mayor of Chicago, was published in the Chicago Daily News *newspaper on the 74th anniversary of Chicago's charter, March 4, 1912. (Chicago History Museum DN-0058274)*

Cyrus Hall McCormick, *a prominent owner of lakefront property, whose granddaughter and nephew will live at 999. (Photographer: H. Rocher. Chicago History Museum ICHi-59696)*

OPPOSITE: *Map of the area between Lake Michigan and the Chicago River showing modest development of the land south of Chicago Avenue. (Chicago History Museum ICHi-65925)*

In 1857, Ogden and McCormick started a company called Chicago Dock and Canal. The State of Illinois issued a special charter that authorized it to construct wharfs and docks on their land and in the navigable waters of Lake Michigan. The shore was expanded by their efforts and the natural accretions caused by the lake's currents.

The lakefront gradually meandered northeast. Near Superior Street was the largest brewery west of the Atlantic seaboard—Lill and Diversey, which mixed its hops and barley with Lake Michigan water. At Chicago Avenue, the site of the Water Tower and the Water Works, the water's edge was within kissing distance of Pine Street. At Oak Street, the shore turned north and headed toward Lincoln Park. The shoreline was never as straight as a hog-butcher's blade. With each successive wave, grains of sand were deposited and taken away—a few more here, a few less there.

From the river to Lincoln Park, the land on the west side of Pine Street had been platted and every lot was owned. The owners were individuals, estates or companies. The presence of the Water Works on the east side of the street led people to assume the city owned the land under it and the tiny bit of property to the east of it. But that assumption was far from settled law.

The shore itself was not exactly *terra firma.* It was marshy, a concoction of sand and clay commingled into slop, and home to a menagerie of insects and an assortment of birds, and the occasional frog, snake, rodent, wild dog, feral cat and, every so often, a man down on his luck. Here, erosion worked like a quiet thief. A person would be standing in the muck, thinking it was a wetland, and the next day it was gone, washed away and exported a few blocks to Kinzie's Addition or farther south, to the foreign shores of Indiana or Michigan.

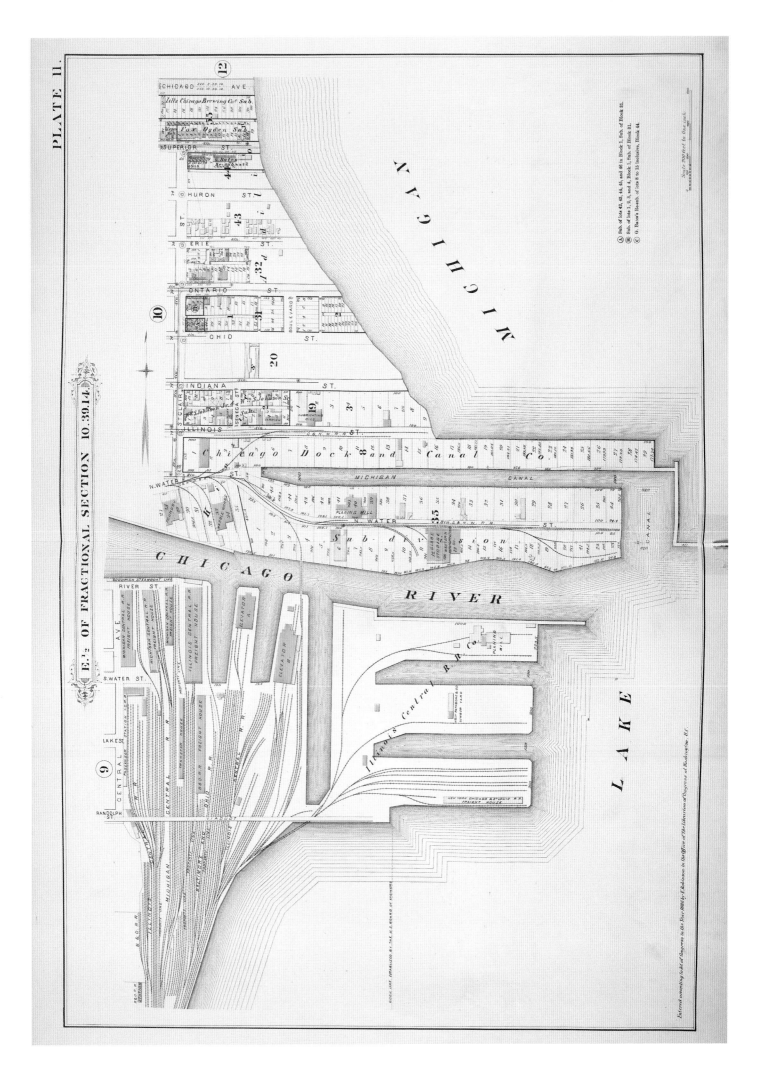

PLATE II.

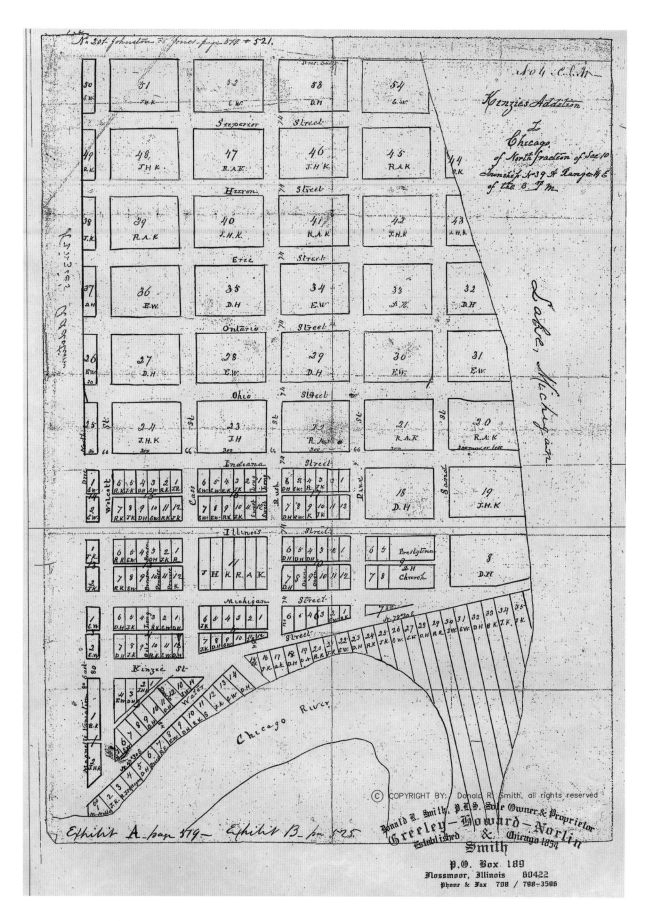

Kinzie's Addition to Chicago of north fraction of sec. 10, township no. 39 N., range 14 E. of the 3rd p.m. Photocopy of anonymous and undated manuscript, traced by Chicago surveyor Samuel Sewell Greeley circa 1858 from earlier undated manuscript of circa 1833. Attorney Abe Lincoln used it as an exhibit in the legal suits of Johnson v Jones et al. (1853-61) and Bates v. Illinois Central Railroad Co. (1854-61), both involving property rights on the shore of Lake Michigan. (The Newberry Library, Chicago. map4F G4104.C6A 18-.C6 2010, sheet 5 of 8. © 2014 Greeley-Howard-Norlin & Smith, GHNS131.)

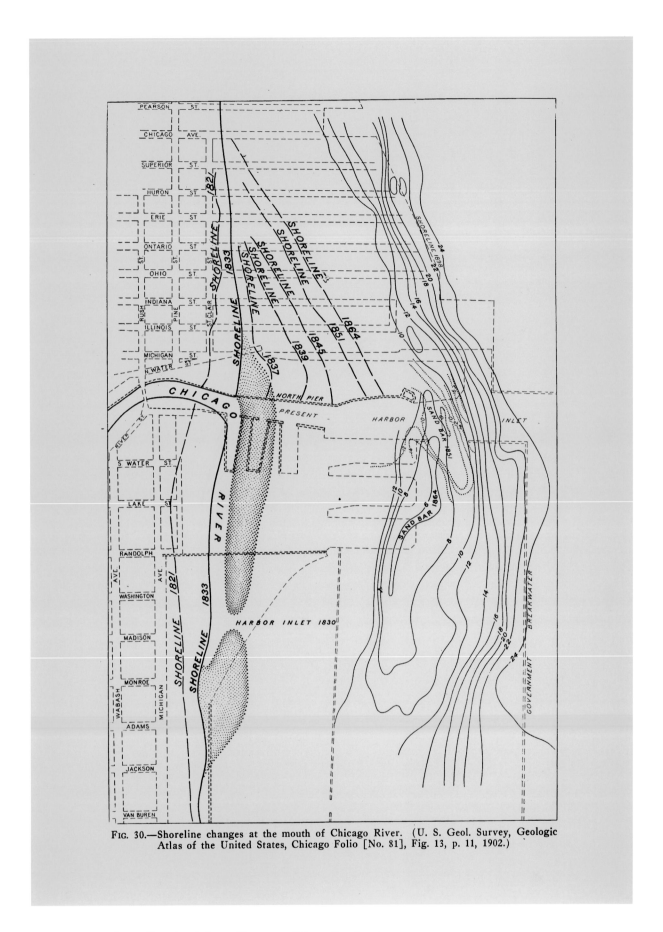

FIG. 30.—Shoreline changes at the mouth of Chicago River. (U. S. Geol. Survey, Geologic Atlas of the United States, Chicago Folio [No. 81], Fig. 13, p. 11, 1902.)

CHAPTER THREE

A Prescient Plan

After the Fire, the men who owned lots on the shore held the cards that would determine the fate of the north side. Their options were many, any one of which would have affected the city's future. Had they sold their property to the War Department for training purposes or turned the lakefront into a succession of resort hotels, it would have led to different outcomes for the entire area. The shore owners toyed with two realistic and divergent directions.

The first option was easy to divine. The lake was filled with ships. One line of thought was to turn the lakefront on the near north side into a great commercial harbor with a large number of docks and wharfs, and then repopulate the devastated neighborhood behind it with storage facilities, factories, taverns and cheap hotels for thirsty, lovelorn sailors. A minority of shore owners supported this vision. But they included Cyrus McCormick.

The majority wanted to transform the same territory into an upscale residential garden. The idea pre-dated the Fire, and seemed to be gathering momentum. As so often has been the case, economic factors change neighborhoods and reconstitute urban America. Chicago's wealthiest families were ripe for greener pastures. Many of them lived on Prairie Avenue between 16th and 22nd Streets. The historic allure of the Prairie Avenue enclave had been open spaces, the availability of double and triple lots, and its proximity to both the lake and business interests downtown.

But that smug upper class neighborhood was already sliding downhill. Within walking distance, a red-light district thrived. Adjacent neighborhoods were suddenly over-crowded with working-class families who had come to Chicago to clean up and rebuild the city. The fashionable ladies of Prairie Avenue shied away from contact with these strange new people chattering in undecipherable

William Lill, chairman of an 1872 public meeting where a plan to build a roadway in the lake was first revealed. (Chicago History Museum ICHi-68174)

languages and off-putting brogues, or the dark-skinned men and women from the Deep South. And, perhaps most odious of all to the refined sensibilities of the wealthy was the foul air and smoke generated by around-the-clock factories, and the putrid stench and horrifying squeals of death emanating from the nearby stockyards.

On September 16, 1872, less than a year after the Fire, a meeting of the North Side Improvement Association was held at the new office of William Lill on the corner of Chicago and Pine. In attendance was a large contingent of north side property owners. Among those present were William B. Ogden, always interested in investing in Chicago's future; William Lill, the co-owner of Lill &

In one of those prescient moments
on which destiny often hitches a ride,
someone unknown to us described
an alternative route—the construction
of the Drive in Lake Michigan

Diversey, who had decided not to rebuild his brewery; John B. Calhoun, a builder of railroads; B. F. Culver, a major property owner in Lake View, an independent town north of Chicago; attorney W. H. Bradley and many others.

The men in this room decided the post-Fire fate of the neighborhood so quickly that it appeared to be a forgone conclusion before Lill, the president of the association, gaveled the meeting to order. The attendees resolved that everything east of Clark Street—between the river and Walton Street—would no longer be used for business purposes. Henceforth, whereas and herewith, they agreed to turn the near north side into a posh district lined with one imposing mansion after another.

Next on the agenda was extending Lake Shore Drive in all directions. The Drive already existed in bits and pieces along the lakefront. An old idea was revisited; how old is unclear. The members of the Improvement Association resolved to build a continuous Lake Shore Drive, beginning at Whitney Street and running southward to either Ohio or Indiana streets.

In one of those prescient moments on which destiny often hitches a ride, someone unknown to us described an alternative route—the construction of the Drive in Lake Michigan. In this iteration it would start near Lincoln Park and continue over submerged land to about Huron Street. Engineers and lawyers had been working on the plan for weeks, maybe months. They recommended locating the Drive approximately 400 feet east of Pine Street—near the front entrance to the current Museum of Contemporary Art. The submerged land would rise to the surface by filling in the gaps between the new roadway and the old shore with sand, clay and dirt. To head off any objections to so monumental a task, the engineers assured those in the room that the average depth of the water that far out in the lake was a mere three feet, six inches. Everybody jumped on this idea.

The intricacies of constructing the Drive in the lake were explained. Oak piles would have to be driven into the lakebed. They would serve as supports for the new roadway and create a formidable breakwater, which would trap sand and contribute to the landfill.

When finished, Lake Shore Drive would be 150 feet wide and subdivided into north/south lanes. There would be a center walkway in case of emergencies. Shades trees would be planted on both sides of the Drive 30 feet apart. Promises were made that someday Lake Shore Drive would stretch all the way to Evanston.

Widening Pine Street into a proper thoroughfare also came up for discussion. This was risky, a make or break issue for the shore owners. The city would have to condemn some of the land on the shore—their land—to acquire the right of way for a more glorious Pine Street. But the millionaires had a remedy in their hip pocket. They offered to donate their rights of way in exchange for the deeds to the newly created land.

Well-coached by their lawyers, the shore owners knew they had a legitimate legal claim to any new land abutting their existing property. It was based on a widely accepted tenet of British common law—long embedded in the American legal canon—known as riparian rights, which states that if you own land adjacent to a body of water, you have the right to make reasonable use of it, e.g., swim in it, put up a diving board, dock a boat, build a pier, etc. And if the land beneath the water suddenly appeared on the surface, well, that would be yours, too.

The shore owners also understood that riparian rights did not guarantee a court would award them the land. Both the Federal Government and the State of Illinois could muster strong arguments on their behalf. And perhaps, other people or entities could conjure up plausible claims for themselves.

The nineteenth century ushered in the age of Manifest

To help cement the deal, the shore
owners offered to underwrite
the construction of Lake Shore Drive.
They raised $50,000 on the spot.

Destiny in America. The United States implored its people to populate the country from the Atlantic to the Pacific. A host of new government programs came into existence to facilitate this grand movement. Land was taken from the Indians and easily given to almost anyone who raised his hand. Perhaps somebody somewhere had been given the right to the lakeshore a long time ago. This could be a problem if one hung his derby on riparian rights.

To help cement the deal, the shore owners offered to underwrite the construction of Lake Shore Drive. They raised $50,000 on the spot as a good faith expression of their good will.

The final discussion centered on value. Everybody agreed that this plan would add immensely to the value of north side property. A letter was read from a Mr. Goodwin, a property owner in Lake View. He pledged to pay for 1,000 feet of Lake Shore Drive, recognizing that improvements undertaken south of his land would benefit him as well.

A document memorializing the agreements was signed by Ogden, Lill and the other large property owners. Work was to begin upon the resolution of legal issues, which included persuading the city, or some other appropriate governmental body, to support their plan. Construction was expected to begin before winter. On paper, the near north side had been reinvented.

Unfortunately, the North Side Improvement Association's proposal died on the vine. It was too ambitious and controversial for a city focused on lifting itself up from the ruins. It was the right idea, but the wrong time. Lawmakers in Springfield eventually made it possible for the idea to become reality. And it would take a full-scale scrum before the playing field could be cleared of unwelcome combatants fighting for a piece of the action. Lake Shore Drive did happen, along the lines outlined by William Lill and his friends in 1872.

After a brief interlude, the project resurfaced in 1875. On September 11, a severe rainstorm damaged a wide unpaved path called Lake Shore Drive that ran from North Avenue to Lincoln Park. The Lincoln Park Board of Commissioners, which was created in 1864 to deal with erosion, had installed a series of wooden boxes filled with sand, dirt and rubbish in the lake. It ran from North Avenue to within two or three blocks of the Water Works. This wacky contraption was supposed to serve as a low cost breakwater, but, as the wind grew in intensity, the waves acted like vast scooping machines, tearing apart the flimsy boxes and disemboweling large chunks of Lake Shore Drive.

The next day the *Chicago Tribune* ran an editorial, encouraging the Park Board to undertake the immediate construction of Lake Shore Drive elevated on piles about a quarter-of-a-mile from the shore as a barrier against erosion. The commissioners ignored the *Tribune*'s advice. Acting on authority given to them by the State Legislature, they left the Drive where it was. But they raised it high enough to avoid the waves, and fortified its base with rocks to withstand the punishment doled out by Chicago weather. As a side benefit, the commissioners had the road veer off inside Lincoln Park to the west to form an elliptical track, suitable for leisurely carriage rides around a flower garden. Its easternmost section stopped at North Avenue—a vestige of it still exists and runs past the memorial to Ulysses S. Grant.

Around this time, a visionary with a Midas touch—a man of uncompromising integrity and thoughtfulness—who defied the robber baron reputation that clung to his peers like sweat, quietly reinvented the north side without the blare of trumpets or the spotlight of self-promotion.

CHAPTER FOUR

The VISIONARY

P otter Palmer came to Chicago in 1851 to seek his fortune. By the time he died in 1902, he had made more than one.

With a $5,000 gift from his father, he opened a dry goods store—a precursor to the full-scale department store—on poorly lit, crowded and foul-smelling Lake Street. His store, P. Palmer and Company, would cater to women, an insight that seems self-evident today. But in the 1850s, Palmer was pioneering a new business model. Every woman who walked in the front door was personally greeted by him— often by name—and introduced to a well-mannered male "floorwalker." If an item she wanted couldn't be found on a shelf, the floorwalker would apologize for its absence and bring it up from the basement. In that fleeting moment, Palmer raised the bar on what would constitute an acceptable shopping experience in the next century.

Palmer made the store look successful by deliberately leaving one-fourth of the shelves empty. A few shawls were casually opened and tossed on counter tops, ribbons were scattered on tables, and fabrics were hung from bolts and draped over chairs, as if the store were too busy to straighten up. The best merchandise was displayed in the windows, drawing women into the store like hunters.

He introduced a free delivery service and invented the "money-back guarantee," "the customer is always right," low fixed-prices and a liberal return policy. Competitors guffawed and waited for him to go bankrupt. In short order, he created more loyal customers than the competition had customers. He managed the store's reputation through regular advertising and relied on word-of-mouth, gladly given from a host of happy customers.

As the 1850s were drawing to a close, Palmer anticipated the Civil War. To protect his need for a large and steady supply of fabrics, he spent nearly every dollar he had cornering the market on cotton and wool. His

Potter Palmer, Chicago.
(*Chicago History Museum ICHi-26498*)

enormous purchases filled warehouses he either had to rent, buy or build. He kept his customers satisfied throughout the bitter conflict. With his huge surpluses, he made uniforms for the Union Army. When the war ended, Palmer was a multi-millionaire.

He immediately compounded his new fortune by purchasing most of the existing properties and empty lots on State Street, at the time unpaved and no wider than an alley. By the time his buying frenzy was satiated, Palmer's State Street holdings stretched from Randolph to Congress. Retaining the east side of the street for himself, he gave the west side to the city. In exchange for his generosity, Chicago agreed to widen the street by 27 feet, making it more gracious, tree-lined and Parisian. The presence of a refined State Street reoriented Chicago on a North-South axis, which paralleled the lakeshore, instead of its historic East-West axis that followed the river. He moved his store to State and Randolph, and sold it to two of his younger associates, Levi Z. Leiter, who stepped aside shortly thereafter, and Marshall Field, who changed the name. The rest, as they say, is history.

Potter Palmer was one of the original investors—along with George Pullman and Albert Spalding—in what would become the Chicago Cubs. He enjoyed horse racing. He was a force in the Democratic Party and became the only positive memory legendary actress Sarah Bernhardt had of her sole visit to Chicago.

In 1870, Potter married Bertha Honoré. He was 44; she was 21. She was a skilled musician, linguist and writer. Historian Ernest Poole described her as "beautiful, dashing, quick, and smart; and, more than that, she was sure of herself." Bertha would become the Queen of Chicago society, the woman who taught Chicago's hog butchers and railroad kingpins how to dance before the opening of the World's Columbian Exhibition in 1893.

For a wedding present, Palmer gave his bride the "world's most luxurious hotel," the Palmer House at State and Quincy. At eight stories, it was the tallest building in Chicago. It opened on September 26, 1871. Thirteen days later, the Fire destroyed it.

Within days, Palmer borrowed $1.7 million from the Connecticut Mutual Life Insurance Company on the strength of his signature—at the time the largest single loan ever made in the United States. He used the funds to rebuild his vast portfolio of properties. He vowed to make the new Palmer House safer and more spectacular than the original. He built it to the highest possible standards, and, when he embedded silver dollars in the barber shop floor, he added a drawing card for the curious. People who could

*Mrs. Potter Palmer (Bertha Honoré).
(Photographer: Charles Delevan Mosher.
Chicago History Museum ICHi-12031)*

only dream of such flamboyant wealth came to fawn, but they often bought something—a beard trim, a newspaper, a cigar, a postcard—for the vicarious thrill of spending money at the Palmer House. Promoted as the "world's first fireproof building," Palmer publicly dared anyone who agreed to his terms to try to burn it down. The catch: if you failed, you had to pay for all the damage you caused. If the entire hotel went up in flames, you had to rebuild it

TOP: *Stereograph of the Palmer House at the corner of State Street and Quincy Street, before the Chicago Fire of 1871. (Chicago History Museum ICHi-39580. Image cropped.)*

BOTTOM: *View of the ruins of the Palmer House Hotel after the Chicago Fire. (Chicago History Museum ICHi-26749. Image cropped.)*

The celebrated Palmer House barber shop. Eight hundred silver dollars were inlaid in the marble floor. J. Ottmann Lith. N.Y., published 1887. (Courtesy of Library of Congress Prints and Photographs Division Washington, D.C.)

exactly as it was. There were no takers.

On October 4, 1872 at the height of the post-Fire restoration of Chicago, 4,000 union bricklayers went on strike. Demanding $4.00 for an eight-hour day, the strikers closed down almost every construction site in the city. Screaming extortion, the general contractors refused to bow to the bricklayers' demands, reasoning that it was more important to beat back collective bargaining than to bring Chicago back to life. Many of their developer clients agreed. The rebirth of Chicago stopped with a dull thud.

Potter Palmer had resolved to finish the replacement Palmer House before the onset of winter. He fired his contractor and, in a disarming move, appeared at a striker's meeting. He got right to the point. He promised to hire only union bricklayers and pay them their asking wage of 50 cents an hour. The union accepted his offer. Despite some offstage wringing of hands from the stunned contractor community, the strike was over. The Palmer House reopened on November 8, 1873. Among its many guests were Bertha and Potter, who had decided to make it their home.

As the Palmer House was handing out room keys to its first patrons, Potter Palmer focused his attention on the roasted haunts of the German and Scandinavian immigrants on the *Nord Seite*. He quietly began buying burned out vacant lots on Astor and State streets north of Division Street. He couldn't buy all of them. He had competition. The Catholic Church led by the Most Rev. Patrick Augustine Feehan, first Archbishop of Chicago, was trying to rescue the Church from the financial instability caused by the Fire. The plunge into north side real estate helped both men enrich their respective coffers.

His safe overflowing with new deeds, Palmer announced to everybody's absolute astonishment that Bertha and he were going to build a home on the lakefront on the north side. Not exactly a home, but a castle complete with turrets and minarets. Not exactly on the lake, but on a frog pond, which, at the time, couldn't be differentiated from the lake. Not exactly anywhere, but precisely where Schiller and Lake Shore come together today.

What was so startling was Bertha's complicity in the decision. The socially active Palmers would have no neighbors. They would be isolated from the rest of Chicago. This may have suited Potter, who often left swanky parties early, retiring to his chambers to work. But Bertha was the brightest light in all of high society. Hers was the first name on the A-list. She—and virtually she alone—determined who else was on it. But she wasn't concerned

The Palmer residence. (Photographer: J. W. Taylor. Chicago History Museum ICHi-39490)

about the off-putting nature of her new address. At the right time, she would send out invitations to one of her parties-of-the-year and everybody would flock to her door.

Construction on their home began in early 1882. The frog pond was buried under tons of sand and black dirt imported from central Illinois. Three years later, the Palmers moved into their Norman Gothic castle, the largest and most ornate house in the city. The Canadian gray limestone, Wisconsin brown granite, Ohio sandstone, the ivy-covered exterior and 80-foot tower were overshadowed by the grandeur of its interiors.

The entrance provided an immediate and overwhelming gasp. An octagonal hall stood three stories high and was topped by a glass dome. Visitors walked on a floor of polished marble formed into a spectacular mosaic and gazed at walls covered with authentic Gobelin tapestries. The public rooms on the main floor represented a whirlwind tour of Europe: an English dining room that sat 75, a Victorian library, a French drawing room, a Spanish music room, a Moorish corridor that led to Turkish and Greek parlors, and a 90-foot-long dance floor that doubled as an art gallery with enough paintings by Pissarro, Renoir, Manet, Monet and Degas later to form the nucleus of the Art Institute's world-class collection of French Impressionism.

The first private elevators in Chicago transported the Palmers to their sumptuous living quarters. The family's living room was above the library. Bertha's boudoir opened on to a 500-square-foot piazza with a commanding view of the lake. Several suites were reserved for guests. The third floor sported a stage where private concerts, recitals, ballets and plays were performed for elite audiences. The rooftop held a full-scale ballroom. And, of course, the castle was absolutely fireproof. Nothing was too good for a man who had given his wife a collar made of 2,268 pearls and seven diamonds as large as grapes.

Almost immediately after Potter announced his intention to build his home on the north side, Prairie Avenue millionaires followed his stunning example, often buying their lots from his cache.

The Gold Coast—as this part of Chicago north of Oak Street came to be called—needed to refurbish its rundown, unpaved Lake Shore Drive. The Lincoln Park Board of Commissioners agreed to do the work and the new property owners agreed to pay a supplemental assessment to rebuild and pave the drive and to extend it to Bellevue. In addition, they improved the breakwater off the shore. The work was completed quickly. The Park Commissioners offered to rename the street Palmer Drive.

TOP: Gold Room of the Potter Palmer residence, 1350 North Lake Shore Drive, Chicago, circa 1900. (Chicago History Museum ICHi-68175)

BOTTOM: Main Gallery of the Potter Palmer residence, circa 1900. (Chicago History Museum ICHi-01266)

*Potter Palmer made the near north
side fashionable, a considerable
contribution to the transformation
of the neighborhood.*

The millionaire demurred. Property values doubled and then tripled. Palmer had made his final fortune.

The repair job on the drive brought the millionaires and the Park Commissioners closer together, setting up a cozy relationship for the future. It would lead to amending the 1872 plan and a predisposition to get it done.

It is unlikely that Potter Palmer, who also owned land on the St. Clair shore, William Ogden, the estate of Cyrus McCormick or any other circumspect shore owner negotiated hat in hand with the Park Board. At least three men carried their water. Attorney Henry N. Cooper, who made a career out of getting Lake Shore Drive built in the lake; General Charles Fitz-Simons, who owned a dredging and bridge building company; and Henry I. Sheldon, whose family was close with the Ogdens—indeed the Ogden and Sheldon Company owned lots on the St. Clair shore.

It has been speculated that Tobias Allmendinger, a German immigrant who invested in real estate, also interfaced with the Park Board on behalf of the project. But, years later as the development of Lake Shore Drive was nearing fruition, Allmendinger would be reluctant to throw his lot in with the Yankee millionaires. He is worth noting, however, because his lakefront property was at Oak and Michigan. If he had had a crystal ball, he might have seen that when the submerged land about 1,000 feet from the shore broke through the plain of the water, it would become the site of 999; and according to riparian rights, Allmendinger would have owned it. Instead he sold his rights.

Potter Palmer made the near north side fashionable, a considerable contribution to the transformation of the neighborhood. But another man, equally famous, was about to challenge the *hoi polloi* for supremacy of the made land. George Wellington "Cap'n" Streeter, a flimflam fabulist in a shiny top hat and tobacco-stained green frock coat, drove his boat into the middle of their riparian dream.

Painting by Anders Zorn (1860-1920) of Mrs. Potter Palmer, 1893, oil on canvas. (Potter Palmer Collection 1922.450. The Art Institute of Chicago)

George Wellington Streeter.
(Courtesy of University of Illinois
at Urbana-Champaign Library)

CHAPTER FIVE

The Con Man *Cometh*

On July 10, 1886, Cap Streeter and his tough as rawhide second wife, Maria Mulholland Streeter, beached their commuter boat, the *Reutan*, on a sandbar 463 yards from the Pine Street shore, about where Chicago Avenue and Lake Shore Drive intersect today. After dropping off passengers in Milwaukee, they were returning to Chicago empty. According to Streeter, a violent storm drove his vessel into shallow water where it became lodged on a sandbar.

A born showman, he enjoyed an arm's length relationship with the truth. His insistence on a storm is questionable. The weather forecast for July 10 called for a typical summer day—hot, dry and sunny. But Chicago's weather is notoriously capricious. Maybe the wind and rain weren't an imaginary contrivance. Or, maybe George, who years later seemed to forget his commuter-trip-to-Milwaukee story and switched it to a yarn about practicing gun running for an eventual voyage to liberate Honduras, maybe that George shipwrecked his rickety boat on purpose. It is likely Streeter had heard stories about landfill and maybe something called rip rights, and decided to make some of that good stuff for himself.

Shortly after the *Reutan* ran aground, city workers told Streeter to move his boat. They told him that it was stuck on city property. A few bystanders volunteered to help Marie and George pole and push their boat a few yards to the south, closer to Superior. When the city employees were satisfied that the *Reutan* had been correctly repositioned, Streeter must have chuckled. If the submerged land beneath his boat did not belong to the city, it must belong to him. Mr. and Mrs. Streeter made no effort to abandon ship. Instead they opted to live on it. They stayed for years, homesteading on water.

Friends helped build a footpath from the boat to the shore made of branches, twigs, bricks, stones, dirt and sand. Without a building code to constrain their construction efforts, human excrement and dead animals were tossed into the mix. Soon the Streeters had enough squishy landfill to walk to the shore without wading in the water.

George Wellington Streeter (right) repairing his ship, the Reutan. *(Courtesy of University of Illinois at Urbana-Champaign Library)*

The Reutan, *the boat in which Streeter was stranded near Chicago Avenue. In this photograph, it had already been moved to the shore. (Courtesy of University of Illinois at Urbana-Champaign Library)*

Immediately Streeter's battered craft began to act like a miniature breakwater. She captured grains of sand and held them close to her bow. Gradually, a small island formed around the *Reutan*. To augment his growing landmass, Streeter paid the drivers of garbage wagons to dump their loads on his property. Soon contractors hauling dirt from excavation sites were incented to join in. Over the years Streeter boasted that the presence of the *Reutan* created 186 acres of landfill, a hopelessly exaggerated engineering feat. Whatever, he didn't care. It was his.

Years drifted by. The Streeters eventually left their water-logged home. They repaired the vessel, rechristened it the *Maria* and put her to work as a sight-seeing boat. For a place to live, Cap bought an old scow, dragged it to where the John Hancock Building now stands, and turned it into the foundation for his new two-story house. He began dividing "his" made land into lots and sold them on the cheap. A tent city sprang up around the Cap'n and his wife, who woke up every morning thinking they were on the cusp of becoming tycoons.

One big problem sullied Streeter's fantasy. He did not own the land in anybody's eyes but his. The owners of the lots on the old shore were fairly certain riparian rights gave

them control of the landfill. A war was about to begin. It would play out on two distinct battlefields: the courtroom, where numerous lawsuits by shore owners and Streeter alike were paraded before weary-eared judges, and on the made land itself with fists, knives, pistols, machine guns, cannons and pots of boiling water.

Streeter, a former circus ringmaster and front man for a shady dance hall, argued with mock eloquence that before the *Reutan* arrived, the bed of the lake was the property of Illinois. No person owned it, until he made it appear. At which point, he was the natural owner based on—uh, oh—the right of discovery. This historic declaration of international law must have sounded plenty sophisticated to Streeter. Roughly speaking, it meant, whoever gets there first and plants a flag owns it. With only a year or two of formal schooling, he had no idea that "Discovery" grew out of a 1493 Papal Bull, which gave the New World to Spain. It established the precedent that the United States Supreme Court used to justify the right of colonial powers to strip indigenous peoples of their sacred lands in *Johnson v. M'Intosh* (1823).

Streeter had a gift for lawyerly-like debate without understanding a thimble-full of law. When the discovery

View looking west from foot of Pearson Street, showing Chicago
Water Works tower and garbage wagons filling in the property
in Streeterville. (Courtesy of University of Illinois at Urbana-
Champaign Library)

argument fell on deaf ears, he waved a map from 1821
under a judge's nose. Drawn up by the federal government,
it clearly showed that the Illinois boundary stopped at the
water's edge and that Streeter's land was in the lake at the
time of statehood. Therefore the lakebed actually belonged
to the United States of America, under whose laws it
belonged to him. Lower courts were reluctant to dismiss
that line of thought. Maybe the crazy-looking old coot
had something there. But they never affirmed Streeter's
grasping at straws.

Over the years, Streeter pulled many strange and fanci-
ful arguments out of his top hat, probably with the help
of William H. Cox, who had bought land from Streeter.
Cox wrote lengthy treatises in a jumbled parody of legal
jargon. They had become allies. If squatter's rights didn't
carry the day, how about a deed from an Indian tribe
or a petition filed under the Homestead Act that was
denied because the Act only applied to land west of the
Mississippi River or a land warrant Streeter received after
the Civil War in recognition of his service to the Union,
which might have held sway had Streeter not been a
deserter. Streeter also asserted that he had acquired the
land from the estate of a veteran of the War of 1812, the

proof of which was locked in a safe, which he refused to
open, fearful that some criminal would steal it. When
all that failed he produced a letter signed by President
Grover Cleveland granting him the land. It turned out
to be a crude forgery, probably the work of Cox's steady
hand and fine penmanship. The Cap'n ballyhooed a patent
signed and sealed by federal land commissioner Silas W.
Lamoreaux. That, too, was forged. As the battle over the
reclaimed land unfolded, Lamoreaux would become a bit
of a forgery himself.

Streeter's antics in civil court were delightfully silly
and so patently devious that they endeared him to a public hungry for a folk hero. He made good copy. Publishers
knew they sold more papers with Streeter in the headlines,
so they tooted his man-of-the-people horn at every opportunity. The Chicago Examiner, in particular, loved him,
wrote of his exploits in the vernacular and designed political cartoons that showed Streeter humiliating his big city
opponents. However, the actions that brought him into
criminal court raised doubts about the evenness of his keel.

Around the time a small portion of Streeter's supposed landfill merged with the original shore, the millionaire owner of that property, Nathaniel Kellogg Fairbank,

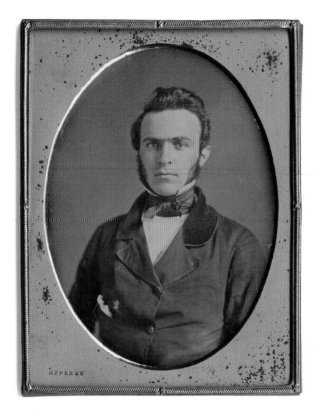

John Villiers Farwell, Jr., an active
participant in the war with Cap Streeter.
(Chicago History Museum ICHi-36225)

ABOVE: Nathaniel Kellogg Fairbank, circa 1845-1869.
(Chicago History Museum ICHi-68132)

RIGHT: A marketing piece, "Fairbank's Cherubs," presented
with compliments of N. K. Fairbank & Company, lard reformers, Chicago & St. Louis, circa 1890. (Library of Congress
Prints and Photographs Division Washington, D.C.)

Chicago's king of lard, soap and cottonseed oil, rode his horse and buggy on to the made land to evict Streeter personally. Their confrontation turned into a shouting match. Streeter reached for his shotgun and Fairbank, the gentlest of souls, fled for the safety of civilized Chicago. He met with his lawyer. Much to his surprise, his lawyer warned him that riparian rights were ambiguous, akin to shadow boxing with the law. Taking Streeter to court might be a lengthy and expensive procedure, and the outcome was far from certain. Fairbank decided to bide his time.

Through an intermediary, another shore owner John V. Farwell, one of the leaders of retail stalwart Carson, Pirie, Scott & Company, hired thugs to serve eviction warrants to Streeter and the small community of malcontents, drifters, drug dealers, pickpockets and prostitutes who had gathered around him. Farwell's son directed the police to tear down a fence Streeter had built. Maria poured boiling water on their heads. Streeter protested and threatened to shoot the cops. They arrested him and charged him with carrying a concealed weapon and assault. Nothing came of this. It was the first of many curious legal decisions where

the courts let this obviously guilty man walk free.

In 1891 a fluky incident gave Streeter a thread of hope. The captain drew a map depicting his claim, everything from Superior to Ontario. Sometimes bureaucracies create needless procedural steps and sometimes they fall asleep at the wheel. Somehow the recorder's office accepted his map. The Rascher Company included Streeter's land in an insurance map of Chicago.

In 1893, police constable Charles Vogel organized a war party of carpenters and teamsters and entered Streeter's property. They began destroying the few flimsy structures, quickly reducing them to rubble. The reusable wooden boards were thrown into a pile and hauled away in horse drawn wagons. Streeter warned the interlopers that he would shoot them. Maria beat up one of the raiders. The couple was arrested and released. They moved to the south side. Streeter's retreat turned out to be a strategic withdrawal. In less than a year he was back on his land. This time he would act like a latter day John Wayne, jaw set, guns drawn, in a movie without moorings, directed by the Marx brothers.

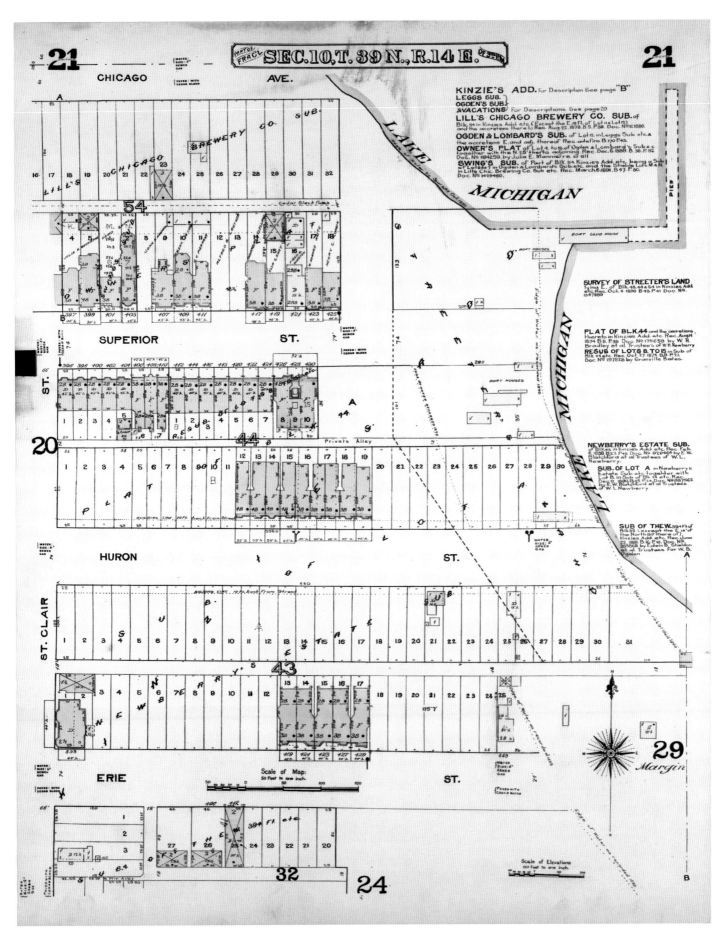

A map that erroneously labeled a parcel of land west of Lake Michigan as Streeter's, causing years of confusion.

From Atlas of Chicago published by Rascher, Volume 1, 1891, Sheet #21. (University of Illinois at Chicago)

CHAPTER SIX

STOP *and* GO *and* STOP

Persistence was the key to getting Lake Shore Drive off the ground and into the lake. The 1872 plan was stillborn but not forgotten. The 1875 *Tribune* editorial was ignored. The next time the plan surfaced was on April 27, 1886. On that day, Henry I. Sheldon representing Ogden, Sheldon & Co., large holders of property south of Pearson, reacquainted the Lincoln Park Board of Commissioners with the broad brush strokes of the 1872 agreement to extend Lake Shore Drive east into Lake Michigan at Oak Street, and then turn it south for an eventual rendezvous with Ohio Street.

Submerged land would rise like dough through natural accretion and man-made landfill. The shore owners on St. Clair would submit to a special assessment and pay for the entire project. The commissioners would then transfer title to the uncovered land to the shore owners as compensation for funding the project. Although the commissioners accepted the proposal, the Illinois Attorney General George Hunt blocked the deal.

With frustration steaming from every pore, the owners, commissioners, their lawyers and agents began knocking on doors in Springfield. They pushed for legislation specifically authorizing the scheme. On June 4, 1889, the General Assembly voted to give the Park Board the authority to build the road. The bill was entitled "An Act Enabling Park Commissioners Having Control of Any Boulevard or Driveway Bordering Upon Any Public Water in This State to Extend the Same."

The bill required the commissioners to get the written consent of the people or legal entities that owned two-thirds of the shore. In a complex series of steps, the Park District would own Lake Shore Drive and the riparian rights east of the drive, and the current shore owners, who would pay for the project, would own the reclaimed land.

When lawmakers pass a new law, they rarely admit

Judge Joseph E. Gary, Chicago, circa 1886, presided over the Haymarket Anarchist Trail and served on a blue-ribbon panel that recommended building a road in the lake. (Photographer: C. D. Mosher. Chicago History Museum ICHi-18750)

they did a bad thing. But these legislators understood the dubiousness of their actions and disclaimed the Act from the get-go. They characterized it as a "pretended" act, not passed in accordance with the articles of the Illinois Constitution. It could not be used as precedent for any

*The Army Corps of Engineers
was asked to verify or, if need be,
modify the technical plans, and
to confirm that the Drive did not
interfere with navigation.*

future laws. When it went into effect on July 1, 1889, the surest bet in Springfield was that someday its legal footing would be challenged.

To ameliorate the oncoming onslaught of criticism, the commissioners appointed a panel of esteemed men to decide if Lake Shore Drive built in Lake Michigan served the public interest. The panel consisted of Judge Joseph Elbert Gary, who had heard the Haymarket Riot case; Lambert Tree, an attorney, judge and diplomat; and E. S. Dreyer, a banker, who, a few years later, would trade his blue-ribbon status for prison garb. He would be convicted of embezzlement. The panel was asked to determine the value of the submerged land. They concluded that the question was too speculative and conjectural to venture a guess. In their final report, they urged the Board to strike a deal with the property owners, even if concessions had to be made.

The Army Corps of Engineers was asked to verify or, if need be, modify, the technical plans, and to confirm that the Drive did not interfere with navigation. Soundings were made and a harbor line established at the eastern edge of the nascent Lake Shore Drive. The Army's chief engineer filed a report with the War Department stating that he had no objections to the plan.

In 1891, the Lincoln Park Board of Commissioners signed a contract with General Charles Fitz-Simons of Fitz-Simons and Connell to build a breakwater near Oak Street. Fitz-Simons also was instructed to create landfill five feet six inches above the water. This would become the surface over which Lake Shore Drive would skim across the lake. For whatever reason, Fitz-Simons dawdled over the breakwater. Instead he laid the groundwork for the wedge-shaped Oak Street Beach

On Wednesday January 20, 1892, the Lincoln Park Board of Commissioners met the shore owners, or, more precisely, their high-priced attorneys and the stiff-collared trustees of their estates. Every agreement reached behind closed doors would be reviewed and ratified in an open session.

Alfred Hitchcock coined the term "MacGuffin" in 1935 to explain his art. Like a conjurer, he would misdirect the viewers into thinking his movie was about one thing, when actually it was about something else. *Psycho* starts out as a film about a heist. That's the MacGuffin. And then Norman Bates pulls back the shower curtain.

As far back as 1872, Lake Shore Drive was the MacGuffin. It concealed the real story—a land grab. True to form, the meeting began with a detailed discussion of the Drive. "A gentle curve from Bellevue to Oak...1,000 feet east into Lake Michigan...turns southeast...maintains an average distance of 1,000 feet from the old shore...travels 8,800 feet...links up with Indiana Street."

It's unclear how many shore owners actually attended the meeting. The Pine Street Land Association, a lobbying group and mutual interest society, was there. They spoke for the millionaires who owned lakefront property south of Chicago Avenue. So confident was the Association that they had already platted the submerged lands. The North Side Land Association represented the owners north of Pearson. They had more members and, as a result, moved more slowly.

The presentations continued. Praise was heaped on the shore owners. Their retainers must have nodded appreciatively.

The landowners "will fund the construction...estimated at $100 per running foot...pay for curbs and all paving of cross streets...no Chicagoan will pay taxes for the 'finest boulevard...ever laid out in any city'...will vacate voluntarily their property to widen Pine Street...turn over to the Park Board the deeds to the land the drive will occupy...surrender their rights to any submerged land east of the finished drive...bear the expense of the landfill...will

*A tip of the hat must go to Potter
Palmer for gentrifying the north side.
Bertha and he moved to an area as
desolate as the far side of the moon, an
act that attracted other millionaires.*

*Lake Shore Drive, circa 1890, looking north from about
Goethe. The Palmer mansion is in the background on the left.
(Chicago History Museum ICHi-37286)*

What did the shore owners get
in return? On the east-west streets,
21,000 feet of frontage and title
to $12 million worth of made land—
a 600% return on investment.

cost them in the range of $2 million...for everything." That was the MacGuffin.

What did the shore owners get in return? On the east-west streets, 21,000 feet of frontage and title to $12 million worth of made land. Nobody mentioned that it was a 600% return on investment. That was the movie.

General Fitz-Simons promised to complete the job by October 1, 1892. When paving and landscaping were finished, the Lincoln Park Board of Commissioners would take charge of the parks and roads. The area between the river and Indiana retained its commercial flavorings. Docks, piers, stables and houses costing less than $15,000 were prohibited. The property east of the Water Works would become a public park. It is still municipal property—a fire station; the Seneca Play Lot; the Museum of Contemporary Art, previously the site of the 1st Cavalry National Guard Armory; and Lake Shore Park. With regard to the bulk of the new land, the residentialists had triumphed over the harborites. The McCormick estate had capitulated a long time ago.

After the meeting adjourned, the lawyers for the shore owners surrendered their deeds to the Park Board. The Board peeled off a 200-foot wide strip of land and reserved it for Lake Shore Drive. In due course, the deeds were returned to the millionaires. The Pine Street Land Association, which served the landowners with holdings near the river, hired Chicago Title and Trust to hold the deeds. The North Side Land Association represented owners north of Pearson and put their deeds in escrow at the Northern Trust Company. Upon completion of Lake Shore Drive and the landfill, every deed would be returned to its beneficial owner.

The *Chicago Tribune* credited Henry I. Sheldon and two members of the Park Board—General Richard Stockton, one of five original commissioners, and John Worthy, a stone dealer, all of whom spent the better part

of six years overseeing the process. Soon, a third commissioner's name would surface as a behind the scenes force—Horatio N. May, a retired city controller and wholesale grocer. The *Trib* especially admired how these fine gentlemen prescreened every deed, every transfer of property, every contract, and every word, comma, dash and period with the most respected lawyers in the city. They neglected to mention that Worthy and May had a conflict of interest. They owned property on the shore.

A tip of the hat must go to Potter Palmer for gentrifying the north side. Bertha and he moved to an area as desolate as the far side of the moon, an act that attracted other millionaires to North Lake Shore Drive. His neighbors now included Honest Abe's son, Robert Todd Lincoln, the former Minister to England; a protégé of Marshall Field, Harry Selfridge, who took what he learned from the master to London, where he opened his own department store, Selfridge's; suburban real estate developer Samuel Gross, who claimed Edmond Rostand stole *Cyrano de Bergerac* from him; Reverend David Swing, the most popular Chicago preacher of his time; William Borden, whose dairy provided one-fourth of Chicago's milk; and Harold McCormick, the son of Cyrus and the husband of Edith Rockefeller, whose father was the world's richest man.

Two spoilers, however, were about to take center stage. An irate Illinois State Senator, Henry Bartling, was about to investigate the theft of the lakefront. Illinois Attorney General Maurice Thomas Moloney would sue the millionaire shore owners, challenge their riparian rights and demand that they return the shore to the people.

CHAPTER SEVEN

SENATOR BARTLING *and* ATTORNEY GENERAL MOLONEY *Go to* WAR

The Democrats won the election of 1892. Nationally, Grover Cleveland, a former President of the United States (1884–88), barely beat the incumbent Benjamin Harrison in the popular vote and cruised to victory in the Electoral College. His running mate was Adlai Ewing Stevenson of Illinois, whose favorite son coattails pulled many lackluster Illinois Democrats across the finish line.

Across the nation, the Republican loss was fueled by their support of high tariffs. The working class translated that into fewer jobs for them at lower pay. The GOP's posture as the anti-immigration party cost them dearly in big cities, including Chicago, particularly in German and Irish neighborhoods.

President Cleveland's personal reputation was crafted during his battles with Tammany Hall in New York City. Known for challenging corrupt practices in politics and business, he attracted similarly inclined men to his party. In Illinois, two self-styled reformers heard his call, campaigned as crusaders against corruption and were swept into office—Attorney General Maurice Thomas Moloney of Ottawa and State Senator Henry Bartling from a German Lutheran district on the North Side of Chicago.

Both men expressed a growing curiosity over the Lake Shore Drive submerged land deal. They smelled rats on the Lincoln Park Board of Commissioners and among their wealthy cronies.

Bartling struck first, spurred to action when General Fitz-Simons' men drove piles into the lake 180 feet farther from the shore than the agreement called for. That looked to him like theft of the people's property. Under the auspices of the State Legislature, he formed a committee to investigate the affair. The first hearing occurred on May 14, 1893. The committee went on record that they were going to "get at the true inwardness" of the deal. Their working hypothesis was that the well-heeled shore owners were spending no more than $500,000 on improvements to receive property valued at $10 million. That was too large a sum of money for everything to be on the up and up.

"It was an illegal deal," assumed Bartling, before gathering his first fact. "And we are going to do what we can to restore (to) the people their rights."

In Bartling's theory of the case, the Lincoln Park commissioners lacked the constitutional authority to build Lake Shore Drive—notwithstanding the 1889 special legislation. In his opinion, the Federal Government controlled navigable water and not Illinois, riparian rights only extended to the water's edge, and the Park Board had no right to sell the people's submerged land.

The first witness was ex-commissioner N. E. Liecht. He testified that he was in Europe when the drive was authorized. He passed the buck to fellow commissioners John Worthy and Horatio N. May, and asserted that they engineered the deal and that the idea came from the property owners. Liecht made Bartling's morning when he revised the value of the submerged land up by 50%.

Bartling couldn't believe his ears. "Then the land will be worth $15 million," sputtered Bartling, overcome with delight. "Will it not?"

Subsequent witnesses, however, kept lowering the perceived value of the land. When the guesstimates sank to $3.75 million, Bartling stopped asking for expert opinions.

Every witness associated with the Lincoln Park Board testified that they did nothing wrong, that it was the shore

In Bartling's theory of the case, the Lincoln Park commissioners lacked the constitutional authority to build Lake Shore Drive—notwithstanding the 1889 special legislation.

Honorable Maurice T. Moloney, Attorney General of Illinois.
(The Newberry Library, Chicago. F 8395 .03, vol. 16)

Honorable Henry C. Bartling. (Courtesy University of Illinois
at Urbana-Champaign Library)

owners who instigated and lobbied for Lake Shore Drive. A former secretary of the Board, E. S. Taylor, told the committee that the first time a Drive was discussed was "contemporaneous with the opening of the park" in 1865. Taylor informed the committee that both Worthy and May would profit from this deal. He confirmed Bartling's suspicion that the shore owners had helped to write the 1889 State law.

Already a villain in Bartling's eyes, Horatio May was sworn in. He testified that the shore owners had informed the Board that they were building the Drive farther out in the lake. No one on the Board told them "no." So they plunged ahead. Who can blame them? He added that the money set aside to build a seawall had been diverted into making a beach. May assured the committee that if and when the Drive was completed, the commissioners could reject the work for good cause. Then the Drive and made land would revert to the State.

When Bartling tried to call the shore owners as witnesses, he was stonewalled. Apparently, the trusts that held their deeds were "hidden trusts." The identities of the individual owners were confidential. Lawyers for the trusts stood behind their ironclad walls. Senator Bartling threatened to exercise his subpoena power and generate more negative publicity than the millionaires probably

wanted. After a few days of bargaining, the lawyers turned over the names of some of the shore owners.

Among those on the list were the Chicago Dock and Canal Company, the estates of Cyrus McCormick and William B. Ogden. They shared ownership of the submerged land between Grand Avenue and Ohio Street. Ontario to Erie was controlled by Ogden, Sheldon and Company. Erie to Huron was divided up among the Newberry Library, attorney Horace Hulbert, socialite Jessica McCreery and the enterprising Potter Palmer. The shore between Huron and Superior belonged to the Newberry family and N. K. Fairbank. John V. Farwell owned the shore from Superior Street to Chicago Avenue. In accordance with the rules of riparian rights, the Farwell and Newberry families built piers off their property that were never used in the hope of establishing a precedent for ownership of the land covered by Lake Michigan.

Chicago to Pearson belonged to the public. There were many owners of the lots between Pearson and Oak, among them, B. F. and A. C. McNeill; Mrs. Minnie Allmendinger, Tobias' widow; General Charles Fitz-Simons, whose access to inside information led him to buy whatever land was available; the reprehensible Cuthbert W. Laing, a real estate dealer, who in a decade's time would be sued by his own daughter for not telling her that she had inherited

Walter L. Newberry (1804-1868) gave his lakefront property to the Newberry Library. (Chicago History Museum ICHi-68173)

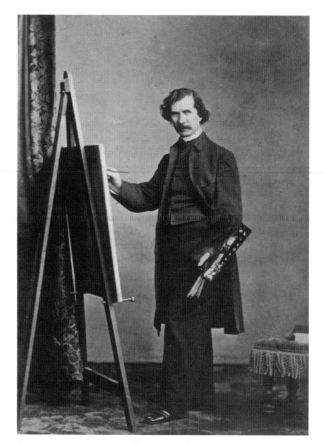

George Peter Alexander Healy, famed society portrait artist and lakefront property owner. (Photographer: John Corbut. Chicago History Museum ICHi-68128)

a small fortune from her deceased mother; and George P. A. Healy, one of America's most accomplished portrait artists. Bertha Palmer treasured his painting of her, even more than the one done by Anders Zorn, which the Art Institute has in its permanent collection.

Five months on the job, the first-term State Senator must have realized he was tangling with some of the most formidable men in America. They represented a mix of Democrats and Republicans, all of whom could snap his political twig with large contributions to a rival. To make matters dicier for Bartling, many of the titans had gifted a portion of their submerged holdings to charities. The ultimate beneficiaries included St. Luke's Hospital, the Newberry Library, the Home for the Friendless, the Chicago Historical Society, Graceland Cemetery, the Legal Aid Society, Children's Memorial Hospital, the Art Institute of Chicago and United Charities of Chicago.

For the good of his career, Senator Bartling could have abandoned his investigation, turning it loose in a frosty Chicago wind, watching it fly away in the night sky. Instead he issued a report that described the project as a "theft from the navigable waters of Lake Michigan" motivated by avarice. Bartling passed the baton to the Attorney General of Illinois, recommending that he "take all necessary steps to obtain possession of the lands created

in the waters of Lake Michigan and do all in his power to prevent greedy "shore owners from encroaching on the people's water."

In 1867, at 18 years old, Maurice Thomas Moloney emigrated from Ireland to the United States. Four years later, he graduated from the University of Virginia with a Bachelor of Law degree and moved to Ottawa, Illinois. There he served as a city attorney and later as state's attorney before his election to Attorney General of Illinois in 1892.

Two years earlier in 1890, the United States Congress passed the Sherman Anti-Trust Act. It breezed through the Senate 51–1 and the House 242–0. Its avowed purpose was not to regulate business, but to protect ordinary people from unfair business practices. The theory: competition tends to foster lower prices and safer products, and trusts limit competition. The Act tried to ensure a level playing field with many competitors duking it out for market share. Almost overnight, "trusts" became a bad word, on equally bad footing with monopolies and conspiracies.

Bartling had discovered trusts at the center of the lakefront wheeling and dealing. Now Moloney picked up the cudgel. He believed that the owners of these particular trusts used their wealth and influence to secure favorable legislation. In an inherently non-competitive manner, the

Sure, they pledged their own money,
because what they were buying was
worth five times what they were
putting up.

shore owners acted as one to wheedle the Park Board out of the people's land. Sure, they pledged their own money, because what they were buying was worth five times what they were putting up. Maybe more. In February 1894, Moloney informed the press that he questioned the primacy of riparian rights and the constitutionality of the 1889 law. He was considering a lawsuit.

Attorney Henry N. Cooper, who had worked for the shore owners for years, ridiculed Moloney. Acting befuddled, he said that the Attorney General had seen the details of the project in a private meeting a year earlier and had openly expressed his satisfaction "with the legality of the Lake Shore Drive extension."

In mid-April, Moloney wrote an opinion denying the legitimacy of the entire project. He argued that the legislature had no right to transfer State property to private parties. He announced that the case he was building would soon be presented to the court. He felt the people needed a cease and desist order to shut down construction of Lake Shore Drive. His list of possible defendants included the City of Chicago, the five current members of the Lincoln Park Board of Commissioners and the millionaire members of the Pine Street Land Association.

Serendipitously, the United States Supreme Court gave Moloney a reason to gloat. They had "just handed down a decision of portentous importance." The court redefined the doctrine of riparian rights. Shore owners now needed authorization from their State to build a pier even in shallow water. One can imagine Moloney waving the ruling in the air for all to see, breaking into an old country jig before regaining his composure.

Moloney obsessed over the size and value of the potential landfill, as if a very large number proved impropriety, instead of a good business deal. He wrote, "Aggregated wealth is aggregated selfishness."

Cooper brushed off Moloney's attempt to manufacture

a quotable sentence by suggesting that he was measuring the shore from the wrong place, that he was confusing natural occurrences with landfill. In a bombshell announcement, Cooper warned that, if Moloney pressed his case, his clients would work side-by-side with the Attorney General to prove that the legislature had acted unconstitutionally. They would demand that the Park Board return their riparian rights. Then they would build a harbor approachable by large vessels, put up wharfs and warehouses and turn the near north side into a low rent commercial district, complete with drunken sailors and barroom brawls.

General Fitz-Simons also chimed in. If a lawsuit were brought against him, he would sue the commissioners for damages—$100,000 on the button—for failing to fulfill their contracts. On April 14, 1894, he sent a letter to the Park Board affirming his intention.

Once again, the commissioners responded that they had done nothing wrong. Whatever happened, they would abide by the decision of the court. They scoffed at Fitz-Simons' letter, telling the *Tribune* that his contract was with the property owners, not them. "That is a good game of bluff," laughed one commissioner.

On April 26, 1894, a meeting was held at the Newberry Library between representatives of every owner and the AG and his staff. The owners had asked for the meeting. They wanted to present reasons why the suit should be quashed. Instead, they offered no objections to an immediate trial. Moloney nodded and explained it was his duty to conserve the interests of the people of Illinois. He went on to say that he would ask the court to order the removal of "every remnant of the Drive and landfill." One could construe that by every remnant, Moloney meant every grain of sand, every molecule of concrete. Total obliteration. Self-righteous and sanctimonious, Moloney seemed to prefer an exorcism instead of a trial. But instead he announced that

the case was on the calendar of Judge Thomas G. Windes. It was called the *People* ex rel. *Moloney v. Kirk.* Charles S. Kirk must have been stunned. He was the newest member of the Board. He had had nothing to do with Lake Shore Drive. He made soap. Nevertheless the trial would begin in May.

George Wellington Streeter knew how to read, and he was aghast at newspaper accounts of the impending trial. They failed to mention him or his claim. The Commissioners, the millionaire dandies and the Attorney General were pulling on his land like it was taffy. But he didn't jump into the fray. He had a wealthy surrogate.

Ed Pardridge, a legendary short-seller of wheat and a successful speculator in real estate, hired attorney Francis E. Burton to represent a number of persons who had purchased lots on the landfill from Streeter. The Cap'n liked to brag that he had sold over 200 lots—most certainly a crime since he had never owned any of them. Burton said his clients were only seeking recognition of their interests.

A map from 1818—the year Illinois became a state— fixed the boundary line on the western shore of Lake Michigan. Illinois had no right to any new land made in the water.

Followers of Pardridge's activities—and there were many—assumed that he knew Streeter's landfill was an unsettled legal question worth millions, and that he had a chance to cash in big time. Why else would he gamble his own money to join the fight?

Burton met privately with Moloney and asked him to add a few defendants to the suit. One of them would be the United States of America. They had legal superiority over Illinois and its rinky-dink Park Board. Using a selection of maps, plats, abstracts and various other official looking miscellanea, Burton walked Moloney through the arguments advanced by Streeter and Peter J. Johnson, who claimed land south of Streeter's property nearer to

the river. Between them, Burton explained, they own a big chunk of land east of St. Clair.

Moloney leaned back in his chair. This could be interesting. It turned out that a man named Lewis H. Van Diver administered the estate of the late John Scott, a private in a Maryland regiment during the War of 1812. For his service in the early wars of the Republic, Scott was awarded a land warrant for 40 acres to be applied anywhere in the United States or its territories. Scott never used it. Burton showed the document to Moloney. It was seamed and battered, full of erasures, and dim with age. On April 1, 1892, Cap Streeter brought the warrant to the office of the Recorder of Deeds and had it placed in the official record. Streeter located the 40 acres of ground 451 feet east of St. Clair, between Chicago Avenue and Erie Street. The captain got his hands on another warrant or two and used them to secure more adjacent land. This was genuine proof—these grants from a grateful nation—that Streeter really did own his land.

Burton had more. A map from 1818—the year Illinois became a State—fixed the boundary line on the western shore of Lake Michigan. Illinois has no right to any new land made in the water. The title was still vested in the United States, not Illinois.

Burton told Moloney that Streeter did not care for the lawsuit, the Attorney General, the courts, the State or the City of Chicago. He only cared for the United States of America. He did not want to become a defendant himself.

Burton mentioned that Peter Johnson also was one of his clients. For many years, Johnson had lived south of Erie Street near the lakeshore as a squatter. He laid claim to the ground between Erie and the North Pier. Johnson

Silas W. Lamoreaux, corrupt Federal Land Commissioner. (Image from the Library of Congress, Chronicling America: Historic American Newspapers site. Courtesy of the Ohio Historical Society)

SILAS W. LAMOREAUX.

had not attracted the celebrity of Streeter, but he was just as cocksure that his claim was valid.

Burton discussed another possible defendant—William H. Cox, who had purchased some lots from Streeter and wanted more. Cox had written to the General Land Office at Washington, D.C. in October 1893, seeking permission to acquire 130 acres of land in Kinzie's Addition. The particular parcel of land had not been surveyed. He enclosed $162.50 to pay for the land and asked the government to execute an official survey. The Commissioner of the Land Office, Silas W. Lamoreaux replied to Cox with a coldly formal letter. The land in question did not belong to the United States. Therefore Illinois has to conduct the survey and make such determinations as it sees fit. Lamoreaux returned the money to Cox and suggested he read up on the law.

Ignoring the letter from Lamoreaux, Burton told the *Chicago Tribune*, "No one has produced anything to show that the Lake Shore Drive land does not belong to the United States."

"Your clients want to get into the case to get a quasi-recognition of their claims, don't they?" asked the *Tribune*.

"No sir, nothing of the kind. I had a long talk with the Attorney General. He doesn't think that those Pine Street Land Association people have any right to the property, and he wants to hear about Streeter's claim. In the interest of justice all should be included."

Later that day Cap Streeter held court in his office on the thirteenth floor of the Chicago Title and Trust building, a space probably secured for him by Pardridge.

"I got my title from the government and I don't want anything to do with the city," said Streeter. "I and Johnson are the only people owning that property, and we'll hold it."

"I got my title from the government and I don't want anything to do with the city," said Streeter. "I and Johnson are the only two people owning that property."

"Is your map on file at the City Hall, Captain?" asked a reporter.

"I have all the maps there I need or am ever going to have. I am outside the City of Chicago."

Representatives of the Pine Street Land Association ridiculed the claims of Streeter and Johnson. Again Cooper was the spokesman. "The Supreme Court had settled Streeter's claim. The Scott warrant is full of flaws and will never stand (up to) a judicial examination."

After numerous continuances, the *People v. Kirk* trial began on November 28, 1894 before Judge Windes. Burton's petition had been rejected—he had a federal claim and he should have been in federal court. Moloney's case was built around five contentions.

First, the shore owners were not building Lake Shore Drive as a public works project. Profit was their motive.

Second, the riparian rights of an owner do not extend into navigable water.

Third, the act of the Legislature sanctioning the Drive and new land was class legislation. It granted privileges to the Lincoln Park Board Commissioners and the shore owners unavailable to everybody else.

Fourth, the special act passed by the legislature violated Article 4, Section 13 of the Illinois Constitution, which states that "No act...shall embrace more than one subject and that shall be expressed in the title." The law is often a literal game. Since the title of the 1889 bill only mentioned extending roads near water and not the sale of submerged land, it was *ipso facto* unconstitutional.

Fifth, filling in the waters of the lakeshore was an encroachment upon the domain of the United States. Illinois did not have the authority to give it away.

EXHIBIT C.

MAP OF THE OHIO STREET EXTENSION OF THE LAKE SHORE DRIVE.

ISHAM RANDOLPH, Consulting Engineer.

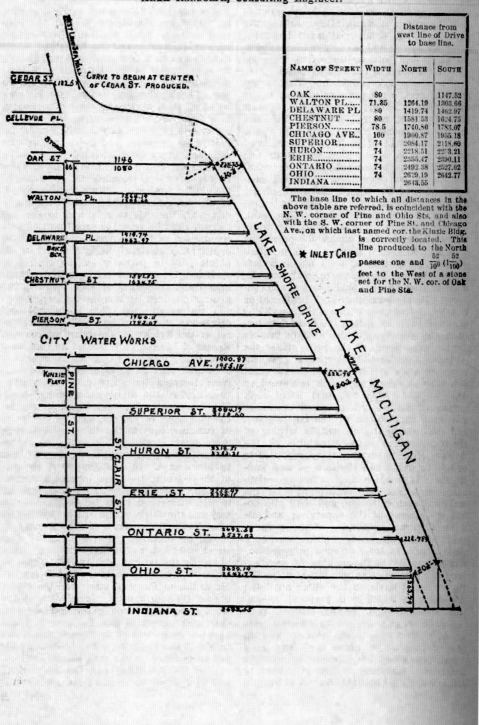

Map of Lake Shore Drive, circa 1897, shows that the last section of the Drive to be completed was East Lake Shore Drive and the connection to North Lake Shore Drive. (Courtesy of Rinn Law Library, DePaul College of Law)

View looking north from the foot of Superior Street captures the emptiness of Streeterville in 1910. Lake Michigan is on the right. (Courtesy of University of Illinois at Urbana-Champaign Library)

The lead attorney for the Park Board denied every allegation in the Attorney General's suit. The lawyer for the Ogden estate said the profits to be derived from the landfill were exaggerated. The counsel for the North Side Land Association pointed out that the War Department had approved the project. Therefore, there was no encroachment on Federal water.

From the beginning, Moloney seemed to be drowning in his own spittoon.

Every time he tried to make a point and a plaintiff's lawyer objected, Judge Windes sustained it. When Moloney objected to something, he was overruled. Windes wouldn't allow the prosecution to discuss land values. It was opinion, not fact. He wouldn't sit still for a 55-year history of the shore. Immaterial. Moloney tried to prove that the owners and their contractors began working before contracts had been signed. Immaterial. Again.

On January 30, 1895, Judge Windes rendered his verdict and dismissed Moloney's entire suit. The shore owners were allowed to keep the submerged property sold to them by the Park Board. Riparian rights, however, did not carry the day. Windes agreed with the Attorney General that Illinois owned the submerged land. But the State Legislature had acted within its constitutional rights.

They represented both the State and the people, and determined what was in the best interests of each. They had every right to convey public property to private individuals. What's more, there was no compelling evidence that the landfill would interfere with navigation or fishing. In his summary, the judge lobbed a zinger at Moloney. If he believed that a felony had been committed, he should have brought the case to criminal court.

Judge Windes also ruled in favor of the Lincoln Park Board of Commissioners. They had the right to determine the latitude, longitude, length and breadth of Lake Shore Drive. He referred the issue of ownership of the land adjoining city property near the Water Works to a Master of Chancery.

In 1896, the Illinois Supreme Court affirmed Judge Windes's decision, and the citizens of Illinois voted Moloney out of office.

Work on Lake Shore Drive began again. In 1902, the last leg of the drive was completed. It was the extension of Oak Street, now called East Lake Shore Drive. The creation of acres of new land did not lead to a building boom. North of Pearson, no new buildings were added to the still dreary landscape. Other men stilled claimed the land, not the least of them was the indefatigable George W. Streeter.

Exterior view of Captain George W. Streeter's shack and surrounding yard, Chicago, circa 1905. The shack was erected in an area that later became the Streeterville neighborhood. (Photographer: Chicago Daily News, Inc. Chicago History Museum DN-0003554)

ABOVE: Chief Simon Pokagon claimed Streeterville on behalf of the Potawatomi tribe. (Courtesy of the Center for History)

LEFT: A contemplative Captain George Wellington Streeter. (Courtesy of University of Illinois at Urbana-Champaign Library)

CHAPTER EIGHT

STREETER *Redux*

In February 1847, Colonel William McKee of the 2nd Kentucky Volunteer Regiment was killed during the Battle of Buena Vista in the Mexican-American War. In 1853, Congress enacted a special bill giving each of McKee's orphaned children scrip entitling them to a quarter section of land, which could be located on any vacant land in the United States. In need of cash, the orphans sold their scrip. Eventually they ended up with Harvey M. LaFollette, who led a syndicate that tried to use the McKee scrip to acquire the Kinzie Addition to Chicago.

An educator, LaFollette had been the Indiana Superintendent of Public Instruction. He founded the LaFollette Coal, Iron and Railway Company in Tennessee. He was a first cousin of "Fighting" Bob LaFollette of Wisconsin, who in 1957 was voted one of the five greatest senators in U.S. history, along with Henry Clay, Daniel Webster, John Calhoun and Robert Taft.

Harvey LaFollette fell in with a crooked and corrupt politician. Silas W. Lamoreaux, the Federal Land Commissioner who had bluntly rejected William Cox's application for a piece of Kinzie's Addition in 1893, jumped through hoops to accommodate LaFollette's request to use the scrip to boot McCormick, Ogden, et al. off the same land in 1897.

William McKinley and the Republicans had taken back the White House in 1896. Lamoreaux, who came to office under Cleveland, was likely to be out of a job. To ensure that his pals would get the Kinzie Addition, he awarded them a patent for the land. He put his written decision in a sealed envelope to be opened on Tuesday, February 23 and went on vacation. But he made a fatal mistake. He gave a copy of his secret document to Harvey LaFollette, who prematurely leaked it to the press.

Immediately the shore owners learned of the deceit. They were politically connected. The concept of six degrees of separation was not yet understood, but these men were closer than that to just about anybody important. Emergency telegrams dot-dash-dotted out of Chicago bound for Washington. Outgoing President Cleveland was alerted. The incensed incoming Secretary of the Interior, Cornelius Bliss, leapt into action. He gave Lamoreaux an offer he didn't refuse—to avoid public humiliation, prosecution and possibly prison, he was told to order an immediate rehearing of the matter and resign. Lamoreaux complied.

In the new hearing, Bliss sided with the shore owners. Case closed, except for the appeals by LaFollette, all of which failed. But they had wasted time and had held back the development of the land.

One of the most unexpected claimants to the reclaimed land was the Potawatomi tribe. They had lived in the Upper Mississippi Valley. Their hunting grounds had hugged the shore of Lake Michigan from southwestern Michigan to northeastern Wisconsin. In the Treaty of Chicago of 1833 and the subsequent Treaty of 1846, they relinquished their claim to five million acres in exchange for cash and land west of the Mississippi. A band of the tribe, which had converted to Catholicism, was allowed to stay near St. Joseph, Michigan.

With crucifixes around their necks, they became adept at suing the government for breaches of various treaties. In the late nineteenth century, Chief Simon Pokagon and a couple of slick Chicago lawyers tried to reclaim Potawatomi land, including the lakefront property the shore owners had won in *People v. Kirk.* When the lawyers in the scheme didn't realize a quick buck, they wandered away. Chief Pokagon sold his quitclaim deed to William H. Cox, the sometime ally of Streeter. Cox filed his claim with the Indian Bureau of the Department of the Interior. It was rejected.

In the spring of 1901, Chief Simon's son, Charles, announced that he was planning an invasion of Streeterville to retake tribal land. His warriors would come on a

Captain George Wellington Streeter holding dog, standing with group of unidentified men, Streeterville, Chicago, 1918.

(Photographer: Chicago Daily News, Inc. Chicago History Museum DN-0070544)

chartered steamer from St. Joseph. It might have been the last great battle between the indigenous people and their Anglo conquerors. But it never got off the dock.

The most ornery, rambunctious and tenacious claimant remained Cap'n George Streeter. He went berserk after the courts awarded his land to the millionaires. His attempts to regain the uncovered land turned violent and seemed to escalate with each passing year.

In 1894 three sheriff's deputies stepped onto Streeter's supposed property. He shot them in the legs and buttocks with buckshot and was arrested for assault with a deadly weapon. A judge with a gift for irony dismissed the case on the grounds that buckshot was not deadly.

On April 5, 1899, Streeter seceded from the City of Chicago and the State of Illinois. His bailiwick now had a name, the District of Lake Michigan. Its dimensions ran from Oak Street to the river, from the lake to roughly St. Clair. Streeter pronounced district "deestrict," and the local newspapers made sure that goofy spelling and collo-quial mispronunciation stuck. "Deestrict" residents voted to retain the Constitution of the United States as the bedrock of their legal system. Streeter appointed himself

governor. William Niles, who had purchased land from him, was appointed military governor. Niles ordered his men to build a stockade and a courthouse out of two-by-fours. Streeter placed a small arsenal of revolvers, repeater rifles and ammunition in the stockade: an informal declara-tion of war. An American flag was raised in front of the courthouse. A large crowd gathered to watch the unfold-ing events from the safety of Pine Street. They cheered the insurgents' pluck. But they had to wait a month for the rhetoric and symbolism to boil over into action.

The 38 liberated male souls of the District celebrated their Independence Day on Thursday, the Fourth of May. Streeter stationed guards on the imaginary bor-der between the District and the city. His men hoisted the stars and stripes. Streeter read his version of the Declaration of Independence, which began with the famil-iar, "When in the course of human events," before veering from Jeffersonian flourishes to the vernacular to expound on a litany of grievances against the upper crust and the city that enabled them.

Two hundred policemen advanced on the celebrants. The onlookers rooted for a Streeter victory and shouted

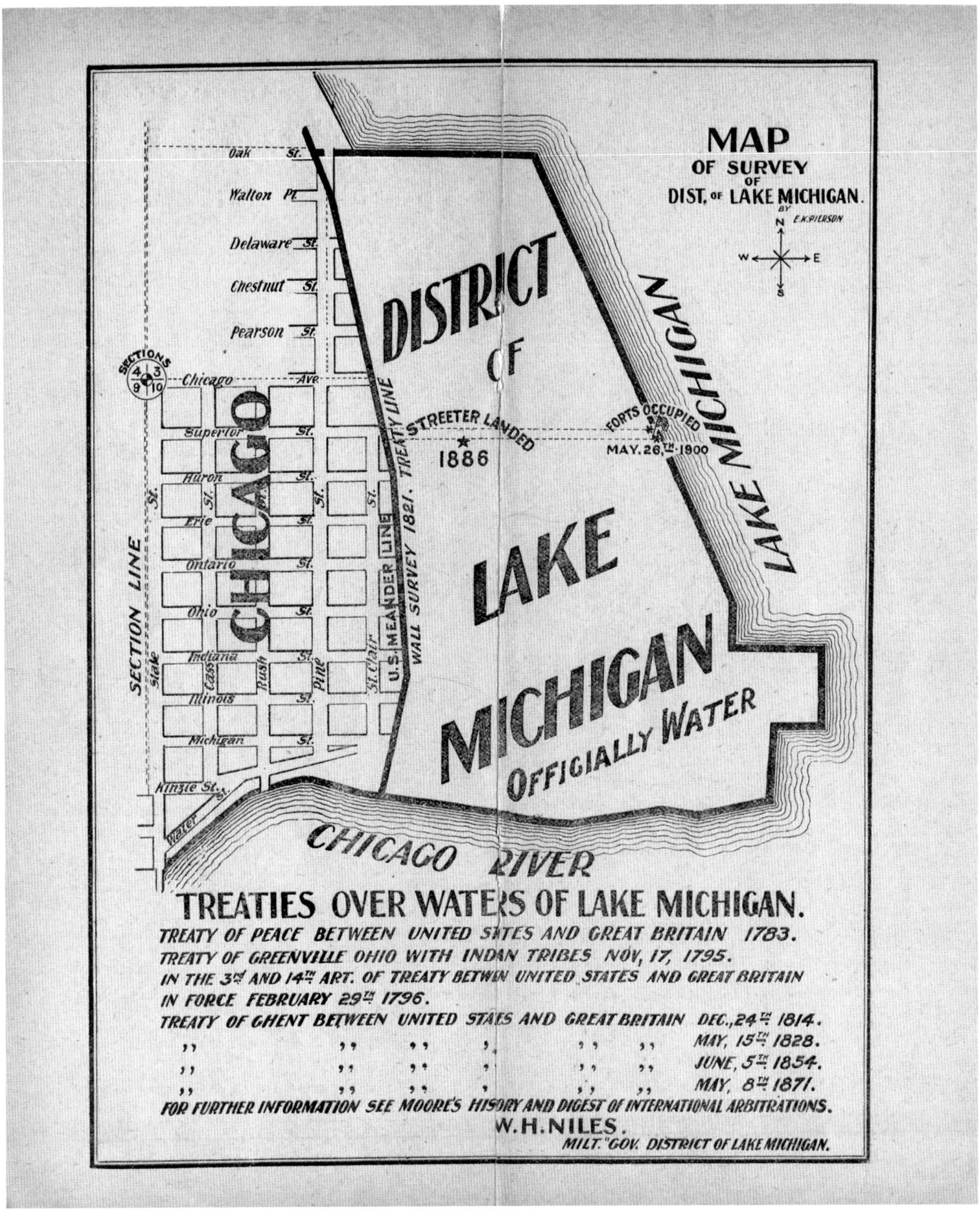
MAP
OF SURVEY
OF
DIST. OF LAKE MICHIGAN.
BY
E.K.PIERSON
N
W
E
S
Oak St.
Walton Pl.
Delaware St.
Chestnut St.
Pearson St.
SECTIONS
4 3
9 10
Chicago Ave.
Superior St.
Huron St.
Erie St.
Ontario St.
Ohio St.
Indiana St.
Illinois St.
Michigan St.
Kinzie St.
SECTION LINE
State St.
Cass St.
Rush St.
Pine St.
St. Clair St.
CHICAGO
DISTRICT OF LAKE MICHIGAN
OFFICIALLY WATER
U.S. MEANDER LINE
WALL SURVEY 1821. TREATY LINE
STREETER LANDED
1886
FORTS OCCUPIED
MAY. 26TH 1900
LAKE MICHIGAN
Water
CHICAGO RIVER
TREATIES OVER WATERS OF LAKE MICHIGAN.
TREATY OF PEACE BETWEEN UNITED STATES AND GREAT BRITAIN 1783.
TREATY OF GREENVILLE OHIO WITH INDAN TRIBES NOV. 17, 1795.
IN THE 3RD AND 14TH ART. OF TREATY BETWIN UNITED STATES AND GREAT BRITAIN
IN FORCE FEBRUARY 29TH 1796.
TREATY OF GHENT BETWEEN UNITED STATES AND GREAT BRITAIN DEC., 24TH 1814.
" " " " " " MAY, 15TH 1828.
" " " " " " JUNE, 5TH 1854.
" " " " " " MAY, 8TH 1871.
FOR FURTHER INFORMATION SEE MOORE'S HISORY AND DIGEST OF INTERNATIONAL ARBITRATIONS.
W.H. NILES.
MILT. GOV. DISTRICT OF LAKE MICHIGAN.

Map of the District of Lake Michigan. From a pamphlet, "The Military Government of the District of Lake Michigan: Its Legal Standing..." circa 1905. (Chicago Public Library, Special Collections and Preservation Division, SRT Box 1, Folder 43)

their support for the armed rebels, as they marched back and forth in front of their courthouse, weapons shouldered, trying to look like disciplined bad asses. Fearless police inspector, Max Heidelmeier walked into the enemy territory, grabbed Streeter by the collar and hauled the founding father off to jail. One by one the entire population was arrested, ending the battle without a shot being fired. The crowd retired to nearby saloons to relive their brush with history. The following Monday the police passively looked on as several men brandishing torches reduced the District of Lake Michigan to ashes. The defenders of the District were released on bail and never brought to trial.

Later in 1899, a man named Samuel Avery, a squatter like Streeter, built a boathouse about where 999's current private parking area is located. Streeter drove him away with a shotgun and claimed the boathouse as his own. A court ruled that Streeter was merely protecting his

Kirk talked tough, wore a cowboy hat,

carried a gun and lived in a hut about

where 999 stands today. Arguably,

he was a hit man posing as

a security guard.

property and let him keep the boathouse. Streeter did not seek clarification or base future arguments on what the precedent setting phrase "his property" meant.

Broad scale hostilities resumed on May 26, 1900 with a naval invasion. Thirteen brave men who owned lots in the District, including several Spanish-American War veterans in uniform, pushed off in two boats from the south side and headed for Superior Street without Streeter, who presumably stayed in bed. District commander William Niles planned and organized the attack. The boats carried beans, meat, shovels, axes, rifles and a Gatling gun. They landed at two o'clock in the morning, unopposed. Again an American flag was raised. An earthwork 12 feet high was built. A few rounds were fired from the Gatling gun to announce their readiness to die for their pretend district. At dawn the police trickled over. The rebels shot at them, wounding a horse and a 14-year-old bystander. By noon the police had regrouped. A force of 600 cops, some with Winchester repeaters, others with pistols and clubs, descended on the out-numbered, out-gunned rebels. A Chicago fireboat armed to the gills raced to the scene. Two of Streeter's enlisted men lost their nerve and deserted, taking the Gatling gun with them.

From a law enforcement perspective the days of molly-coddling Streeter's land-baron fantasies were over. Lincoln Park policeman, William Hayes, swinging his baton on a leather thong, approached Niles and offered him a make-up-your-mind-right-now choice: immediate arrest or a terrible beating. Niles seemed to capitulate but refused to turn over his rifle. The cops charged, and Niles tried to bayonet them. They gang-tackled the commander, pounded him with fists and clubs, slapped him in manacles and fast-walked his bruised and bleeding body to the police station. Niles' confederates were more docile and surrendered at the first opportunity, but they, too, were beaten sense-less. Weeks later a jury acquitted the invaders of assault

and lesser charges. If the police were reprimanded, it was with a wink.

After that decisive defeat, Streeter moved to the Tremont Hotel. He continued to sell lots, sometimes to undercover cops. He bragged that an army of 1,000 men would retake the District, as soon as he sold 1,000 lots, but when Streeter tried to recapture the land in 1901, only 15 men rallied to his side. Some of the liberators came on foot; others rode in two covered wagons with women and children on board. They respected the handful of fences that had been erected by agents for the millionaires. Quickly, quietly, Streeter and his band repossessed the land and set up a tent village in open spaces, the largest of Cap's reign. In the next few days the enterprising settlers built a makeshift windmill.

Louisa Healy, the widow of the famed portrait artist and an owner of lots on the old shore, obtained a court order demanding that Streeter and his cohorts evacuate her property. Streeter tore up the eviction notice. He was arrested for contempt of court. Once again he was released and the charges dropped.

But he returned in October 1901. A hundred supporters cheered him on. For some reason, he was allowed to stay, as the shore owners tried a dangerous alternative strategy. Attorney Henry Cooper hired armed watchmen to live on the landfill to keep Streeter in check. One of those men, John A. Kirk, no relation to the Kirk in the *People v. Kirk*, was brought in from the same rough and tumble territory in western Missouri that spawned the legendary outlaws Jesse and Frank James, Cole Younger and his brothers and the Dalton Gang. Kirk talked tough, wore a cowboy hat, carried a gun and lived in a hut about where 999 stands today. Arguably, he was a hit man posing as a security guard—a step or two below hired killer in the criminal hierarchy. Streeter's bodyguards lived in a white tent near Delaware Street. Both sides

TOP: Captain Streeter with his first wife, Maria Mulholland, Billy McNamara and two unidentified cops, Chicago, 1902. (Chicago History Museum ICHi-22283)

BOTTOM: Captain George Wellington Streeter and his wife, Elma, standing on a sidewalk, Chicago, 1915. (Photographer: Chicago Daily News, Inc. Chicago History Museum DN-0065393)

TOP LEFT: *Captain and Mrs. George Wellington Streeter (Elma), Chicago. (Chicago History Museum ICHi-12593)*

BOTTOM LEFT: Chicago Examiner *cartoon September 17, 1910, page 4.*

ABOVE: *Captain Streeter jailed for 60 days for contempt of court.* Chicago Examiner *April 5, 1918, page 9.*

(Both Chicago Examiner *images courtesy of Chicago Public Library, Special Collections and Preservation Division*)

periodically fired their guns at nothing in particular as a form of intimidation.

Streeter and his men practiced reconnaissance maneuvers, slithering on the ground, guns drawn, to see how close they could get to the enemy's encampment. At dusk on February 11, 1902, Henry Cooper and James O'Malley, a police officer, met with Streeter in an effort to tamp down any hostilities. Streeter knocked Cooper to the ground with the butt of his rifle. Cooper and O'Malley were enticed to leave with guns pressed tightly against their backs.

An hour later, Kirk stepped outside his shanty and was shot at by three or four men crawling toward him. There

was no return fire. One of the bullets passed through Kirk's skull. He died a few hours later. Streeter and three associates, Billy McManners, Henry "Klondike" Hoeldtke and William Force, were arrested and charged as accessories to murder.

After a mistrial, a second jury found Streeter and McManners guilty. They received indeterminate sentences, the equivalent of life. Streeter entered Joliet Prison on January 23, 1904, slightly more than a year after he was convicted. Maria Mulholland Streeter died that year from injuries suffered when she fell off a streetcar. Under armed guard Streeter attended her service at Holy Name Cathedral.

*"The government deeded me this land
and, by cracky, there ain't nobody livin'
who's going to hornswoggle me
out of it."*

Streeter was ultimately given his freedom based on a technicality; the authorities had taken too long to commit him to prison, a violation of an obscure Illinois law. His ambition to live out his days as a member of the landed gentry would not die easy. In 1909, he made news by purchasing the "battleship" *Favoris Rouges* in Morris, Illinois to attack Streeterville. How ironic! They gave the neighborhood his name but wouldn't give him the deeds. The *Favoris Rouges* would belch smoke on its journey from Morris to make war on the lakefront. Sadly, Streeter beached another boat. This time on the foul smelling banks of the drainage canal, an inland waterway largely composed of fecal matter and urine.

A month later, Illinois dispatched a real warship to roust squatters from Illinois shores.

In the summer of 1910, Streeter retrofitted a narrow three-room house on top of an automobile. He mounted two enormous Gatling guns on a pole, each pointing in the opposite direction. He painted it a glowing green. He called his contraption the "Streeterville Steamer." He planned to use it to invade the still empty land and capture anybody he found there. He talked about starving them out through some kind of half-baked blockade.

"I am going to win this time," he declared. "I am the owner of that property and I intend to claim my own. The government deeded me this land, and by cracky, there ain't nobody livin' who's going to hornswoggle me out of it."

Streeter bragged about the size of his new army. But it appeared to be composed of three unimposing women—his new wife, Elma, and two attractive nieces from Montrose, Michigan, Miss R. D. Streeter and Miss Carrie Heehn.

On the eve of the battle, he demonstrated his weaponized home for a few members of the press. The Captain pulled several levers. His gasoline engine gave a few short coughs. The machine turned around until it faced the District, now occupied by stooges for the millionaires.

"At ten o'clock tomorrow morning, this cruiser will crash through the iron fence around that stolen land. We'll see if the police can stop me."

Representatives of Chicago Title and Trust complained to the Chief of Police. He asked them to put their demands in writing, which they must have done. Streeter's promised assault on the "financial gangsters" never happened.

Over the years Streeter was arrested hundreds of times on a variety of charges: trespassing, assault, assault with a deadly weapon, battery, possession of concealed weapons, selling alcohol on Sundays, selling alcohol without a license, contempt of court, wild and riotous conduct, fraud, forgery and numerous other affronts against society. However the authorities always found an excuse to let him go, as if he were little more than a serial nuisance. In all likelihood, the well-heeled shore owners were unwilling to test their rights versus his in a neutral courtroom where justice is blind and juries have been known to come to unpredictable and irrational verdicts.

Meanwhile by 1910, the shore owners could see the completed Lake Shore Drive and laugh at Cap Streeter's boast that he created 186 acres of land. Gigantic pylons had been driven into the land beneath the water. Roadbeds had been laid and concrete poured by Fitz-Simons and his workers, as Streeter continued to flip twigs, stones and cow pies into the water. His handiwork paled next to the tons of sand dredged up from the lake bottom. No one would dispute that the builders of Lake Shore Drive had made more land, much faster than Streeter.

In reality, Streeter really did contribute to the landfill. Guesstimates from the time put his share at four acres out of 186.

In their article entitled "Contested Shore: Property Rights In Reclaimed Land and the Battle for Streeterville" published in 2013 by the *Northwestern Law Review*, Joseph D. Kearney and Thomas W. Merrill posed the most

City's Forces Take Captain Streeter's Stronghold

✠   ✠   ✠   ✠   ✠   ✠   ✠

Defender of 'Deestrict' of Lake Michigan Yields

"Streeterville's" defending army, which went down to defeat yesterday before the City of Chicago's forces. Left to right, Major Mrs. G. W. Streeter, the wife; Captain George W. Strecter, himself; First Lieutenant Miss R. D. Streeter, and Second Lieutenant Carrie Heehn, nieces of the captain.

Work on New Office Building
Stopped; Warring Forces
Sociable Truce.

(Bulletin.)
STREETERVILLE, Deestrict of Lake

Chicago Examiner *September 16, 1910, page 10.*

(Courtesy of Chicago Public Library, Special Collections and Preservation Division)

befuddling question of the early history of Streeterville: "Why did it take so long for the struggle over the newly formed land to be resolved?"

They suggest the most plausible of answers. "As long as the reclaimed land stood vacant, it remained, in the minds of many, a resource that was up for grabs—and as long as it was perceived as being up for grabs, competition to establish property rights...continued. The competition, in turn, discouraged development of the land, which

meant that it remained vacant and hence continued to be perceived as up for grabs. The matter was resolved only when the claimants with the most resources started to build substantial structures on the reclaimed land."

The first claimants with the resources and courage to build were Ogden Trevor McClurg and Stuart Gore Shepard. They were the developers of the building that ended the war—999 Lake Shore Drive.

*Captain George Wellington Streeter, wearing a tophat and
sitting in a hallway, Chicago, 1915. (Photographer: Chicago
Daily News, Inc. Chicago History Museum DN-0065391)*

CHAPTER NINE

The MILLIONAIRES' *Colony*

By 1910, a few residential structures had been built south of Pearson. Near the Chicago River, the St. Clair warehouse and manufacturing district was thriving. The area was described as "attractive and convenient." The made land north of Pearson, on the other hand, was still a wasteland. It vacillated between windswept, icy and forbidding and a sea of mud, punctuated by patches of weeds. Other than the ancient Water Works, man had left no trace of his presence. The *Chicago Tribune* wrote, "No building on the land has been made." The side streets were already there, paved and waiting for a purpose.

Most of the original advocates for an upscale residential enclave were dead. Their estates maintained an ongoing interest in the legal kerfuffles that plagued the reclaimed land. Their trustees and lawyers were the conservative voices that argued for a go-slow approach to development. One old-timer, still alive and kicking, was attorney Henry N. Cooper. On July 10, 1910, he sold 84 front feet on East Lake Shore Drive to 36-year-old architect Benjamin H. Marshall for $42,000.

Marshall told the press he intended to construct a ten-story apartment building on the property. He hoped to form a small syndicate of investors to infuse $400,000 of capital into the project. He promised to draw up plans later in the year. No one doubted Marshall's ability to create luxury apartment buildings that catered to the needs of the very wealthy. He already had 40 East Cedar and 1100 North Lake Shore Drive under his belt. Joy Morton of Morton Salt; William J. Chalmers of Allis Chalmers, manufacturers of industrial machinery; and Samuel Insull, protégé of Thomas Edison and head of the Commonwealth Edison Co., lived at 1100.

Marshall's newest purchase would one day blossom into 199 East Lake Shore Drive. But it would not be the first building on its block. Before Marshall could get around to 199 he received a commission to build a different building.

On December 16, 1910, the *Chicago Tribune* published this headline, "O. T. McClurg and S. G. Shepard Will Build Eight Story Apartment House. Site Right On The Bend." The two young friends (Ogden Trevor McClurg was 31; Stuart Gore Shepard, 35) had acquired the vacant land from John McGillen for an undisclosed sum of money. McGillen, manager of Stephen A. Douglas's campaign for U.S. Senator against Abraham Lincoln in 1858 and mayor *pro tem* after the assignation of Mayor Carter Harrison in 1893, had bought it from the estate of Tobias Allmendinger. Based on what Marshall paid for the 199 land, McClurg and Shepard must have laid out somewhere between $60,000 and $70,000 for the property. The *Tribune* article went on to say that plans were being prepared by the architectural firm of Marshall and Fox, and would "include every modern convenience that can contribute to the comfort and luxury of the tenants. The rents will be correspondingly high."

McClurg and Shepard had already decided that they would live in two of the building's 24 apartments—the first floor apartments and the penthouse were not yet part of the concept. "Four other north siders...have given assurance...that they will buy into the transaction and... have apartments in the building." It was estimated that it would cost $500,000 to build 999.

And still nothing happened. One can imagine the testy arguments inside the Lake Shore Drive Land Association. As new landowners, Marshall, McClurg and Shepard had become members. They had the money and the shovels, and they were ready to go. The old guard resisted. Maybe more claimants were hiding in the woodwork. Versions of "Let's wait" versus "What are you afraid of?" bounced off the rafters, until a real reason surfaced. Over the years,

John McGillen, former mayor pro tem of Chicago, who sold the land where 999 would be built to McClurg and Shepard. (Courtesy University of Illinois at Urbana-Champaign Library)

messy little details like deaths, divorces, changes in secondary beneficiaries like charities, sales to outsiders and transfers within the group had taken place. Wills and official city and county records had to be read and reread to confirm that everybody's wishes were strictly obeyed. Lots had to measured. New surveys were needed. Every piece of property had to be re-deeded before anybody could build. That task fell to Chicago Title and Trust. After that, with all plausible obstacles out of the way, development could begin. The old guard acquiesced; the young Turks agreed to wait a little while longer.

On September 8, 1911, McClurg and Shepard agreed on 999's western boundary with Orrin J. Holbrook, of the Chicago Telephone Company and the landowner of the future 229. The southern dividing line was settled with John H. S. Lee, who controlled the land that today is 990 North Lake Shore. McClurg and Shepard formed the Lake Shore Building Company, which actually owned the land and eventually the building at 999.

On October 6, 1911, the Lake Shore Drive Land Association changed its name to the Lake Shore Drive Improvement Association. Implicit in the new name was a change in mission—from an organization that defended the owners' right to the reclaimed land to one that wanted to build, build, build. Among those present at that crucial meeting were Adrian C. Honoré representing his sister, Bertha Palmer; William J. Chalmers; Henry N. Cooper; DeWitt C. Cregier, a former Lincoln Park Commissioner; the Marshall Field estate; David B. Lyman, Jr., the president of Chicago Title and Trust; George Healy, the son of the portrait artist; architect Louis Guenzel; the quartet

of Shepard, McClurg, Marshall and Marshall's business partner, Charles E. Fox, among others.

On October 11, a new agreement defined the exact boundaries of 14 contested lots, including 999's, and sorted out ownership for nine widows or widowers. A few new names of owners emerged; among them, Francis A. Hardy, a real estate magnate and chairman of the board of B. F. Goodrich Rubber Co.; five adult members of the Eiger family, which manufactured women's hats; and Samuel E. Bradt, the future superintendent of Illinois roads and highways.

On December 6, 1911, the curtain rose on the last act of the 40-year drama over reclaimed land. Chicago Title and Trust announced they were issuing new deeds to 43 prominent Chicagoans. Together these deeds accounted for every lot east of Michigan Avenue from Pearson to Oak.

The officers of the new association—some were children when Palmer built his castle on a frog pond—were president Stuart Gore Shepard, vice-presidents Adrian C. Honoré and architect Louis Guenzel. For his sheer endurance and long service on behalf of the shore owners, Henry Cooper was appointed secretary. Benjamin Marshall became the treasurer. Those five men, along with Ogden T. McClurg and David B. Lyman, Jr. comprised the executive committee.

The press release also contained an historic agreement that turned the long residential dream into reality. It bound the new deed-holders and future owners of those deeds to a business plan that allowed for only "private residences, apartment buildings and hotels" in the area. Private stables, garages and central stations that generated and distributed electricity were also permitted, but only for the exclusive use of the owners or their lessees. This agreement was to remain in force until January 1, 1940.

The *Chicago Daily Tribune* called the plan the creation of a "millionaire's colony." It didn't matter that the lots were empty and desolate. That's exactly what one would expect when the smoke finally clears the battlefield. With the ink barely dry on their freshly printed deeds, developing the land was now the priority.

On Thursday, December 11, 1911, the city of Chicago issued Permit No. A 98, File No. 50.18 to Ogden Trevor McClurg and Stuart Gore Shepard. Secured by their agent, the architectural firm of Marshall and Fox, it gave McClurg and Shepard permission to build a nine story apartment building on a plot of land they owned between 944 and 956 North Lake Shore Drive, the most desirable location on the entire landfill, occupying a vista with a panoramic view of the lake. Surveyors had determined that the vacant double lot was an asymmetrical 126′ x 122′ x 116′. The contractor of record was E. L. Schneider Jr. & Son. At some point during construction, another floor was added and the address was changed to 999 Lake Shore Drive.

OGDEN T. McCLURG

Edgar Rice Burroughs

HOUSE OF A. C. McCLURG, ESQ., LAKE SHORE DRIVE, CHICAGO
FRANCIS M. WHITEHOUSE, Architect.

CLOCKWISE FROM TOP LEFT:
Ogden T. McClurg. (Chicago History
Museum ICHi-67636)

Dr. W. E. B. Dubois. (Courtesy
of Library of Congress Prints and
Photographs Division, Washington,
D.C. LC-DIG-ggbain-07435)

Dustjacket from 1914 hardcover
edition of Tarzan of the Apes.
(Copyright ©2014, Edgar Rice
Burroughs, Inc. All rights reserved.
Tarzan™ owned by Edgar Rice
Burroughs, Inc. and used by permission.)

Exterior of A. C. McClurg's residence,
1444 North Lake Shore Drive, boyhood
home of son, Ogden Trevor, Chicago,
circa 1890s. (Francis M. Whitehouse,
architect. Chicago History Museum
ICHi-65095)

CHAPTER TEN

Who Were THOSE GUYS?

Ogden T. McClurg was the son of Alexander C. McClurg, an ardent bibliophile and scholar who began clerking at Chicago's first bookstore S. C. Griggs & Co. in 1859. The Civil War interrupted his career. He joined the 88th Illinois Infantry and was elected captain. His promotions came as rapidly as cannon fire. By the time he scorched Southern earth with General William Tecumseh Sherman, he was a general and chief-of-staff of the 14th Army corps. Personal bravery, fearlessness almost to the point of irrationality and a profound devotion to his men were the pillars on which he built his fighting reputation.

Throughout the war, General McClurg carried a copy of *A Golden Treasury of English Verse* on his person. Even though his horse had been shot out from under him twice during the battle of Mission Ridge, the book was spotless after four bloody years in the field, as if it had never left the bookshelf in his store.

After the war General McClurg returned to S. C. Griggs. Ultimately the general came to own the store and changed its name to A. C. McClurg & Company. Along with novelist Theodore Drieser, poet Eugene Field and other literati who called Chicago home, the general frequented the Saints and Sinners Corner of his own bookstore, a magical place where rare books, both sacred and profane, stood side by side in a formidable collection. The store rapidly expanded into one of the nation's biggest publishing houses and its largest distributor of printed materials.

In 1876, General Alexander McClurg married Eleanor Wheeler, a niece of William B. Ogden. Three years later their son Ogden Trevor was born. Alexander believed in classical education and imported two teachers from Roxbury Latin School in Massachusetts to tutor his son. When Ogden was old enough to take the grand tour of

Europe, the general decided not to dismiss the tutors. Instead he established a new school in Chicago where they could continue teaching. The school began as a seedling. It sprouted into the Chicago Latin School.

When Ogden was summoned to his father's deathbed in 1901—he arrived too late—he was in his final year at Yale's Sheffield Scientific School. After graduation, he joined A. C. McClurg's middle management and worked his way up the ranks to president, a title he held until his death. On his watch, the company signed W. E. B. DuBois, the first African-American to earn a doctorate from Harvard, the co-founder of the NAACP, and a fearless activist who stared racism in the face and never blinked. McClurg published DuBois' *The Souls of Black Folk*, a seminal work in sociology and the cornerstone of African-American literature. A few years later Ogden McClurg brought to market the first Tarzan novel, *Tarzan of the Apes*, by Edgar Rice Burroughs. Burroughs was prolific, a boon to his publishing house. In the next 15 years, he turned out ten more Tarzan novels, helping to make the lord of jungle a sustaining cultural sensation, and another 12 novels—some of which were set on Mars and introduced the world to superhero John Carter; others took place in the Earth's core or on the moon. A book of short stories played with the emotions of its readers, ranging between horror, humor, Westerns, murder mysteries and spoofs. Burroughs stayed with A. C. McClurg until Ogden's accidental death in the mid-1920s.

Ogden juggled work and play with aplomb. The playboy bug bit him early and he became a fashionable participant at Newport News, Virginia during the summer seasons. He squired the prettiest young women to the most well-bred parties. He entered yacht races on the Eastern seaboard and the Great Lakes, progressively acquiring faster boats.

Ogden had grown up at 1440 North Lake Shore Drive in one of those elegant mansions inspired by Potter

Palmer's bold move to the north side. The McClurg homestead was patterned after the French chateau of Françoise d'Aubigné, known at court as Madame de Maintenon and much better known as the woman who rose from poverty to decorate Versailles as the second wife of the Sun King, King Louis XIV. McClurg knew every one of its 33 rooms by heart. But something modern in him, something as carefree and reckless as his father's battlefield demeanor, attracted him to unproven luxury high-rise living and he acted on that impulse. To help finance the development of 999, Ogden sold his father's mansion.

Like McClurg, Stuart Gore Shepard had recently lost a distinguished father. Judge Henry Martyn Shepard, a former law partner of the late Melville Fuller, chief justice of the United States Supreme Court. Judge Shepard was one of earliest promoters of Chicago's park system. He understood the importance of having a park in every neighborhood for a city with a huge working-class population. The field house could double as a community center. The groomed green lawns would be gathering places in the summer, host to picnics and games. He also conceived the 1893 World's Columbian Exposition and announced the idea in a speech at the Iroquois Club. In a landmark legal decision, he upheld the eight-hour workday, bringing balance and fairness to the workplace.

His studious son Stuart followed him into law. He founded a law firm with Robert R. McCormick, a great grandnephew of Cyrus. In 1915, Shepard and McCormick would hire two young lawyers, Weymouth Kirkland and Howard Ellis. When McCormick left law to become the publisher of the *Chicago Daily Tribune* and brought Shepard with him as the paper's chief legal officer, Kirkland

When Benjamin H. Marshall (Benny to his friends) stood on the empty site of 999, he likely imagined the future by looking northwest at the past.

and Ellis renamed the firm after themselves. It remains one of the most successful and respected law firms in the United States. Little is known of Shepard's recreational endeavors, other than he crewed on the *Alice*, a schooner owned and skippered by McClurg in the Chicago to Mackinac race of 1905.

Having already bought the land under 999, McClurg, Shepard, Marshall and Fox purchased another 25 frontage feet on East Lake Shore Drive from the Healy estate on June 13, 1911. Eventually additional purchases would augment this prime location. The four partners would eventually transform it into 209 East Lake Shore Drive. In all likelihood, McClurg and Shepard put money into Marshall's plan for 199. Those four men had found each other.

Perhaps because McClurg and Shepard had the deepest pockets, it was agreed that ground would be broken first at 999.

When Benjamin H. Marshall (Benny to his friends) stood on the empty site of 999, he likely imagined the future by looking northwest at the past. Between Oak Street and Lincoln Park, strung along North Lake Shore Drive were the muscular mansions of the super-rich, beginning at Oak and Michigan with the home of Harold McCormick and Edith Rockefeller McCormick. Their front gate originally stood at the entrance of the World's Columbian Exposition of 1893. Next door to them lived John Borden, whose dairy supplied one-fourth of the city's milk, butter and cream. Up the street was the Palmer Castle—where Bertha's sister, Ida, now lived with her husband Major General Frederick Grant, the son of the 18th President—and Alexander McClurg's homage to the wife of the King of France. Marshall would have glanced at the swanky domiciles of cabinet officers, senators, congressman, publishers, retail moguls, and even a wealthy silver-tongued preacher. Marshall would have scanned the Romanesque, the Florentine, the Venetian and the Gothic and seen only one apartment building—his creation—at 1100 North Lake Shore Drive.

Marshall knew in his bones that one day single family mansions would disappear from the lakefront—far too many people would demand a view of the lake. Multi-storied buildings would rise up in their place and stand as tall as new technologies would allow—and he would be the visionary who would push the cornerstones of tomorrow into place. He would show the rich and famous that life in the city got better when they moved from 30 or more stuffy and dusty rooms from another century into the sunlit splendor of ten or more rooms with spectacular views in one of his buildings. He believed that the apartments at 1100 were the model for the future with elevator access, walls of English Oak, a billiard room that doubled as a library, a fruit and wine closet, an *orangerie*—French for greenhouse or conservatory—large, gracious common rooms and quarters for three maids and an optional butler's room. Committed to teaching Chicago's wealthiest families how to live in an urban setting, Marshall's ambition was simultaneously strange and prescient. As he dreamed of high-rise apartment buildings hogging the shoreline, only immigrants and factory workers seemed content living in apartments.

Benjamin H. Marshall was born in 1874, the only child of Caleb Howard Marshall, a man of "unimpeachable honesty and an incorruptible code of business ethics." His father was the controlling shareholder of Blake, Shaw & Company, the owners of Dale Bakery, which was sold to Nabisco. The transaction brought in enough money to bankroll the rest of his life with plenty left over for his wife and son to carry on without financial worries. His mother was Celia F. Le Baillie Marshall, "a woman of culture and refinement."

Benjamin H. Marshall. (Courtesy of University of Illinois at Urbana-Champaign Library)

Unlike most sons of affluent families, Benny Marshall dropped out of high school at 17 to pursue a career designing men's clothing, which should have been the last anybody ever heard of him. But in 1893 he attended the Columbian Exposition and was thunderstruck by what he saw. The gravitational pull of the gleaming White City with its Beaux-Arts symmetries altered the arc of his life. On the spot he decided to become an architect. He landed a job as an office boy—probably with his father's help—at the architectural firm of Marble and Wilson. His starting salary was $5.00 a week. He overcame a lack of technical training with a sincere appreciation of architecture, his father's connections to men who invested in important buildings and his inherent flair for the artistic and the dramatic. He became an unstoppable salesman. Two years after he joined the firm he was promoted to partner. At 28 he started his own architectural business. Within three years he was working on millions of dollars worth of projects.

His career almost didn't survive one of the worst disasters in American history. He designed the Iroquois Theatre on Randolph between State and Dearborn. The opening was delayed in part because of "the unexplained inability of architect Benjamin Marshall to complete required drawings

He accepted a shovel from
contractor E. L. Schneider
and turned over a layer of dirt.
The excavation of 999
had begun.

on time." But the Iroquois did open, to rave reviews in November 1903. "The Iroquois is the most beautiful theater...in Chicago, and competent judges state that few theaters in America can rival its architectural perfections." One horrifying afternoon on December 30, 1903, over 600 people, many of them children, were incinerated in a fire of epic proportion. Marshall committed himself to building only fireproof buildings, well in excess of whatever was the prevailing code.

In addition to 1100 North Lake Shore and 40 East Cedar, Marshall's early masterworks included the South Shore Country Club (1905) whose exterior became the fictitious Palace Hotel Ballroom in *The Blues Brothers* movie and the recently renovated Blackstone Hotel (1909) and theater (1910).

Looking out at the bareness of Streeterville, Benjamin Marshall knew he was about to transform Chicago. He accepted a shovel from contractor E. L. Schneider and turned over a layer of dirt. The excavation for 999 had begun.

In December and January, the bones of 999 rose above its snow encrusted surroundings—a broad, powerful skeleton made of steel columns and beams, concrete balconies and clay tile floors. With the strength of Atlas holding a mountain up to the sky, the brick and stone cladding were supported by continuous shelf angles attached to steel spandrel beams at every floor.

The construction of 999 moved at a steady clip. On January 29, 1912, the iron framing for the brick walls was completed for the first and second floors to the satisfaction of building inspector J. F. Carroll. On March 3, the iron framing reached the roof. The exterior walls from the first to the fifth floors were finished on March 12. The inspector approved the partitioning up to the fourth floor on May 17. Six days later the walls were done through the seventh floor. The roof was completed by June 17. The roof on the penthouse went up on July 1. The windows were installed by January 18, 1913. Inspector Carroll gave his final approval to 999 on March 17, 1913. It was ready for occupancy. Nevertheless some families had moved in as early as October, 1912. In addition to its peculiar address, the building was also known as The Lake Shore Apartments. The *Chicago Examiner* described the location as "one of the best known of its kind in Chicago, occupying as it does, one of the most prominent corners on the 'Gold Coast'—the only corner on the Drive that has Lake frontage on two sides."

999 was built in the shape of an L and divided into three tiers of apartments across eight residential floors. "A" and "B" units contained ten and nine rooms respectively, and shared front and rear elevators. "A" units faced north with views of the lake, the beach and the buildings on North Lake Shore Drive. "B" apartments were on the corner and offered both northern and eastern views, the most expansive in the city. "C" had six rooms, separate elevators and eastern views. The estimated square feet for those apartments were: A Tier—3,720; B Tier—3,800; and C Tier—2,650. Every modern device for the convenience and comfort of the tenants was installed. The woodwork and interior finishes were dazzling.

The first floor was devoted to spacious reception halls, administrative offices, butlers' quarters, a waiting room for chauffeurs and a large boiler room. There were two doorman stations in the lobby. Uniformed staff opened doors, greeted residents and their guests and operated all of 999's high-speed elevators.

The tenth floor was reserved for a labyrinthine network of rooms, which were used as servant quarters, daylight laundry rooms, guest bedrooms and storage. A small bungalow, expanded in the 1970s into the penthouse, was placed on the roof and was accessed from the tenth floor. Nine skylights were embedded in the roof. Most of them were closed and covered over during the air-raid blackouts of World War II.

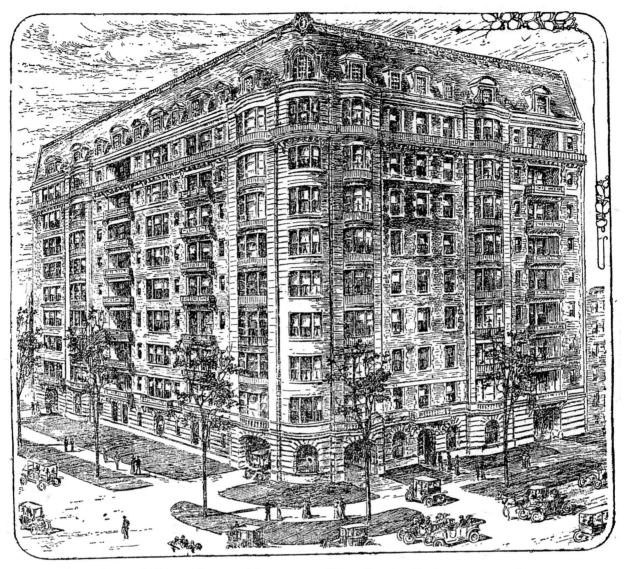

Artist's rendering of 999, probably created as part of the original advertising for the building.

Chicago Examiner *October 25, 1911, page 8.*
(Courtesy of Chicago Public Library, Special Collections and Preservation Division)

All 24 apartments on floors two through nine had two outdoor balconies each. One faced the lake and the other overlooked a courtyard in the rear. In the first hundred years, residents enclosed all but a few balconies, a reaction to the shortness of Chicago's warm weather season. These changes created more internal square footage for every apartment. In the early days, the courtyard contained a small stable. When the automobile replaced the horse as the most popular means of transportation, the space in the back became a small parking area for residents and guests. A tunnel connected the courtyard to the outside world. True to his desire for positive post-Iroquois publicity, 999 contained the latest in fireproofing. Two easy-to-access fire escapes were placed on the courtyard side of the building.

Consistent with the business needs of Marshall, Fox, McClurg and Shepard to attract tenants who grew up in mansions, the public rooms inside each apartment

were grand and spacious. Beginning in the entry foyer, the coffered walls were paneled in the finest African mahogany and extended into the library, living room and dining room. An elegant parquet pattern danced from room to room across oak floors. The floors of the solarium were crafted of white marble. The design on the coffered ceilings was molded into an octagonal and square motif. Decorative crown molding with evenly spaced dentils embraced these rooms.

The libraries in every apartment featured a stone fireplace with pointed arch openings and decorative coursing at the mantel. Brass sconces shaped like torches flanked both sides of the fireplace. Buzzers were placed in the dining room floor, enabling diners to summon the wait staff. There were three entrances to the dining room. The doorway nearest to the kitchen had a moveable obstruction that shielded the guests from the staff. Every one of these was removed during the

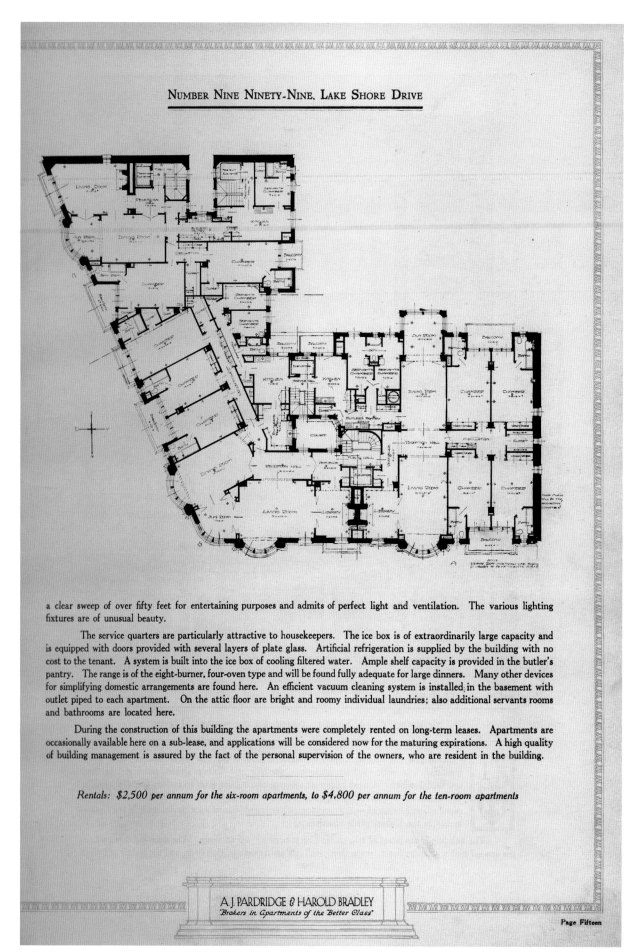

a clear sweep of over fifty feet for entertaining purposes and admits of perfect light and ventilation. The various lighting fixtures are of unusual beauty.

The service quarters are particularly attractive to housekeepers. The ice box is of extraordinarily large capacity and is equipped with doors provided with several layers of plate glass. Artificial refrigeration is supplied by the building with no cost to the tenant. A system is built into the ice box of cooling filtered water. Ample shelf capacity is provided in the butler's pantry. The range is of the eight-burner, four-oven type and will be found fully adequate for large dinners. Many other devices for simplifying domestic arrangements are found here. An efficient vacuum cleaning system is installed in the basement with outlet piped to each apartment. On the attic floor are bright and roomy individual laundries; also additional servants rooms and bathrooms are located here.

During the construction of this building the apartments were completely rented on long-term leases. Apartments are occasionally available here on a sub-lease, and applications will be considered now for the maturing expirations. A high quality of building management is assured by the fact of the personal supervision of the owners, who are resident in the building.

Rentals: $2,500 per annum for the six-room apartments, to $4,800 per annum for the ten-room apartments

A. J. PARDRIDGE & HAROLD BRADLEY
"Brokers in Apartments of the Better Class"

Floor plan showing all three apartments on a floor at 999, 1917. From the book Directory to Apartments of the Better Class on *the North Side of Chicago compiled by Albert J. Pardridge and Harold Bradley. (Chicago History Museum ICHi-68179)*

Three views of a "B" apartment,
circa 1917. (Courtesy of Trevor Potter,
grandson of Odgen Trevor McClurg.)

Florenz "Flo" Ziegfeld, close friend of "Benny" Marshall's.
(Billy Rose Theatre Division, The New York Public Library for
the Performing Arts, Astor, Lenox and Tilden Foundations)

TOP: The tropical pool that formed part of Benjamin
Marshall's home at 612 Sheridan Road, Wilmette, built in 1921.
Photo dated 1929. BOTTOM: Benjamin Marshall residence and
Wilmette harbor. (Both photos Wilmette Historical Museum)

more relaxed, intervening decades. The kitchens had butler's
pantries and eight-burner stoves. Every apartment had rectangular bays with three windows in each.

Everything was geared to the comfort and physical and
emotional well-being of wealthy people—who were willing
to take a chance on apartment living—and to smooth their
transition from gloomy, ponderous mansions to large rooms
with extraordinary views.

Initially 999 was a rental building, which struck Benjamin Marshall as the wrong construct for ownership.
As a condition for his participation in future projects,
Marshall bought or was given stock in every apartment
building he designed. Upon completion his partners and
he immediately turned them into co-ops. Not only did
Marshall earn his architectural fee but he also collected
his fair share of the developer's profits.

After 999 was finished, Marshall didn't rest. He walked
up the block to oversee the completion of 199.

As Marshall's reputation grew he befriended powerful
businessmen, the top shelf of society swells and a wide
cast of characters from the theater. He was attracted to
people of intelligence, style and wit. He enjoyed the best
of everything his time had to offer.

The Impresario Florenz "Flo" Ziegfeld became his best

friend, facilitating Marshall's legendary escapades with
women. He dated showgirls from the Ziegfeld Follies, sometimes two at a time, and gave unsuspecting chorus girls
bathing suits of his own invention that turned transparent
in water. Giggles abounded. Champagne glasses clinked.
For his nights on the town, sometimes Benny wore all
white suits, white shoes and a white panama hat with a
black band. He drove a white Packard Touring Car with a
white canvas top. On others evenings, he was seen driving
a custom-built yellow Packard of his own design as he gal-
livanted from club to club in ruffled shirts and red-velvet
pants under a soft green hat turned down at the brim.
When he walked into a room, everybody knew who he was.

In his spare time, Marshall staged lavish floorshows
at both the Blackstone and Drake Hotels, with dancing
girls, feathered headdresses and stairways to the heavens.
He was a celebrated golfer, an accomplished fisherman and
a gentleman chef whose recipes were served at the Cape
Cod Room for years.

The body of work generated by Marshall and Fox
does not conform to the conventions of any one school.
The South Shore Country Club was designed in the
Mediterranean Revival style. The Edgewater Beach
Hotel was Italian Renaissance. Some experts describe the

Captain George Wellington Streeter's coffin, draped in an American flag with a top hat sitting on it, in a room with his relatives, Chicago, 1921.

(*Photographer: Chicago Daily News, Inc. Chicago History Museum DN-0072926*)

Blackstone Hotel as neoclassical Beaux-Arts; others think it is Second Empire. Marshall prided himself on advocating ideas that had never been done before.

His eclecticism reached its zenith in the studio/home he built for himself in Wilmette. He turned a hodgepodge of fantasies into a celebrated oddity beginning with the drawbridge over the man-made moat. The two story tropical garden with hundreds of colorful birds and real palm and banana trees was accessed through an ornate iron gate. The floor of the Chinese love temple was a thick mattress covered in satin. Fiery dragons inhabited the ceiling. The Mandarin bed was rumored to be 500 years old. The Parisian cafe had a talking parrot. The year-round pool had a turquoise floor and a retractable glass ceiling. The bar had portholes, which created the illusion that you were sailing on the ocean in a glittering ship. Tables rose from the floor. Push a button and a glass wall receded letting in the perfumed night air. There was also the largest architectural library in the United States. Those were the twenties, showy and excessive without a need for limits. And a party at Benny's was the incarnation of its roar.

Happily for the residents who lived at 999, Benjamin Marshall tapped into an inner reservoir of restraint when designing its living spaces.

CODA:

With the help of a friendly alderman, Cap'n Streeter and his common law wife, Elma (nicknamed "Ma") opened a makeshift sandwich and soda shop at Delaware and Lake Shore. The former governor of the "Deestrict" of Lake Michigan was now a tourist attraction. He regaled anyone who would listen with tall tales and half-truths of his incredible career in law, real estate and street warfare. Streeter died in 1921. He had a swell funeral. Mayor William Hale Thompson led a 40-car motorcade to Graceland Cemetery. The president of Chicago Title and Trust delivered a eulogy:

"The Cap'n's ideas of law were somewhat at variance with that of the preponderant legal opinion. We shall miss him more than can be imagined. He kept two lawyers and one vice-president busy for 21 years."

Members of his family and people pretending to share his blood sued and kept on suing to regain their land. The final case was resolved in 1940.

They lost.

Lake Shore Drive looking south from Oak Street with partial view of 999 on the right, Chicago, 1915. (Chicago History Museum (ICHi-19834)

View of Lake Shore Drive from Erie Street, 660 North, Chicago, 1915. (Chicago History Museum ICHi-62385)

HISTORY

CHAPTER ELEVEN

The ADDRESS

WHERE DID IT COME FROM?

Two different published stories of equal weight tell how 999 got its address. One of them ran in the *Chicago Tribune* in 1958. "The 999 Lake Shore apartment building, the first edifice... erected on Captain Streeter's former domain, does not bear { a } true address." The building "was named after the famous locomotive No. 999," the first power-driven vehicle to go more than 100 mph.

Emmett Dedmon, the former editorial director of the *Chicago Sun-Times* and *Chicago Daily News* tells another story in *Fabulous Chicago*, his 1953 history of the city. "Ogden McClurg built his first apartment house at the far end of a sandy strip reaching eastward to the lake from the Harold McCormick mansion. McClurg numbered the building 999 Lake Shore Drive, indulging the same superstition which led him to locate McClurg's warehouse at 333 East Ontario.* Nine was his lucky number. When 999's ornate walls towered lonely against the lake sky, the area was considered desolate; maids refused to cross the windy stretch to get to work. But in a few years there was a row of buildings in the area, numbered 179, 199, 209 and 219, carrying out the theme of nines and confusing Chicago taxi drivers for all time."

Two stories. Take your pick.

*Marshall and Fox were also the architects for the McClurg warehouse at 333 East Ontario.

IS IT CORRECT?

For all intents and purposes, yes. But...

The United States Post Office officially lists 999's address as 944–956 North Lake Shore Drive. This is also the address on the permit issued to McClurg and Shepard allowing them to begin construction. A letter directed to any even numbered address between 944 and 956 should be delivered to 999. Possibly as long ago as 1913, the Post Office grandfathered McClurg's fictional address.

The recorder of deeds would tell you a different story. The deed clearly states that the precise location of 999 is "44, Holbrook's & Sheppard's Subdivision of part of Block 8 in Canal Trustees' Subdivision of South Fractional, 1/4 of Fractional Section 3, Township 39, North Range 14, East of 3rd Prin., Lot 12, Sister Lot 1, 117.73 west x 229.33 south x 110.34 east x 182.10 north, line as per agreement with Lincoln Park Commissioners October 11th 1911."

Try telling that to a cab driver.

HOLBROOK & SHEPPARD'S SUBDIVISION

of part of Block 8 in Canal Trustees' Subdivision of South Fractional 1/4 of Fractional Section 3 Township
39 North, Range 14 East of 3rd Prin. Mer.

44

8

THE LAKE   SHORE   DRIVE

| 7 | 8 | 9 | 10 | 11 | 12 |
| 6 | 5 | 4 | 3 | 2 | 1 |

LAKE SHORE DRIVE

E. WALTON   PL.

State of Illinois } s.s.
County of Cook }

I, Emil Rudolph, do hereby certify that I have surveyed lots one (1) two (2) three (3) four (4) five (5) and six (6) in Fitz Simons' Addition to Chicago, being a subdivision of part of block eight (8) Canal Trustees' Subdivision of the South fractional quarter of fractional Section three (3) Township thirty-nine (39) North, Range fourteen (14) East of Third Principal Meridian;— Also that part of accretions to said Block eight (8) lying East of a line seven hundred and fifty (750) feet East of and parallel to Lincoln Park Way and not included in said Fitz Simons' Addition and that I have subdivided the same into twelve (12) lots all of which is correctly represented upon the plat hereon drawn.

Chicago, December 26th A.D. 1911.

Emil Rudolph Surveyor
All distances are shown in feet and decimals of a foot.

Orrin J. Holbrook

Francis A. Hardy

Lake Shore Building Company
by Stuart G. Shepard
Vice President

Attest

Ogden T. McClurg
Secretary

State of Illinois } s.s.
County of Cook }

This day personally appeared before me Elmer O. Troeger a Notary Public in and for said County in the State aforesaid Orrin J. Holbrook and Francis A. Hardy personally known to me to be the persons herein named and whose names are hereon subscribed who acknowledged that at the time of such appearance they were the owners of a portion of the tract of land hereon described and that the subdivision thereof hereon drawn was their free and voluntary act and deed and that they signed their names hereon as their free and voluntary act and deed for the uses and purposes hereon set forth. Given under my hand and Notarial Seal this 19th day of Feb. A.D. 1912.

Elmer O. Troeger
Notary Public

State of Illinois } s.s.
County of Cook }

I, Harris Carman Lutkin a Notary Public in and for said County in the State aforesaid do hereby certify that Stuart G. Shepard, Vice President of the Lake Shore Building Company and Ogden T. McClurg, Secretary of the said Company, personally known to me to be the same persons whose names are subscribed to the foregoing instrument as such Vice President and Secretary respectively appeared before me this day in person and acknowledged that they signed and delivered the said instrument as their free and voluntary act and as the free and voluntary act of said Company for the uses and purposes therein set forth, and the said Secretary did then and there acknowledge that he as custodian of the corporate Seal of said Company did affix the said Corporate Seal of said Company to said instrument as his free and voluntary act and as the free and voluntary act of said Company for the uses and purposes therein set forth.

Given under my hand and Notarial Seal this 10th day of January A.D. 1912.

Harris Carman Lutkin
Notary Public

Approved Feb. 24, 1912. Jno. T. Riley
Examiner of Subdivisions for City Chicago Cook Co. Ill.

No. 4918125 Recorded February 24 A.D. 1912 at 11⁴⁸ o'clock A.M. Abel Davis Recorder

Official Plat that determined the exact boundaries of 999's lot,
February 24, 1912. (Chicago Recorder of Deeds)

999 Lake Shore Drive, circa 1916. (Photographer: Chicago Architectural Photographing Company. Chicago History Museum ICHi-21187)

Chicago aerial photo, circa 1925, reveals how underdeveloped Streeterville continued to be. (The Newberry Library, Chicago. Midwest MS Sloan, Bx. 1, Fl. 1)

CHAPTER TWELVE

A RENTAL BUILDING
to a CO-OPERATIVE to RENTAL
to CO-OP

Ogden McClurg and Stuart Shepard ran 999 as a rental building. Financing the first building on East Lake Shore Drive, watching it rise above the nothingness of Streeterville and successfully renting 100% of the apartments must have been deeply satisfying. The highest rent they received was $700 a month, nothing to scoff at in those days. 999 paid a substantial and safe net return on investment. On the other hand, acting as landlords must have been a chore, especially with World War I taking control of their lives. In 1917, Shepard moved to Washington, D.C. to serve as general counsel to the War Risk Insurance Bureau. A special act of Congress conferred on McClurg the rank of Commander in the U.S. Naval Reserves. His commission required him to spend much of his time at the Great Lakes Naval Station, 37 miles away. By 1919, if not earlier, the partners went looking for a buyer.

The Great Depression was about to savage the dignity of millions of Americans. It wouldn't take long before hard times rode the elevators of 999.

In 1920, they found their angel in Frederick Stanley Oliver, co-founder of the Oliver Company—a large real estate management and brokerage firm—and former president of the Chicago Realty Board. Oliver incorporated the 999 Lake Shore Drive Building Company, and, as its principal shareholder, directed it to buy McClurg and Shepard's Lake Shore Building Company.

Al Chase, the *Tribune*'s real estate reporter, informed his readers that, "The valuation made by the appraisers for the purchaser was $1.4 million." If McClurg and Shepard received anything near that figure, their joy would have put them over the moon. Their total investment in 999 was estimated between $500,000 and $700,000. The actual purchase price paid by Oliver was not disclosed. He partially financed the deal with a mortgage for $875,000 underwritten by S. W. Straus & Co., who in turn sold serial bonds backed by 999 to its investors. The bonds paid 6%.

Even better days were predicted for the building in the immediate future. The Michigan Avenue bridge would open that year. The downtown business district would soon be five minutes away by motorcar. A plan to connect Lake Shore Drive to an outer drive in Grant Park was in the works, which would "add very materially to the value of the property."

Frederick Oliver now owned a prestigious rental building, but he was determined to turn 999 into a co-op. That would take some time. First he had to wait until all current leases expired. The *Tribune* explained Oliver's plan. He would give the current tenants an opportunity to buy shares in the building for $67,500 per apartment. Those tenant-owners would pay a nominal rent of one dollar a year and share in any deficit that might arise. While waiting for the leases to run their course, Oliver raised everybody's rent, prompting an indignant letter from Ogden McClurg.

In 1924, Oliver began pursuing co-operative ownership in earnest. He sold the 999 Lake Shore Drive Building Company to a syndicate, which included two real estate speculators, Leander J. Dodd and H. H. Decker, and himself. The purchase price was approximately $1.5 million. They replaced the $875,000 mortgage from Straus with another mortgage of identical size, also from Straus. By 1930, this triumvirate had sold equity in 999 to more than half of the tenants, who were now the proud owners of stock certificates and the happy occupants of their apartments. Unfortunately the stock market had crashed and

Cartoon featuring Frederick S. Oliver, Chicago, 1923.
Verses by J. P. McEvoy and illustrations by a cartoonist for the
Chicago Evening Post. (*Chicago History Museum ICHi-68186*)

George W. Borg, circa 1948, bought 100% of 999 in 1944.
(Chicago History Museum ICHi-68196)

the Great Depression was about to savage the dignity of millions of Americans. It wouldn't take long before hard times rode the elevators of 999.

The stock market crash of 1929 only lasted four business days, but it was one of the most traumatic experiences ever to afflict the United States' national psyche. Beginning on Black Thursday October 24, 1929 through the closing bell on Black Tuesday October 29, 1929, the Dow Jones Industrial Average dropped 25%, losing $30 billion in market value (around $400 billion today). It was more than the total cost of World War I. The public was terrified. Wall Street bankers feverishly bought stocks to prop up the market only to see it continue to plummet.

Faith in the American economy dissipated, as did the hopes and dreams of ordinary folks and millionaires alike.

Since 1922, the stock market had been an arrow shot into the sky. The marvel of the world, it kept going up and up and up in defiance of gravity and common sense. The market grew almost 20% every year, encouraging increasingly larger numbers of people to buy stocks. The Dow reached an all-time high of 381.2 on September 3, 1929. Times were so good Wall Street concocted a new financial innovation, "buying on margin," which enabled people without sufficient cash to make a down payment of 10% to 20% and borrow the rest of the purchase price for individual stocks from their broker. When the market collapsed, brokers called in their loans. Investors sold what they could, but were unable to raise enough money to cover the margin call. When they went to their banks to tap into their life savings, they discovered that banks had invested their nest eggs in the stock market. Only a fraction was left. Everywhere, people were wiped out.

The market bottomed at 41.22 on July 8, 1932. From its all-time high, it had lost almost 90% of its value. The crash led to the Great Depression. Unemployment rose to 25%, wages fell 42%, economic growth plunged 50%, and world trade dropped 65%. Deflation caused prices to tumble 10% a year, depressing already meager earnings.

The residents of 999, caught up in the gluttony of the rising market, were not impervious to the sorrows of the crash. As individuals many were hurting. To make matters worse, in late 1927, 999 borrowed $700,000 in the names of its shareholders through a bond issue underwritten by the Metropolitan Life Insurance Company. The exact purpose of the loan remains a mystery. Did the money go into the operating fund? Was it earmarked for capital improvements? Or did the board speculate in the overheated market?

Whatever happened, on November 28, 1934 the building defaulted on the interest owed to Met Life. It also owed $12,000 in back taxes to Illinois. A foreclosure suit was filed in Circuit Court on February 5, 1937. Twenty-five residents were named as co-defendants. A settlement was negotiated and Metropolitan Life ended up owning 999. They turned it back into a rental building.

After foreclosing, Met Life rejected several offers to sell the building. However, on June 22, 1944, 16 days after D-Day, they agreed to let 999 resident George Borg, the chairman of Borg-Warner, buy it for $300,000. In a

A foreclosure suit was filed in Circuit Court on February 5, 1937. Twenty-five residents were named as co-defendants. Metropolitan Life ended up owning 999.

display of unfettered optimism in an uncertain world, Borg paid $150,000 in cash and assumed a mortgage for the balance. The terms were negotiated by Great Lakes Mortgage Corporation for the seller. Sudler & Company represented Borg. In addition to their fee, Borg rewarded Sudler by hiring them to manage the property. Once again, 999 transformed into a rental building.

During World War II, 15 Gold Coast buildings had carved large apartment suites into smaller units to accommodate the housing needs of the wartime civilian work force. Borg ignored that trend, insisting he bought 999 as an investment. He announced his decision to monetize his risk on November 12, 1946. He would be selling 999 Lake Shore Drive to those tenants who wanted to retain their apartments and to go outside the building to sell whatever was left vacant. *The Chicago Sun-Times* reported, "The new co-op policy of 999 Lake Shore Drive holds little hope for apartment hunters." The writer of the article argued that current tenants loved the building and their apartments. They would gobble up the stock to continue living there. The newspaper concluded that those tenants were about to become their own landlords.

In the end, 20 of the 25 tenants, including Borg, bought stock in the new 999 Lake Shore Drive Corporation. They paid nearly $15,000 each to sign proprietary leases and keep their apartments. 999 became a co-op for the second time. The other five apartments were sold to non-residents. A loan to the building of $300,000 at 4% was negotiated with General Mortgage Investments, Inc. The board of directors approved the purchases and the loan. On January 18, 1947, 999 entered the modern age.

They Lived
at 999

A GUIDE TO READING
THE RESIDENTS' ENTRIES

The next four chapters are devoted to the roll call of the residents of 999. Chapter 13, "The Originals" covers the years 1912–1919. For almost every family that lived in the building during those years, there is a list of family members, their guests and their servants, followed by biographical sketches of individuals or a general history of the family. There are holes in the record. For some entries a rich source of information was available. For others, nothing could be found beyond a few names.

For clarity's sake, let's look at few examples.

1913
Mr. and Mrs. Springer Brooks

Here, we learn that Mr. and Mrs. Springer Brooks lived at 999 in 1913. They may have moved in in 1912 or moved out in 1917. All we know definitively is their presence at 999 for one year, and nothing else.

1913–24
William Wood "Secor" Cunningham (1864–1946)
Althea Stone Cunningham (1870–1953)
Secor Cunningham, Jr., son
Emma Carlson, maid; Rita Swanson, maid

For reasons that may be entirely sexist, a husband's name is listed before his wife's. In this case, William before Althea. Children comprise as many lines as necessary. With the Cunninghams there is only Secor, Jr. They may have had other children who spent a few months in 999 before college, marriage or career. Their existence would have evaded our sources. Boarders and long-term houseguests (in this case there were none) and live-in help are shown next.

Unlike the elusive Mr. and Mrs. Brooks, we know the first and middle names of Mr. Cunningham, as well as his nickname; the years of his birth and death; and the names of his wife, son and live-in household help. The family left enough tracks in the snow to warrant a write-up—where they lived before 999, Mr. Cunningham's preference for "Secor," some bland facts about his career, Mrs. Cunningham's relationship with Children's Memorial Hospital, the title of a paper Junior wrote and the annexation of "Secor" by novelist Edgar Rice Burroughs. It is not

the stuff of which movies are made, but it's more than we learned about Springer Brooks.

1913–17 (9A)
1913–26 (PH)
Ogden Trevor McClurg (1878–1926)
Gertrude D. Schwarz McClurg
Eleanor Wheeler McClurg (1920–99), daughter
Barbara Ogden McClurg (1925–2012), daughter
Margaret Dockery, maid; Margaret McLean, nurse
Nellie Chambers, cook

You've already met Ogden T. McClurg. But there is more coming on page 102 about him, his family and their two apartments—9A and the Penthouse. Through the good graces of Ogden's grandson—Trevor Potter—you will see photographs from his remarkable and well-preserved family album.

Chapter 14, "Settling In" and Chapter 15, "The Difficult Years" cover 1920–29 and 1930–46 respectively and follow the same format as Chapter 13.

Chapter 16, "The New Status Quo," 1947 to the present day, takes advantage of better record keeping by the two real estate management firms 999 used during that time—Sudler & Co. and Wolin-Levin, now FirstService Residential. The family entries are now organized by apartment starting with 1A and ending at 9C. People who lived in the building prior to 1947, whose apartments we just happen to know, are included again in an abbreviated form.

If you happen to be 999's newest residents—Sir Mogan Lourdenadin and his family—for what it's worth—you were preceded by the Bauers, the Lydons, Ms. Scott, Mr. Gabreez, Mr. Anderson, the Dodges, the Tuckers, the Dahlbergs, the Walls, the Dickasons and the McClurgs. Between 1912 and 1919, 40 families and 151 people lived at 999. Forty families in seven years may seem like an excessively high turnover of apartments. But 999 was a rental building in those years. Apartment living was an experiment. Leases were probably short. A number of families were only living there until their new suburban homes were finished. With 20/20 hindsight, the turnover rate seems appropriate.

The ORIGINALS

1912-13
Abraham Rosecrans Baldwin (1877-1950)
Helen Poole Baldwin

"Prithee, sweet lady, would you accept these sweets, a slight token of my esteem?" asked the handsome leading man of his beautiful co-star in an amateur production of *Makeshifts* by Gertrude Robbins. The audience giggled. Rosecrans Baldwin, the flummoxed actor, accidently dropped his box of candy. The actress, Helen Poole, blushed.

A few hours earlier, Rosecrans had proposed to Helen and she had accepted. The audience included a large number of their friends. They saw past the footlights to the real life romance on stage. They were married in Lake Forest on September 11, 1912, honeymooned in Europe and, upon their return, moved into 999. The newspaper account of the ceremony and the couple's post-nuptial plans is the earliest known published reference of anyone committed to living at 999.

They eventually had three children. Hardly anybody in Chicago knew that Rosecrans Baldwin's real first name was Abraham. As far as he was concerned, his father was Abraham Baldwin. Rosecrans was the co-founder of Tenak Products Company, manufacturers of electrotype molding materials.

Helen Poole Baldwin. Chicago Examiner, July 13, 1912, page 3. (Courtesy Chicago Public Library, Special Collections and Preservation Division)

1912-13 (Apartment unknown)
Colonel Livingston Thomas Dickason (1843-1913)
Elizabeth Gilbert Barber Dickason
Dorothy Dickason (1894-1918), daughter
Livingston Thomas Dickason, Jr. (1903-74), son
Margaret Murphy, maid; Catherine Moore, cook;
Audon Kinsella, maid

9A
1917-29

Of all the families that lived at 999, keeping track of the Dickasons is the most challenging. Widows became wives. Sons became fathers. Family members moved out of the building only to return. In lieu of a list of names, here is a prose version of their meanderings.

Colonel Dickason died in 1913. Almost immediately, his widow Elizabeth took their two children to a house farther north in the city. In 1917, she had a change of heart and purchased 9A. The same year, her daughter, Dorothy, got married at 999 and moved to New Orleans with her new husband. Livingston, Jr. continued to live with his mother. In 1926, Elizabeth married Dr. Francis X. Walls. They moved to 219 East Lake Shore Drive. Livingston, however, was now a grown up. He stayed at 999 and later married Katherine Hogg Maxwell. After having a baby, Mary Elizabeth, at 999, they relocated to New Jersey. Decades later, Mary Elizabeth returned to 999 as a married adult. It was as if 999 had cast a boomeranging spell on the Dickasons.

In 1861, Livingston Dickason joined Company H of the 4th Ohio Volunteer Infantry as a private. He fought in some of the deadliest battles of the Civil War from bloody Shiloh—23,746 casualties—to the river of death at Chickamauga—34,624 killed, maimed or missing. At Chickamauga, Dickason was so severely wounded that he almost died. He was sent home a colonel. He married Syble "Sibbie" Tinkham in 1866. They had four children. Two survived infancy.

In 1867, the colonel moved his family to Fairmont, Illinois, where he bought and sold grain. He relocated to Danville, Illinois and successfully entered the coal, timber and railroad industries. The citizens of Danville hadn't seen anyone as focused, determined and prosperous as Dickason; so they elected him mayor in six straight elections. He also owned real estate and a stone quarry in Bloomington, Indiana, a hotel in French Lick, Indiana and another in Pass Christian, Mississippi.

Sibbie died in 1891. Dickason took his sorrows to Chicago, where he met and married a younger woman—Elizabeth Gilbert Barber—moved into a huge new mansion on the south side and had two more children. He worked as a special advisor to the brokerage firm C. W. Canby & Co. The colonel bought a 1907 Thomas Flyer and became a motoring enthusiast. The *Chicago Examiner* seemed amazed that the automobile "travelled 126,000 miles on its own power...on all conditions of road and in all sorts of weather." They speculated that Dickason must have broken a mileage record.

By 1913, Livingston Dickason, Sr.'s entire body was locked in paralysis. He wanted to see Italy before he died, and his family granted his wish. He passed away shortly after arriving in Naples. Almost immediately after bringing his body back for burial, Elizabeth moved to 2200 North Sheridan Road. A few years later, she returned and sublet 9A from Ogden McClurg for five years at an annual rent of $4,800.

The colonel's death delayed his daughter's debut. Petite, slender and beautiful, Dorothy Dickason was a charmer from an early age. Her favorite possession was an umbrella she bought in Paris as a child. The handle was carved into the head of a bulldog with jeweled eyes and ears that moved. The jaws opened mechanically and it was supposed to say, "Votes for Women." But it broke, which forced Dorothy to say it herself in her loudest and most determined suffragette voice.

Dorothy was brave. As a teenager, she stopped a pair of runaway horses that were charging at a group of her friends. True to her station, they were polo ponies.

Imagine one of those old black and white movies where a ditzy young heiress is caught up in a screwball situation of her own making. To collapse time and make the story move faster, the director shows a succession of newspaper headlines. The following from 1917 were written about 21-year-old Dorothy, and they were all true:

"Heiress to Marry Wealthy New York Man." His name was Walter Henry Stauffer. He was in the army, stationed near the Mexican border.

"Plans to Join French Red Cross Despite Betrothal." Dorothy's mother explained to the press that her daughter wanted "to help humanity across the sea."

"Miss Dickason Halts War Trip. Society Girl Decides Not to Sail to France as a Nurse." Her mother flew to New York to drag her back to Chicago.

"Society Girl Trains For Air Corps. Miss Dorothy Dickason Foregoes Duties as War Nurse to Offer Services as Pilot of Aeroplane." By golly, she would go to war.

LEFT: L. T. Dickason from The National Tribune *(Washington, D.C.) June 18, 1908. (Courtesy of The Library of Congress, Washington, D.C.)*

BELOW: Ad for C. W. Canby & Co., L. T. Dickason, Special Partner. Chicago Examiner, *January 1, 1910, page 14. (Courtesy of Chicago Public Library, Special Collections and Preservation Division)*

Dorothy Dickason. Chicago Examiner, *June 13, 1917, page 9. (Courtesy of Chicago Public Library, Special Collections and Preservation Division)*

This time as an aviatrix, maybe become a flying ace, send German Fokkers into a tailspin spewing smoke. Dorothy Dickason versus the Red Baron!

"Her Decision Made." In the end, she married Stauffer at 999. It took 138 days for her saga to run its course. Seven months later she died from a sudden illness.

1913
Mr. and Mrs. Springer Brooks

1913-24
William Wood "Secor" Cunningham (1864-1946)
Althea Stone Cunningham (1870-1953)
Secor Cunningham, Jr., son
Emma Carlson, maid; Rita Swanson, maid

On October 8, 1912 the *Chicago Daily Tribune* reported that the Secor Cunningham family had moved to the Virginia Hotel in Chicago "pending the finishing of the apartment at 999 Lake Shore Drive now nearing completion."

As if he were shaking off a curse, Cunningham, Sr. abandoned his first and middle names—William Wood—in favor of "Secor." Having reinvented himself, he stopped using William or Willy or Billy or Woody. His tombstone contains only his adopted first name. Born in Altoona, Pennsylvania, Cunningham was the Cook County broker for many Pennsylvania insurance companies, among them Fireman's Fire of York, American Fire of Philadelphia and Reliance of Philadelphia.

Althea I. Stone Cunningham, the only daughter of a socially prominent Chicago family, served as a long time board member for Children's Memorial Hospital. Secor, Jr. authored a paper with the yawn-inducing title, "The Economy of Water Transportation." Loyal to their help, the Cunninghams employed their maid, Emma Carlson, into perpetuity. She was 91 in 1920.

Edgar Rice Burroughs may have met Secor through Ogden McClurg. He borrowed his made-up name, as well as McClurg's real one, for his novel *The Girl from Farris's*. He created an irksome cad—Ogden Secor—whom he killed off in a bordello.

1913-15
Ernest H. Eversz, Ethel Wood Eversz
Ernest Wood, son; Barbara Eversz, daughter

Ernest Eversz founded an investment bank in Chicago and married Ruth May Swift, the beautiful daughter of Gustavus Swift, the world's most famous meat packer. She divorced Ernest in a page one story before the construction of 999. At 999 Ernest was married to the former Ethel Wood.

"Secor" Cunningham
(Courtesy of University of Illinois
at Urbana-Champaign Library)

1913–15
Addison G. Fay, Emily W. Fay
A. Orville Fay, son; R. Arshman Fay, son
Martha Fay, daughter

The press referred to the Fays as "wealthy socialites." They owned a second home—fairly common for 999 residents then and now—in Marblehead, Massachusetts, where they docked their 76 foot yacht, the *Shawnee*. A 1920 ad for the Scripps Motor Company featured a photograph of Fay's *Shawnee III*. Addison ran the Aetna Explosives Company at 188 West Madison. Munitions were a family obsession. In the years immediately following the War of 1812, Addison's great grandfather, also named Addison, a pioneer in the emerging industry of pencil manufacturing, blew himself to smithereens experimenting with gunpowder.

ABOVE: *Scripps used Addison G. Fay's* Shawnee III *to advertise their Model D-6 motor.*

RIGHT: *Fay's company maunfactured Aetna Blasting Caps. (Courtesy of Hal Post)*

9C
1913–15
David G. Hamilton (1842–1915)
Mary Jane Kendall Hamilton
Bruce P. Hamilton, son

The first chance 18-year-old David Hamilton had to vote for President of the United States he picked Abraham Lincoln. Later in life, he invested heavily in railroad companies. Hamilton's extensive holdings eventually were folded into the Atchison, Topeka and Santa Fe. As president of the Chicago City Railway Company, at the time the largest and most profitable cable car system in the world, Hamilton replaced horse drawn passenger wagons with the city's first electric powered cable cars. Newspapers referred to him as "the street car magnate." He found time to serve as president of the board of trustees for the University of Chicago. A daughter, Adelaide, no longer living with her parents in 1913, would move to 999 as the wife of future resident, Dr. Edwin Ryerson.

*David Gilbert Hamilton, 1892.
(Chicago History Museum ICHi-67676)*

1913-20
Alexander D. Hannah (1843-1913)
Catherine Grady Hannah
Ida Anderson, maid; Mildred Johnson, cook

Alexander Hannah may have been the first resident of 999 to die in his apartment. He passed away on December 15, 1913. Hannah had been a traveling salesman, who formed a partnership to distribute booze with David Hogg called Hannah & Hogg. In 1898 they sold their company and bought the luxurious Brevoort Hotel at 120 West Madison Street. They razed the hotel in 1906 and built a new 14-story Brevoort Hotel in the same location. The new Brevoort was famous for its dazzling circular crystal bar and its art collection. Paintings were everywhere—walls, ceilings and windows. The hotel catered to a fast growing profession—salesmen—a business model so lucrative that the Brevoort was one of the few Loop hotels never to go through bankruptcy. Non-salesman Frank Lloyd Wright lived there before he built his home and studio in Oak Park.

In 1889 Hannah built a cottage on Mackinac Island. He spent summers there with his wife and children. He took a deep interest in the development of the island and was a director of the Grand Hotel.

Alexander D. Hannah's Hotel Brevoort. (Lake County, Illinois Discovery Museum, Curt Teich Postcard Archives)

1913-24
George Cooley Hixon (1871-1923)
Blanche Kelleher Hixon
Tillie Behring, housekeeper
Caroline Cannier, cook

George Cooley Hixon was the son of Gideon Cooley Hixon, a millionaire lumberman and state senator from La Crosse, Wisconsin. George oversaw the eastern section of the family business, dealing in grain, lumber, and their investments in commodities and stocks. Part-timers at 999, the Hixons' primary residence was in La Crosse.

1913-20
James C. Hutchins, Agnes Hutchins
James C. Hutchins, Jr., son; John M. Hutchins, son
Grace Stone, maid; Elsie Nowan, maid
Jennie Rollander, cook

James Hutchins co-founded the securities firm of Mitchell, Hutchins & Co., which survived for almost a century. Sold to Paine Webber in 1977, the brand name continued until 1990.

Cartoon featuring portrait of James C. Hutchins, Chicago, 1923. Verses by J. P. McEvoy and illustrations by a cartoonist for the Chicago Evening Post. *(Chicago History Museum ICHi-68184)*

John Lee Mahin (1869–1930)

Julia Graham Snitzler Mahin

Margaret Mahin, daughter

Marian Mahin, daughter

John Lee Mahin, Jr. (1902–1984), son

Originally a newspaperman, John Lee Mahin, Sr. started the Mahin Advertising Company, one of the first agencies in Chicago. A spellbinding public speaker, the *Los Angeles Times* wrote that a Mahin speech brought into play "an unusual amount of personal magnetism, combined with hard business sense, and a shrewd and kindly exploitation of human nature." He banged the drum loudly on behalf of the power of advertising. He wrote two books *Advertising: Selling the Consumer* and *Mahin's Advertising Data Book*, which he sold through magazine ads. In 1916, Mahin moved his business and family to New York.

Julia Mahin helped direct a costumed pageant on the Northwestern campus honoring the birth of the country. Young people portrayed Huguenot and English settlers, and the indigenous people they slaughtered. The only performer not in costume was a black bear. Mrs. Mahin was in charge of creating an authentic Indian camp. Her younger society friends posed as squaws.

Eleven years old in 1913, John Lee Mahin, Jr. grew up in 999, moved to Hollywood and became a prolific screen-writer and producer of movies. Often the un-credited script doctor of other people's unacceptable work, he saved many wayward projects. Whether or not his name appeared in the credits, some of the many award-winning movies he worked on included *Scarface: The Shame of the Nation* staring Paul Muni; *Red Dust* with Clark Gable and Jean Harlow; the original *A Star Is Born* with Janet Gaynor and Frederick March; *Captains Courageous* starring Spencer Tracy as Manuel Fidello, a role for which he won the Oscar for Best Actor in 1937; *Woman of the Year*, the first pairing of Tracy and Katharine Hepburn; and a timeless classic with Bert Lahr, Ray Bolger, Jack Haley, Billie Burke, Margaret Hamilton and Judy Garland called *The Wizard of Oz*.

One of his better lines was written for Clark Gable in *Mogambo*. Gable's character was asked if he wanted to make a move on Ava Gardner. "That's playgirl stuff, Brownie. I've seen them in London, Paris, Rome. They start life in a New York nightclub and end up covering the world like a paid advertisement. Not an honest feeling from her kneecap to her neck."

An archconservative, he ran the Screenwriter's Guild and helped drive presumed Commie sympathizers out of Hollywood.

CLOCKWISE FROM TOP LEFT: John Lee Mahin, Jr., (Courtesy of Alvin Hulse); Original Wizard of Oz poster, 1939, (Wikimedia Commons); Julia Mahin in costume third from left, Chicago Examiner, September 30, 1909, page 3. (Courtesy of Chicago Public Library, Special Collections and Preservation Division)

How an Advertising Account is Handled by the "Mahin Method"

Accounts come to us in two ways. One of our solicitors calls upon a manufacturer whose business, we believe, can be made more profitable by systematic, scientific advertising; an inquiry comes to us from a manufacturer asking for plans that will increase his profits.

We ask for details, the character of his product, price, quality, to whom it is sold, jobbers, retailers or customers, salesmen employed, margin of profit, the attitude of the trade. We secure as complete information as possible.

We then go a step farther, commence a thorough investigation through our established connections, study the problem in different localities.

Armed with this information, the solicitor visits the manufacturer, both getting a better understanding of the situation. They discuss sales methods and plans, and the solicitor prepares an advertising estimate, showing the cost of covering the desired territory, based upon the facts gathered.

The preparation of **advertising copy that will sell the commodity advertised,** is the next step. This it will do, because it is based on an intelligent understanding of the entire situation — each and every detail. Circumstances determine its nature, whether it be light and catchy or serious. "Spotless Town," "Ham What Am," "Let the Gold Dust Twins do Your Work," are examples of the catchy, effective advertising we

Examples of John Lee Mahin's advertising and business philosophy from Mahin's Magazine. (*The Newberry Library, Chicago. H 711 .54, vol. 3, (Apr–May) 1904, page 186)*

1913–20
Dr. George Paull Marquis, Emily C. Marquis
Anna Marquis, daughter
Mary Sebush, maid

Around 3:00 p.m. on May 4, 1902 Potter Palmer drifted into unconsciousness. At 4:00 p.m. Dr. Marquis was admitted to the Palmer residence. He tried to keep the great man alive by administrating oxygen, but it was too late. Marquis pronounced Palmer dead at 5:40 in the afternoon.

9A (1913–17)
PH (1913–26)
Ogden Trevor McClurg (1878–1926)
Gertrude D. Schwarz McClurg
Eleanor Wheeler McClurg (1920–99), daughter
Barbara Ogden McClurg (1925–2012), daughter
Margaret Dockery, maid; Margaret McLean, nurse
Nellie Chambers, cook

After subletting 9A to Elizabeth Dickason, Ogden McClurg moved his family to the penthouse, at the time no larger than a modest bungalow. Standing on the roof deck today, you can see an obvious change in building materials where McClurg's bungalow evolved into something greater in the 1970s, thanks to Donald C. Hannah. McClurg may have decided to live on the roof for its commanding view of Lake Michigan, the body of water he was determined to conquer. And he did. Three times in the 1920s he won the Chicago to Mackinac race. Even today his skill as a yachtsman redounds. Starting in 1941, the winner of Section Nine of the Mac has been awarded the Ogden Trevor McClurg Cup.

McClurg married twice. His first wife, Marian Gordon Ewen McClurg, was an accomplished yachtswoman. She died unexpectedly in 1909. In 1916, he married Gertrude

Left to right, back row: McClurg, Spinden; front row, Mason, Whiting, Griscom. Note malarial expressions of Mason and Whiting

The leaders of the Mason Spinden exploring the Yucatan. From The Silver Cities of Yucatan. (*The Newberry Library, Chicago. Ayer 656.9 .Y9 M2 1927, pg. 272*)

Ogden Trevor McClurg in naval uniform. (Courtesy of Trevor Potter)

LEFT: The Ogden Trevor McClurg Memorial Trophy is awarded to the winner of Section Nine of the annual Chicago to Mackinac Race. (Courtesy of Chicago Yacht Club)

McClurg's yacht, the Alice, in the background on the right. (Photographer: Chicago Daily News, Inc. Chicago History Museum SDN-007955)

RIGHT: Ogden Trevor McClurg and Gertrude Schwarz in love. (Courtesy of Trevor Potter)

Schwarz of New York. They had two daughters—Eleanor and Barbara. But family life did not deter him from being named co-respondent in John P. Wilson's divorce from his adulterous wife June, described by *The New York Times* as "a noted beauty."

In 1926, *The New York Times* sponsored the Mason-Spinden Expedition to search for Mayan ruins in Northern Mexico. McClurg accepted the role of shipboard navigator and hydrographer. For two months journalist Gregory Mason, anthropologist Herbert Spinden, ornithologist Ludlow Griscom, artist Francis Whiting and McClurg sailed a schooner up and down the east coast of the Yucatan Peninsula, dropping anchor from time to time to go ashore and search for rare birds, undiscovered flora and ancient ruins, all of which the team found in abundance. Newspapers around the world covered the story with breathless full-page hyperbole, line drawings and photographs of their exotic findings, and hand-drawn maps with dotted lines depicting the course of the ship.

A few weeks after his return from the Yucatan, McClurg died in a car crash in Elmhurst, Illinois. Newspapers speculated that the accident was caused by an ancient Mayan curse.

Gertrude McClurg in apartment 9A at 999 with daughters, Eleanor (standing) and Barbara (on mother's lap). (Courtesy of Trevor Potter)

McClurg's daughters also led interesting lives. Eleanor served in the Red Cross Motor Crops during World War II. In 1948 she married Bostonian James F. Hunnewell, an investment manager and avid sailor. Eleanor became a recognized expert in the restoration of historic manor homes in New England. She was the longtime chairman of the Ellis Memorial Antiques Show in Boston, one of the two or three most prestigious shows in America.

After graduating from Smith College, sister Barbara volunteered for the Visiting Nurse Association in Appalachia and delivered backwoods health care on horseback. She earned her aircraft pilot's license at Great Lakes Naval Training Station. During the Korean War, she worked for the C.I.A. An accomplished athlete, she skied for *Sports Illustrated* photo shoots, sailed, hunted and was an avid tennis player and golfer. In 1954, she married Charles S. Potter, president of the Union Stockyards in Chicago. She died peacefully at home in 2012.

1913–24
Homer W. McCoy (1859–1923), Jessie O. McCoy
Elisabeth Knapp, cook; Matilda Thyes, maid

Homer was an investment banker who enjoyed traveling. In 1919 alone, Mr. and Mrs. McCoy spent six weeks in Castle Rock, Arkansas, three weeks at a large ranch in Wyoming and another three weeks in downstate Illinois visiting her family. They also had a second home in Wausaukee, Wisconsin, which they visited frequently.

1913–15
Roy McWilliams (1875–1957)
Elizabeth McWilliams

The son of an associate of Marshall Field, Roy McWilliams was an attorney and U.S. consular agent at Biarritz, France during World War I. He returned to Biarritz as vice-consul, 1924–6.

During the first 25 years of the twentieth century, Elizabeth and Roy threw some of Chicago's most memorable costume parties. Newspapers continued mentioning them decades after the last guest had staggered home. Two of their best were held at 999.

Prior to the first Cubist exhibition at the Art Institute in 1913, they held a future-of-art party. It was arranged to honor composer John Alden Carpenter, who would live at 999 in the 1940s, and his wife Rue Winterbotham Carpenter, a cutting-edge interior designer. Among the two most modern Bohemian artist types in Chicago, they were sailing for Europe in a week, so this was a bon voyage celebration of sorts. Bror Julius Olsson Nordfeldt, a Swedish painter, also attended the party. His recent painting of Rue was currently hanging in the Art Institute—a brilliant colorful figure against a dead white background was shown as a forerunner of the futurist exhibit.

The noted artist, William Penhallow Henderson draped the walls of the McWilliams' apartment in black canvas and covered it with meaningless splashes of color, dots, dashes and circles—poor mimicry of the unfamiliar and disorienting breakthroughs of Cubism. The guests

Futurist Party, Newest Thing in Functions, Given in a Maze of Colors
Society Dances Weirdly in the Grotesque Garb of Imagery

A "Paris art student" at the Futurist ball.

The feast of the masqueraders at the McWilliams' fancy dress party.

Three images from "The Future of Art Party" held in the Roy and Elizabeth McWilliams apartment at 999 in 1913.

TOP LEFT: Roy McWilliams in black face with unidentified woman.

ABOVE: Artist Bror Julius Olsson Nordfeldt, third from left.

BOTTOM: Unidentified woman contemplates modern art.

Chicago Examiner, *February 26, 1913, page 11. (Courtesy Chicago Public Library, Special Collections and Preservation Division)*

dressed in costumes of their own design depicting what they imagined the art of the future would look like.

Henderson was the rage of many art devotees at the turn of the century. He had painted separate portraits of Roy and Elizabeth. The McWilliams also collected other works by him. They lent four of their paintings to the Art Institute of Chicago for its celebration of Henderson in January 1913.

A few months later, the McWilliams hosted another costumed bash. Count Kurt von Reiswitz, the German consul, attired in immaculate evening dress and presented himself as a suicide victim. His right temple bore fake black powder burns. A stream of blood ran down his face soiling his starched shirt. A young newly married couple dashed into the A-side apartment impersonating Adam and Eve. Wearing only a few leaves to cover their obvious nudity they danced around the room to giggles and wild applause.

In 1916, Roy McWilliams and Rue Carpenter would appear in a play, *Cousin Jim* at the Casino Club. Their performance was released as a movie. The proceeds went to the American Red Cross.

Society Folk in a Desperate Struggle to Increase the Funds of the American Red Cross Organization

Roy McWilliams and Rue Winterbotham Carpenter demonstrate their acting chops in the one and only performance of the play Cousin Jim *at the Casino Club in 1916. Chicago* Examiner, *April 21, 1916, page 10. (Courtesy Chicago Public Library, Special Collections and Preservation Division)*

ABOVE RIGHT: Miss Dollie Chesher, the live-in nurse for Clarence Parker, who disappeared from 999 in 1919. (Photographer: Chicago Daily News, Inc. Chicago History Museum DN-0070784. Image cropped.)

1913-20
Clarence Farleigh Parker (1865-1920)
Harriet Crangle Parker
Virginia Parker Straw, daughter
H. Foster Straw, Virginia's husband
Anna Lopakta, cook; Nellie Laughlin, maid
Dollie Chesher, nurse; Ray Woodward, chauffeur

Clarence Farleigh Parker retired early from the Illinois Central Railroad as vice-president due to a prolonged illness. In February 1919 his name was plastered all over the city's newspapers in connection with the disappearance of his nurse, Dollie Chesher, who left Parker's apartment at 999 to walk the family's Pekingese, Sunee. She never returned.

Too infirm to be considered suspects, Clarence and Harriet Parker supplied the authorities with general information—Dollie's hair and eye color, her approximate height and weight and the like. Some of Dollie's friends, however, pointed their fingers in the direction of a certain Mr. Rockwell, a mysterious silver salesman from Connecticut who called on Dollie whenever he brought his sparkling wares to Chicago. An eyewitness claimed he saw Dollie standing on the lakeshore with a uniformed army officer. A few residents of 999 suggested that the army officer was really Ray Woodward, Dollie's presumed lover and the Parker's chauffeur, dressed in his livery uniform. Oddly, Woodward quit his job the day before Dollie vanished. Rumors circulated that Dollie had run off with the chauffeur. But the police discovered her clothes in a suitcase in the Parker apartment and Woodward turned up alone in Washington, D.C. He had left Chicago before she walked the dog. The police interviewed people living in every building in the neighborhood, including everybody at 999. They searched every square inch of Streeterville and could not find her body.

Months later the missing Dollie washed ashore. The police never knew if her demise was an accident, suicide or murder. Her death drifted into the cold case files and was soon forgotten.

In the 1920 census the Parker's daughter Virginia, 24, lived with her parents at 999, as did her new husband, H. Foster Straw, a salesman for a radiator company. Eventually the Straws moved to Lake Forest. A Navy man, Foster served as a Lieutenant Commander in World War II.

1913-24
Frances Welles Shepard (1830-1932)
the widow of Henry Martyn Shepard (1825-1904)
Perry M. Shepard, son; Stuart Gore Shepard, son
Wayne Chatfield-Taylor
Adele Blow Chatfield-Taylor
Mrs. Robert S. Hotz and
her daughter Lila Hotz, houseguests
Nellie Creedon, maid; Harriet Bias, cook

Frances Shepard, the mother of Stuart Gore Shepard, was the Illinois regent for the Daughters of the American Revolution. In 1915 Perry Shepard was an officer of the Washburn Company, a wire and iron goods firm. By 1920 he managed Peabody Fairbanks, an investment bank.

When their mother went on an extended vacation, Perry and Stuart would take rooms at the University Club. Their apartment was lent to people who were in-between homes. Newlyweds Lt. Wayne Chatfield-Taylor and Adele Blow Chatfield-Taylor lived in the Shepard apartment in 1917. Wayne would serve in a variety of senior positions in both FDR's and Harry Truman's administrations. He became the Assistant Secretary of Treasury and Under Secretary of Commerce. Adele's family came to Virginia in 1609. She was the co-founder of the National Women's Democratic Club and served as vice-chairman of the United Nations War Relief. She also restored old historic houses.

The Hotz women lived in the Shepard apartment in the summer of 1919, while waiting for their house on Sheridan Road to be completed.

1913
Bertrand Walker (1868-1962)
Ida Fleetwood Drew Walker (d 1946)

Born in Indianapolis, Indiana, Bert Walker graduated Harvard with an A.B. in 1890. After a year at Harvard Law School, he entered the law school of the University of Michigan, graduating in 1893. He was an attorney for the New York Central Railroad and general counsel for the Chicago, Indiana and Southern Railroad. He married Ida F. Drew who attended the Ogontz School for Girls in Elkins Park, Pennsylvania.

Frances Welles Shepard. (Courtesy of University of Illinois at Urbana-Champaign Library)

Adele Blow Chatfield-Taylor. Chicago Examiner, August 17, 1917, page 9. (Courtesy Chicago Public Library, Special Collections and Preservation Division)

In the late nineteenth and early twentieth centuries, Francis S. Peabody was a colossus of American industry. After graduating Yale in 1881, he found employment as a messenger boy at a bank. Two years later at age 24, he founded the Peabody Coal Company with an investment of $100. When he died of a heart attack during a fox hunt in 1922, Peabody was the nation's largest coal company and Francis was worth $100 million. He was a power in Democratic politics for a quarter of a century. In 1908, he led the movement, which resulted in Adlai E. Stevenson's nomination for vice-president of the United States. In 1916, he ran the financial operation and was the head fundraiser for Woodrow Wilson's successful campaign for President.

A widower, he met a widow, in Europe. Marian G. Bryant had been married to a wealthy mining operator in Montana. Mary—as she preferred to be called—and Francis married in 1909 in New York. They lived at 999 briefly, while they were building a huge country estate near Hinsdale called Mayslake.

Francis Stuyvesant Peabody.
Chicago Examiner, *May 2, 1917,*
page 3. (Courtesy Chicago Public
Library, Special Collections
and Preservation Division)

A lawyer, banker and real estate baron, Charles Pike was best known for his association with the Chicago Historical Society's museum, now called the Chicago History Museum. He arranged its rooms chronologically. All the artifacts from an historical event were displayed together. The events followed one another in the same order that they had occurred. Pike's ordered approach told stories and spread to other museums around the country. He was also a life member of the Art Institute and Field Museum, and a devotee of the opera and symphonic concerts.

Frances Alger Pike was the daughter of Russell A. Alger, the twentieth governor of Michigan, a U.S. senator and the secretary of war during the Spanish-American War under President William McKinley.

Banker and bond dealer, Manny Simmons married a chorus girl, Kitty Pope, at the Plaza Hotel in New York. At ages 16 and 14 respectively, Miss Pope and her sister were orphaned. They learned to high kick, joined a chorus and slept backstage. Kitty sang and danced in *The Time, the Place and the Girl; The Girl Question;* and *The Honeymoon Trail.* She met Manny while performing with the La Salle Theater Company in Chicago.

Charles B. Pike with historic fire wagon and firefighter's helmet, Chicago, 1932.
(Photographer: Chicago Daily News, Inc. Chicago History Museum DN-0101459)

Alexander Smith, Mary Smith
Anna Sandquist, maid

By 1928 Mary was a widow. Looking for information about somebody named Mary Smith is pointless, thankless and answerless.

1914
John Kerwin Stewart
a.k.a. Terence O'Brien (1870–1916)
Julia Pearl Butler Stewart
Marian Stewart Honeyman (1902–1988), daughter
Jeanne Stewart (1911–21), daughter

When John K. Stewart died on June 1, 1916, he left behind two wills. The first was filed in Chicago in 1914. He wrote the other in New York ten days before his life ended of natural causes. It was a draft and ultimately discarded by the courts. However, the investigation conducted into the viability of the contending documents led to the discovery of his birth name—Terence O'Brien of Nashua, New Hampshire. The O'Brien family had lost track of Terence. The Stewarts apparently had no idea John K. was somebody else.

In the early 1890s, Terence was fired from his job as a laborer for whistling. Under his own name he tried prospecting without much success. In Seattle he met Arthur and Michael Conlon. The three men invented a horse clipper with a flexible shaft. They demonstrated their horsehair-cutting device at county fairs. A lawyer named Stewart patented the flexible shaft for O'Brien. Hoping it would improve his luck, O'Brien adopted the lawyer's name and reinvented himself as John K. Stewart. His fortunes changed immediately. The Conlons drifted out of his life.

With a friend named Thomas J. Clark, Stewart manufactured horse clippers, sheep clippers, bicycle handlebars and flexible shafts. They formed a company called Chicago Flexible Shaft. They introduced their first home appliance, the Princess Electric Iron, under the brand name Sunbeam, which eventually became the name of the entire operation. Mrs. Stewart's half-nephew, Leander H. La Chance, was appointed president of the company in 1916. Shortly afterwards, he would add greatly to the confusion over Stewart's two wills.

Stewart used his flexible shaft to manufacture cables for his newest invention—the speedometer, soon a stable in every automobile. In 1908, it was installed in the Ford Model-T. This led Stewart to start another company devoted to automotive component parts. It underwent many name changes—a process that came naturally to Stewart. After buying out a rival—the Warner Instrument Company—the firm became known as the Stewart-Warner Speedometer Corporation. A decade after Stewart's death, it merged with a company owned and operated by George Borg, also a 999 resident, and Borg-Warner was born.

Stewart's Chicago will—the official will—left half his estate to his wife, Julia, and the other half was to be split between his two daughters, Marian, 14 and Jeanne, five. The executors were Leander La Chance and Martin Taylor, an attorney. Determining the size of the estate took years. A clerk at the speedometer company discovered deposit slips on six Chicago banks that turned up $1.8 million nobody knew Stewart had. When La Chance received at $7.50 bill for a safety deposit box, he had the box opened and found another $250,000. Nine months after her husband's death, Mrs. Stewart died at a hotel in Aiken, South Carolina. The hotel opened her suitcase and $690,000 in gold certificates fell out. Inside they also found $296,000 in certified checks.

Before the estate was settled, the youngest daughter Jeanne also died, leaving Marian, the 19-year-old wife of New York attorney, Robert B. Honeyman, as the sole heir. She sued her uncle, Leander La Chance, and Martin Taylor charging them with mismanagement and incompetence. Six years after John K. died Marian received her entire inheritance—over $6 million.

Marian Stewart, age eight, future heiress. Chicago Examiner, *January 3, 1910, page 8. (Courtesy Chicago Public Library, Special Collections and Preservation Division)*

1914-15
Charles J. Trayner, Elizabeth Trayner

Charles J. Trayner followed his father, John Trayner, into the real estate business. John Trayner came to Chicago in 1846 and started buying and selling real estate. He sold the site of the Palmer House to Potter Palmer. Shortly thereafter he became indignant when, at Palmer's behest, the city widened State Street, reducing the size of Trayner's neighboring lots. Trayner could scream and yell into the wind. Palmer had the clout and prevailed. In addition to Charles, John's other son, Owen R. Trayner, Sr. (1862–1956), also went into real estate and lived at 999.

1914-15
Landon Cabell Rose (1872-1931)
Louise Grout Hill Rose

A native of LaPorte, Indiana, Landon Rose graduated from Wabash College in 1893 and immediately entered Rose & Co., a private banking house run by his family. Over the course of his career, he helped run the Colonial Trust & Savings, the Central Trust Company, the Michigan Avenue Trust Company, the Continental Casualty Company, the Life Insurance Company of Virginia and the North Avenue Bank. He belonged to the Society of the Sons of the American Revolution and the Society of Colonial Wars. He married Louise Hill in the English countryside where she owned an estate. She was the widow of Arthur Hill, a millionaire politician from Michigan. It was the second marriage for both of them. She sued Landon for divorce in 1925, claiming he deserted her.

1914
Frederick W. Upham (1861-1925)
Helen Hall Upham

F. W. Upham was politically active in the Republican Party. He rose from 22nd Ward alderman to delegate at the 1892, 1908, 1912, 1916 and 1920 national conventions to treasurer of the Republican National Committee in 1918. He made his money in coal, ice, building materials, lumber and timberlands. A close friend of his ideological opposite, Francis S. Peabody, he was elected a director of Peabody Coal.

Fred W. Upham.
Chicago Examiner, *March 24, 1911, page 9.*
(*Courtesy Chicago Public Library,*
Special Collections and Preservation Division)

Reducing somebody's life to a blurb in the society pages is a little absurd. But not much was written about Mrs. John Winterbotham, other than "She wore a chic little dress embroidered in silver or gray with a sash to the Rex Ball" in 1922. We know considerably more about the public-spirited and art-conscious family she had married into.

Husband John Russell Winterbotham (1843–92) was a warrior. He was commended "for gallant and meritorious service" fighting for the Union at Cold Harbor and in the Wilderness Campaign. Amelia's sister-in-law, Rue Winterbotham Carpenter, was Chicago's most celebrated interior designer. In 1910, she redid the interior of the Auditorium Theater and made it more glorious than the 1889 original. Brother Joseph Winterbotham left an undisclosed sum of money to the Art Institute of Chicago, specifying that it had to be spent on 35 pieces of art executed by foreign artists over a 25 to 35 year period. The works were to be scattered throughout the museum as the curators saw fit. But once a year they have to be reassembled in their entirety and displayed as the Winterbotham Collection. Joseph Winterbotham's son, Joseph Jr., donated the bulk of his art collection to the Art Institute, including works by Renoir, van Gogh (six paintings, among them the *Self-Portrait*), Gauguin, Cézanne, Matisse, Picasso, Modigliani, Toulouse-Lautrec, Braque, Chagall, Pollock, Lipchitz, Motherwell and Noguchi.

1915–20
Alice Rebecca Hughlett Corwith (1845–1930),
the widow of John E. Corwith
Alice Blixt, maid; Emily Lindberg, cook

Two of Galena, Illinois' leading citizens, John E. Corwith and Alice Hughlett, exchanged marriage vows in 1868, the same year their friend and neighbor General Ulysses S. Grant was elected president of the United States.

Corwith co-founded the Galena National Bank with his brothers. Eventually John and Alice moved to Chicago, where he invested the money he earned in banking in several Chicago businesses, including the Chicago Railway Company. He became its principal shareholder. He also invested heavily in real estate across the United States. When he died in 1898, Alice became a well-to-do widow.

Mary Hempstead grew up in Evanston and was a Daughter of the American Revolution.

1915–20
James McHenry Hopkins, Sr., Anna F. Hopkins
Farley Hopkins, son
James McHenry Hopkins, Jr., son
Mary Gleason, maid; May Brunen, maid
Catherine Powell, cook

James McHenry Hopkins, Sr. was the president of the Ryan Car Company, manufacturers and re-builders of railroad cars. He was also the chairman of the Camel Company, which made fixtures for railroad car doors. Camel advertised his wares in the *Daily Railway Age Gazette*, entertaining readers with popular comic strip styled ads. The copy in the first ad set the stage for the series:

"Behold, oh worthy ones! Behold the Sheik Kahrdor and his wonderful Camel Phixtures, engaged in traveling the ever-busy land of American railroads, on an errand of erudite research. Their adventures in this glorious land of the free will form a series of most interesting Camelogues. Come sit at their feet, Oh worthy ones of the railroad world."

Junior became the president of a coal company.

Self-Portrait *by Vincent van Gogh, 1887.*
Oil on artist's board, mounted on cradled panel,
(Joseph Winterbotham Collection 1954.326
The Art Institute of Chicago)

5C
1915–30
Frederick Clayton Letts, Marjorie Dodd Letts
Marie Benson, maid; Agnes Swanson, cook

Frederick Letts sold wholesale groceries for Western Grocery, which was run by his father. Marjorie Dodd Letts was one of the best American women athletes of the early twentieth century. A tennis prodigy, she won her first major doubles championship at the Cincinnati Masters in 1906 when she was 12 years old. She appeared in eight finals at the Masters winning the singles and doubles titles twice each. After her tennis career ended, she switched to golf, winning the Women's Western Golf Championships three times (1916, 1917 and 1920) and reaching the finals in 1910 and 1919. Her most notable victory came in the 1921 U.S. Women's Amateur Championship when she beat Cecilia "Cecil" Leitch, called by *The New York Times*, "the greatest golfing woman the world has ever seen."

1915
Kersey Coates Reed (1880–1929), Helen S. Reed
Mary C. Reed, daughter

Kersey Reed was a lawyer. Helen's maiden name was Shedd. Her father donated an aquarium to the city.

1915
Mr. and Mrs. Charles Donald Thompson

1917
Thomas W. Bowers (1888–1950)
Louise Hellen Bowers

Thomas Bowers was the son of Lloyd W. Bowers, the Solicitor General of the United States. Thomas became an attorney after matriculating at Yale (AB) and Harvard (LL.B.). He lived most of his life in New York City. While in Chicago, he worked at the law firm of Holt, Cutting & Sidley. His brother-in-law was Senator Robert A. Taft of Ohio, who ran for and lost the Republican nomination for President in 1940, 1948 and 1952.

Marjorie Dodd Letts, a champion at golf and tennis.
Chicago Examiner, *August 25, 1916, page 11.*
(*Courtesy Chicago Public Library, Special Collections and Preservation Division*)

1917-24
William Merriam Burton (1865-1954)
Kean Burton
Olga Hallberg, maid; Hilda Anderson, cook

In 1913, William Merriam Burton, a Ph.D. from Johns Hopkins and the first chemist hired by Standard Oil of Indiana, was awarded the most important patent in the history of petroleum refining. U.S. Patent 1,049,667 was given to Burton for a process called thermal cracking, which doubled the amount of gasoline that could be extracted from a barrel of crude oil. Burton and his team of scientists worked under life-threatening circumstances. The crude oil was placed under 75 pounds of pressure per square inch and heated to 850 degrees Fahrenheit in improvised steel cauldrons that were prone to explode.

Earlier in 1896, when there were only four automobiles in the entire United States, Burton had his first breakthrough at Standard Oil when he helped figure out how to remove sulfur from crude. His discoveries directly influenced the rise of the automobile, the importance of gasoline and the spread of highways in every inhabited area of the world. Burton was the president of Standard Oil from 1918 to 1927. He was inducted posthumously into the Inventors Hall of Fame, the same Hall that also has honored the likes of Louis Pasteur, Alexander Graham Bell, Thomas Edison, the Wright Brothers, Charles Goodyear, Enrico Fermi and Steve Jobs.

William M. Burton, Chicago, March 9, 1927. Burton was president of the Standard Oil refinery in Whiting, Indiana. (Photographer: Russell. Chicago History Museum ICHi-68135)

Reuben H. Donnelley. (Chicago History Museum ICHi-67694)

1917
Reuben Hamilton Donnelley (1864-1929)
Laura Belle Thorne Donnelley (1867-1918)
Eleanor Donnelley (1859-1959), daughter

Reuben H. Donnelley published telephone directories for many of America's biggest cities. He was also a vice-president of R. R. Donnelley, his father's business and the world's largest printing company. In 1891 he took a sabbatical from ink and paper to start the brokerage house of Knight, Donnelley & Co. In 1905 the firm failed. Reuben returned to printing and publishing. Twenty-two years later he repaid in full the investments of every one of Knight, Donnelley & Co.'s shareholders, as well as the money owed to every creditor, plus compounded interest.

Laura Donnelley was the daughter of one of the founders of Montgomery Ward & Co. Her sister-in-law, Mrs. James Ward Thorne, conceived the miniature Thorne Rooms at the Art Institute.

1917
Joseph H. Geraghty

Ralph Martin Shaw (1869-1949)
Louise "Lola" Shepard Shaw
Ralph M. Shaw Jr., son; Louise T. Tyler, daughter
Thomas Shaw, son
Agnes Cawley, maid; Anne Carlson, cook
Katherine Clancy, maid

Early American history flowed through Ralph Shaw's veins. His great grandfather, Hiram Shaw, was born in 1776 in North Adams, Massachusetts—named after Samuel Adams, the rabble-rousing patriot and signer of the Declaration of Independence. In 1798, with only a crude map to guide them, Hiram and his brother took a post-revolutionary hike on the Wilderness Road and walked from Massachusetts to Kentucky. Ralph's paternal grandmother had two brothers who fought under General "Mad" Anthony Wayne in the War for Independence. Another brother was an Indian agent in the Van Buren administration. Ralph's grandfather, Nathaniel Shaw, captained a Mississippi River boat, the *Brandywine*, before returning to Lexington, Kentucky to start a successful business making coonskin caps, beaver skin top hats and fur coats. Ralph's father spent his career in the fur business. From 1776 to coonskin hats, the Shaws were a cornucopia of Americana.

Ralph Martin Shaw, Chicago, circa 1920.
(Chicago History Museum ICHi-68180)

Born four years after the end of the Civil War in Bourbon County, Kentucky, Ralph Shaw graduated from Transylvania Normal School in Lexington, received a B.A. from Yale and a law degree from the University of Michigan. In 1892, he moved to Chicago. He practiced law at Winston & Meagher. When he was promoted to partner, the firm's name changed to Winston, Payne, Strawn and Shaw.

Ralph combined his legal acumen with a head for business to become chairman of the board and general counsel of the Chicago Great Western Railway, general counsel and director of the United States Pipe and Foundry Company, and counsel and director for the Union Stock Yards & Transit Company, the Stewart-Warner Corporation, the Chicago Junction Railway, Dy-Dee Wash, Inc., and the Live Stock National Bank. He was also chairman of the Illinois Division of the Association Against the Prohibition Amendment and an active opponent of FDR's New Deal.

In 1896, he married Mary Stephens who in 1913 traveled to Africa with their son, Ralph Jr. During her trip home, she died in Geneva, Switzerland on September 29, 1914. The following year, Ralph married Louise "Lola" (Shepard) Tyler, the widow of Theodore Tyler. Together they raised three children, Ralph, Jr. (his), Louise (hers) and Thomas (theirs).

1919-20
Harry Milne McIntosh, Callas McIntosh
Marjorie McIntosh, daughter
Donald McIntosh, son
Margaret McCarthy, cook; Margret Tully, maid

Harry McIntosh was the president of an investment bank. The McIntosh's summer residence in Lake Forest was called the "Belmont," where every Tuesday afternoon Mrs. McIntosh and her friends gathered to play bridge in French under the tutelage of Mme. Marie Antoinette Walker.

1919-20
Charles D. Townsend, Mary H. Townsend
Emma Johnson, maid; Anna Gorman, cook

Charles Townsend was the president of an "instruments" company, although the census taker's handwriting leaves open the possibility that it was an "investment" company. Either way the name of the firm is unknown.

Settling In

Nineteen families (or in some cases individuals) were holdovers from the prior decade: Burton, Corwith, Cunningham, Elizabeth Dickason and her children, Hannah, Hixon, Hopkins, Hutchins, Letts, Marquis, McClurg, McCoy, McIntosh, Parker, Shaw, Frances Shepard and her sons, Smith, Townsend and Winterbotham. Thirty-eight new families encompassing 143 new people lived at 999 for the first time in the 1920s. This brings the number of people confirmed to have lived in the building through 1929 to 291 individuals from 77 families.

1B

1920-40

Thomas Clemens, Myrtle Clemens, first wife

Margetta Clemens, second wife

Eva Clemens, third wife

Howard Clemens, son; Ralph Clemens, son

Tom Clemens was the building's superintendent for the better part of three decades. He had a different wife (Myrtle, Margetta and Eva) every time the census taker knocked on his door. His son Ralph became an elevator operator for the building.

Are these two of the reindeer Colonel Daniel Devore brought to Alaska? (Comstock)

1920

Colonel Daniel B. Devore (1861-1956)

Helen G. Devore (1871-1960)

Bessie Coughlin, maid; Julia Beck, cook

Walter Mathews, chauffeur

Daniel Devore's military career lasted almost 75 years. A native of Woodfield, Ohio, he entered West Point in 1881, received his commission as a second lieutenant in 1885 and taught at his alma mater from 1894 to 1897. After serving in the Spanish-American War, he was sent on a special mission to Norway to purchase 537 reindeer and relocate them in Alaska, which was the beginning of the Alaskan herd. It is not clear—one way or the other—if Santa Claus' reindeers from Dasher to Blitzen were part of the initial group. During the rest of his career, Colonel Devore was stationed all over the world with a variety of assignments. While living at 999, he was in charge of National Guard affairs for the Army's Central States Department. He retired a brigadier general but remained in the Army Reserves until his death in 1956.

Helen G. Devore was the daughter of Alexander Stewart, a lumberman who amassed a large fortune and became a three-term congressman from Wisconsin. When Helen died in 1960, she left $10 million to underprivileged children.

In November 1920, after transferring to the Washington, D.C. area, the Devores bought Chatham House outside Fredericksburg, Virginia. Chatham House was built in 1730 from a plan created by Christopher Wren for the original Chatham House in England. The list of houseguests who had previously stayed in the Devore's new home reads like a who's who of American history. George and Martha Washington honeymooned there. Marquis de Lafayette was a guest of honor. Robert E. Lee courted his future wife at Chatham House. General Ambrose Burnside used it as his headquarters. And Abe Lincoln slept there after reviewing the Army of the Potomac.

Albert Younglove Gowen
Jeanne Bouchet Lyle Gowen
Anna Johnson, maid

Albert Gowen married Jeanne Bouchet in New York City in 1919. Shortly thereafter, they moved to Chicago and 999. The couple embarked on a belated honeymoon from a New York City harbor aboard Gowen's ship *Speejacks* on August 19, 1921. Almost every newspaper in the world covered their voyage.

Jeanne was a charming, outgoing, auburn-haired beauty from Texas. Albert, originally from Cleveland, Ohio, started as a laborer in a stone quarry, worked his way up the ranks to management and made a fortune in the cement business. The well-liked millionaire enjoyed an expensive hobby—ocean-going vessels—five of them christened *Speejacks*, which was his nickname at St. Paul's and Harvard. Joining the Gowens were Chicago friends Jay Ingraham, a professional motion picture cinematographer, and Burney Rogers, an accomplished still photographer and taxidermist. The crew consisted of a wireless radio operator and a navigator—both from Australia; a chief engineer, Jack Lewis, who had designed and supervised the construction of the *Speejacks*, and his assistant; a Belgian cook who later was replaced by a Chinese cook; a French all-purpose sailor; an official chronicler; a stock broker from New York City who signed on as a common seaman; and the captain and ship's master, Frank Hogg, a former all-American football player at Princeton. Their destination was, well, everywhere. They planned to circumnavigate the globe in the smallest boat ever to accomplish that feat.

In Albert's circle of friends, wagging tongues suggested the adventure was a flight from social problems. Jeanne didn't fit in with their crowd. Apparently she had also cooled to her husband's affections, and this was his attempt to win her back by turning her into a woman envied the world over.

Their itinerary covered the four corners of an oblong planet: a 34,000 mile journey from New York to Miami to Jamaica to Panama; from Takaroa to Tahiti to Samoa to Fiji to New Caledonia; Sidney; Brisbane; New Guinea; Samara; the Solomon, Admiralty and Hermit Islands;

The *Speejacks*, the first motor boat to sail around the world. She measures 98 feet long by 17 feet beam by 6 feet draft. She is shown here entering the harbour of Sydney, Australia.

Mrs. Gowen on a "desert taxi" near the Pyramids.

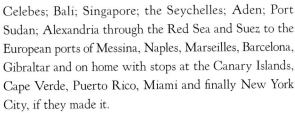

(Courtesy of The Library of Congress)

Mr. A. Y. Gowen, of the *Speejacks*, with Balinese dancing girls

(Courtesy of The Library of Congress)

Celebes; Bali; Singapore; the Seychelles; Aden; Port Sudan; Alexandria through the Red Sea and Suez to the European ports of Messina, Naples, Marseilles, Barcelona, Gibraltar and on home with stops at the Canary Islands, Cape Verde, Puerto Rico, Miami and finally New York City, if they made it.

Twice newspapers reported the ship lost at sea, once on the Pacific and later in the Atlantic. The men on the *Speejacks* heard the news on the ship's radio that they had twice disappeared and twice they replied that they were alive, well and on course. Built of wood with teak decks and a coppered bottom, 98 feet in length by 17 feet wide, she had a straight stem, rounded fantail, a single dummy stack, a full-length awning and a mast on which a steadying sail could be set. Powered by two 250 horsepower gasoline engines, the *Speejacks* had a top speed of 14 knots. As one of Standard Oil's largest shareholders, Gowen arranged to have thousands of gallons of fuel waiting for them at strategic locations around the world.

The ship's interior was a little world unto itself with modern conveniences like inter-cabin telephones, wireless communications, electric heating and lighting, refrigeration, freezers stocked with months' worth of provisions,

an assortment of state-of-the-art life-saving equipment and two machine guns in case they were attacked by pirates.

The voyage encountered its fair share of difficulties. From the outset, there wasn't enough fuel on board and the ship had to be towed for 3,400 miles. Unfortunately the *Speejacks* wasn't built for long-range towing. She pitched and rolled, leaving everybody continuously nauseated. After only 18 days their drinking water ran so low, it had to be rationed. They survived on coconut milk from the ship's store. In Panama, a Peruvian oilman tried to pick up Jeanne, thinking she was Albert's daughter. When they crossed the equator the weather was surprisingly cold and wet. The rudder cable broke and an emergency tiller had to be jerry-rigged. *En route* to Samoa the electrical system temporarily short-circuited. In spite of these nagging woes, the things they did and saw made the trip memorable.

On a beach in Takaroa, Burney Rogers and Jeanne wound up their gramophone and demonstrated the latest dance moves to puzzled natives. The master of the ship married a couple from Tahiti who, in the eyes of the governing French, had not been properly divorced from their prior spouses. Captain Hogg sailed the ship into international waters, performed the ceremony and returned everybody to the beach for a wedding feast. In Fiji they canoed on the Wainibuka River for ten days and ate turtle flippers with their indigenous island guides. They gasped at the firewalkers of Bequa and were repulsed by the beheading of a Chinese man on Pago Pago. They met hermits, aborigines, beachcombers, missionaries, sultans, bearded Indians, Malays in colorful sarongs, Arabs in gold-topped round white hatches, Dutch colonials hanging on to vestiges of civilization in the sweat and stink of jungle heat, high-rolling Chinese gamblers and preachers spreading the word of Mahatma Gandhi. They danced at country clubs and drank beer on the wide verandas of baronial estates. They inhaled the myriad scents of spices, perfumes and unwashed flesh. In Singapore they were given three monkeys as traveling companions. The monkeys were cute and playful, until they became unruly. The crew chloroformed them and tossed their limp bodies into the sea. They sailed through uncharted waters past herds of great whites and hammerheads, and the ship-swallowing whirlpools of the Malay straits. They rode elephants and visited the Taj Mahal. They stood next to the Pyramids. In Monte Carlo, Albert won a small fortune at roulette, betting only on 35 and 26, the Broadway address of Standard Oil of New York. His winnings were sufficient to offset some of the cost of the trip and to buy himself a sporty Italian car.

On December 1, 1922, they arrived in New York at 11:15 a.m. A large fleet of private craft traveled several miles out to sea to greet the *Speejacks*. The voyagers had taken 93,000 feet of film and used 73,000 gallons of fuel. Indeed the *Speejacks* was the smallest ship—and the first motorized one—to circumnavigate the globe. It was also the recipient of the longest tow in history.

Jeanne wrote in her journal, "All that I long for is a fireplace, perfectly stationary scenery, a bathtub that remains level, food on dishes that stays put—and nice dry clothes!"

Once in port, she checked into a hotel by herself and, after 467 days in confined quarters, began planning her divorce from Albert.

1920
Rudolph Hemming, Yvonne Hemming

Rudolph Hemming told the census taker that he was a clerk.

1920-24
Harriet G. Hall Keith
the widow of Elbridge Gallet Keith
Henry Glover Hall, brother
Mr. and Mrs. Marquette Healy, houseguests

Harriet Hall of LaSalle, Illinois married Elbridge G. Keith in 1865. Elbridge was born in Barre, Vermont in 1840. At 17 he followed his older brothers to Chicago. They formed the Keith Brothers Company dedicated to selling the finest hats, caps and buckskin gloves. Elbridge drifted away from haberdashery in the late 1880s to pursue banking. He subsequently became the president of the Metropolitan National Bank and Chicago Title and Trust, and a member of the Chicago Board of Education. Widely read, he became an authority on history and finance. His competence with numbers led to his appointments as the treasurer of the Chicago Bible Society, the Bureau of Charities and the Home for the Friendless. An active Republican, he was a delegate at the 1880 national convention, which nominated James A. Garfield. An ardent lover of art, he possessed a notable collection of masterpieces. Elbridge died in 1905.

Harriet Keith organized lectures in her apartment on an array of highbrow topics from "Dutch and American Art before the Twentieth Century" to "The Great Transition in English Poetry."

Her brother Henry Glover Hall had been a farmer in LaSalle County, Illinois. He was 63 years old in 1920.

Mr. and Mrs. Marquette Healy lived in the Keith apartment in 1922 while they waited for the opening of their summer home in Lake Geneva.

1920
Carl H. King, Marjorie King

Carl King was one of the building's live-in custodians.

George Alexander McKinlock (1857–1936)
Marion Wallace Rappelye McKinlock
Muriel Rockefeller McCormick,
daughter-in-law, sort of
Nanny Williams, maid; James Harris, butler
Lillian Hill, cook

At the dawn of the twentieth century telegraphy, telephony and electricity were growth industries similar in importance to the Internet, the computer chip and the database at the end of the last century. If an opportunistic young man wanted to help shape the future and make a good buck in the offing, those were the industrial sectors to enter. In his career George Alexander McKinlock participated in all three. He began building his résumé as the business manager of the American District Telegraph Company in Detroit. Later he became the cashier and auditor of the Bell Telephone Company in the same city.

He moved to Chicago in 1887 and started the Central Electric Company, a manufacturer of products that required electricity to operate. He eventually sold the business to General Electric. With the proceeds he purchased real estate in the loop, including the McKinlock Building

at 208 West Jackson Boulevard. He and his wife, the former Marion Wallace Rappelye, were pillars of society in Chicago, Palm Beach and Bar Harbor, Maine. Their estate in Palm Beach was called Villa Alejandro. Marion was the founder and president of the Palm Beach Garden Club.

Their son, George Alexander McKinlock, Jr., called Alex by his friends and family had been a Harvard student and football hero, intercepting a pass and returning it 80 yards for a touchdown against Carlisle in 1914. When the United States entered World War I, he enlisted in the Army. An intelligence officer, Alex was killed by German machine gun fire during a reconnaissance mission at Berzy-le-Sec in Soissons on July 21, 1918. Marion McKinlock received the news while working as the director of the Red Cross Canteen.

Distraught, the McKinlocks focused their philanthropy on projects that honored Alex's memory. In his name they built a new freshman dormitory at Harvard. They funded a sunken garden and its surrounding terraces at the Art Institute of Chicago. Later they increased their donation to add statuary to the courtyard. It is called the George Alexander McKinlock, Jr. Memorial Court. They purchased nine acres of land in Streeterville and donated it to Northwestern University. They erected an ornate gate at

Wilhelm Heinrich Funk, Mrs. George Alexander McKinlock, Sr. (*Harvard Art Museums/Fogg Museum, Harvard University Portrait Collection, Gift of the Estate of Muriel McCormick Hubbard in memory of Mr. and Mrs. George A. McKinlock, H595. Photo: Imaging Department © President and Fellows of Harvard College*)

Ellen Emmett Rand, George Alexander McKinlock Sr., 1929. (*Courtesy of Northwestern University Archives*)

Chicago Avenue and Lake Shore Drive and named it the George Alexander McKinlock, Jr. Gate. It was to be the grand entrance to Northwestern's downtown campus. The stock market crash of 1929 severely diminished the family's assets and they were unable to fulfill their commitment. Alexander's gate was moved two blocks south to Huron and Lake Shore Drive. It is still there.

TOP: Lt. George Alexander McKinlock, Jr. (Lake Forest-Lake Bluff Historical Society)

BOTTOM: The George Alexander McKinlock Gate was to have been the entrance to the downtown campus of Northwestern University. Today it stands at Huron Street and Lake Shore Drive. (Courtesy of Samuel Yellin Metalworkers)

THE HEIRESS
WHO MARRIED A GHOST

Miss Muriel McCormick with her father, Harold Fowler McCormick.
Muriel was one of McCormick's children by his first wife, Edith Rockefeller.
She was a favorite of maternal grandfather, John D. Rockefeller.
(Photographer: Chicago Daily News, Inc. Chicago History Museum DN-0073771)

THE MARRIAGE OF Muriel McCormick to Alexander McKinlock, Jr. was a screwball comedy begging to be filmed by the likes of Frank Capra or Ernst Lubitsch. The plot goes something like this. Muriel was a flamboyant redhead comfortable in the jazzy excesses of the Roaring Twenties. She also was the granddaughter of both Cyrus McCormick, the founder of International Harvester, and John D. Rockefeller, whose wealth has been estimated at $663 billion in today's dollars. Muriel, John D's favorite grandchild, spent much of her teenage years on a grand tour of Europe. She ridiculed a parade of panting suitors desirous—in all likelihood—of her fortune. Her ultimate rebuke of these unsolicited declarations of interest occurred in the late 1920s when she announced her decision to marry Alex McKinlock, who would have been unable to attend his own wedding because he was dead, and had been for almost a decade.

Muriel's moorings began to fray when her parents filed for divorce. Muriel sided with her mother (the former Edith Rockefeller) because her dad, whom she called "doddsie," had abandoned his family for the arms of a gorgeous Polish opera singer, Madame Ganna Walska, whose voice was deemed so awful an audience in Havana threw vegetables at her, a scene Orson Welles incorporated into *Citizen Kane.*

Before the long departed Alex blew in Muriel's ear, the call of the theater was her siren. Her stage debut had come in April 1922. In the fall, Hollywood knocked on her door, offering her a million dollars to star in four pictures. She turned it down, declaring, "My heart is set on opera," possibly an Oedipal gesture designed to lure her wandering father back home. She adopted the stage name Naranna Micor and rented a walk-up apartment in an attic on Chicago's north side. She ran a dress shop, eventually abandoning it to join a troop of nomadic singers. She gravitated to the occult, a predilection she may have inherited

The last family portrait of Harold McCormick and Edith
Rockefeller McCormick and their children taken in Switzerland
where all of them, except their youngest daughter, were undergo-
ing psychoanalysis with Carl Jung or one of his assistants.
From left to right standing are Mathilde, Fowler and Harold.
Seated from left to right are Muriel and Edith.
(Wisconsin Historical Society 102045)

Polish opera singer Ganna Walska in operatic costume
holding a lyre. Ms. Walska was the second wife of Harold
Fowler McCormick. (Wisconsin Historical Society 8789)

in the womb. During an upscale dinner party, her mother
stunned the guests by asserting that in another life she
had been the wife of King Tut.

Muriel had never met or even seen Alex in life. Their
paths first crossed at a séance when a spirit called her by
name, *Muriel...Muriel.* In subsequent sessions the voice
was identified by the medium as Alex's. She told Muriel
that Alex had been one of the handsomest of Chicago's
young men. More séances followed, each contact growing
more sure-footed and passionate than the last. Eventually
Alex's own mother Marion McKinlock became convinced
that her dead son was wooing Muriel.

Muriel and Marion's mutual desire to contact Alex
made them inseparable. They went everywhere together—
the opera, theater and Casino Club. Nobody dared invite
one without the other. The McKinlocks became Muriel's
godparents and she began living with them at 999. Marion
gave her a miniature photograph of her son, which Muriel

wore in a locket on a chain around her neck, touching it
often. The two traveled to Europe, located Alexander's
grave and brought his remains back to America. His
ashes were placed in an urn and displayed in one of the
McKinlock homes.

Overcome by the faux heat of their romance, Muriel
declared Alex her "spiritual bridegroom." She began wearing a ring of platinum, which, according to one newspaper,
"warns all young men with ambitions that she considers
herself bound to the fallen war hero as if he were alive
and waiting for her at home." The "marriage" lasted a
few years, a long time considering Alex brought nothing
to their relationship.

In 1931 Muriel gave up the ghost and married a living
person, Elisha Dyer Hubbard, a gentleman farmer from
Connecticut. The McKinlocks were the only witnesses
as the couple knelt on a Spanish shawl under an ash tree
in Bar Harbor, Maine.

1920-24
Dr. Edwin Warner Ryerson (1872-1961)
Adelaide Hamilton Ryerson
Mary Hamilton, mother
Selma Johnson, maid; Emma Johnson, maid

Born in New York, Dr. Edwin Ryerson received a medical degree from Harvard and worked as house surgeon at Children's Memorial Hospital in Boston. In 1899, he relocated to Chicago. Seven years later he joined the staff of St. Luke's. During World War I, he served as a major in the army medical corps. From 1927 to 1935, Dr. Ryerson was a professor of orthopedic surgery at the Northwestern University Medical School. He was elected president of both the American Orthopedic Association and American Academy of Orthopedic Surgeons. He authored over 60 research and clinical papers.

As the president of the Antiquarian Society of the Art Institute of Chicago, Adelaide Ryerson was instrumental in obtaining the Beveridge Collection of porcelain objects and the Helen Birch Bartlett collection of post-Impressionistic and modern paintings, including Seurat's *A Sunday on La Grande Jatte*, van Gogh's *Bedroom at Arles*, Toulouse-Lautrec's *At the Moulin Rouge*, Cézanne's *Basket of Apples*, Gauguin's *Day of the God*, Picasso's *The Old Guitarist* and Matisse's *Woman on Rose Divan*. She was a member of the women's board of St. Luke's and the National Society of Colonial Dames of America. The Ryersons retired to Fort Lauderdale, Florida in the 1950s. After her husband's death, Mrs. Ryerson donated $500,000 to Northwestern to endow a professorship in orthopedic surgery

Mary Hamilton was Adelaide's mother and the widow of David G. Hamilton, a deceased former resident of 999.

Henri de Toulouse-Lautrec, 1864-1901, At the Moulin Rouge, 1892/95, Oil on canvas. (Helen Birch Bartlett Memorial Collection 1928.610. The Art Institute of Chicago)

Georges Seurat, 1859-1891, A Sunday on La Grande Jatte, 1884, 1884-86, Oil on canvas

(Helen Birch Bartlett Memorial Collection 1926.224. The Art Institute of Chicago)

1920
Louise M. Shepard
Matilda Pearson, maid

Louise Shepard was the widow of Henry Shepard, a farmer from Warren, Illinois in Lake County, and the mother of Louise "Lola" Shepard, Ralph Shaw's second wife.

1920
Addison H. Stillwell (1889-1942)
May Peabody Stillwell
May Henderson Stillwell, daughter
Addison E. Stillwell, son
Johanna Katria, maid; Elaine Lundin, nurse
Irma Gibson, cook

Addison Stillwell was the president of Stillwell Lumber, which operated five large mills in Mississippi. He joined the Navy when the United States entered World War I. He was sent to the Naval Academy at Annapolis, Maryland for intensive training. He emerged as a lieutenant, junior grade.

May Peabody Stillwell was the daughter of Francis Stuyvesant Peabody, the founder of Peabody Coal, one of the largest coal companies in the world, and a former resident of 999. May married Addison in 1914. They honeymooned in Egypt. In 1920, the Stillwells had apartments at both 999 and 199 East Lake Shore Drive. The couple divorced in 1922, so perhaps they were already living apart.

Group of men on a boat, including Addison Stillwell (second from left) believed to be Mackinac Island, Michigan, October 26, 1933. (Chicago History Museum ICHi-68134)

9A
1920-25
Dr. Francis "Frank" X. Walls
Elizabeth Dickason Walls
Livingston Dickason, Jr., son
Margaret Murphy, maid; Catherine Moore, cook
Audon Kinsella, maid

1926-29
Livingston Dickason, Jr.
Katherine Hogg Maxwell Dickason
Mary Elizabeth Dickason, daughter

999 resident Elizabeth Dickason was widowed when her husband Colonel Livingston Dickason died in 1913. She moved out of the building, but returned in 1917 after subletting 9A from Ogden McClurg. She married Dr. Frank Walls in Paris in 1926. He was an Army physician during the Spanish-American War. The couple owned a summer home in Nantucket. They moved to 219 East Lake Shore Drive, while Livingston Dickason, Jr. remained at 999.

After graduating Yale, Dickason, Jr. became a production engineer and married Katherine Hogg Maxwell of Rye, New York. He was considered a great catch and "there were many disappointed hearts when the news broke that he was to marry an Eastern girl." Their first child, Mary Elizabeth Dickason, was born in 1927. Mary spent her early years at 999 before moving with her parents to Short Hills, New Jersey sometime in 1929. She returned to 999 in 1983 as the wife of Dr. Donald West King. She, too, was a doctor.

1921
Margaret Allan Pullman (1870–1932),
the widow of William C. Pullman
William Allan Pinkerton Pullman, son

Margaret Pullman was the widow of William C. Pullman, an executive of the Pullman Company and the nephew of founder George Pullman. She was the granddaughter of the great American detective Allan Pinkerton. Mrs. Pullman focused her philanthropy on the County Home for Convalescent Children. Her son, William, married Madeleine Childs in 1925. He is regarded as the father of the Chicago Botanic Garden in Glencoe.

BELOW: Wedding of Madeleine Childs and William A. P. Pullman, Lake Forest, Illinois, July 1, 1925. (Chicago History Museum ICHi-68178)

ABOVE: Mrs. William A. Pullman, Chicago, 1925. (Photographer: Chicago Daily News, Inc. Chicago History Museum DN-0079641)

TOP ROW, LEFT TO RIGHT: William A. P. Watkins, John McIlvaine, Clymer S. Bowen, Thomas C. Dennehy, Jr., E. Ogden Ketting, Hale Holden, Jr., Mrs. C. Frederick Childs, Samuel Insull, Jr., Richard Robertson, Edison Dick. SECOND ROW: Helen Isham, Anne Beebe, Mary Park,

Claire Childs, William A. P. Pullman, Madeleine Childs Pullman, Harriet Lowden, Louise Mitchell, Laura Thompson, Alice Carpenter, Marion Warner Dennehy. FRONT: George Roberts, Jr., L. Newell Childs, and flower girls Peggy McIlvanie and Anita Smith.

Herman Armour Nichols, Lynette Craven Nichols
Marie Louise Nichols, daughter

1923-24
Mr. and Mrs. Otto W. Lehmann

Otto Lehmann's father, Ernst, co-owned a dance hall with George Wellington Streeter. In 1875, Ernst Lehmann went legit when he founded the Fair Store in Chicago, one of the first discount department stores in the country. His son, Otto, raised prize-winning show horses and competitive thoroughbreds.

In 1923, the *Chicago Daily News* photographed a house and identified it as "the home of O. W. Lehmann, located at 999 North Lake Shore Drive," which begged the question, were there two 999s in 1923? A close examination of the words at the bottom of the image revealed the home was on Lake Shore Drive and Diversey Boulevard, still a mistake. The actual address was 2748 Lakeview Avenue. In 1923, Lehmann sold it for $500,000 and moved to 999, which probably explains the sloppy note taking by the *Daily News*. Today it is the site of the Benevolent and Protective Order of the Elks National Memorial and Headquarters.

Home of O. W. Lehmann at 2748 Lakeview Avenue in 1923. The Chicago Daily News *misidentified the address as 999 Lake Shore Drive, where Lehmann had leased an apartment. (Photographer: Chicago Daily News, Inc. Chicago History Museum DN-0075761)*

2B
1924-31
Frederick Stanley Oliver (d 1931)
Frances Oliver, daughter
Frances Hart, mother-in-law
Sarah W. Brown, housekeeper

Frederick Stanley Oliver bought 999 in 1920, and turned it from a rental building into a co-op. One of the least sophisticated poems ever written was about him.

"Down along Michigan Avenue,
He spreads the soothing and saving salve,
Have they lent an ear to his words of cheer?
They have indeed, indeed they have."

(*See page 90 for a cartoon of Oliver and the poem.*)

Frederick Stanley Oliver.
Chicago Examiner, *December 21, 1911, page 8. (Courtesy Chicago Public Library, Special Collections and Preservation Division)*

4B
1924–86

George Stuart (1843–1943), father
Charles Stuart, son; Harold Leonard Stuart, son
Harriet Barnes Stuart, daughter
Elizabeth Barnes Stuart, daughter
Arthur Anderson, butler
Fannie Anderson, maid; Rudolph Bricking, butler
Anna Jenkins, housekeeper; Linda Moran, maid

The Stuarts were lineal descendants of the Duke of Rothesay who became King James the IV of Scotland and later King James I of England, the same King James who commissioned the translation of the Bible into English. James' mother remains famous to this day: Mary Queen of Scots, who changed the spelling of the family name from Stewart to Stuart when she was the Queen of France so that her subjects would not have to struggle pronouncing "w." Mary's head was removed from her body on a nod from Queen Elizabeth I of England, her first cousin once removed, which means George Stuart and his children were related to the Virgin Queen as well as her father, Henry VIII. Following the family tree farther back in time, we get to Robert the Bruce, the legendary King of Scotland, whose daughter Marjorie married Walter, the 6th High Stewart of Scotland. The Stewart/Stuart ancestry can be traced back to Alan FitzFlaad, a Breton, who sailed to Great Britain not long after the Norman Invasion of 1066. Before that the trail grows cold. Not wishing to denigrate anybody else's family, the Stuarts of 4B have the most imposing pedigree in the history of 999.

The Stuart art collection consisted of paintings of their ancestors. The painters varied depending on the century in which the work was commissioned. The artist was always among the acknowledged greats of their time—Holbein, Gainsborough, Whistler and their like. The art on the walls of 4B was—there is no other way to put it—priceless.

The Stuarts lived as if there were still a moat around their castle. Each of them had their own set of servants.

George Stuart, a retired investment banker, died 51 days after his 100th birthday in 1943. Born in Rhode Island and educated at Eton and Oxford, he interrupted his education to serve in the American Civil War. He married Harriet Barnes during Reconstruction. They had five children, the four listed above and Margaret Stuart Doig who lived in New York. Wife Harriet died in 1923, which led to the Stuarts taking an apartment at 999.

As a young man Harold Stuart worked for the investment firm of N. W. Halsey & Co., specialists in bonds. At 20, he became its president after Halsey's death in 1911 and the company's name changed to Halsey, Stuart &

Mary, Queen of Scots, a linear ancestor of the Stuarts of 999. (Photos.com)

Co., which in its heyday commanded a vast clientele. One relationship in particular towered above all the others. During the first 25 years of the twentieth century, Samuel Insull attained legendary status as a businessman who performed the impossible on a daily basis. It was said that if you were seen talking to him, your net worth went up a million bucks. As luck would have it, Harold Stuart spoke with Insull nearly every day, which was good for Stuart's business—and Insull's—until the bottom fell out and both men, along with 14 others, stood shoulder to shoulder in the dock, accused of mail fraud and embezzlement.

The story begins on February 28, 1881, when a short, unimposing, rail-thin, pallid young man of 21, exhausted from his two-month journey across the Atlantic from England, shook hands with his new employer, the Wizard of Menlo Park. The bantamweight was Samuel Insull. The wizard, of course, was Thomas Alva Edison—the inventor of the phonograph, motion picture camera and incandescent lighting. Insull was to be his personal secretary. Back then, secretary meant more than being a crack stenographer and typist—Insull was both—but also someone who would manage his bosses' finances. Edison's were a mess. He couldn't be bothered with making deposits, balancing a checkbook or paying bills. His mind was occupied with thoughts of electricity. He was about to light a few blocks of New York City, a parlor trick prior to his lighting the world. Edison didn't know it at the time, but the young fellow with the cockney accent standing in front of him was good with numbers and a budding genius when it came to running a business.

Huge investment banks and deep-pocketed financiers with out-sized egos led by J. P. Morgan and the Vanderbilt family stood behind Edison. But they were not Edison's principal source of capital. That honor fell to Henry Villard, a German financier, who seemed to have a sixth sense understanding of Edison's vision. But, in the end, Villard's pockets weren't deep enough. Morgan began buying stock in various Edison companies. There were many. Every invention seemed to get its own publicly traded company.

A debate ensued over the best method for bringing electricity to market. Edison insisted on building central stations and locating them in neighborhoods. From there electricity would be sent out to the streets, offices, stores and homes in the area. Edison was already hard at work inventing every item a central station would need, "switches, sockets, cables, junction boxes, wires, insulators, fuses, meters, filaments, voltage regulators, and scores of other devices." Edison's needs for capital were growing Gargantuan.

Meanwhile, Morgan and his colleagues shared a different vision regarding the distribution of electricity. They favored putting small generators inside large buildings shooting electricity up from basements, much like a steam and radiator heating system. That way electricity would be rationed to people with money. It would be expensive and profitable. Siding with Edison was the untested rookie Samuel Insull. Edison prevailed, but at a high cost. He had to surrender control of his companies to boards of Morgan's choosing and to relinquish the rights to many of his most valuable patents. Insull watched with a growing mistrust of New York bankers and a smoldering fury directed at the greedy men who tormented his idol.

Rapidly, Insull became Edison's most trusted business associate. In 1889, Edison asked him to rescue one of his troubled companies, Edison General Electric (shortly thereafter, just plain General Electric). In one year, Insull improved the performance of the company so dramatically that the number of employees had to be increased from 200 to 6,000. The bankers approved of Insull, but fired the company's other managers. They offered Insull the second vice-president's job. He considered it an insult and resigned.

He went to Chicago in 1892 to run the Chicago Edison Company. He brought with him a fundamental understanding of electricity so counterintuitive and profound that competitors wouldn't grasp it for at least another decade. Insull realized the obvious. Electricity could not be warehoused. For all practical purposes, it had to be manufactured, sold, delivered and used in the same instant. This insight released Insull from the bonds of convention. He was free to invent new business models.

He believed that electricity was for everybody, including the humblest consumer. He wanted to bring electric power to more places than downtown commercial districts and upscale neighborhoods in big cities, but to small towns and unincorporated areas as well. Philosophically he was J. P. Morgan's opposite. Insull believed that electricity should be sold at the lowest possible price. He kept putting bigger and bigger generators inside central stations to lower the unit cost of his lightning bolts, which helped him sign up new customers at an unheard of clip.

Insull violated conventional wisdom in other ways. He respected labor unions, often paying workers more than they asked for. After all they were his customers, too. He fought for government regulation of public utilities and turned skeptical politicians into allies. He devised the open-ended mortgage and began a revolution in how American businesses were financed. At one point he bought Chicago Elevated Railways, thereby owning his largest customer. He also could be tough. A group of bipartisan alderman known as the "Gray Wolves" started a shell electric company. They called it Commonwealth Electric and passed a law giving their bogus business a 50-year exclusive franchise to sell electricity to Chicago. They tried to extort money from Insull, promising never to operationalize their electric company in exchange for a very large bribe. "Be my guest," replied Insull. When the politicians tried to create a central station they discovered Insull owned the entire inventory of every electric equipment manufacturer in the United States, as well as their near-term future production. The wolves were forced to sell their company, its name and its exclusive contract to Insull for a modest sum of money. He renamed his electric company, Commonwealth Edison, comforted that it could now operate until 1947 without competition.

After six years at the helm, Com Ed was ten times as large as the day Insull took charge. During that time, it had paid 24 consecutive months of dividends. He began buying other utility companies. At the suggestion of one of his financial advisors, Ed Russell, he organized these new acquisitions inside various holding companies. Some of these acquisitions included providers of gas and public transportation. To pull this juggernaut together, Insull needed a river of money flowing past his office. He refused to deal with the scoundrels in New York. He wanted somebody smart in Chicago.

He found that person in 26-year-old Harold Stuart, an expert in bonds, who explained to Insull how he could get the funds he needed using methods New York didn't preach or practice. One could raise a million dollars from one institutional investor or get four rosy-cheeked fat cats to toss $250,000 each into the pot, approaches favored by the House of Morgan. Or you can get it from 100 people

Harold L. Stuart.
(Paul V. Galvin Library,
Illinois Institute of Technology)

President Theodore Roosevelt standing in a car during a visit to Chicago, 1917. Samuel Insull is standing next to him.

or 1,000 or even 1,000,000. Previously other financiers had told Insull that it was impossible to raise funds for a power plant located near a hamlet you could barely find on a map; Stuart smiled and said, no problem.

Stuart pioneered the mass market retailing of bonds. The team of Samuel Insull and Harold Stuart amazed the financial world. Stuart actually could raise any amount of money with ease and Insull's operational genius turned every acquisition into a profit-generating dynamo. In due course Stuart no longer had to sell Insull's bonds, he rationed them. By 1927 he had become Insull's principal financial advisor and a very wealthy man in his own right. As Forrest McDonald, the author of the book *Insull*, put it, "Financing utilities was many times more profitable than running them." As business boomed for Halsey, Stuart, Harold Stuart sent his older brother Charles to New York to open a branch office and siphon customers from the old dogs of Manhattan.

On August 23, 1929, Insull controlled five huge holding companies, each with numerous subsidiaries, included some that sold a competitive form of energy: gas. The holding companies were publicly traded and ran their subs

for long-term growth and profits. Insull's public utility properties had a combined value of $3 billion, astronomical in those days. They had six million shareholders, 500,000 bondholders and four million customers. They generated one-eighth of the electricity and gas used in the United States. Insull's holdings were growing at the astonishing rate of $7,000 a minute. His personal fortune was estimated at $150 million and climbing.

However, Insull had made a fundamental mistake that would cost him dearly. He deliberately kept the value of the holding companies down. The assets inside of them were worth many times more than their parent.

Off stage, the New York crowd muttered in frustration; fortunes were being made in Chicago and they were not allowed in the game. So they began buying and holding Insull's publicly traded securities, the undervalued holding companies. J. P. Morgan became a competitor, investing broadly in East Coast public utilities with some success, but he lacked an Insull to run things.

The stock market crash on October 29, 1929 handed New York the cudgel to metaphorically bash in Insull's brains. At first Insull fared well during the Depression. At

one point he even raised money to create a safety net to help Chicagoans weather the storm. Even though the underlying assets of his subsidiary operating companies remained strong, the value of his holding companies began to slide. As their prices grew cheaper, New York bought more and more shares. Soon they owned enough of Insull's stock to bully some large Chicago shareholders into agreeing to let the great man go. They forced the once mighty Insull to resign from every one of his companies on the same day.

The country needed a scapegoat for the Depression and, with a push from New York, the federal government tried to pin the tail on Insull and his associates, including Stuart, who were indicted for embezzlement and using the United States mail to defraud investors. The latter charge was based largely on Insull's $500,000 annual salary. The government put its best prosecutor, Leslie E. Salter, on the case. Salter accepted the evidence provided to him by the SEC and FBI as gospel, a monumental mistake.

Government witnesses were made to seem like idiots, admitting time after time that the way Insull kept his books was the way everybody kept their books, including the federal government. When Salter raised Insull's $500,000 salary as a signpost of malfeasance and greed, he discovered—apparently for the first time—that Insull had donated all of it to charity. Insull took the stand and was mesmerizing. Starting with his personal relationship with Edison, a genuine American hero, through every business decision he ever made, Insull beguiled the jury. He came across as good and as great as his reputation before his fall from grace.

A former vice-president of the United States testified as a character witness for Stuart, as did Cardinal Mundelein, even though Stuart was not Catholic. During a recess, Salter found himself next to Insull's adult son at a urinal and said, "Say, you fellows were legitimate businessmen." It took the jury five minutes to acquit Insull, Stuart and all the other defendants of every charge. In all subsequent

trials the results were identical. In one of them the judge ordered the jury to return a verdict of not guilty.

But Insull had gone broke defending himself and now other men owned his companies. He retired to Paris and died on the Metro in 1938. His estate was found to be worth $1,000. He owed his creditors $14 million.

As for Harold Stuart, after his acquittal he testified before Congress on the practices of firms like the House of Morgan, how their interests were not aligned with the interests of the American people. His testimony helped convince Congress to pass a host of new laws designed to rein in big investment banks. In 1952, at a time when Halsey, Stuart was responsible for the most IPOs in the United States, Harold appeared before the U.S. Supreme Court on behalf of the government in its antitrust case against Morgan Stanley and 16 other competitors of Halsey, Stuart. Harold was not an economic populist or an anti-capitalist or a friend of New Deal regulators, but his evidence helped the government break up one of J. P. Morgan's institutions. Revenge must have been sweet.

The family had its quirks. Forty-three years after he passed away, George Stuart's phone number at 999—787-3550—was still listed in the telephone book.

Harriet and Elizabeth Stuart were spinsters who lived together with Harold their entire lives. A widely believed rumor that Harriet smothered Elizabeth with a pillow could not be verified.

After midnight, on an evening shortly after Harriet, the last of the Stuarts, died, a large number of small trucks, cars and U-Hauls parked in front of 999. Men in dark clothing went up to the Stuart apartment. They individually wrapped each painting from their extraordinary collection in blankets. They brought them downstairs, loaded them into the waiting transports and drove them away, where they faded from view and disappeared into the art market of the netherworld.

1924-28
Livingston Fairbank, Jr. (1871-1934)
Miriam Patterson Fairbank
Jane Boyce, Mrs. Fairbank's daughter from
a prior marriage; Livingston Fairbank III, son

Livingston Fairbank was the son of N. Kellogg Fairbank, one of the Pine Street shore owners. He also was a descendant of Phillip Livingston, a signer of the Declaration of Independence. Livingston Fairbank graduated Harvard and seems to have devoted the rest of his life to pleasure, living off the interest from a trust fund set up by his father. At least once, in 1925, he dipped into principle to purchase shares in Frederick Stanley Oliver's 999 cooperative. Fairbank was already living on the eighth floor with his wife and family.

Miriam Patterson Fairbank created Musical Sundays at 999. She invited 15 to 20 society friends to listen to afternoon concerts in her apartment. The *Tribune* reported, "Tea and other refreshments are served, the atmosphere is one of informality and friendliness, and the walls of the Fairbank's...library, wainscoted and paneled in dark woodwork, rang with the voices of the singers."

A gifted singer with a rich soprano voice, Miriam studied singing in France, Germany and Italy and frequently sang at charitable events in Chicago. She made her formal musical debut in April 1926 in Paris. A London recital followed two years later.

In the 1920s, if you had gobs of money, the place to be was Paris. So in addition to their apartment at 999, the Fairbanks annually joined the American colony in the City of Lights. Every year they rented a different apartment "on the Left Bank in historic houses filled with old world charm and atmosphere." They threw fabulous parties. At one of them, the guests of honor were the Grand Duke and Grand Duchess Boris of Russia—a country where they would never again hold the reins of power. Ganna Walska, the would-be opera singer and rival of Muriel Rockefeller McCormick for the attentions of Muriel's father, attended, very much in love with herself. At another soiree held to celebrate the visiting American composer Chicagoan John Alden Carpenter, the guests included conductor Pierre Monteux of the Boston Symphony Orchestra, the widow of Claude Debussy and composers Darius Milhaud, Maurice Ravel, Arthur Honnegger and Edgar Varese.

LEFT: Miriam Fairbank in her kitchen at 999, 1928. Notice the ice box to her right. (Photographer: Chicago Daily News, Inc. Chicago History Museum DN-0084587)

OPPOSITE: Miriam Fairbank appeared in ad for Pond's® Two Creams. The photograph of her was taken by the great fashion photographer, Edward Steichen.

Pond's® is a registered trademark used with the kind permission of Unilever PLC and group companies.

Portrait of Mrs. Livingston Fairbank
© Permission of The Estate of Edward Steichen.

(The Newberry Library, Chicago. Case TX1 .G7 v.80, no.6, Good Housekeeping, pg. 105)

As Mrs. Livingston Fairbank of Chicago Sees It

"*Today women are better groomed, just as they are healthier and more efficient than ever before. Their skins, particularly, are kept clear, fresh, youthful. Pond's two delightful Creams are responsible for thousands of lovely complexions.*"

Miriam Fairbank

ONE may always recognize Mrs. Livingston Fairbank's winsome smile in her box at the Chicago Opera. One sees her at the Twelfth-night Balls which mark the height of the social season. And her Sunday evening musicales, at which one meets and hears a distinguished company of artists and musicians, mingling with the music-lovers of Society, are occasions of rare delight.

Mrs. Fairbank had just returned from Palm Beach when I encountered her on the Boulevard one March morning.

"How could you leave blue sea and magnolias for this—dust, soot and gales?" I asked her, gesturing at the atmosphere. "They're disastrous to one's skin. But you seem to thrive!" I added. "You're like a Dorothy Perkins rose this morning. Did Palm Beach teach you a new secret?"

"When you've lived in Chicago as long as I," laughed Mrs. Fairbank, "you'll know you can have a perfectly good complexion—even a lovely one—right here, in spite of unfriendly elements."

"What *do* you do," I begged her, "to keep so unblemished in the midst of soot and dust?"

"I JUST use Pond's Two Creams," she answered, "the very same two that I found so many of my friends were using. A simple method—requiring only a few moments each day." And then she told me how: *Every day, and more frequently than once if you have been out a great deal*, cleanse your face, neck, throat, arms and hands with Pond's Cold Cream. Let it stay on a few moments. Remove every vestige with a soft cloth which reveals how much dirt

THE TWO CREAMS *society women are using today*

Steichen

MRS. LIVINGSTON FAIRBANK

of a Chicago family whose wealth and prominence date from pioneer days. She is a leading favorite in Chicago's most exclusive social set, because of her social charms and her lovely lyric soprano voice.

To the right, the music-room of her apartment at 999 Lake Shore Drive, which commands a superb view of Lake Michigan. On her dressing table, Pond's Two Creams.

Among the other women of distinguished position who have expressed enthusiasm for the Pond's method are:

Her Majesty, Marie, The Queen of Roumania; The Lady Diana Manners; Mrs. Reginald C. Vanderbilt; Mrs. Gloria Gould Bishop and Mrs. Marshall Field, Sr.

the pure oils of this delicate cream have brought from the depths of your pores. Do it all over again. Now close the pores with a dash of cold water or a light massage with ice.

If your skin is dry, use more Pond's Cold Cream after cleansing, before retiring, and leave it on all night. Your skin will be softened, yet toned to elasticity, too. And how white and soft your hands! If your skin is oily, Pond's Cold Cream will free the pores from all accumulated oils.

THE *complementary step in the Pond's Method of skin care* is to smooth over the skin of your face, throat and hands a gossamer of Pond's Vanishing Cream. It gives your skin a soft even-toned finish, a new lustre. It protects it—denying the power of wind and sun to coarsen and burn, of soot and dust to mar the fineness of its texture. And it keeps the soft whiteness of your hands! Now, too, your powder and rouge go on with smoothness and blend with natural charm. So always use it before powdering and before going out.

Try Pond's for yourself. The unfailing results which have commended this method to Mrs. Fairbank and the loveliest, most perfectly groomed Society leaders everywhere, will also endear these Creams to you.

Free Offer

Mail coupon for free tubes of these two creams and a little folder telling how to use them.

The Pond's Extract Company, Dept. F
135 Hudson Street, New York City.

Please send me your free tubes of Pond's Cold and Vanishing Creams.

Name.................Street............

City.................State............

4C
1924–25
Terry Druggan (1902–1954) and Hassel as "Mr. and Mrs. Edward Mulvihill"

999's residents and staff had every reason to believe the couple in 4C was Mr. and Mrs. Edward Mulvihill. That's what they said their name was. They had moved into the building in the spring of 1924. Previously, the Mulvihills had lived at 219 East Lake Shore Drive under the name Mr. and Mrs. Richard Phillips. While there, Mr. Phillips violated his neighbors' propriety by casually displaying guns in their presence. He owned many—from handguns to Tommy guns. He was summarily evicted.

By the time the Mulvihills got to 999, they were living apart. She idled away her hours in 4C, while Mulvihill/Phillips was incarcerated in Cook County Jail, which didn't stop him from enjoying periodic conjugal visits to 999. Jail guards drove him to his rendezvous. They waited outside in their parked car until their passenger finished his business and was ready to be returned to his home away from home.

Reporters from the *Chicago American* got wind of the prisoner's special treatment and blew the whistle on the corrupt and slipshod practices running wild at the county clink. When the story broke, the denizens of 999 learned the true identity of their tenant. Chills ran down their collective spine. Mulvihill's real name was Terrance Druggan, a.k.a Terrible Terry. Even though he was only

22, he had been a regular on the front pages of Chicago's newspapers for years. His fame approached that of movie stars and baseball heroes. But he was a gangster. Only his friend, Al Capone, eclipsed his reputation for immorality.

Druggan's criminal career began at the bottom as a street urchin stealing fruit off vendors' wagons. With his buddy, Frankie Lake, he joined the notorious Valley Gang, which controlled the near west side with the no-questions-asked authority that comes from the beat-down end of a lead pipe. Rapidly, Druggan and Lake graduated to assault, armed robbery and murder. While still in their teens, the boys gained control of the Valley Gang and its little black book of political connections. Druggan separated himself from most thugs by speaking in whole sentences. Like Lake he wore round, horn-rimmed eyeglasses, at the time a fairly common look for men in the darker professions. He couldn't completely suppress the punk in him; even in front of judges, he jiggled coins in his pants pocket.

With the advent of Prohibition, Druggan and Lake muscled their way into the control of five breweries. Combining his hair-trigger temper and native intelligence, Druggan proved to be a master of the post-Volstead Act beer business. By the third year of Prohibition, he had succeeded beyond his wildest dreams. Lake and he were multimillionaire beer barons, who gave every member of their gang a chauffeur driven Rolls Royce. They forged a lucrative business relationship with Johnny Torrio and his scar-faced import from New York City, Alphonse Gabriel Capone. For all intents and purposes, the well-connected Druggan

Reputed gunmen Frank Lake (left) and Terry Druggan (right), Chicago, 1925. (Photographer: Chicago Daily News, Inc. Chicago History Museum DN-0079320)

Alphonse Capone. (Courtesy of University of Illinois at Urbana-Champaign Library)

ran the west side for Big Al, and when he needed a good lawyer he summoned Clarence Darrow to stand by his side.

In 1924, when Druggan and Lake refused to answer questions about their business dealings, they were sentenced to one year each in Cook County Jail for contempt of court.

Reporters at the *Chicago American* heard about the unlimited liberties for Druggan and Lake from the Lake County states attorney's office. They had gone to Cook County Jail to question both inmates about the bullet-riddled body of a gangster deposited in Waukegan and found the Valley Gang leaders missing. From that moment, the Druggan-Lake jail story inflated like the universe in the aftermath of the Big Bang.

Elevator operators from 999, R. C. Conway and J. T. Barrow, testified that Druggan made about 30 trips to his love nest. On the stand, Druggan revealed that the woman who played his wife was Hassel. He didn't clarify if that was her first or last name, or merely what he thought of her. When their trysting place became public knowledge, an embarrassed Hassel left Chicago.

Druggan, accompanied by guards, also left jail for reasons beyond sexual dalliance: to visit relatives, patronize popular cabarets, eat lavish dinners in downtown restaurants, review the contents of his safety deposit box at the Continental and Commercial Bank, or bump into one or more of his associates while strolling down a quiet street. Amazingly, Druggan had been furloughed 90 times in less than a year to see his dentist, Dr. Franklin Percival, who later was asked, "Why so many visits?" He replied, "Mr. Druggan is very nervous. I can only work on his teeth a few minutes at a time." When Dr. Percival's bill came, Druggan gladly forked over $3,200.

Five times Terry Druggan left jail without any guards and returned when he felt like it. Nobody knows what he did on those excursions. Morris Eller, a member of the sanitary district and a Republican leader, issued those passes. Was Eller the force behind the extreme laxity at Cook County Jail? Not really; the five passes seem to be the extent of his involvement.

Shortly after Druggan and Lake arrived culture at the jail changed. Lake's sister had been hospitalized with a terminal illness. He asked the warden, Wesley Westbrook, for permission to visit her. Westbrook charged Lake $1,500 for the privilege. His sister died not long after Frankie said his goodbyes.

A few days later, the warden's secretary, Henry Foerst, approached Terry Druggan and told him that Westbrook would entertain regular furloughs and early releases for the two lads for a price—$100,000. Druggan thought Westbrook was a bloodsucker, but that didn't stop him from negotiating the price down to $60,000 and a paid

Film poster for *The Public Enemy* (1931), directed by William Wellman shows James Cagney (1899–1986) and Jean Harlow (1911–1937). (Warner Bros./Courtesy of Getty Images)

vacation to Mexico. Before the deal was finalized, lesser sums were also agreed upon for the warden's secretary (who handled the money) and two other assistants, as well as four guards and the sheriff.

True to his word, the warden set Druggan and Lake free early based on their good behavior. But soon Westbrook and his co-conspirators were behind bars themselves.

On the outside, Druggan and Lake went on with their criminal lives, although they eventually parted company over a redhead they met at a tea party. In 1930, the Chicago Crime Commission officially named both men "Public Enemies," along with Capone, "Machine Gun" Jack McGurn, "Bugs" Moran, "Three-Fingered" Jack White and "Greasy Thumb" Guzik, among others. In the same year, a raid on Druggan's suite at the Morrison Hotel turned up a letter implicating him in a plot to kill Al Capone. Somehow Druggan was allowed to live. Like Big Al, he spent years in federal prison for tax evasion

In 1931, James Cagney played Tom Powers, a character loosely based on Terry Druggan, in the classic American gangster film, *The Public Enemy*. Only one other 999er had a movie made about his life but he won't arrive until the 1940s.

In 1954, Druggan died of natural causes.

5B
1925-28
George Milton Seaman (1876-?)
Adelaide M. Herzberg Seaman
Margaret Seaman, daughter
Mary Seaman, daughter
Mary Clark, cook; Delia Walsh, maid

In 1905 George Seaman co-founded the Great Lakes Paper Company, later renamed the Seaman Paper Company. He was also president of Henrotin Hospital. Mrs. Seaman had her $10,000 mink coat stolen from a philanthropic event she attended at 1524 Lake Shore Drive. She told the police that she knew the identity of the thief and no charges were filed. After a three-day courtship their daughter, Mary, wed William Folds in 1936. She and the groom were regarded as "among society's best young bridge players."

9A
1927-48
Bror Gustave Dahlberg (1881-1954)
Mary Alexander Dahlberg (1901-38), first wife
Gilda Krieger Lichtle Dahlberg, second wife
Alma Lee Dahlberg, adopted daughter
Craig Johnson, foster son
Basil Rathbone, houseguest
Mable Anderson, housekeeper

An impoverished boy from a humble background, Bror Dahlberg could have been a character in a rags-to-riches novel by Horatio Alger. He was ten when he migrated to the United States from Sweden with his parents. His father died shortly after arriving in America, forcing the young Dahlberg to find a job. His career path was a steep incline upwards: elevator operator, stenographer, factory worker, general manager of a paper company, inventor, industrialist.

Dahlberg discovered a process for making synthetic insulating board out of the fibrous residue of sugar cane, a celluloid glop called bagasse. Before Dahlberg, it was considered garbage and tossed out with the coffee grounds. He formed the Celotex Corporation to produce bagasse-based insulation at a time when the sugar cane industry was in financial trouble. Successive crops had been infected with a disease caused by inbreeding. Dahlberg helped introduce new and hardier cane stocks and revived the industry. As Celotex grew he purchased sugar plantations and refineries in the South, and drained vast areas of Florida swampland for sugar cane production. Celotex boards were used as heat and sound insulation in buildings around the world, including Rockefeller Center and the White House.

By the 1920s, Bror Dahlberg had become a wealthy establishment figure incapable of keeping his messy private life quiet. Some of his problems could be laid at the bedpost of his first wife Mary Alexander Dahlberg. If paparazzi had existed in the twenties they would have camped outside 999 waiting for a glimpse of the girl from San Saba, Texas who slinked into the corridors of power with a flash of leg, a dangling curl and a dash of daring-do. Her accomplishments, however, may well have exceeded her looks. She competed in international bobsled races at St. Moritz, canoed 218 miles through uninhabited North Hudson Bay and wrote a novel entitled *Dagger*.

Mary made headlines in 1927 when she was robbed of an estimated $72,000 in jewels from her suite at the Ritz-Carlton in New York. An inventory of the missing gems listed an assortment of bracelets, rings, collars, lockets, plaques, necklaces, hat pins, watches and earrings made of platinum, diamonds, black and white pearls, sapphires and emeralds. The perpetrators were never caught. Insurance fraud was a possible scenario.

Bror G. Dahlberg, Chicago, 1932.
Chicago History Museum (ICHi-67638)

The newspapers had a field day when the Dahlbergs entertained the photogenic Spanish Princess Marie de Bourbon, every bit as attractive as Mary, and an assortment of fawning guests at 999, and later at their ranch in Minnesota. As a sideshow to the whirlwind parties, Mary and her friends received poison-pen letters accusing Mrs. Dahlberg of using personal publicity to raise the profile and price of a tract of land in Florida that Bror and she were trying to sell. The Dahlbergs openly accused Mrs. Frank Townley Brown, a wealthy Florida widow, of writing the letters. Brown sued them for $200,000 in retaliation.

In a subsequent confrontation with Mrs. Brown, Mary Dahlberg pointed to a flashy bracelet on her arm and proclaimed, "See this thing, it was given to me by the Spanish King. It means that if there is anyone I want killed, he'll have it done, and my husband has money enough to put you out of the way without your being missed." Consistently imprudent, Mary Dahlberg once called Chicago socialites "washtub aristocrats."

On January 23, 1931, Mary walked out of her apartment at 999 in the middle of the night and deserted her husband. She left with their adopted daughter Alma Lee and sailed to Majorca. She rented an apartment in a monastery, the very place where Chopin composed his preludes and nocturnes, and lived with the cross-dressing French novelist George Sand. Rumors flew across the Atlantic that Mary was romantically involved with the Spanish princess. When queried about her love life, Mary replied, "The newspapers have had me about to marry a Polish prince, then a master of the hounds, a bearded sea-captain and once even a bootlegger...who thought he was going to be Al Capone's successor. Emphatically I have no intention of marrying anybody. I am much more interested in literature than love."

In the divorce Bror won custody of Alma Lee.

Unable to keep her covenant with the literary life or her nose in a book, Mary broke her promise to remain single. She married Huntley Chapin, a Yale graduate, artist and self-proclaimed capitalist, and moved to New Mexico. Huntley got into in a barroom brawl in San Antonio and

Mrs. Mary Alexander Dahlberg (right), who was accused of deserting her husband. She is shown with the Princess Marie of Bourbon, a cousin of the former king of Spain, who was entertained by Mrs. Dahlberg when she visited this county in 1925. (From Chicago Tribune, March 24, 1932 © *1932 Chicago Tribune. All rights reserved. Used by permission and protected by the Copyright Laws of the United States. The printing, copying, redistribution, or retransmission of this Content without express written permission is prohibited.)*

was shot in the face by a former city detective with a film noir name, Skinny Baker. Huntley somehow survived and divorced Mary in 1935, claiming she hired gangsters to murder him. Her counter suit charged him with having her falsely arrested in Mexico.

Meanwhile Bror Dahlberg continued to attract trouble. He was accused of bribing United States senators to insure passage of a bill guaranteeing high tariffs for imported sugar. A New York tailor took him to court because Dahlberg refused to pay for several custom-made suits he routinely wore. He claimed that they were too tight. Celotex shareholders sued him for concealing Celotex profits. Dahlberg was the appointed guardian for his foster son, Craig Johnson, 13. The boy's real parents sued Dahlberg for $40,000. Mary popped back into his life and tried to collect $41,250 in back alimony. Bror's lawyers proved that she had been married to another man at the time she wed Dahlberg. That husband's name was John Marcus, a.k.a. John Martin of Cincinnati, an associate of George Remus—"the king of the bootleggers." Unfortunately John Marcus/Martin was unable to testify at the hearing. He had been murdered. Occasionally Dahlberg did the suing: $300,000 in damages for a car accident.

Dahlberg remarried. This time to a beauty named Gilda. Walking home from a play with two other couples, they were all kidnapped at gunpoint by two men wearing handkerchief masks in front of Drake Tower. The hostages were forced into a taxi driven by another masked man. The cab slowly wandered through the streets of Streeterville while the kidnappers debated what do with their victims. Finally they robbed them of $30,000 in jewelry and cash, and released them on Superior near Fairbanks.

Bror co-founded the Damon Runyon Cancer Fund with Walter Winchell, a nationally known newspaper columnist and radio personality. Dahlberg was an active backer of Dwight Eisenhower for President, an advocate for low-cost housing and a member of the Chicago Zoological Society and the National Institute of Social Science.

BASIL RATHBONE, DAHLBERG HOUSEGUEST

Actor Basil Rathbone was a friend of Bror and Gilda Dahlberg and a frequent visitor to 999. They met in 1944 when the Dahlbergs helped stage two Christmas parties at the Hotel Biltmore in Santa Barbara, California honoring wounded veterans. Among the celebrity hostesses were Lana Turner, Betty Grable, Hedy Lamarr and Eva Gabor. The Andrews Sisters and Dinah Shore sang their recent hits. Basil Rathbone read Christmas poems. And Mrs. Dahlberg played Santa Claus.

In 1948, Rathbone lived at 999 while the Dahlbergs went on an extended vacation. He was starring in a theatrical production of *The Heiress* at the Selwyn, which was located in the same building where the Goodman stages plays today.

He rose to prominence as a Shakespearean stage actor, who also appeared in over 70 films. He is best known for his portrayal of the travelling con-man Edward Murdstone in *David Copperfield* (1935), the suave villain Sir Guy of Gisbourne in *The Adventures of Robin Hood* (1938), and the master of elementary deduction *Sherlock Holmes* in 14 Hollywood movies made between 1939 and 1946.

Basil Rathbone on the set of
The Hound of Baskerville, *1939.*
(© Sunset Boulevard/Corbis)

3C
1928
H. L. Baumgarden, Mabel Baumgarden

9B
1928–47
George W. Borg (1887–1960), Effie Borg
George W. Borg, Jr., son
Albert N. Lauenstein, butler
Augusta Lauenstein, cook; Merie Quiding, servant

As a teenager George Borg worked in a machine shop in Moline, Illinois owned by his father, Carl, and Marshall Beck. Borg & Beck manufactured woodworking equipment. While never officially hired, George was frequently fired for doing things without asking permission. Ignoring his many terminations, he would show up the next day ready to work. In 1911, George and chief machinist Gust

Nelson invented and patented the original sliding automobile clutch, transforming his father's business from producing a handful of tongue shaping machines annually to manufacturing clutches for an automotive industry growing exponentially with each new model year.

In the early 1920s, George decided to move the company to Chicago. He took Beck and his father to a big Windy City bank and asked them to finance the expansionistic dreams of Borg & Beck. George talked so incessantly and fast that the banker couldn't break into the monologue. Turning to the two older men he asked, "Who owns this business, anyway?" The elder Borg, formerly a two-fisted sea captain, replied in his thick Swedish accent: "Well, Mr. Beck and I own the horse and buggy, but George, he drives it just the same." The loan was made. A few years later George paid both men millions to retire.

Borg & Beck evolved into the Borg-Warner Corporation with George at the helm. He retired in 1941 but remained a board member until 1958. He turned his attention to the George W. Borg Corporation, a maker of automotive clocks

Carl W. Borg, father of George W. Borg (left) and Marshall Beck (right). (Chicago History Museum ICHi-68194)

and electronic timers widely used in cars and home appliances. He purchased a faltering knitting mill, produced fabrics for the armed forces during World War II and, in the post-war years, developed deep-pile fabrics with the self-referential names of *Borgana* and *Borglura*. After a merger the company became Amphenol Electronics.

Between 1944 and 1947, George rescued 999 from receivership and converted it to a co-op.

RIGHT: *"The Borg and Beck Clutch,"*
one of the greatest breakthroughs in
the early history of the automobile.
(Chicago History Museum ICHi-68197)

BELOW: *Page from first timekeeping*
book of Borg and Beck, 1906.
(Chicago History Museum ICHi-68195)

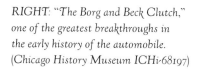

looks more like fur than fur itself BORGANA T.M.

As warm as fur, too. But so light it floats on your shoulders like the flutter of a feather. Borgana is the first word in cream-soft luxury, the last word in smartness. Only Borgana (an exclusive blend of Orlon and Dynel) looks and feels like Borgana. You'll love it so, you'll hate to see cold weather go. At fine stores everywhere in Cognac (as shown), Champagne, Moonstone, Black . . . in misses, junior, petite and children's sizes. For name of store nearest you write any of the makers listed below.

MODELIA, INC., 205 W. 39th St., N.Y. • **KRAELER-FRASCA,** 500 Seventh Ave., N.Y. • **ALBRECHT FURS,** 21 W. 5th St., St. Paul • **ROTHMOOR CORP.,** 22 W. Madison St., Chicago • **ANNIS FURS,** 130 W. 30th St., N.Y. **GORDON MFG. CO., LTD.,** 423 Mayor St., Montreal, Canada • **LINKER & HERBERT,** 205 W. 39th St., N.Y. • **MODE KIDDIE COATS,** 520 Eighth Ave., N.Y. • **ROSENBLATT & KAHN** (children's coats), 520 Eighth Ave., N.Y.

a **BORG** fabric   Borg Fabric Division, The George W. Borg Corporation, Delavan, Wisconsin.   *Patented

George Borg went into the fabric business after World War II.
Borgana was one of the brand names he used to market faux
fur coats.

6B
1928–30
Anna May Cairns
Anna M. Cairns, daughter

1930
James E. Cairns

In January 1928, Anna May Cairns and James Cairns were divorced. According to the divorce papers, James had a drinking problem. When sober, James worked at various brokerage firms. When he was inebriated, he frequently beat up Anna May, sometimes in front of witnesses. Once when Anna May moved back to her mother's house, he cut her clothing into little pieces with a scissors. The court granted Anna May custody of their 11-year-old daughter, all of his shares in 999 and ownership of the lease on their apartment. By 1930 they were living together again.

4C
1928–30
William E. Clarke
Bertha Holbrook Clarke (1862–1946)

The Clarkes were married in 1909 and divorced in 1929. Bertha accused William of infidelity.

6A
1928–30
W. C. Cook, Mary G. Cook
William Lake, stepson; Esther Cook, daughter
Mary Naughton, maid; Christina Johnson, maid

W. C. Cook was the vice-president of a bank. William Lake was a chemist.

7B
1928
E. A. Coyle, Violet Coyle

8B
1928–30
B. H. Edwards, Marion Edwards
Betty Edwards, daughter; B. H. Edwards, Jr., son
John P. Cook, butler; Estella Cook, catering

B. H. Edwards was the president of a lumber company.

8A
1928
George Wilson Kretzinger, Jr. (1880–?)
Louise Kretzinger (1851–1930)

G. W. Kretzinger was a corporate lawyer who had attended Vanderbilt, the University of Chicago and Harvard. Louise was a critic of public school education. In 1899, she accused public school teachers of practicing psychological experiments on their pupils. She called what went on in the classroom, "Mental vivisection more cruel and with worse results than any practiced in dissecting rooms." Her campaign to filet public schools did not gain much support.

4A
1928–37
Royden James Keith, Marie Morrisey Keith
Marie S. Bosse, mother-in-law
Julius Balke, Jr. (1857–1936), boarder
Lucy Roller, cook; Rose Naughton, maid

Stanford graduate, Royden James Keith was an actor. In 1915, he appeared in Jerome Kern's *Nobody Home* at the Playhouse in Hudson, New York. A local reviewer noticed his performance, "Royden Keith and Mabel Withee, juvenile leads, played their roles in fine manner and sang and danced their way into the hearts of the audience." In 1917, he replaced the male lead in the theatrical production of *Dew Drop Inn* at the Illinois Theater in Chicago. The play closed a few weeks later and with it died Royden's active infatuation with the smell of greasepaint and the roar of the crowd. By 1930, he was working for his boarder Julius Balke, Jr. Later he was a territorial manager for the Westinghouse Electric Supply Company.

Prior to her marriage to Royden, Marie Morrisey was a singer who toured extensively in the United States. She entertained the troops during World War I, giving 74 concerts in 90 days. She broke with classical concert tradition by building her repertoire exclusively of songs written in

English, which enhanced her popularity. The *New York American* described her voice as, "A delightfully warm rich contralto, appealing and sympathetic." The *Chicago Tribune* identified her strengths as "Her voice, her interpretation, her first class English enunciation, her looks and her manner."

In 1947, she became the president of the National Federation of Music Clubs. In that capacity she helped fund the rehabilitation of Nathaniel Hawthorne's cottage in the Berkshires, where he wrote *The House of Seven Gables*. In 1950, Mrs. Keith inaugurated a campaign to increase the number of radio broadcasts featuring fine music and presented an award to Standard Oil of California for sponsoring quality musical programing broadcast to children.

TOP RIGHT: Julius Balke, Jr.
(Chicago Billiard Museum.
Courtesy of Bob Jewett collection.)

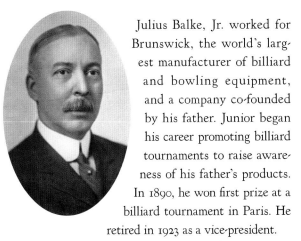

Julius Balke, Jr. worked for Brunswick, the world's largest manufacturer of billiard and bowling equipment, and a company co-founded by his father. Junior began his career promoting billiard tournaments to raise awareness of his father's products. In 1890, he won first prize at a billiard tournament in Paris. He retired in 1923 as a vice-president.

IA
1928–29
J. W. Kiser

Royden James Keith. (Billy Rose Theatre Division, The New York Public Library for the Performing Arts, Astor, Lenox and Tilden Foundations)

Marie Morrisey Keith. (The Newberry Library, Chicago. V 205 .97, vol. 1)

9C
1928–38
Colonel George Tayloe Langhorne (1867–1962)
Mary Waller Langhorne

Born into a wealthy Virginia family, Colonel George T. Langhorne graduated from the United States Military Academy at West Point in 1889. He fought in the Spanish-American War and in the Philippine insurrection. To his credit, the townspeople of San Paulo on Luzon presented his battalion with a satin flag showing 45 stars in appreciation of the thoughtful treatment given to them by Langhorne's soldiers. Fifty-four years later Col. Langhorne donated the flag to the military museum at West Point.

Prior to the United States' entrance into World War I, Langhorne, a major at the time, served for two years (1914–15) as the military attaché to the United States embassy in Berlin. His primary responsibility was to monitor the European war. He was openly embedded inside the German army in France, Belgium and Galicia. He reported his observations of their strategies, tactics, troop movements and weaponry to Washington, D.C. His return to the United States garnered considerable press coverage. Langhorne was ordered to keep what he knew to himself. He could talk openly and honestly only when debriefing the Secretary of War, the senior members of the army general staff and the chairmen of the Senate and House Committees on Military Affairs.

When he finished testifying, Langhorne was reassigned to Fort Worth, Texas, just in time to engage the paramilitary forces of Mexican revolutionary Pancho Villa in a bloody border war fought between March 1916 and February 1917. For two epic weeks in May 1916, newspapers in the United States followed Langhorne's daring exploits inside Mexico.

He returned to the Philippines as the acting governor of Morro province. He also was appointed assistant to General Leonard Wood, the governor general of the island, for all intents and purposes an American colony. Langhorne retired from the army in 1931.

In 1928, Langhorne married Mary Waller of Chicago at Hedsor Parish Church, Cliveden, England, near the country home of his first cousin, Lady Astor (the former Nancy Witcher Langhorne of Virginia). Her sister, Irene, who married Charles Dana Gibson, was the original model for the Gibson girl, and America's first mass-marketed sex symbol, sent her regrets. Colonel and Mrs. Langhorne settled in Chicago where he was elected president of the Army and Navy Club and of the American Friends of China. He died in 1962 at 94.

Gibson Girl. The model was probably Langhorne's first cousin, Irene Gibson. (Clipart.com)

Major George T. Langhorne in civilian clothes, 1916. (Library of Congress Prints and Photographs Division Washington, D.C.)

General Francisco "Pancho" Villa on horseback, during the Mexican Revolution. Possibly taken at the time of the Battle of Ojinga, Chihuahua, January 1914. (Library of Congress Prints and Photographs Division Washington, D.C.)

THE FLYING SQUADRON
LED BY A CADILLAC

Col. George T. Langhorne, 8th Cavalry, Commanding Big Ben District,
Presidio, Texas, seated in the Cadillac Touring Car he employed to chase
Pancho Villa's men. In the background is part of the Carranza force of Ojinaga,
Mexico. They evacuated the town when attacked by Villa.
(National Archives photo no. 111-SC-82715)

THE INCIDENT that catapulted Major George Langhorne into the headlines occurred on the night of May 5, 1916, when two groups of Mexican raiders aligned with Pancho Villa attacked the Texas villages of Glenn Springs and Boquillas. Three American soldiers and the young son of a shopkeeper were killed. Two other Americans were kidnapped—Jesse Deemer, the owner of a general store, and Monroe Payne, "a huge half-Indian, half-Negro" rancher—and taken south of the border. Col. Fredrick Sibley ordered Langhorne's cavalry to cross the Rio Grande in hot pursuit. Langhorne's invading party consisted of 80 men, two wagons, three newspaper correspondents and Langhorne's personal chauffeur driven Cadillac touring car. His men were divided into "flying squadrons," a centuries-old tactic where small groups of soldiers are organized for maximum speed either on foot or horseback. Langhorne led them into battle in his Caddy, which he filled with oats for the horses.

The following excerpts from *The New York Times* were filed from inside Langhorne's advancing force:

May 8—"A strict censorship is enforced to screen the troop movement in the field campaign in whatever form it takes..."

May 11th—"Major George T. Langhorne and his command are well over the river into Mexico."

May 15th—"Langhorne waits to attack."

May 18th—"Major George T. Langhorne and his little flying squadron of the Eighth United States Cavalry have rescued the two Americans who were kidnapped from Texas in the Glenn Springs raid...killed five of the raiders...seriously wounded two others....three escaped...not an American was hit...a tall thin Virginian...Major Langhorne and his men had been riding night and day. The miles they covered had already established a record for cavalry...the men sometimes had eaten once a day, sometimes not at all...great herds of white goats formed a considerable part of Major Langhorne's rations...with such odds against them it was inspiring to see."

For the final assault Langhorne placed 12 sharpshooters inside his Cadillac and raced into the breach, rifles and pistols firing at will, followed by his flying squadrons on horseback moving in from the flanks. The image of the swashbuckling Langhorne leading his men into battle is so cinematic it's a wonder no studio ever put the scene into a movie. Unbeknownst to Langhorne, a band of Yaqui Indians aligned with Villa had been trailing him waiting for an opportunity to massacre his troops. Thanks to the intervention of Col. Sibley, the potential slaughter never occurred.

The invasion of Mexico was the first time motorized vehicles were used as part of a flying squadron. Langhorne, however, wasn't the innovator. In the same border war, Lt. George Patton of World War II fame beat him to it. Patton got a movie.

1928-29
Cassius Clay McBurney, Geraldine McBurney

Cassius Clay McBurney sold stocks and bonds. He married Geraldine some time after his divorce from another woman in 1924.

7A
1928
Mrs. Elizabeth D. Parkinson

7C
1928-30
Louis A. Rang, Eugenie "Jean" Farrow Rang

1930
Elmer M. Judd Jr., Eugenie "Jean" Farrow Judd
Henry Andrew, butler; Elizabeth Andrew, maid

In an infamous love triangle that titillated newspaper readers, Louis Rang, a member of the Chicago Board of Trade, was married to Fifi Schultz Rang, and, at the same time, was caught up in a torrid affair with Eugenie (Jean) Farrow. "I went to see her," recalled Fifi, discussing a conversation she had with her husband's mistress. "She gave me two months to win him back—my own husband."

"If you win, I'll step out of his life," promised Jean. Fifi lost and divorced Louis in 1917.

Louis married Jean in the 1920s and bought shares in 999 for around $18,000, which entitled them to live in apartment 7C. Louis died in 1929 and left Jean an estate worth in excess of $1.3 million, about $150 million in today's dollars. A few months later the market crashed.

Enter Elmer Judd who earned a comfortable living selling cars. He married Jean and moved into her apartment. After a few years Jean passed away. In probate court, Elmer learned that his wife's inheritance had lost 90% of its value.

8C
1928-40
Frank Kennicott Reilly, Carlin Walker Reilly

Mr. Reilly shot himself in the head and died in 1932. According to a report in the *Tribune*, he was depressed over the Depression. They were careful to point out that he was not financially troubled personally. He was the president of Reilly & Lee, the original publishing house of Frank L. Baum, creator of the *Wizard of Oz* series.

6C
1928
J. E. Rogers

3A
1928-74
Walter D. Willett (1880-1931)
Florence Collins Willett (ca. 1899- ?)
Alvin T. Willett, son; Helen Willett, daughter
Charmain Willett, daughter
Frances Goetz, maid

Walter Willett owned and operated the largest trucking and busing company in the world. After high school, he joined his father's teamster business, which consisted of six teams of horses, a few wagons and a mounting debt. Walter instituted a number of innovations. He put ball bearings in the wagon wheels, reducing the number of horses needed to pull it. He devised new and faster unloading methods and was the first to employ six-wheeled trucks. He also operated a passenger bus line with special buses for transporting sick or disabled children. Under his leadership, the company withstood the disastrous fire of 1871, the hard times of the 1880s and the panic of 1893.

By 1930, the Willett fleet straddled two worlds: the horse drawn wagon and the motorized truck. Willett inventoried 1,000 trucks, 85 buses and 500 horses. The horses would be phased out and the number of trucks and buses would multiply.

If you grew up in the Chicago area in the post-World War II era, chances are you rode in a yellow school bus operated by an arm of the Willett Company. Today the Willett brand continues to lease buses and haul freight around the United States.

Willett bus at Chicago Municipal Tuberculosis Sanitarium, 1921. (Courtesy of Frances Archer)

A testimonial ad for Kirk's American Family Flakes featuring
Miss Frances Goetz, maid to Mrs. W. D. Willett. (Digitized
image courtesy of the Michigan State University Libraries.
Used by permission of The Procter & Gamble Company.)

The DIFFICULT *Years*

In a departure from the prior two chapters, each of which covered a decade's worth of residents, the chapter on the 1930s extends through 1946. Those were difficult years financially for the country and many of the tenants. As previously noted, 999 suffered during the Depression. In 1937, both the State of Illinois and Metropolitan Life Insurance foreclosed on 999—Illinois for back taxes and Met Life for failing to make interest payments. Met Life owned the building, rented the apartments to cover costs and managed it with benign disinterest. In 1944, tenant George Borg played the good knight and rescued 999. In 1947, he turned it once again into a co-op. The building rode the wave of post-World War II prosperity to regain its financial health.

During those 17 years of hard times, there were 14 holdover families from prior decades. The longest tenured were Fred and Marjorie Letts, and the mystery resident Mary Smith. By 1930, Letts and Smith had been in the building for a record-breaking 15 years. From 1930–46, 23 families and 87 people were introduced to 999, bringing the totals through 1946 to 101 families and 381 individuals.

4C
1930
Florence LaVictorie Addington
the widow of the late Keene Harwood Addington
James Addington, son
Hartwell Giles, butler; Nora Giles, maid

Keene Harwood Addington battled skunks in Lake Forest with a missionary zeal reminiscent of St. Patrick's banishment of snakes from Ireland. As the town's mayor (1917–19) he had to defend his constituents against an odoriferous invasion of the black and white critters. In his brief encounter with elective office, he also raised money for a sister village in France destroyed by German artillery, and negotiated the town's purchase of the Lake Forest Water Company. He held stock options in that company and was soundly criticized for a shameless conflict of interest. The highlight of his mayoral tenure was branded

Keene H. Addington. (Courtesy of Library of Congress Prints and Photographs Division Washington, D.C.

"Emergency Union," because he successfully coordinated all of the activities of local government under one operational umbrella. On a national scale, Addington helped create the Federal Reserve System during Woodrow Wilson's presidency.

Addington co-founded the law firm Jones, Addington, Ames & Seibold. With a colleague, he annotated the prosaic *Statutes of the State of Illinois: in force January 1, 1913.* He partnered with inventor Reuben Benjamin in a new venture, the Benjamin Electric Company. Benjamin held the patent for the first electric light socket, one of more than 350 devices he patented, mostly in the field of electrical lighting. The prolific Benjamin received the fourth most patents in American history. Benjamin Electric created the flood lighting system used at Westminster Abbey for Queen Elizabeth II's coronation in 1953.

Little is known about Mrs. Addington. The press did report that she once fainted at a performance of the Russian ballet. Son James Addington married Sarah Wood, the daughter of General Robert E. Wood, who became the chairman of Sears, Roebuck and Company. James would meet his second wife at a Singles Sweepstakes party.

1930
Chauncey "Charles" Blair Borland
Beatrice "Belle" McCullough Borland
Chauncey Blair Borland, Jr., son
Belle Borland, daughter
Beatrice Borland, daughter
Richard Fuson, butler; Betty Hutyara, maid

Chauncey Borland spent most of his adult life managing the family's extensive real estate holdings. He also inherited the presidency of Borland Manufacturing. When he stepped outside of family enterprises, he served on the boards of public companies, hospitals and libraries. He was also a member of the Chicago Crime Commission. Daughter Beatrice Borland wrote a travel book.

1930
Joseph C. Flowers, Inez W. Flowers
Gabriella S. Bognar, servant

Census taker Mary Higgins forgot to include the Flowers' apartment number in her report. Joseph Flowers was a publisher.

Dr. Horace Lyons, true to his profession in the 1930s, smokes a cigarette. Seated next to him is his second wife, Jeanette Jennings Gartz Lyons. (Courtesy of Gloria Garvey-Hanington)

3B
1930
Dr. Horace R. Lyons, Alice Lyons
Alice Lyons, daughter
Signe Land, cook; Anne Boork, maid

In 1925, at the 31st annual meeting of the American Laryngological, Rhinological and Otological Society at Atlantic City, New Jersey, Dr. Lyons presented a paper on "The Anatomic Relations between the Upper Teeth, Especially the Lateral Incisor and the First and Second Molar." At the 39th annual meeting in Chicago, he chose a subject with a shorter title "The Use of Amniotic Membrane as a Transplant following Radical Mastoidectomy." Audience reactions to either speech have been lost to history.

At least once, however, pulse-pounding excitement found him. A couple of Al Capone's goons barged past his receptionist and entered his office. They demanded that he perform emergency surgery on Big Al's young son, Albert Francis "Sonny" Capone. Dr. Lyons politely refused. The hoods pulled out their guns, which clarified any possibility of misunderstanding. Lyons quickly acquiesced. After the successful operation, Lyons was paid $10,000 in cash, which he turned over to the Feds.

7A
1930-63
Walter Paepcke, Elizabeth Nitze Paepcke
Anina Paepcke, daughter; Paula Paepcke, daughter
Antonia A. Paepcke, daughter
Margaret Mullarkey, nurse
Leona Roephenack, nurse and maid
Teresa Koch, cook; Fred Miller, butler
Dora M. Frank, governess
Nelly Kaltenmark, maid; Helen F. Schleh, cook

Lifetime learners, Walter and Elizabeth Paepcke (PEP-ka) never stopped studying history's great thinkers. They actively sought ways to apply the canonical ideas of the past to the dilemmas of the present. Walter may have been the most culturally enlightened corporate executive of his generation. When *The New York Times Magazine* devoted the entire January 1, 1995 issue to "Lives Well Lived," they put Elizabeth's picture on the cover.

Their great gift to the world began humbly in 1939 with frozen water pipes at the Paepcke ranch in Larkspur, Colorado. To distract her three houseguests—Walter was working in Chicago—Elizabeth proposed a ski outing to a once prosperous silver mining town that had fallen on hard times. She and her guests hitch-hiked part of the way in the back of a flat-bed truck, put sealskins on their skis to provide greater traction and walked herringbone style up a mountain for five hours.

"At the top, we halted in frozen admiration," Elizabeth wrote. "In all that landscape of rock, snow and ice, there was neither print of animal nor track of man. We were alone as though the world had just been created and we its first inhabitants." Down below hidden by clouds sat the dilapidated, nearly deserted Victorian town of Aspen, Colorado. The intellectual side of what it would become sprang from Elizabeth's imagination and persistence, and Walter's organizational acumen, the goodwill of his friends and the depth of his bank account.

Subdued—almost detached at times—Walter acted the patrician. He could be overbearing, officious and arbitrary. Also brilliant, he repeatedly challenged conventional wisdom as outmoded and outdated. He won people over with reason and will. By contrast Elizabeth's fierce intelligence revealed itself through charm and wit. They made a hell of a team.

Walter was the son of a German immigrant, Herman Paepcke, whose American dream was satisfied by a thriving lumber business. Walter went to the city's finest lower, middle and upper schools, University and Latin, before graduating from Yale, class of 1917. He joined his father's

Walter Paepcke. (Photo by Ferenc Berko/berkophoto.com)

Robert Maynard Hutchins, the Chancellor of the University of Chicago, and Elizabeth Paepcke. (Aspen Historical Society)

The New York Times Magazine

JANUARY 1, 1995 / SECTION 6

LIVES WELL LIVED

Some people who
made a difference, and why.

ELIZABETH PAEPCKE
By Ted Conover

HENRY GELDZAHLER
By David Hockney

LINUS PAULING
By Watson and Crick

WILMA RUDOLPH
By Evelyn Ashford

KARL POPPER
By Ryszard Kapuscinski

NICKY HOPKINS
By Ray Davies

ANDREW KOPKIND
By Calvin Trillin

RICHARD NIXON
By Daniel Schorr

KURT COBAIN
By Jim Carroll

RALPH ELLISON
By Roger Rosenblatt

JACQUELINE ONASSIS
By Wayne Koestenbaum

Plus: the creators of Teflon,
Woody Woodpecker
AND MORE

Elizabeth Paepcke made the cover of The New York Times
Magazine *devoted to Lives Well Lived. (From* The New York
Times, *January 1, 1995 © 1995 The New York Times.*
All rights reserved. Used by permission and protected by
the Copyright Laws of the United States. The printing, copy-
ing, redistribution, or retransmission of this Content without
express written permission is prohibited.)

company out of college.

When Herman Paepcke looked at his lumberyard he saw cords of wood piled high, wide and deep. Walter, on the other hand, imagined cardboard boxes. In 1926, he started his own business and called it Container Corporation of America. He successfully took it public the following year. Walter satisfied shareholders with a reliable stream of dividends, ran a profitable ship and never lacked capital. CCA emerged from the Great Depression, stronger than ever, without having borrowed a dime. An example of his disdain for conventional wisdom came when he violated the basic principle of economies of scale by decentralizing his factories. He located them near customers to hold down freight costs and to respond rapidly to their problems and opportunities. He also differentiated CCA from the competition through his use of advertising. He didn't advertise to announce promotions or a new-sized carton, but to create a memorable image for his brand, pioneering a polite, less boastful approach to marketing. He hired fine artists to bring to life ideas from history's great writers: Shakespeare, Thoreau, Whitman, Lincoln and other masters of the pen. Walter understood that people might buy his products, even his stock, without ever realizing how his ads predisposed them to his offerings.

Elizabeth's grandmother nicknamed her "Pussy" and it

stuck. It is what she called herself. The daughter of William A. Nitze, a professor of romance languages at the University of Chicago, she grew up in a home that celebrated the life of the mind. Her brother, Paul, became an expert in defense and disarmament, and was appointed to positions of high rank and broad authority by five presidents: Franklin Roosevelt, Truman, Kennedy, Nixon and Reagan.

Elizabeth studied painting at the Art Institute, worked as a decorator and theater designer, and evolved into a guiding light for Chicago's intellectual elite. In 1922, she became Mrs. Walter Paepcke in Santa Fe, New Mexico. Already brainy, she was now wealthy. And, oh yes, she was beautiful. "She had cobalt blue eyes and a dazzling smile...the first thing people noticed," extolled *The New York Times*. The woman smiling from the cover of their Sunday magazine could have passed for a movie star. Elizabeth pooh-poohed references to her looks and dismissed them as shallow.

Walter and Elizabeth devoted themselves to the Greek concept of the complete life: a combination of hard work, vigorous play and never-ending inquiry and education. They participated in the Great Books seminars run for captains of industry by author Mortimer J. Adler and Robert Maynard Hutchins, the Chancellor of the University of Chicago.

As Elizabeth's spiritual encounter with Aspen lingered,

Friedl Pfeifer, the head of Aspen Skiing; Walter Paepcke; Herbert Bayer, a Bauhausian architect and designer; and Gary Cooper, movie star, circa 1955. (Aspen Historical Society, Ryan Collection)

Albert Schweitzer walking arm in arm with Walter Paepcke during the Goethe Bicentennial, 1949. (Aspen Historical Society)

she wanted to share it with Walter. But the area had become the training slopes for the 10th Mountain Division and was off-limits during the entirety of World War II. A few days before they left for their first joint visit, the couple participated in a group discussion about how a place can tease out great ideas and give birth to enduring works. Think Greece in the time of Socrates, Plato and Aristotle; Florence and Rome as Leonardo, Michelangelo and Raphael reimagined blank walls, blocks of marble and empty canvases; the London of back-to-back-to-back first run plays by the likes of Marlowe, Shakespeare and Jonson; the Philadelphia courthouse where Franklin, Jefferson, Adams and others invented a revolutionary form of government. For the first time on Memorial Day 1945, Walter Paepcke saw the mountains, the valley and the potential. For long-time residents of Aspen, this was their town's Ur moment.

Not quite a ghost town, close to 700 people lived in the Aspen area. But many houses were deserted, their facades cracked, the paint faded. The few streets were in disrepair, victims of neglect and weather. The only restaurant served food fit for dogs. The one hotel, the Jerome, was rundown and mostly empty. The Paepckes stayed there for 50 cents a night, as they contemplated a town without a fire department, sewers, a laundry or a doctor.

The next morning, Walter bought Elizabeth a birthday present, one of Aspen's largest unoccupied houses, the first act in a miracle. Convinced that Aspen's greatest resource was snow, they partnered with Friedl Pfeifer, formerly the head of the ski school at Sun Valley and a veteran of the 10th Mountain Division, to create the Aspen Skiing Company. Outside investors purchased shares in the new company. Their capital turned into ski lifts and a variety of spectacular runs. William Patterson, the head of United Airlines, and hotelier Conrad Hilton jumped in on the theory that if the plans for Aspen panned out, visitors would need ways to get there and places to stay. Walter and his friends improved the town's plumbing, heating and electricity, bought the core of what would become downtown Aspen and rehabbed nearly every home in sight.

Aspen hosted a coming out party in 1949, a 20-day celebration of the 200th anniversary of Johann Wolfgang von Goethe's birth, an event initiated and planned by the Paepckes along with key administrators and academics from the University of Chicago. The organizers erected a huge tent where guests could listen to classical music and mind-expanding lectures. Invitations went out to the country's business leaders and many of the world's greatest performing artists and deepest thinkers. Among those who RSVP'd "yes" were violinist Nathan Milstein;

Arthur Rubenstein, pianist, tries his luck on the original Lift #1 during a break at the Goethe Bicentennial Convocation in Aspen. (Photo by Ferenc Berko/berkophoto.com)

Walter and Elizabeth Paepcke in tent during Goethe Bicentennial. (Photo by Ferenc Berko/berkophoto.com)

cellist Gregor Piatigorsky; pianist Arthur Rubinstein; philosopher José Ortega y Gasset; playwright Thornton Wilder; poet Stephen Spender; and organist, theologian, philosopher, humanitarian and doctor of medicine, Albert Schweitzer, who rarely left the hospital he ran in the jungles of French West Africa, but whose presence lent early credibility to the festival. The Paepckes had envisioned a place where artists, thinkers and musicians could gather. And there they were.

Within a year, the Paepckes began expanding the concept of Aspen. They created the Aspen Music Festival, where the careers of Renée Fleming, Leonard Slatkin, Philip Glass, Nadja Salerno-Sonnenberg, Joshua Bell and Itzhak Perlman took root, and the Aspen Institute for Humanistic Studies, "where the human spirit can flourish... amid the whirlwind and chaos of modernization...to help... leaders recapture...eternal verities, the values that guide them intellectually, ethically and spiritually."

Over the years the Paepckes helped expand the Aspen brand into dozens of organizations devoted to improving the quality of life for every person on the planet. The Aspen Center for Environmental Studies identified the causes and effects of global climate change in 1962, well ahead of the curve. The Aspen Center for Physics has hosted over 10,000 physicists, including 52 Nobel Laureates, who came to Aspen to share, ponder and debate new ideas. Thousands of articles and books have been published citing the Center for contributions in particle physics, condensed matter physics, astrophysics, cosmology, biophysics, mathematics, gravitational wave physics, and nonlinear dynamics. A petition by the Aspen Institute led to a ruling that permitted presidential debates in the United States. Russian president, Boris Yeltsin, cited an Aspen presentation on "Television and Elections" in a decree requiring fair media coverage of his country's parliamentary elections. The Aspen Program on World Economy helped launch the concept of micro-enterprise development, which is revolutionizing the economies of third world countries.

A virtual who's who of twentieth century movers and shakers beat a path to Walter and Elizabeth's door to inspire and to be inspired, among them presidents Carter, Bush, Bush and Clinton; myriad heads of state; composers Igor Stravinsky and Benjamin Britten; Chief Justice Warren Burger; Supreme Court Justices Hugo Black, John Marshall Harlan, Harry Blackmun, Thurgood Marshall and John Paul Stevens; artists Jasper Johns, Robert Rauschenberg, Roy Lichtenstein and Andy Warhol; theologian Reinhold Niebuhr; secretary of state Henry Kissinger; historians Arnold Toynbee and George Kennan; photographers Henri

Left to right: Andre Roch, Elizabeth Paepcke, Ted Ryan and Friedl Pfeifer at the 1987 Aspen Hall of Fame Dinner in which they were all inductees, 1987. (Aspen Historical Society, Aspen Skiing Co. Collection)

Elizabeth Paepcke. (Aspen Historical Society)

Cartier-Bresson, Ansel Adams and Dorothea Lange; writers Clare Boothe Luce and Saul Bellow; systems theorist, architect, engineer, author, designer, inventor and futurist Buckminster Fuller; literary critic Lionel Trilling; journalists Norman Cousins and Bill Moyers; violinist Isaac Stern; physicist Enrico Fermi, and many, many others the Paepckes called by their first name.

Walter died in 1960, Elizabeth in 1994. She lived long enough to realize that not everything was perfect in paradise. She decried the ostentatious lifestyles and overpriced homes and stores that contradicted her vision for Aspen. She confronted excess with a sharp tongue and a smile. Everybody loved her. Lady Margaret Thatcher, for example, would not begin her book signing at Stuart Brent's on Michigan Avenue until she could say hello to her dear friend Elizabeth.

Aspen was the Paepcke's passion. But their headquarters was apartment 7A, 999 Lake Shore Drive. During her widowhood, Elizabeth lived in 8C, where she hired her longtime friend, Mies van der Rohe, as her interior designer. She could have lived anywhere in the world, but reaffirmed her love for 999—64 years in a row. Today Walter and Elizabeth sleep side-by-side in the Aspen Grove Cemetery. Lives well lived, indeed.

7B
1930
Johanna Widermann, housekeeper

With the residents of 7B out of town, the census taker could only verify the presence of the housekeeper, Johanna Widermann, who was 99 years old and not as good with a broom as she used to be.

Interior of the Paepcke apartment, Chicago, 1950. (Photographer: Hedrich-Blessing. Chicago History Museum HB-13061-A)

William Wilms, Lydia Paepcke Wilms (1881–1932)
Herman Wilms, son; Paula Wilms, daughter
Paul Becker, chauffeur; Hermione Becker, cook
Marie Hermann, maid

Born in Germany, William Wilms became an American citizen in 1897. He settled in Chicago and collaborated with Herman Paepcke on a variety of successful timber projects. He became the vice-president of The Paepcke-Leicht Lumber Co. His relationship with the Paepcke family deepened when Wilms married Herman's daughter Lydia in 1904.

Before the United States formally entered World War I, Wilms was involved with a high-ranking German spy and a plot to foment a Hindu uprising in colonial India to draw Great Britain's attention away from the war in Europe.

The sordid facts emerged during Wilms' testimony at a page-one criminal trial in October 1917. The presiding judge was Kenesaw Mountain Landis, soon to be the first commissioner of baseball. Wilms was not charged with a crime, perhaps because he was a critical prosecution witness against the plotters.

Wilms testified that Baron Kurt von Reiswitz, the German consul-general in Chicago, recruited him. Von Reiswitz reported to His Excellency Count Johann Heinrich von Bernsdorff, the Imperial Ambassador to the United States in Washington, D.C. Von Bernsdorff's orders came via encrypted messages from a mysterious Dr. Fischer in Berlin. Fischer's instructions were conveyed to him directly from the German high command—Kaiser Wilhelm II and his closest advisors. Wilms may not have realized it but he was dancing to a tune scored by the Kaiser.

"Baron von Reiswitz asked me on May 5, 1915 to transfer $20,000 to the credit of Ferdinand Hotz, a Chicago jeweler," testified Wilms. "He said it was for the purchase of a letter of credit."

Von Reiswitz handed Wilms a certified check for $20,000. Wilms put it in one of his bank accounts, and issued two personal checks for $10,000 payable to Hotz. The consul general asked Wilms to deposit the checks in two different banks. In a subsequent conversation, von Reiswitz informed Wilms that the money was used in the East Indies for propaganda purposes.

In reality, German senior leadership was trying to get Great Britain to withdraw from the war to tamp down a drummed up revolution in India. For the same reason, Germany also tried fostering an Irish revolt. To keep the United States out of Europe, the Kaiser's men attempted to get Mexico and Japan to form an alliance and declare war on the United States. They hoped to rile up Philippine nationals to rebel against us. The same spy organization was ordered to blow up key war-making factories in Canada and the States. The initiatives were imaginative. Wilms had fallen in with a clever bunch of bad guys.

William Wilms, circa 1906. From the cover of American Lumberman *magazine, Chicago, January 20, 1906. (Chicago History Museum ICHi-68181)*

Johann Heinrich Andreas Hermann Albrecht, graf von Bernstorff (1862-1939), circa 1910, was leader of the German spy ring stationed in the United States during World War I. (Library of Congress Prints and Photographs Division, Washington, D.C. LC-USZ62-68292)

When a respected man of means walks like a money launderer, acts like a money launderer, and talks like a money launderer, he must be a money launderer. Wilms never discussed in a public forum whether or not his actions weighed on his conscience.

William Wilms' testimony carried on, "On June 30, 1915, Baron von Reiswitz said he had been instructed by cable to transmit $20,000 to Manila and asked if I could arrange this with bankers, as he did not want to be identified with it."

"Ordered by whom?" Wilms was asked.

"By Washington," replied Wilms.

Wilms understood that meant Count von Bernsdorff. Wilms handled the request. The money jumped the Pacific Ocean and surfaced in the Philippines on time. Was he a money launderer or a chump? Who knows? Wilms escaped prosecution and continued living the dream in America.

Ironically in 1933 Wilms' daughter, Paula, sided with the Allies and married the British vice-consul general assigned to Chicago. When Wilms died the following year, his obituary said he was the chairman of the board of the Bloomington Limestone Company. He listed his occupation as financier.

1937–40
John V. Farwell III (1896–1992)
Margaret Willing Farwell
Joan Farwell, daughter; John V. Farwell IV, son
Inga Baasek, maid; Margaret Schroeppel, maid

The Farwell family planted their roots in Chicago sand and swamp in 1838. The first John V. Farwell opened a dry goods store in 1856. It later merged with Carson Pirie Scott & Co. His grandson, John V. Farwell III, attended Yale. In 1916, he became the 76th naval aviator in our nation's history. A daredevil pilot, he performed an unauthorized stunt by flying his plane under five of New York City's bridges, claiming there was less turbulence near the water. In 1926, he purchased the Sanitary Scale Company, a manufacturer of grocery store scales. He developed one of the first compensating-spring scales to achieve higher accuracy by adjusting for temperature changes. He was a founder of National Builders Bank, which became LaSalle National Bank. He was a director there for 33 years.

Farwell III had a vigorous libertarian streak. In 1950, he was charged with failing to comply with the government's 1947 census of manufacturers. The purpose of the census was to obtain statistics useful to trade associations, business research institutions and the government. The penalty was a $500 fine or 60 days in jail or both. We do not know the results of his trial, but he died in 1992: a free man at 96.

1937
Eugene Francis "E. F." McDonald (1886-1958)
Inez Riddle McDonald
Jean Marianne McDonald, daughter
Eugene McDonald "Skipper" Kinney, nephew

A high school dropout at 14, E. F. McDonald (Gene to his friends) floundered before he found his footing. He lost money trying to manufacture a better automobile starter. He tried the credit-finance business and failed. He joined the Navy and rapidly earned the rank of Lieutenant Commander because he understood how to operate a device the Navy used to record radio and telephone conversations. That narrow-cast skill became his key to fame and fortune. The recording device's manufacturer went out of business. Suddenly McDonald was indispensable, the only man in the Navy who could use and repair the recorder.

After his tour of duty was over, he took his newfound interest in communications into civilian life. In 1921, he entered into a partnership with the Chicago Radio Laboratory. They called their new enterprise Z-nith. McDonald was put in charge. In 1923, the loose partnership was incorporated as the Zenith Radio Corporation and for the next 35 years, until his untimely death in 1958, the charismatic McDonald would be the only boss the company knew. In the first four years on the job, Zenith pioneered AM and FM radio broadcasting, introduced the first portable radio, the first mass-produced radio that used alternating current and the first push-button automotive radios. The first Zenith TV set appeared in 1939, followed by the first 21″ TV with commercial color. Along the way they invented the wireless remote control. McDonald also approved the slogan, "The quality goes in before the name goes on."

Lt. Comdr. E. F. McDonald (on left) with explorer, Lt. Cmdr. R. E. Byrd, April 6, 1925. (Library of Congress Prints and Photographs Division, Washington, D.C. LC-DIG-npcc-13318)

McDonald went to the end of the earth to prove a point about radio. He was second in command to explorer Donald McMillan on a 1925 expedition to the Arctic. On July 5, McDonald delivered the following message via short-wave radio, "All well on board. Spirits high in anticipation of next stop." That brief broadcast convinced military experts that Zenith's short wave approach traveled farther and came in clearer than the Navy's long wave radio sets.

In 1946, Commander E. F. McDonald joined Ogden McClurg as a 999 winner of the Chicago to Mackinac race. He shattered the official record, covering 345 miles in 12 hours, 55 minutes. At the time passenger ships required 22 hours to cover the same distance.

1937
M. M. More

1937
George Eaton Scott

George Eaton Scott was president of American Steel Foundries. He also enjoyed a national reputation as a leader of the American Red Cross and director of the Boys Clubs of America. He was an active supporter of wildlife conservation. Scott's collection of antique oriental porcelain and silver was well known to experts. He was a close friend of Theodore Roosevelt. In 1931, before state or federal money became available to combat the deleterious effects of the Great Depression, he and four other business leaders raised $8.8 million for the Emergency Relief Fund.

1937
Samuel Slade, Alma L. Slade

Samuel Slade was an executive for a company that sold supplies of some sort. In 1917, with the help of 60 suburban women, Alma Slade started one of the first thrift shops in the country. Through the resale of clothing, it raised money for wounded French soldiers.

1937
Edward Foster "E. F." Swift, Jr. (1900-1963)
Kathryn Thompson Mather Swift

E. F. Swift, Jr. was the grandson of Gustavus Swift, the founder of the meatpacking giant Swift & Company, who once bragged that his slaughterhouses were so efficient that they used "everything but the squeal of the pig." E. F.'s father became chairman of the family business. Junior doesn't appear to have had a career in anything, which might be an oversight of research, because at the end of his life he had more money than he inherited.

E. F. married Marion Atchison in 1918 in Atlanta. He was an ensign in the U.S. Navy. They divorced in 1924. Marion alleged that she had no choice, due to her husband's "extreme and repeated cruelty." In 1933, he was married a second time to Kathryn Thompson Mather Swift. This marriage lasted for the rest of their lives.

Born in Chicago in 1902, Henry Field grew up at Baggrave Hall in Hungarton, Leicestershire, England. Educated at Sunnydale, Eton and Oxford, he moved back to Chicago in 1926, and launched a sterling career as an anthropologist and archaeologist. He began his career as the assistant curator of physical anthropology at the Field Museum of Natural History, endowed by his great uncle Marshall Field. Landing a job at a museum with his family name on the door was not nepotism; Henry had real talent.

His first excavation was at Kish, which is part of modern day Iraq but was once the ancient Babylonian city of Sumer (ca. 3100 BCE). The general area had been destroyed by a massive flood (ca. 7500 BCE), arguably the very flood where Noah and a ménage of animals were saved by an ark. The 1927–28 expedition uncovered thousands of stone implements some 50,000 years old, including what was then the oldest wheel ever found. Field and his team also discovered over 200 skeletons of humanoid men, women and children—estimated to be older than one million years. (Carbon dating had not been developed yet, so one million years might have been an error on the extremely high side.) Field shipped them back to Chicago. He supervised the creation of two permanent exhibitions at the museum for the 1933 World's Fair, officially named *A Century of Progress International Exposition*. The "Hall of Prehistoric Man" had nine full-size dioramas depicting the everyday lives of early humans, complemented by artifacts collected by Field. The "Hall of the Races of Mankind" contained over 100 life-size sculptures by Malvina Hoffman. In 1934, Field was promoted to head curator of physical anthropology at the museum. In that capacity he acquired "Magdalenian Girl," which is still on display and remains the most complete Upper Paleolithic skeleton in North America. Field returned to Iraq to conduct landmark studies of Marsh Arabs, Shammar Bedouins and Kurds. His many expeditions over six decades unlocked the secrets of man's ancient past.

In 1941, Franklin Roosevelt asked Field to serve as the "Anthropologist to the President" as a member of the top secret M project. "M" stood for migration and the project anticipated the massive dislocation of refugees during and after World War II. Field's task was to identify potential re-settlement areas in North Africa and the Middle East.

Around 1950, Field left Chicago to become a research fellow at the Peabody Museum of Anthropology and Ethnology at Harvard. He continued to go on important expeditions to Africa, the Near East and Pakistan. He taught at the University of Miami in Coral Cables, Florida. In 1966, he published his autobiography, *The Track of Man*, a surprise bestseller. His third wife, Julia Allen Field, was a lion tamer.

LEFT: Henry Field dressed for an archeological dig in Iraq. (© The Field Museum, #CSA75912.)

BELOW: Replica of Neanderthal man from the Hall of Prehistoric Man commissioned by Henry Field for the Field Museum, Chicago. (© The Field Museum, #CSA67016)

THE BIRDS AND BEASTS
WERE THERE

"I went to the animal fair,
The birds and the beasts were there,
The little raccoon by the light of the moon
Was combing his auburn hair
The monkey he got drunk
And sat on the elephant's trunk
The elephant sneezed and went down on his knees
And what became of the monk?"
(Anonymous children's song; sailors sang a bawdier version)

HENRY FIELD threw the weirdest party in the history of 999, and probably 99.99% of every other building as well. On Easter Sunday 1938, he gathered into his apartment a smattering of creatures that growled, hissed or chirped. Field and his co-host, Guy Murchie, Jr., decided to mingle their penchant for a good time with their interest in zoology. They threw a party for animals and as an afterthought invited some people. The invitations implored guests to bring 25-foot pythons or other beasts of their own choosing. The RSVPs had an I-accept-but-you-must-be-kidding ring to them. Fearing that nobody would comply with their wishes and bring a beast, the hosts recruited a menagerie on their own.

The Cole Brothers Circus provided Mary, a fully-grown camel. Field placed her in the center of his dining room at 999 and surrounded her with straw. Very few people—perhaps none—have ever walked around in a camel's hooves. But imagine how disorienting this indignity must have been for Mary. Perhaps we, too, would have hissed and spat at the guests.

The handler of the singing sea lion insisted she was too dangerous to take out of her cage. Besides, the cage didn't fit in the freight elevator. So they kept her imprisoned in the lobby, where she entertained other tenants returning home from a night on the town with her rendition of "America" in the loudest sea lion tenor any apartment dweller ever heard.

A sad-eyed organ grinder with a walrus mustache named Giuseppe amused Field's partygoers with a monkey dancing wildly on his shoulder.

Many guests showed up with animals on leashes or in their hair or pockets. Harriet Higginson wore a flowery hat with a cellophane crown. Nestled inside were two baby chicks dyed purple and green. A married couple arrived with a huge female goat and tethered her by an open window. Dr. Lewis Robbins and his date, Mary Laughlin, brought two kids unrelated to the first goat. Nevertheless, they left the little goats near the big mama goat. No one reported if this attempt at impromptu family planning was a success.

Mrs. Byron Harvey could have been accused of advocating animal miscegenation. She arrived with two mammalian mice and a crustaceous red lobster. They did not interact. Indeed a few cynics thought the lobster was deceased.

Henry Field was not a snob. He invited one of the building's elevator operators, who came dressed as a tramp and escorted Eczema, a noisy duck. A few squeamish guests carried stuffed lions. A 999 neighbor, Colonel George Langhorne wore a lion costume with a head as big as a sofa. He roared ferociously and scared no one. One man came as the Republican Party. He wore two red elephant trunks made of cloth posing as horns and a purple sequined butterfly as a mask. It was hard to tell if he was for or against the GOP.

There was a deodorized skunk, a live lobster in a paper bag on the bed, a guinea pig in the bathtub, a plumaged gamecock near the front door uttering long raucous shrieks, a pair of mice in a red harness and chickens on the mantel.

The caterer, if there was one, came up with the perfect touch. Animal crackers served with cocktails. Whoever cleaned up the mess and aired out the apartment deserved a medal.

(*Illustration: Clipart.com*)

1940
Edward M. Bertha (1887–1964)
Agnes Hanes Bertha
Edward M. Bertha, Jr.
Alma Weber, servant

Edward Bertha owned apartment buildings in almost every neighborhood in Chicago. He also had a seat on the Chicago Stock Exchange.

1940
Frank Byram, Mary Byram
Allie O'Neal, maid

Frank Byram was an executive for a construction company.

1940
William A. Elliott, Kathryn Elliott
Klotylda Matuszczak, maid

William Elliott was a salesman for a power plant. The spelling of Klotylda Matuszczak's name was confirmed by the inscription on her tombstone at Madison Oakridge Cemetery in Madison County, Florida.

1940
Lt. Colonel Milo Pitcher Fox (1887–1951)
Agnes Fox
Segunda Suito, servant

Milo Fox was in the U.S. Army Corps of Engineers. He was awarded the Silver Star for gallantry in action during World War I. His first wife Helen Heyl Fox attended the 1916 Army-Navy football game with Major Douglas MacArthur.

1940
Raymond Garbe
Clyde A. Stoody

Raymond Garbe and Clyde Stoody were architects, roommates and co-owners of 999 stock certificates. Garbe graduated from Wheaton College and the Harvard School of Architecture. He found his niche designing interiors of hospitals so that they could be reconstituted as medical care expanded and evolved. Garbe's innovations included centralized service cores for nursing and surgery units, and the use of modular construction to achieve maximum adaptability. He taught hospital planning at Northwestern, and endowed a professorship in design at Harvard. He married Ruth Moore Garbe, an internationally known writer on evolution and anthropology. Stoody won an honorable mention in the 1931 Prix de Roma, an architectural competition.

1940
John H. Kraft, June Kraft
Elsie Gerde, cook; Erick Gerde, chauffeur
Lillian Gerde, daughter

John processed, packaged and sold cheese. Then he did it again and again and again. In 1909, he founded a cheese company with four of his brothers. They named it after themselves. Even wife June got into the act. She was a "cheese industry librarian."

John H. Kraft, co-founder of Kraft Cheese Company, April 8, 1942. (Chicago History Museum ICHi-68133)

Edward Perry Russell. (Courtesy University of Illinois at Urbana-Champaign Library)

1940
John J. Ready
Mary Stumpel, housekeeper

A widower at 49, John Ready owned an investment securities firm.

Edward Perry Russell (1857-1940)
Mary L. Russell Christie, daughter
Doris Russell Curtis, daughter
Theodore Curtis, grandson
Diane Curtis, granddaughter
Amanda Larson, housekeeper

In 1885, Edward P. Russell went to work for Edward L. Brewster & Co., the first Chicago brokerage house to acquire a seat on the New York Stock exchange. He spent his entire career working for this firm, which eventually changed its name to Russell, Brewster & Co. He was to Samuel Insull in stocks what George Stuart was in bonds. One day Russell casually suggested "holding companies" to Insull, a suggestion that Insull casually accepted. Insull put various operating units of his empire into a variety of different holding companies, which he shockingly undervalued making it possible for J. P. Morgan and the rest of his New York crowd to eventually buy them on the cheap.

Russell committed suicide at 83.

1946-47
Whipple Jacobs (1898-53)

In 1943, Whipple Jacobs, president of the Belden Manufacturing Co., was cited for his contributions to progressive management on the WGN radio program "Distinctive Service." His career with Belden, a manufacturer of electrical cable, began in 1914 as a cost clerk making $9.00 a week. He took a leave from Belden during World War I to serve as a first lieutenant in a field artillery unit. He left Belden in 1949 to become president of Phelps Dodge, the world's largest fabricator of copper products.

1946
Willard Fiske Lochridge
Florence Sturges Lochridge

On Tuesday November 12, 1946, the *Chicago Sun-Times* in its "At the Moment" column included the following tidbit: "Another celebrity the tenants... {of 999} ...see often in the elevator is Bing Crosby, who comes to call on the W. F. Lockeridges." Other than this tantalizing reference connecting 999 tenants to one of the most popular entertainers of the twentieth century, no trace of W. F. Lockeridge or his wife could be found in the United States census or through Google and other search engines.

David Robson of Ampersand discovered the problem—spelling. Lockeridge was really Lochridge. Willard Lochridge was a vice-president and account executive for J. Walter Thompson. He worked on the Kraft account. Bing Crosby was the star of the Kraft Music Hall, which he took over from Al Jolson in 1935. Crosby personified cool

and casual. He was also hot headed. When the *maître d'* of a hotel restaurant refused to seat him because he wasn't wearing a tie, he bought the hotel, fired the man, sat down at a table and ordered lunch. He was tieless.

In 1945, Crosby decided to pre-record his show. Kraft and NBC put their foot down. They believed the home radio audience wouldn't stand for the lack of spontaneity implicit in canned broadcasts. Crosby wanted to record four shows in a week and take a month's vacation. Lochridge's job was to keep Crosby in line, which was impossible with the stubborn star. The singer wasn't coming to 999 to croon to Florence Lochridge. He was there so Willard could sweet talk him down from his inflexible position. Lochridge failed.

Kraft and NBC sued Crosby and J. Walter Thompson in 1946. A settlement brought Crosby back to the studio for the last 13 weeks of live broadcasts. Then he left the show for ABC and Philco Radio Time. He probably never returned to 999.

Harry Lillis "Bing" Crosby (1904-1977) best-selling recording artist, Academy Award winning actor, host of the hit radio show, The Kraft Music Hall *and periodic visitor to 999. (© Bettmann/Corbis)*

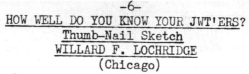

HOW WELL DO YOU KNOW YOUR JWT'ERS?
Thumb-Nail Sketch
WILLARD F. LOCHRIDGE
(Chicago)

Descendant of auld Scotch-Irish stock is square-jawed, gruff but twinkly-eyed V.P. Willard F. Lochridge. After an interesting early-colonial history his family settled in Illinois, where Loch (pronounced Lock) was born early in the gay 90's. His father was the banker in the little town of Pawnee down near Springfield; also the owner of the general store, a grain elevator, and a number of farms around there.

Loch <u>might</u> have found a job at home, but while in high school in Springfield (at the age of 12!), he smelled printer's ink and upon graduation, became a cub reporter getting "Personals" for the <u>Illinois State Journal</u>. Competing papers tried but never equalled the <u>Journal's</u> two full pages of "Personals" in one issue. "Names Make News," said <u>Time</u> much later.

Willard Lochridge went to Illinois Wesleyan, decided not to become a lawyer, took various hitches on UP in St. Louis and Kansas City, and wound up as City Editor of the <u>Kansas City Post</u>. That was when he married happy-hearted Florence Sturges, who shares with him the glory of six (6) stalwart sons.

JWT got Lochridge from the Sales and Advertising Dept. of Stewart-Warner, Chicago, in 1925. Kraft particularly has been his charge -- the Kraft that was a young and hesitant advertiser in 1928 and is now an advertising and sales leader in the nation.

Loch has been a member of the Central Council of AAAA for three years, chairman for one year. He is on JWT's Board of Directors. Still an enthusiastic golfer, he has been Club Champ of Sunset Ridge once and of Briargate three times.

So far, his boys have grandfathered him four times, and one of the babies is the first <u>girl</u> born to the Lochridge clan in 40 years! Loch contentedly resides in Evanston with the whole kit and kaboddle of Lochridges living within a radius of five blocks.

* * *

WHOM WOULD YOU LIKE TO READ ABOUT IN THESE THUMB-NAIL SKETCHES?
Send your suggestions to Jean Hurley

Biographical and thumbnail sketch of Mr. Willard F. Lochridge. (J. Walter Thompson Company Biographical Information, David M. Rubenstein Rare Book & Manuscript Library, Duke University. © J. Walter Thompson U.S.A., Inc.)

The New STATUS QUO

I n 1947, a flurry of proprietary leases was signed within days of each other, one per apartment. Those actions completed the conversion of 999 to a co-op and ended George Borg's ownership of the building.

Between then and now, all subsequent transactions were recorded in the proprietary leases. Both the sellers and the buyers signed the lease, along with the 999 board president, a representative of the management company and a notary public. Theoretically, more than a half-century's worth of such fastidious recordkeeping should have enabled us to identity all of the leaseholders and their apartments for the last 66 years. But as time rolled by many of the original proprietary leases filled up with signatures. There was no more room to add more names. What to do about the situation was left up to the management company. There have been two of them since 1947—Sudler and Company and Wolin-Levin (FirstService Residential). Between them they had two choices: either they could staple extra signature pages to the original proprietary leases or they could initiate a new blank one. Following no discernible protocol, both actions were taken. Randomly, copies were made of some of the leases and not others, and then copies of copies.

Everything relating to a specific apartment was crammed into file folders, along with an assortment of miscellaneous paperwork from tenant applications to construction blueprints to telephone messages from 50 years ago with perplexing instructions like "Ed, call Joe."

Considering the level of hoarding inside the apartment folders, it is hard to believe that anything was lost. But much was. Entire leases disappeared. Almost everything pertinent to this book from 6A and 8B has disappeared. No one remembers when or why. The records for most apartments appear complete, give or take a missing entry here and there. Politicians are fond of saying, "Perfect is the enemy of the good." What we managed to retain from 1947 to the present day is not perfect. It's good.

Other drawbacks made the proprietary leases less than ideal. Unlike the decennial census, where an effort is made to include everybody living at an address, 999 proprietary leases contain only the names of shareholders, not necessarily spouses, and definitely not children, long-term guests or live-in household help.

With so many residents unidentified, the number of people who lived at 999 between 1947 and 2013 is unknowable and clearly understated in this book. Nevertheless, at least 129 families accounting for 296 people lived here during that run of history, from Jackie Robinson's first game in the majors to Barack Obama's second term. Since 1912, we were able to confirm that 230 families lived at 999, bringing the total of identifiable individuals to 677. Taking a somewhat informed guess, both numbers could be 15% to 20% higher, if the records were complete.

For the first time in this chapter, the population of 999 is presented by apartment beginning at 1A and ending with 9C. For those people mentioned earlier whose apartment we know, their names are included again, but not their biographies.

EXCEPTIONS:

The 1952 and 1953 Chicago Cross Directory Phone Books listed William B. Cudahy as a resident of 999. Combining information from different sources, only two apartments were empty in 1952 and 1953—2A and 2B. A third unit, 6C, became available in 1953; perhaps its occupants, the Cowhams, moved out in the middle of 1952 and Cudahy moved in, taking the apartment as is. William Cudahy lived in one of those three apartments. We cannot say with any certainty any more than that.

In the Wolin-Levin records, David Leahy owned shares in the building and lived in apartment 2B in 1977. That was impossible. The Sciaky family lived there from 1959 to 1997. We never found out which apartment was Mr. Leahy's or if he ever moved into 999.

William Brewer Cudahy. (The Historical Society of Palm Beach County)

1952–53
William Brewer Cudahy

William Cudahy was a scion of the Cudahy meatpacking family. Cudahy Packing was established in 1887 by his grandfather and great uncle. The main thrust of their business was supplying European markets with cured pork. High tariffs from Great Britain in the 1920s forced them to focus on domestic sales. Their biggest sellers in the United States were canned ham, sliced dried beef, Italian-style sausage and sliced bacon.

William Cudahy graduated from Harvard and earned a law degree from Northwestern University. He became a financial analyst for the American National Bank. In 1957, he moved to Palm Beach, Florida, where he became head of the trust department for the First National Bank. In 1978 and 1979, he served two one-year terms as the mayor of Palm Beach.

1977
David Leahy

1928–29
J. W. Kiser

1947
Helen K. Edwards
Anne Riedmayer

1949
Samuel Greene, Viola Pryor Greene

Warning: this entry is pure speculation. A Samuel Greene with Chicago roots who was married to a Viola Greene might be Judge Samuel W. Greene, who was a wildly popular Christian Science lecturer.

1961
George W. K. Snyder

George W. K. Snyder was president of Wheaton Grade School 36. He resigned when the board voted against a proposal to build a new school on Wheaton's north side. He later married a resident of 999.

1970–94
Elizabeth H. Paepcke

1994–present
Margaret Z. Bauer

2A

1952
Richard H. Grimm

1966
John R. Zinzow, Dorothy M. Zinzow

Dorothy Zinzow was an active member of the League of Women Voters. In 1966 she helped organize a voter education program for college students at De Paul's Alumni Hall.

1972–2011
Dr. Randolph W. Seed, Deborah Seed
Randy's children from a prior marriage:
Lindon Seed, son; Deeda Seed, daughter
Randy and Deborah's children:
Allison Seed Reis, daughter
Vanessa and Jennifer Seed, twin daughters
Mike Reis, Jennifer's husband
Sverre Melbye, Vanessa's husband
Victoria Melbye, granddaughter
Serena Melbye, granddaughter

Based on an idea developed in the Soviet Union, Dr. Randolph Seed's father, Dr. Lindon Seed, working with Dr. Bernard Fantus, established the first blood bank in the United States in 1937 at Cook County Hospital. Dr. Linton Seed also appears to be the first doctor to use chemotherapy to fight malignant tumors. Initially the mainstream medical community was vigorously opposed to both blood banks and chemo.

Dr. Randy Seed's brother, Richard, a Ph.D. physicist from Harvard, gained global notoriety in 1998 when he announced his intention to clone humans. When politicians openly debated the ethics of cloning—13 states banned the practice—and funding for the project dried up, Dr. Richard Seed abandoned his quest.

Also a Harvard graduate, Dr. Randy Seed was no stranger to controversy. In the late 1970s, he declared his interest in creating test-tube babies. He opened the Reproduction and Fertility Clinic in Chicago with his brother, Dr. Richard Seed. They developed a procedure called artificial embryonation to help women with diseased or surgically removed ovaries have babies. The sperm of the infertile woman's husband was artificially inseminated

into the egg of a healthy woman. Five days into the surrogate pregnancy, the fertilized egg was flushed out and transferred to the uterus of the wife. She then carried the embryo to term, participating in the physiological and emotional aspects of a nine-month pregnancy, minus the first five days.

Most of Randy's career was spent performing traditional surgery in Chicago. But he never totally gave up the pursuit of the extraordinary. In 1972, he entered the *Guinness Book of Records* when he ran up the stairs of a 100-story building in the record time of 14 minutes, 29 seconds.

The Seed children were competitive skiers. At Williams College, Lindon was an all-American in 1991 and Jennifer was a three-time all-American (1990, '93 and '94). Jen, Allison and Vanessa were all ranked #1 in the country when they were 12 years old. All three skied professionally. Vanessa's husband, Sverre Melbye, was on the Norwegian National Ski Team.

Deeda Seed lives in Salt Lake City and was a member of the Human Rights Center of Utah. She was also communications director for the mayor of Salt Lake.

2011–present
David Wilkinson, Brenee Wilkinson

3A

1928–80
Walter D. Willett

1981–Present
James L. Golding, Nancy Golding
Phillip Golding, son; Andrew Golding, son

1928-37
Royden James Keith, Marie M. Keith

1947-53
John Alden Carpenter (1876-1951)
Ellen Waller Borden Carpenter
Mary Elizabeth Borden,
daughter of Ellen Carpenter

Easily 999's most accomplished artist, John Alden Carpenter was born into an affluent Chicago family whose wealth came from shipping and whose ancestors—the Aldens of colonial Plymouth—sailed to America on the *Mayflower*. He studied musical composition at Harvard, and later, in Rome, under Sir Edward Elgar of *Pomp and Circumstance* fame. Carpenter wrote two symphonies, a violin concerto, several tone poems, and over 50 songs, including *Four Negro Songs* scored to texts by Langston Hughes and *Four Poems*

by Paul Verlaine. His first success was the Violin Sonata introduced by virtuoso Mischa Elman in 1912. In 1915, the Chicago Symphony Orchestra, under the baton of Frederick Stock, debuted his *Adventures in a Perambulator*, a suite for orchestra, spiced with wit and satire. Four years later Serge Diaghilev, founder of the Ballets Russes, commissioned Carpenter's *Skyscrapers*, a ballet in six scenes about violence in American. George Gershwin was influenced by the dazzling orchestration of his jazzy 1921 ballet *Krazy Kat* based on the comic strip by George Herriman. Carpenter created *Song of Faith* in 1932 for the George Washington Bicentennial. In 1951, the Chicago Symphony devoted an entire concert to Carpenter's music to celebrate his 75th birthday. He did not have a single style. Instead he experimented with different schools and idioms. His work was considered mainstream and accessible. Carpenter's first marriage to Rue Winterbotham, the city's most adventurous interior designer, ended with her sudden death on December 7, 1931.

Two years later he married the socially prominent and philanthropic Ellen Waller Borden, who shared his love of music. Her father, James Breckenridge Waller, was a Chicago real estate mogul and a staunch Republican. Brother J. B. Waller, Jr. was the GOP kingpin of the 43rd ward. Ellen had been married to John Borden, the heir to

John Alden Carpenter, composer. (Photographer: Moffett Studios. Chicago History Museum ICHi-18508)

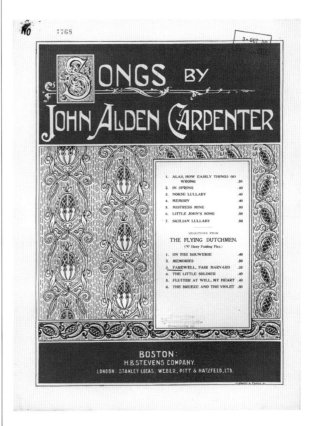

Songs by John Alden Carpenter. H. B. Stevens Co., 1897. (*Library of Congress, Motion Picture, Broadcasting, and Recorded Sound Division.*)

the Borden Dairy estate. In their 1928 divorce, she won custody of their two daughters, Mary Elizabeth, then 15, and her rebellious namesake Ellen, 19, who that same year wed Adlai Stevenson, a future governor of Illinois and two-time Democratic presidential candidate. She divorced him after he was elected governor claiming that she didn't like life on the stump. She publicly declared her preference for Dwight Eisenhower for President and voted for him over her ex—in 1952 and again in 1956. She wrote a book of poems based on her life with a man who resembled Adlai called *The Egghead and I*. She withdrew it from publication because it could not be printed before the '56 election. Fictional or not, she skewered the candidate with this quatrain:

When a man is unable to govern
His wife, his mother, his nurse,
He takes particular pleasure
In running the Universe!

Their son Adlai Stevenson III became a United States senator from Illinois.

Adlai Stevenson, Democratic Presidential nominee and son-in-law of Ellen Waller Borden Carpenter, at the Democratic National Convention, Chicago, July 1952. (Library of Congress Prints and Photographs Division, Washington, D.C. LC-DIG-ppmsca-19176)

1962
Helen Houlahan Rigali

Helen Houlahan Rigali endowed a chair in political science at Chicago's Loyola University. She was the widow of John Emil Rigali, Jr., a University of Chicago graduate and a second-generation dealer in religious art. Like his father, Rigali ran the Daprato Brothers Co., which made plaster of Paris figurines of saints, stained glass windows, marble and bronze statues, liturgical tabernacles and altars, and ornamental mosaics. The firm was headquartered in Chicago at the corner of Van Buren and Canal. Its operations extended to two other cities—New York and Pietrasanta, Italy.

Studio filled with ecclesiastical statues manufactured by the Daprato Statuary Company, 1919. Daprato Company had offices in Chicago and New York, but this view is probably from the New York branch. (Chicago History Museum ICHi-68136)

1964
Jack L. S. Snead, Jr., Kathryn W. Snead

Jack Snead proved wrong the opinionated predilection of the Interstate Commerce Commission, which declared in 1931 that the railroad monopoly over intercity freight would never be shaken. Snead turned Consolidated Freightways, a small Oregonian company, into the nation's largest trucking company. Consolidated offered services in 25 states, as well as Canada. Snead demonstrated that trucks hauling cargo less than 100 miles could move almost anything more cheaply than railroads.

1970
Dr. Geoffrey Kent (1914-2008)
Katharine Mary Ruscoe Kent (1912-2007)
Mrs. A. A. Ruscoe, mother-in-law

On May 10, 1940, Adolph Hitler and Hermann Goering subjected the Netherlands to the first large-scale airborne attack in the history of warfare. Parachutists and troops brought in by air transport landed behind the flooded water lines. A panzer division crossed the common border and added muscle to the assault. Despite a heroic effort to repel the Nazis, the country fell in five days.

In Amsterdam, at the first sound of gunfire, Dr. Gershon Kohn leapt into action. A medical intern, he had graduated with an M.D. from the University of Amsterdam in 1939. On invasion day, Dr. Kohn happened to be in charge of 60 Jewish children from an orphanage. He managed to get them safely to the dock at Ijmuiden. They boarded the freighter SS *Bodegraven*, the last *kindertransport* of World War II. *Kindertransport* was a joint rescue effort between the British government and the Refugee Children's Movement. It began saving Jewish children after *Kristallnacht* in 1938. The *Bodegraven* left port ten minutes before the Netherlands fell. German warplanes raked the decks of the ship with machine gun fire. One person died. A few days later, the rescue ship landed in Liverpool.

Dr. Gershon Kohn joined the British Army and changed his name to Dr. Geoffrey Kent. He served the wounded during the Manchester Blitz. He was awarded a medical license from the Royal College of Physicians of London in 1943, and a Master of Science degree from the University of Manchester in 1944. During World War II, he was stationed in Holland and Belgium as an officer in the Desert Rats Division of the British Royal Army Medical Corps. After his tour of duty, Dr. Kent immigrated to Canada with his growing family to become the Director of Pathological Services for Southwest Saskatchewan. He lived with his family in Moose Jaw.

On September 14, 1952, Dr. Kent was a passenger aboard the Number 10 train bound from Western Canada to Montreal. It crashed into the Number 9 train, spilling two carloads of fish on to the tracks. Dr. Kent tended to the injured. The publisher of the *Sudbury Star*, J. R. Meakes, who was on the train, wrote about Dr. Kent, "I met a hero of the wreck. A fair, slight young doctor whose quiet spoken Oxford English calmed imminent hysteria, while his sure hands made a rapid examination of the injured."

Dr. Kent moved to Chicago in 1953 to become the associate director of pathology at Cook County Hospital. Before he retired in 1976, Dr. Kent had moved from senior pathologist at Cook County to chairman of the Department of Pathology at West Suburban Hospital in Oak Park in 1958, chairman of Chicago Wesley Memorial Hospital in 1969 and pathologist-in-chief and director of laboratories at Northwestern Memorial Hospital in 1973.

Bronze memorial sculpture of the Children of the Kindertransport *outside Liverpool Street Station in Hope Square, London. (Photographer: Yaroslav Radlovsky/Diomedia)*

The *Banco di Roma* Apartment:
1973–78
Mario A. Gabriele

1978–83
Sergio Annovazzi
Maria Louisa Annovazzi

1984
Vittorio Sisto

In the early 1970s, large European banks salivated at thoughts of Chicago. The huge agricultural and manufacturing businesses in Illinois and neighboring states made Chicago a force in world commerce, but a long-standing ban on foreign banks operating inside Illinois prevented Chicago from becoming a global financial engine. That changed on October 1, 1973, when Governor Richard Ogilvie signed into law an act opening the state to international banks. On the same day, Mario Gabriele, the president of the new *Banco di Roma* branch in downtown Chicago, bought shares in 999. *Banco di Roma* had strongly lobbied the Illinois government to change the law, and when it changed, they pounced, becoming the first of 22 foreign banks to enter the Windy City market.

"The most difficult part of the launch was learning how American banks go after individual accounts," observed Gabriele. "Promotion is unknown in Italy." *Banco di Roma* offered a new Maserati to anyone who deposited $250,000 for one year at zero interest. No one qualified for the free car. But the bank got a good deal of free publicity and much needed experience in American marketing hoopla.

4A became a kind of corporate apartment for *Banco di Roma*. 999's bylaws did not allow a company to own shares in the building so Gabriele purchased the stock himself, and when it was time for him to return to Italy, he sold it to his successor Sergio Annovazzi who in turn sold it to Vittorio Sisto.

William J. McDonough.
(*Federal Reserve Bank of New York–Curating Section*)

1989–97
William J. McDonough
Suzanne Clarke McDonough
Paul H. McDonough, son
Lynne Madden McDonough, Paul's wife

In 1993, Bill McDonough was appointed chief executive officer and chairman of the Federal Reserve Bank of New York, the most powerful of the 12 Fed banks. Paul Volcker was one of his predecessors; Tim Geithner was his immediate successor. In Chicago, he was vice-chairman of the First Chicago Corporation and the First National Bank of Chicago. Suzanne McDonough graduated from the Medill School of Journalism at Northwestern University. She founded and developed the Cuernavaca Racquet Club of Fort Lauderdale, Florida, and was a member of the governing board of the Chicago Symphony Orchestra.

Paul McDonough, Bill's son from a prior marriage, lived at 999 with his wife, Lynn, for six weeks in 1994.

1999–present
Robert N. Szalay, Nancy K. Szalay

1930
William Wilms, Lydia Paepcke Wilms

1947–2003
James Wilson Reilly, Annette May Cuneo Reilly
Meric Reilly, son; Madeleine Reilly, daughter

James Reilly and Annette Cuneo were married at the Drake Hotel in Chicago on April 15, 1943. Officiating at the wedding was Rev. "Father Tom" of the Church of the Assumption. The bridegroom, a member of the United States Army stationed in New Orleans, wore his dress uniform. The bride sported a diamond cluster pin given to her mother by her illustrious grandfather, Frank Cuneo Sr., a produce merchant and the organizer of the Italian Chamber of Commerce to promote the importation of Italian products, for which he was awarded the chevalier of the crown by King Victor Emmanuel of Italy. Her uncle Frank Cuneo, Jr. founded Cuneo Press.

James Wilson Reilly was a teacher and a stockbroker. A favorite recipe of his contained liver sausage and whipped cream. When he died, the Bureau of Alcohol, Tobacco and Firearms had to clean up his apartment. Reilly had collected tens of thousands of rounds of live ammunition.

2004–present
Steven Deli, Anne Deli

James Reilly's recipe for Liver-Sausage and Whipped Cream. (Courtesy of Deborah Seed)

1928–30
W. C. Cook, Mary G. Cook

1946–47
Robert Hall McCormick III

Along with business partner, Herb Greenwald, Robert Hall McCormick III developed the Mies van der Rohe buildings at 860–880 North Lake Shore Drive. They were an overnight iconic sensation, the first tall buildings to go up in Chicago since the 1930s and widely praised for their innovative use of steel and glass. McCormick was the great-grandson of Leander McCormick, who, with his brother, Cyrus, co-founded the McCormick Reaper Company and International Harvester, now Navistar.

Ludwig Mies van der Rohe, Chicago, 1969–1971. (Photographer: Hedrich Blessing. Chicago History Museum HB-35283-Q)

1949–77
Rudolph E. Prussing
Florence Whiting Bourne Prussing

Rudolph Prussing studied engineering at Cornell. He ran a company that manufactured heavy-duty machinery, such as cranes and fork lifts.

1977
David K. Sengstack, Arlene Howard

David Sengstack published educational music. When he sold his company to Time-Warner in 1989, the sale included worldwide rights to the Suzuki Method, the Frances Clark Library, the distribution rights for Smithsonian/Folkways Records and the song *Happy Birthday to You* (which, at the turn of the twenty-first century, was still bringing in around $2 million a year in royalties), along with approximately 50,000 other titles. After the sale, Sengstack formed a private foundation that gives grants to various charities interested in creating positive experiences for children in the first three years of life.

1978
James N. Bay, Julie Beich Bay

Using an old family recipe, James Bay's father, George, started the Bays English Muffin Corporation. A wag once remarked, "English muffins are a doughy excuse to eat butter." In 1968, James Bay succeeded his father as president. In 1972 he collaborated with Ray Kroc, the founder of McDonalds, to create the Egg McMuffin. In 1980, the *Chicago Tribune* assembled a panel of nine experts to rate five brands of English muffins on appearance, flavor and taste. Bays muffins were praised for their golden color, coarse texture and porosity, and were declared the winner.

1997–present
Thomas P. Johnson, Jr., Brenda Johnson

7A

1928
Mrs. Elizabeth D. Parkinson

1930–63
Walter Paepcke, Elizabeth Nitze Paepcke

1964–99
Jeremiah Griffin, Abby H. Griffin
Leona "Lee" E. Griffin, daughter

Jeremiah Griffin was a reputed bootlegger. His daughter, Lee Griffin, continued to live in 7A after her parents died. She was a chain-smoking, Chicago public school teacher. In 1999, she passed away in her apartment. The fire department had to break down her door. She left no will and had no known living relatives. Many of her possessions—including a $4,000 purse that still had the price tag inside—were taken from her apartment by agents of the state of Illinois and never returned. A lawyer was retained to search for far-flung family members. A few distant relatives were found in various parts of the world. The bulk of her estate went to the Catholic Church.

1999–present
Thomas Haynes, Connie Hsu Haynes
Antonia Haynes, daughter

(Photo ©iStock.com/Lauri Patterson)

1928
G. W. Kretzinger, Jr., Louise Kretzinger

1930
Sarah E. Brown, housekeeper

1947
William T. Young, Jr., Margaret Wilson Young

Leone Baxter sitting with her husband and business partner, Clem Whitaker. Behind them is a poster of The Doctor *designed to fight "socialized medicine" for their client, the American Medical Association. (Photo by George Skadding/ Time Life Pictures/Getty Images)*

1950–53
Clement Sherman Whitaker (1899–1962)
Leone Baxter Whitaker (1906–2001)

Ideological opposites Karl Rove and David Axelrod owe a huge debt to Clem Whitaker and Leone Baxter Whitaker, a husband and wife team that invented modern political consulting. Before the Whitakers opened Campaigns, Inc. at the Fairmont Hotel in San Francisco, politicians ran their campaigns pretty much by themselves. At critical times they might augment their staffs with freelance speechwriters or media buyers. But the Whitakers made that obsolete by bundling all the services a candidate could possibly need inside one company, and for the first time politicians could present a consistent, coherent face to voters across all forms of communication.

With Clem and Leona at the helm, Campaigns, Inc. did everything. They conducted research, crafted strategy, made ads and staged events. They wrote speeches, planned and executed media buys, handled public relations and fundraising, scheduled public appearances, secured endorsements, oversaw all field operations, authored newspaper articles, editorials and cartoons that favored their clients and distributed them through their wholly-owned wire service. They even recruited and trained "volunteers" to knock on doors and put placards on front lawns. They

Keep politics out of this picture

Reception for the ladies of the 79th Congress. From left to right: Gladey Tillet (Head of the Women's Division, National Democratic Committee), Eleanor Roosevelt, unknown, Mary Morton, Emily Taft Douglas, Chase Going Woodhouse,

Helen Gahagan Douglas. Washington, D.C., 1945. (Photographer: Tenschert Photo Company. Carl Albert Center Congressional Archives, University of Oklahoma)

allocated a campaign's financial resources. Sometimes, by overspending early, they drove competitors out of primaries. Other times they husbanded money until the last possible moment and overwhelmed the opposition at a time when many voters were making up their minds. They majored in negative ads—their specialty—and minored in dirty tricks. They modeled every experience so that the next campaign would be more effective than the prior one. The Whitakers were also skilled lobbyists, committed to small government conservatism and rolling back FDR's New Deal. They enjoyed widespread fame and success. Working exclusively for Republican candidates and conservative causes, the full-service operation of Clem Whitaker and Leone Baxter changed American politics forever.

Clement Sherman Whitaker grew up in a religious home that was also politically progressive. His father was a Baptist minister, as was his uncle, Robert Whitaker, a well-known socialist, a friend of novelist and left-wing activist Upton Sinclair, and a speaker at the funeral of Tom Mooney, a militant labor leader. Clem went to work as a small town journalist at age 13. By 21, he was covering politics for *The San Francisco Examiner*. He leveraged his experience as a political writer into becoming a

left-oriented lobbyist. He tried to raise teacher's salaries and ban capital punishment. Rather quickly, however, Clem flip-flopped to the right, reasoning that was where the money was.

A native of the state of Washington, Leone Baxter wrote for *The Oregonian* in Portland and later landed a job with the Redding California Chamber of Commerce, where she worked on a project with Clem who quickly hired her. In rapid succession their relationship progressed from boss/employee to partners to a couple and newlyweds in 1938, the second marriage for both.

A fast-talking chain smoker, Clem was tall and thin, brilliant, energetic and intense. Leone was an attractive redhead, curvy, genteel and soft-spoken. What they had in common was cynicism and ruthlessness. Clem once summed up their political philosophy: "The average American doesn't want to be educated, he doesn't want to improve his mind, he doesn't even want to work consciously at being a good citizen. But every American likes to be entertained. He likes movies, mysteries, fireworks and parades. So if you can't put on a fight, put on a show." The more succinct version of their professional belief system was "More Americans like corn than caviar."

Richard Nixon, a client of Whitaker and Baxter, on November 8, 1950, declaring victory at the Los Angeles Press Club after a controversial Senate election race against Helen Douglas. (Los Angeles Public Library Photo Collection)

They worked against clean air, against labor's right to picket, against protecting the Pacific coastline, against medical malpractice insurance and against family friend Upton Sinclair's EPIC campaign (End Poverty in California). They claimed Sinclair seduced young girls and that his supporters were pro-Soviet, which, even if true, had nothing to do with his movement. On behalf of the American Medical Association, they fought Harry Truman's attempt to create universal healthcare. To be near the AMA's headquarters they moved to Chicago and 999. As part of their anti-healthcare effort they recorded and distributed a 1949 speech by Ronald Reagan on how nationalized medical care is the first step to socialism.

Whitaker and Baxter helped elect California governor Earl Warren—a future chief justice of the Supreme Court—and his successor Goodwin Knight, and President Dwight Eisenhower. Richard Nixon's run for the U.S. Senate against Congresswoman Helen Gahagan Douglas in 1950 was the Whitaker's most famous campaign. They claimed she had communist leanings and labeled her "The Pink Lady." The charge stuck, not because it was true, but because this was the heyday of the anti-red hysteria that swept through Hollywood, where she had appeared in one

movie, the inexcusably awful *She*. She was married to a movie star, Melvyn Douglas. Although she lost, Douglas ripped a page from the Whitaker's playbook and called Nixon a name that helped define him for the rest of his life, "Tricky Dicky."

Love them or revile them, there is no denying the impact the Whitakers had in their lifetime or their lasting contributions to campaign management. Their success with negative advertising continues to bedevil American political discourse.

1954
Jacob Mayo Lenz (1881–1959), Mary Lenz

J. Mayo Lenz founded the Lenz Manufacturing Company, which made electrical equipment. Prior to that, he ran the Chicago Telephone Supply Company.

Robert Stuart List. (Colonel Robert R. McCormick Research Center, First Division Museum at Cantigny)

1959
Robert Stuart List, Claire List

Robert Stuart List, who preferred to be called by his middle name, was the publisher of the *Chicago American*, a Hearst publication and the city's largest afternoon newspaper. The *American* was sold to the Tribune Co. in 1969 and was renamed *Chicago Today*. In 1974, they discontinued its publication. In the 1980s, List was the chairman of the Citizen's Committee for Passage of the Gun Responsibility Bill and an advocate of gun-registration laws.

Ralph Charles Wagner, star running back on 1938 Western Illinois football team. (Western Illinois University)

1971–00
Louise H. Benton (1937–1999)
Ralph C. Wagner (1915–1999)

Louise Benton's father was William Benton, the son of missionaries and educators and a man of extensive bandwidth. After graduating Yale, he turned down a Rhodes Scholarship to take a job as a lowly advertising copywriter at Albert Lasker's Lord & Thomas (later Foote, Cone and Belding) in Chicago. He moved to New York and started Benton and Bowles with his friend Chester Bowles. It grew into one of the nation's largest ad agencies. He pioneered market research and the use of radio to build brands. Keeping a promise he made to himself, he retired at 35, and entered public service as Nelson Rockefeller's policy advisor. He returned to Chicago as vice-president of the University of Chicago. Benton negotiated a brilliant deal with General Robert E. Wood, then the chairman of Sears, Roebuck and Company. He arranged to buy the Encyclopedia Britannica, at the time a property of Sears. Benton bought the common stock with his own money and the University of Chicago received the preferred stock plus royalties as a donation from Wood. In 1939, he was part of a triumvirate that purchased Muzak from Warner Brothers. A liberal Democrat, Benton was appointed United States Ambassador to UNESCO by Harry Truman, and later Assistant Secretary of State. When Chester Bowles was elected governor of Connecticut,

Seated: Louise Benton; her mother, Helen Hemingway; her father, William Benton; her sister, Helen. Standing: brothers Charles and John, Southport, Connecticut, 1952. (Chicago History Museum ICHi-68198)

Benton filled his vacancy in the U.S. Senate. He introduced a resolution that called Senator Joseph McCarthy a liar and a thief, unworthy of the Senate, which eventually led to McCarthy's censure. To complete his résumé, Benton was regarded as one of the ten to 20 best card players in the world.

His daughter, Louise, whose godmother was Elizabeth Paepcke, went to work for Britannica, eventually becoming president and chairman of the Encyclopedia Britannica Education Corporation. Louise's trust contributes funds to the Cradle, a Chicago adoption agency that is well regarded for its ethical approach to adoptions.

In 1979, Louise married a colleague from the office, Ralph Wagner. They had been living together at 999. Ralph was an ex-football player whose career was ended by a back injury during training camp with the Chicago Bears in the late 1930s. According to Wagner, his greatest athletic achievement, however, came in track. He beat Jesse Owens, who once set five world records in a single day, in a race. Owens later won four gold medals in the 1936 "Hitler" Olympics in Berlin. The speedy Wagner, a graduate of Western Illinois, became a high school teacher of history and mathematics. He went to work for Britannica's educational division. In due course, he was promoted to president and CEO, the position he held when he married Louise. Wagner became a recognized leader in educational films, overseeing Britannica's production of hundreds of documentaries. He supervised the distribution of 2,000 titles, including an award winner about monarch butterflies.

2000-01
Bill Miller

2001-10
Dr. Constantine Mavroudis, Martha Mavroudis

2011-present
John Jostrand, Beth Jostrand

9A

1913-17
Ogden Trevor McClurg (1878-1926)
Gertrude D. Schwarz McClurg
Eleanor McClurg, daughter
Barbara Ogden McClurg, daughter
Margaret Dockery, maid; Margaret McLean, nurse
Nellie Chambers, cook

1917-19
Elizabeth Dickason
Dorothy Dickason, daughter
Livingston Dickason, Jr., son

1920-25
Dr. Francis "Frank" X. Walls,
Elizabeth Dickason Walls
Livingston Dickason, Jr., son
Margaret Murphy, maid; Catherine Moore, cook
Audon Kinsella, maid

1926-29
Livingston Dickason, Jr.
Katherine Hogg Maxwell Dickason
Mary Elizabeth Dickason, daughter

1927-47
Bror Gustave Dahlberg (1881-1954)
Mary Alexander Dahlberg (1901-38), first wife
Gilda Krieger Lichtle Dahlberg, second wife
Alma Lee Dahlberg, daughter
Craig Johnson, foster son
Basil Rathbone, houseguest
Mable Anderson, housekeeper

1947
Preston Tucker, Vera Tucker
Shirley Tucker, daughter; Preston Tucker, Jr., son
Mary Lee Tucker, daughter; Noble Tucker, son
John Tucker, son

Preston Thomas Tucker (1903–1955) was the second 999er to have his life story turned into a movie—Terry Druggan was the first. Tucker inspired Francis Ford Coppola's 1988 biopic *Tucker: The Man and His Dream* starring Jeff Bridges. Arguably the real star of the movie was a car, the Tucker 48, popularly known as the "Tucker Torpedo."

Preston Tucker's heart pumped motor oil. He grew up in a suburb of Detroit. The first car he ever saw ran over his foot. He learned to drive at 11. At 16, he began purchasing broken-down automobiles, repairing, refurbishing and selling them at a profit. He quit high school to work as an office boy for Cadillac. Attracted to high-performance police cars and motorcycles, he became an under-aged cop. He labored on the Ford assembly line and sold Chryslers in Memphis. He owned and operated a gas station. Tucker loved cars and knew them backwards, forwards and upside

down. He dreamed of someday manufacturing his own line of cutting edge automobiles.

A born salesman, cheerful, affable and optimistic, always talking, always smiling, Preston Tucker seemed to believe his non-stop palaver. Andrew Jackson Higgins, the builder of the landing craft that deposited our soldiers on Omaha Beach on D-Day and, for a brief time Tucker's employer, called him, "The world's greatest salesman. When he turns those big brown eyes on you, you'd better watch out!"

Immediately after World War II, Tucker began pounding the drum for his then imaginary Torpedo and ballyhooed it into one of the most eagerly awaited automobiles in history. He placed an ad in *PIC Magazine* announcing with more bravado than wherewithal his intention to mass-produce a car so advanced it would make everything on the road obsolete. He labeled it *The Car of Tomorrow Today*. According to Tucker, The Tucker 48 would pioneer the use of a padded dashboard, a laminated windshield designed to pop out during an accident, air-cooled disc brakes, and a third headlight centered on the front hood called the "Cyclops Eye." It changed angles when the

Preston Tucker, seated in a Tucker 48 on the Adams Street side of the Federal Building before his trial, Chicago, February 21, 1949. (Chicago History Museum ICHi-67635)

steering wheel turned more than ten degrees to achieve better visibility rounding corners at night. The 48 and its rear engine, which would generate 150 horsepower, would be able reach a speed of 130 mph and cruise comfortably at 100 mph. Made of aluminum and plastic, it would weigh 2,000 pounds and sell for 50¢ a pound. Within a week after the ad ran, Tucker received 150,000 letters, most of them asking when and where they could buy this fantastic car. The pent-up demand from a car-starved nation wasn't surprising. The Big Three automakers hadn't produced a new car since 1941.

Tucker wasn't an unknown. Before the war Tucker and Harry Miller, a brilliant automotive engineer, designed Indianapolis 500 racing cars. During the war Tucker created a combat car that was "too fast" for the War Department. They didn't buy it, but they gobbled up his electric powered gun turret, which was used in PT boats, Higgins landing craft, and B-17 and B-29 bombers. After the war ended, the War Assets Administration leased Tucker the Dodge-Chicago plant at 7401 S. Cicero Avenue, the world's largest factory occupying 475 acres on the inside. The lease agreement bound Tucker to showing $15 million of assets on the books by March 1, 1947, or risk losing the property. He began to raise money for the Tucker 48 by selling dealerships and floating a $20 million stock issue. With over $17 million in the bank in 1947, Tucker was on his way, scrambling as fast as he could go up the ladder of his American dream.

There was, however, a fly in Tucker's soup, actually quite a few flies. The car of tomorrow existed only in his head. He had never built a prototype. His outlandish claims had never been tested. Competitors owned

many of the patents he said would be integral parts of the Tucker 48. His decision to pre-sell "accessories" as a way to secure priority status for prospective owners before he actually made a car was seen by some as a way to avoid building cars, and quite possibly an elaborate scam. When he tried to buy two steel mills to access raw materials for his cars, the War Assets Administration blocked his bid, leading some observers aligned with Tucker to suggest that General Motors, Ford, Chrysler and their political allies were conspiring against him. Somebody whispered in the SEC's ear that some of the money Tucker had raised ended up in his pocket. The SEC disclosed that the

Tucker Chicago Plant assembly line, circa 1948.
(Courtesy of the Ypsilanti Historical Society Archives)

Page from 1948 Tucker brochure.
(Courtesy The Old Car Manual Project
and Howard Nourse.)

self-proclaimed great man had not put any cash into his own company. Tucker's lead salesman, Abe Karatz, who helped him recruit dealers and investors, turned out to be a convicted felon using an alias.

A prototype of the 48 was finally made out of random parts found in junkyards in time for a well-publicized unveiling. Upon seeing it the press nicknamed it the "Tin Goose" and revealed that it could not go in reverse. Tucker replied that he hadn't finished building the direct torque drive, an oversight that was soon corrected. But his reputation, which had skyrocketed overnight, began to plummet.

Harry Aubrey Toulmin, Jr., the chairman of the board of the Tucker Corporation, resigned in a huff and wrote a letter to the SEC distancing himself from the company. He described Tucker as "a tall, dark, delightful, but inexperienced little boy." Tucker published an open letter to the automobile industry, subtly hinting that his efforts were being stymied by a conspiracy between politicians and the SEC. It amounted to too little, too late. His "dealers" began filing lawsuits to recover their money. Stockholders also sued, alleging that the company was "in danger of collapse." The corporation's stock plummeted to $1.00 a share. A Federal grand jury initiated an inquiry. The corporation was placed in trusteeship under the Federal Bankruptcy Act. Nevertheless, with turmoil and angst as his backdrop, Tucker managed to produce 51 hand-made Tucker 48s, including the prototype.

On June 10, 1949, Tucker and six associates were indicted on 25 counts of mail fraud, five counts of violating SEC regulations and one count of conspiracy to defraud. Otto Kerner, a future Illinois governor, led the prosecution. Attorney William T. Kirby and his team defended Tucker and his colleagues. At the trial, the government

Left to right: Henry Ford, unidentified, Harvey Firestone, Preston Tucker, unidentified, Benson Ford, and Edsel Ford, at the Indianapolis 500 speedway, 1932. (From the collections of The Henry Ford. P.188.8255/THF111173)

argued that Tucker never intended to build a car, except possibly to deflect scrutiny away from his real goal of defrauding dealers and investors. Government witnesses described the internal confusion and financial foibles of the Tucker Corporation. Kerner contended that the large number of problems collectively supported Tucker's guilt. The judge chided the prosecution, reminding them that dysfunction did not a conspiracy make and ordered them to present a chain of facts that proved a conspiracy.

Kerner bet his case on two final witnesses. Daniel J. Ehlenz, a former owner of a Tucker dealership, testified that he had lost his $28,000 investment. However on cross-examination, he admitted that he still drove his Tucker

Front and rear views of Preston Tucker's Tucker 48 in front of the Chicago plant that produced approximately 50 automobiles between 1947 and 1949. (Both photos courtesy of the Ypsilanti Historical Society Archives)

48, a present from Tucker. The car had 35,000 miles on it and cruised smoothly at 90 mph. Joseph Turnbull, an SEC accountant, established that Tucker took in $28 million and spent less than one-seventh of it on research and development. He also asserted that Tucker had pocketed over $500,000 of the investors' money. When Tucker's attorney William Kirby asked Turnbull for proof of deliberate financial mismanagement, Turnbull was unable to cite even one example. To make matters worse for the government, Tucker's defense refused to call any witnesses. In his closing argument, Kirby stated that Tucker "either intended to cheat and that's all he intended to do. Or he tried in good faith to produce a car. The two are irreconcilable." He then invited the members of the jury to go for a ride in one of the eight Tucker 48s parked outside the courthouse.

Was Tucker a flimflamming fraud or a flawed genius? The jury took 28 hours to return a verdict of not guilty on all counts for all accused. Ironically, if there was a conspiracy, it succeeded. The Tucker Corporation had lost its factory, was mired in debt and faced a queue of lawsuits. There would be no more Tucker cars. Six years

later, Tucker the man was also dead; a victim of cancer, pneumonia and, quite possibly, a broken heart.

Otto Kerner, the U.S. Attorney who pursued Tucker, had his comeuppance. Illinois twice elected him governor, and later he was appointed to the federal bench. But he was also convicted of 17 counts of bribery, conspiracy, perjury and related charges for stock fraud. He became the first federal appellate judge in history to be jailed.

Conversely Tucker's defense attorney, William T. Kirby, became chairman of the board of the John D. and Catherine T. MacArthur Foundation.

Original stock certificates for the Tucker Corporation became collectors' items, and are worth more today than they were in 1947. Over 10,000 of those certificates were personally signed by Preston Tucker, making them the most desirable. Of the 50 Tuckers produced (not counting the Tin Goose), 46 are still road worthy. All of the features Tucker said would be standard in his car eventually made it to the market, sometimes decades later, as part of nearly every car on earth. The last Tucker 48 to sell at auction went for $2.915 million.

Preston Tucker and Spike McAdams in front of a Tucker automobile at U.S. Courthouse, Chicago, October 17, 1949. (Chicago History Museum ICHi-67637)

THE CAR OF TOMORROW, TODAY

The Tucker Torpedo (the name changed to the 48 to avoid linking its image to the carnage of war) was the most famous car in the world from the moment Preston Tucker announced his intent to build it. No automobile company before or since had the audacity to claim that their new car would be infused with so many exciting state-of-the-art innovations. Despite the publicity, many of these features never made it to the actual 48, largely because of the myriad distractions that plagued Tucker. Of those that did, Tucker and his engineers didn't invent most of them. Tucker did hold seven patents, a fact that came out after his trial. The 48 was designed mostly from a menu of brilliant ideas developed by others. These innovations fell into four categories: safety, comfort, performance and styling. The following list briefly describes the provenance and importance of the innovations that were hallmarks of the 48.

SAFETY

The pressure to put the Tucker 48 into showrooms, and the chaos caused by bad press, a landslide of lawsuits and a page-one trial, forced Preston Tucker to abandon the use of air-cooled disc brakes. Had he been allowed to realize his dream in its entirety, the Tucker 48 would have been the first mass produced car with disc brakes—beating the Chrysler Crown Imperial to market by one year.

In the late 1920s, Packard utilized a third headlight. Tucker installed the "Cyclops Eye" third headlight, his baby's most defining feature, as a much needed safety feature. Subaru revived the idea in the 1980s.

To avoid misaligned tires scraping against the inside of front fenders, Tucker announced front fenders that would turn with the wheels, allowing headlights to mimic the path of the car as it turned. He never put them in the 48.

Tucker created the first padded dashboard. It would be another 25 years before this innovation was widely used.

While others had experimented with locating instruments within the diameter and reach of the steering wheel, Tucker incorporated this obvious boon to safety into the 48, an idea that would not be mass-produced until the 1976 Aston Martin Lockwood.

Laminated safety glass windshields were invented in 1892. Designing the front window so that it would pop out during an accident appears to have emerged whole cloth from Tucker's active imagination.

Seat belts had been around since the early 1880s. The first manufacturers to offer them as optional equipment were Nash in 1949 and Ford in 1955. They first became standard in the 1958 Saab. The Tucker 48 beat them all.

A roll bar integrated within the roof, a front safety chamber installed inside a steel bulkhead, a steering box behind the front axle to protect the driver in front end collisions and self-sealing tires were ideas Tucker borrowed from his racing days and the shipping industry.

Most of the safety features envisioned by Tucker were intended to protect drivers and passengers in case of an accident. Another Tucker innovation protected the car. The parking brake had a separate key so that it could be locked to prevent theft.

COMFORT

A livery service in New York City offered air conditioning in 1933. Packard offered it as an option in 1939. In today's dollars, Packard charged over $4,000 for this feature. In 1941, they discontinued this costly attempt at luxury. Chrysler was the first company to make a long-term commitment to cooled air in 1953. Tucker had built-in air conditioning in 1948.

Four-wheel drive emerged at the turn of the twentieth century. World War II provided the impetus to create a host of all-terrain vehicles, which required improvements in four-wheel drive. After the war, Land Rover introduced a luxury 4WD Range Rover in 1948. Call this innovation

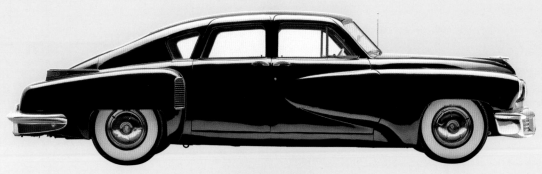

1948 Tucker 48 Sedan.
(From the collections of The Henry Ford. 58.62/THF90624)

a tie between Rover and Tucker. However Tucker's four-wheel drive came with independent spring-less suspension. So maybe he had a slight edge.

With five feet of leg room in the back and four across seating, Tucker favored spaciousness. Five feet is more leg room than one gets in the first-class section of most airplanes.

In 1957, the Chrysler Ghia Limo offered doors that extend into the roof for easy entry and exit. Tucker had the idea first.

PERFORMANCE

Tucker's promise of 30 to 35 miles per gallon compares favorably to these other 1948 vehicles: Lincoln Mark (7 mpg), Willys Jeep (11), Dodge convertible (12.2), Ford Super Deluxe Coupe (12.8) and Cadillac (14). Conversely the 1948 Crosley CC Wagon got 50 miles per gallon and the Fiat 500 Topolino squeezed 60 miles out of a gallon of gas.

To put the Tucker 48's top speed of 130 miles per hour in perspective, the 1948 Jaguar XK120, the car that put Jaguar on the high performance map, had a top speed of 135 mph.

In 1885, Herbert Akroyd Stuart developed the first device that anticipated modern fuel injection, a process where gasoline is metered out and atomized by forcibly pumping it under high pressure through a nozzle to the engine. The Alfa Romeo 6C2500 tested electronic fuel injection in 1940, but never brought it to market. In the 1950s and '60s, the concept was perfected through a variety of experiments. In the 1970s and '80s, automakers began to incorporate fuel injection. Tucker's ideas were clearly ahead of the curve, but the actual 48 came out with conventional carburetors instead of fuel injection.

Aluminum is the earth's most abundant metal, known for its durability, lightness and resistance to corrosion. In Tucker's day, Ferrari used aluminum in its racing cars.

Tucker used an aluminum block in the 48.

The Czechoslovakian Tatra 77 launched in 1933 was the first automobile to have a rear engine, real wheel platform. In addition to the Tucker 48, the Volkswagen Beetle, the Porsche 365 and the Chevy Corvair were early adopters of rear end technology.

Tucker was a pioneer in hydraulic drive systems. Hydraulic torque converters took the place of the clutch in vehicles with automatic transmission. After the almost simultaneous birth and death of the Tucker 48, General Motors began using hydraulic torque converters in the mid-1950s.

In auto racing the speed and efficiency of the pit crew is often the difference between winning and losing. Tucker decided to mount his engine on a separate sub-frame that was secured with six bolts. The entire drivetrain could be lowered and removed from the car in minutes. Tucker envisioned exchanging the troubled engine for a loaner engine in 30 minutes or less.

STYLING

The original drawings for the 48 resembled the Batmobile. Tucker described the inspirations for the car to the Society of Automotive Engineers: "The fender was made to look like a bird's wing to denote fleetness and grace, the bumper style resembles the horns of a Texas longhorn and the chassis follows the contours of a woman's body." Nevertheless, before Tucker, the only automobile to use a teardrop design, the ideal aerodynamic form, was Germany's BMW 328 "Mille Miglia" Kamm Coupe in 1940.

PRICE

Tucker's dream of producing a 2,000-pound car and selling it for 50¢ a pound, almost came true. The Tucker 48 weighted 4,200 pounds and had a manufacturer's suggested list price of $2,450, or 58¢ per pound.

1950-52
Ray Edgar Dodge (1900-1984)
Ada Williams Ince Dodge

According to the mythology of 999 a member of the automotive manufacturing Dodge family bought Preston Tucker's apartment after his demise. The story raises the possibilities that a Detroit blueblood came to Tucker's rescue after his bankruptcy, or, maybe, to give him one more twist of the knife. Unfortunately there does not appear to be anybody in that Dodge family with the name of Ray E.

999's Ray E. Dodge finished sixth in the 800 meter finals at the 1924 Olympic games in Paris. On the voyage home, he watched his teammates exult over the glittering assortment of medals they had won. "Returning home empty-handed was no fun," recalled Dodge. "And right then I saw the demand for a product that will never diminish." With a handful of his Olympic teammates as shareholders, he started a company, which manufactured trophies, medals, bookends and souvenirs.

Bette Davis at Oscar Ceremony. It was rumored that she named the nude male statuette after former husband, Oscar Nelson. (© Sunset Boulevard/Corbis)

Coach Amos Alonzo Stagg with his 400 and 800 Meter Men, 1924 Olympic Games, Paris, France. Roy Edgar Dodge seated, second from left. (Amos Alonzo Stagg Collection, Holt-Atherton Special Collections, University of the Pacific Library)

To fulfill a 1931 commission, Dodge gold-plated a nude statuette of a man. There are many stories about how it got its name. This one may be apocryphal, but it's the best of the lot. When actress Bette Davis saw the statuette, she said that it reminded her of her first husband, Oscar Nelson, a bandleader. Every year the Academy of Motion Picture Arts and Sciences bestows Oscars in recognition of excellence in the film industry. For decades the Oscar was manufactured at Dodge Trophy in Crystal Lake, Illinois.

In addition to Hollywood's highest honor, Dodge also made Emmys, Phi Beta Kappa keys, Heisman Trophies, the Miss America prize, Bowl Game and Vince Lombardi trophies, Gold Phonograph Records, class rings, officer's bars and general's stars, combat medals and many other baubles commemorating the best of this and the world champion of that.

It is possible that Dodge bought shares in the building, but never lived at 999. In 1950, he bought a home in Miami where he also had a factory. Where did he live—Miami or Chicago? The *Tribune* reported that he spent part of every year in Chicago. That was enough evidence to include his story.

1953
Paul J. Anderson

1954
Lewis Gabreez

1955
Edith Wells Scott

1956-74
Eugene K. Lydon (1903-63)
Natalie C. Lydon

In 1954, the same year his wife, Natalie, was elected to the board of Traveler's Aid, Eugene K. Lydon was appointed president of the Great Lakes Dredge and Dock Company, a firm founded by his father, William. Along with his mother and two sisters he inherited the land under the Carbide and Carbon building at 230 N. Michigan Ave.

1976
Marshall Bauer, Margaret Z. Bauer

1990-2013
Margaret Z. Bauer

2013-present
Sir Mogan Lourdenadin
Matrona D'Cruz Tharsis D'Cruz

"B" UNITS AND PENTHOUSE

1B

1920–40
Thomas Clemens

1995–present
William Freivogal, Caroline Freivogal

2B

1924–30
Frederick Stanley Oliver

Cartoon featuring William B. Huey, Chicago, 1923. Verses by J. P. McEvoy and illustrations by a cartoonist for the Chicago Evening Post. (Chicago History Museum ICHi-68183)

1940–47
William B. Huey, Catherine Huey
Elaine E. Leavitt, housekeeper

In 1915, William Huey, comparatively unknown outside of Chicago, defeated George Moore 150 to 138 to win the world championship of three-cushion billiards. He retired without defending his title. He ran the Huey Company, which manufactured blueprints and other drafting materials.

1950
John D. Hill, Alice Hill
John D. Hill, Jr., son
Ellen Hill, mother
Dorothy Nicks, servant

John Hill was a "traveling salesman, advertising." He either sold space in magazines or time on radio.

David Sciaky invented the world's greatest welding machine. Tests conducted by aircraft engineers proved that a Sciaky weld was stronger than the metal itself. It was also uncommonly fast, reducing the number of workers required to produce a quality weld. It was no longer necessary to clean metal before welding. The Sciaky welder produced such intense heat that even a grain of dust or an errant fly would become part of the impossibly strong weld.

David and his three brothers were French of Basque origin. In the run up to World War II, they owned and operated welding machine factories in France, Germany and England. While David—the inventor genius—worked in the backroom improving their product, brothers Mario, Maurice and Sam ran the business. In 1939, two years before the United States entered the war, the American aircraft industry, anticipating our involvement, wanted to make faster, lighter and more durable military planes. They petitioned the War Department to bring the Sciakys to America.

The first brother to come over was Mario, who brought with him one Sciaky welding machine. It was immediately shipped to Douglas Aircraft in California. A few months later, brother Maurice arrived with 50 machines ordered by the Navy. Shortly thereafter the Nazis overwhelmed France, capturing five Sciaky factories, giving them access to the machine's blueprints. Ten days into the Nazi occupation, Sam and David, their families and their mother escaped across the demarcation line with the help of a courageous farmer. The Germans unleashed a barrage of machine gunfire at them and somehow missed. Operatives from the Free France movement helped deliver the Sciakys to the Americans, who relocated them to Chicago and a plant near 67th and Cicero.

When David got to the United States all he had was a lead pencil and his memory. He put both to work immediately. During the war the Sciaky brothers made 3,500 welding machines for factories that in turn produced every American plane and ship, except for submarines, deployed in Europe, Africa and the Pacific. After the war, Maurice boasted, "The Germans had our factories but were not able to make a single welded plane."

David and Yvonne Sciaky
at Niagara Falls, circa 1946.
(Photo courtesy of Samy Zeitoun)

Yvonne Sciaky's recipe for Mousse
Florrie. (Courtesy of Deborah Seed)

Three months after VE day on August 28, 1945, General Charles de Gaulle of France came to Chicago and insisted on adding the Sciaky brothers to his busy schedule. At the Brown Derby Picnic Grounds at 180th and Halsted, de Gaulle personally thanked them for their role in winning the war.

David and Yvette owned an incredible library. Their prized possession was a first edition of Samuel Johnson's *A Dictionary of the English Language*, the first truly comprehensive and reliable English dictionary. They owned a chateau in France where the Dalai Lama was a frequent guest.

Yvette Sciaky, known for her kindness, generosity, elegance and grace, died at 99, giving her enough time to have pursued "her joy," reading the *oeuvre* of literary giants Marcel Proust and Henry James.

1990
David P. Spector, Lorraine Spector

They never moved into 999.

1993–present
Dr. Harvey M. Golomb, Lynn R. Golomb
Adam Golomb, son
Sara Golomb, daughter

3B

1930
Dr. Horace R. Lyons, Alice Lyons

1940–56
Owen R. Trayner, Sr. (1862–1956)
Veronica Trayner
Owen Trayner Jr. (1911–1978), son
Ruth Hagan, housekeeper

Owen R. Trayner, Sr.'s brother, Charles J., lived in the building in 1915. The son of a prominent Chicago real estate operator, Owen, Sr. studied advertising at the University of Michigan, but followed his father into the family business, as did his son, Owen, Jr. In World War II, Junior achieved the rank of lieutenant commander and served as a communications officer aboard the USS *Card*, a carrier escort in the Atlantic, and later on the *Antietam*, a full-fledged aircraft carrier in the Pacific. After returning home, Owen, Jr. scratched the itch that attracted him to harness racing. He became the secretary-treasurer of the Maywood Park Trotting Association. From time-to-time he would tear himself away from the track to build a building or sell a piece of real estate, or to check up on a plant he owned that made decorative tiles and cooking utensils.

1959–74
William Ballard Derby (1903–1987)
Falah Campbell Derby

A graduate of Yale University and Harvard Law School, William B. Derby worked in the real estate department of Northern Trust Bank. He was active in the John Crerar Library and the Chicago Yacht Club. Falah Derby grew up in Chattanooga, Tennessee. The couple married in 1942, as William was about to enter the Navy.

1974-2006
Dr. John S. Graettinger
Elizabeth "Betty" Graettinger

On December 28, 1968, Ervin Cramer, 50, received the still beating heart of the late Reymundo Montez, 24, at Presbyterian-St. Luke's Hospital. It was the second heart transplant performed in Chicago, and Dr. John Graettinger was a member of the elite medical-surgical team that pulled it off.

A native of Ontario, Canada, Dr. Graettinger graduated Harvard College and Harvard Medical School. He joined the Navy and worked on a number of cardiac research projects. In 1953, he joined the staff of Presbyterian Hospital in Chicago, which merged three years later with St. Luke's. He set up the hospital's section on cardiorespiratory diseases and conducted research into how the circulatory system adapts to acute and chronic loads. Dr. Graettinger also served as the executive vice-president of the National Residency Matching Program, and helped revise the procedures and record-keeping used to place U.S. medical school graduates in their first year of residency training.

Betty Graettinger met her future husband after singing *Ein Deutsches Requiem (A German Requiem)* by Johannes Brahms with the Wellesley College Choir, and died in her hospital bed listening to *La Traviata*. "Music fed her soul," recalled her son, John. Betty regularly attended the Lyric Opera, the Chicago Symphony Orchestra and the Music of the Baroque. She was also a political junkie and an avid supporter of civil and human rights. A perfect evening was eating take-out food in front of the television, watching Jim Lehrer on PBS and discussing the issues of the day with her friends and family.

2008-2013
Donald McLucas, Barbara Lyneis McLucas

2013-present
Rob Osmond, Adele Osmond

1924-1985
George Stuart, et al.

1985-2000
R. Todd Vieregg, Carilane Newman Vieregg

Todd Vieregg was an attorney at Sidley and Austin.

2000-present
John Van Horn, Penelope Van Horn

5B

1925
George Milton Seaman

1946-53
Max L. Pray, Mary Sherlock Pray

Attracted to risk, Max Pray was a wildcat oilman, who drilled in areas not known to harbor oil, with enough success to underwrite his philanthropy and his wife's. A prominent socialite in Chicago and Palm Beach, Mary Pray was compared to Pearl Mesta, "the hostess with the mostest," whose lavish parties "attracted artists, entertainers and powerful politicians." A bit of a wildcatter herself, Mary invested in the musical *Plain and Fancy*, a love story set in an Amish community. It turned a profit.

1969-96
Dr. John G. Graham, Jr.
Edna F. Freeman (Hellwig) Graham

Edna Hellwig's first husband, Arthur P. Hellwig, owned Hellwig, Inc., a pharmaceutical manufacturer located at Foster and Ashland. After he died, Edna married Dr. John Graham, Jr. of Grosse Point, Michigan, where he had been living with his mother.

1996-present
Gary Stephen Hopmayer
Marlene (Meme) Esther Hopmayer

Mary Sherlock Pray. (From Chicago Sun-Times, *June 20, 1953 © 1953 Sun-Times Media. All rights reserved. Used by permission and protected by the Copyright Laws of the United States. The printing, copying, redistribution, or retransmission of this Content without express written permission is prohibited.)*

6B

1928-30
Anna May Cairns

1948
Mable R. Baumgarden

1948
John James Munns, Harriet Hollingshead Munns
Gertrude Munns, daughter

J. J. Munns was vice-president of the Kristin Steel Company. In 1950, he flew around the world with his post-debutante daughter, Gertrude, during her summer break before she returned to classes at Wellesley College in the fall.

1954
R. Newton McDowell

On September 9, 1940, Congress passed an act giving the federal government authority to declare private land eminent domain for the purpose of making weaponry. This enabled the government to purchase it from its rightful owners for a few cents on the dollar, clear the land and build munitions factories. As a result, President Franklin Roosevelt authorized the conversion of 20,000 acres just west of St. Louis, Missouri into production facilities for TNT. He put the War Department in charge of the project. The 700 residents of the area read of their fate in the newspaper: the government was going to buy and destroy their homes and farms. The agent selected to handle the individual transactions was R. Newton McDowell, who in short order found himself at the center of a scandal, which ended up in front of the United States Supreme Court.

The War Department agreed to pay McDowell a 5% commission on every property he purchased. In early 1941, the Department of Justice began to scrutinize the transactions. Was Newton jacking up the prices to increase his take? Apparently, yes. And who was this guy, anyway? Who hired him? Suspicions fell on Colonel R. D. Valliant, who was quickly reassigned as far from Newton as possible. The War Department refused to honor McDowell's previous offers. They tried reclaiming the funds already paid to the former landowners, who, for the most part, ignored the government's request to give the money back.

The landowners sued the government, the case reached the U.S. Supreme Court in 1945, and the justices ruled 7–2 in favor of the plaintiffs. Sadly, their property had been burned to the ground years earlier in fires set by government workers. The plants where TNT was manufactured closed after World War II and reopened during the Cold War to process uranium. In 1986, the Department of Energy shut the operation down. They dismantled nearly 50 structures and placed the radioactive debris inside a 45-acre disposal cell, along with mounds of hot sludge and soil. Today the land is called the August Busch and Weldon Springs Conservation Areas.

Nothing much happened to R. Newton McDowell. He moved to 999 and continued his life as the president of the Consolidated Crushed Stone Corporation.

1956
Mildred Swift Snyder
(formerly Mrs. Herbert W. Kochs)
George W. K. Snyder
Herbert W. Kochs, Jr., son
Judith Ann Kochs, daughter

Mildred Swift Kochs moved to 999 after her divorce from Herbert W. Kochs, her husband of 26 years. In 1921, Herbert Kochs co-founded the Diversey Corporation to manufacturer industrial cleaning products. Mildred Swift Kochs was the first mid-western woman elected to the national board of the U.S.O. In 1962, she married her neighbor in 1A, George W. K. Snyder, who, after the wedding, moved into 6B with his bride, her children and her dog Rene, a frisky black poodle.

1965
Phillip B. Stewart, Wilhelmina H. Stewart

1966–89
Phillip S. Neidlinger, Harriet M. Neidlinger
Phyliss Neidlinger, daughter
Eleanor Neidlinger, daughter

The Neidlingers moved to Chicago from Marion, Indiana, where Phillip had been the vice-president of a savings and loan bank.

Hamburg, Missouri property destroyed in a fire instigated by R. Newton McDowell. (National Archives at Kansas City, Missouri)

1989
Joseph D. Madigan, Jr., Carol M. Madigan

Joseph D. Madigan, Jr.'s paternal grandfather established Madigan's, a department store that featured moderately priced clothing for men and women. Madigan's became a fixture in Irish communities on the south and west sides. After graduating Notre Dame and a stint in the Navy, Joseph Jr. expanded the business into the suburbs.

1991-2007
Daniel W. Vittum, Jr., Christine L. Jacobek

Dan Vittum graduated from the University of Illinois in Champaign-Urbana in 1961 with a B.S. in Chemistry and a Phi Beta Kappa key, and from the University of Michigan Law School, first in his class, Order of the Coif in 1964. He joined Kirkland & Ellis the same year, developed a large intellectual property practice, became a partner in 1970 and retired in 2000. Dan was the founding board chairman of the Noble Network of Charter Schools. He also was the chairman and general counsel for the Northwestern University Settlement Association.

2009-present
Stephen Sullivan, Marie Sullivan
Wesley Sullivan, son

Exterior view of Madigan's department store, 4030 West Madison Street, Chicago, January 31, 1953. (Chicago History Museum ICHi-68176 Image cropped.)

7B

1928
E. A. Coyle, Violet Coyle

1930
Johanna Widermann

1940-53
Hubert E. Howard, Helen M. Bishop Howard
Harold and Carrie Thibodeaux, housekeepers

After graduating from Parsons College in 1909 and Harvard Law School in 1912, Hubert E. Howard practiced law. With the passage of the 18th Amendment prohibiting the production, sale and transport of intoxicating liquors in 1919, he was appointed Federal Director of Prohibition Enforcement for Illinois. This would have put him on a collision course with Al Capone, but after a few weeks in office, he avoided his own personal St. Valentine's Day massacre. He was sent to France to captain an artillery unit.

Howard spent the bulk of his career in the coal industry. At various times he was the president of three different coal companies. He served on the National Bituminous Coal Wage Conference. In 1940, the Governor of Illinois, John M. Stelle, appointed him to the Illinois Racing Commission. One of his duties was to allocate horseracing dates to Illinois tracks. Later he headed the Arlington Jockey Club. He also developed the Hillside Shopping Center in west suburban Hillside.

At end of World War II, he was appointed chairman of the Personnel Policy Board of the Defense Department. In 1949, President Truman made Howard a recess appointment to chair the U.S. Department of Defense Munitions Board. One of his accomplishments was to standardize the weaponry used by NATO nations. Howard had three wives. Helen, who lived with him at 999, was the second.

1966
Dr. T. Howard Clarke, Thelma I. Clarke

Doctors die of the same diseases as the rest of us. Dr. Clarke, the president of the Illinois chapter of the American Cancer Society succumbed to cancer in 1973. At the time, he was the medical director of the Illinois Masonic Medical Center. He had been a professor of surgery at both the University of Illinois and Northwestern University.

Hubert E. Howard, standing second from the right, at a National Security Resources Board meeting in a White House Conference Room. Seated left to right: Secretary of Commerce, Charles Sawyer; Secretary of the Interior, Oscar Chapman; Secretary of State, Dean Acheson; National Security Resources Board Chairman, Stuart Symington; Secretary of the Treasury, John Snyder; Deputy Secretary of Defense, Stephen Early; Secretary of Labor, Maurice Tobin; Presidential Advisor, Averell Harriman.

Standing left to right: Under Secretary of Agriculture, Clarence McCormick; Director of the Bureau of the Budget, Frederick Lawton; Assistant to the President, John R. Steelman; Chairman of the Munitions, Board Hubert E. Howard and an unidentified man. (Courtesy of Harry S. Truman Library)

1973–83
Woodbury Ransom, Jr., Christina L. Ransom

The product of a long ago union between two of Kalamazoo's more prominent families—the Woodburys and the Ransoms, Woodbury Ransom, Jr. was related to former Michigan governor, Epaphroditus Ransom, and the founders of the Kalamazoo Laundry and the Global Casket Company. He was a director of the Kalamazoo Stove Company. Woody and Christina endowed the Ransom Arts Center at Eckerd College in St. Petersburg, Florida.

1983–91
Dr. Donald West King
Dr. Mary Elizabeth Dickason King

Dr. Donald King was the Richard T. Crane Professor of Pathology and the dean and vice-president of the University of Chicago Medical School. Dr. Mary King was also a pathologist. She studied at Miss Hall's and was graduated from Smith and the College of Physicians and Surgeons, where her future husband was an instructor. As the daughter of Livingston and Katherine Dickason she had lived at 999 as a newborn and a toddler from 1927 to 1929.

Tench Coxe. Engraving by Samuel Sartain after a painting by J. Paul. (Gratz Manuscript Collection, The Historical Society of Pennsylvania 2469. Image cropped.)

1991–2008
Alexander Brown Coxe, Colleen Coxe
Owen Coxe, son

Alex Coxe is an investment advisor for Merrill Lynch. His family's lineage stretches back to 13th Century England. In the 1600s, Dr. Daniel Coxe, whom Samuel Pepys mentioned in his diary, was granted a vast tract of land in the lower Mississippi valley from King Charles II. During Colonial times the Coxes owned land in the Carolinas, Western New Jersey and in the Mohawk Valley. Another ancestor, Tench Coxe, was elected to the Second Continental Congress, and was appointed to public office by both George Washington and Thomas Jefferson. He served as Alexander Hamilton's Assistant Secretary of the Treasury in 1790.

2008–present
Lawrence Freed, Clarisse Perrette
Adelaide Josie Beauregart Freed, daughter

TOP LEFT: Christina and Woodbury Ransom admiring the dedication plaque of the Ransom Visual Arts Center at Eckerd College, November 8, 1972. (Courtesy of the Eckerd College Archives)

LEFT: Ransom Arts Center. (Courtesy of photographer Robert Barnes)

8B

1928
D. K. Elliott, Marion Elliott

1930
B. H. Edwards, Estella Edwards

1953–91
Dr. Charles B. Puestow (1902–1973)
Lorraine Knowles Puestow

An internationally known surgeon and educator, Dr. Puestow was affiliated with the University of Illinois for nearly 40 years. He was also the chief of surgery for Hines Veterans Hospital and the medical director and head of medical education at Henrotin Hospital. Dr. Puestow was a founder of the Illinois Surgical Society, and its president in 1961–62. He served as a fellow of the Mayo Clinic in Rochester, Minnesota, and worked on the medical and scientific committees of the American Cancer Society, and for the National Research Council's committee on surgery. In 1971, the Veterans Administration named him a V.A. Distinguished Physician, one of seven to receive this honor.

The people who remembered Dr. Puestow best were the crippled and maimed of World War II who received treatment at the 27th Evacuation Hospital unit, which he commanded. The tented battlefield hospital followed the war throughout southern France and in the fierce Italian campaign at Cassino. Dr. Puestow won numerous citations for his military service.

1995–2001
Michael G. Hron, Carol Manzoni (1947–99)

Michael Hron and Carol Manzoni were husband and wife, as well as highly regarded attorneys. Michael was a partner at Sidley & Austin. His practice concentrated on corporate and securities law. In 1999, in addition to his responsibilities at Sidley he was named general counsel for Telephone and Data Systems, Inc.

When Carol Manzoni was named co-chair of the executive committee at Ross & Hardies in 1995, she became one of the first women to head a major law firm. She joined the firm in 1989 and specialized in labor and employment law. She was known for her aggressive leadership style, her toughness, work ethic and sense of humor.

2002
Murray L. Manaster, Ina F. Manaster

They bought shares in 999 but never moved into 8B.

2002–present
William D. Staley, Arlene D. Staley

Dr. Charles B. Puestow.
(American College of Surgeons)

9B

1928–46–47
George W. Borg

1952–89
Le Grand Cannon, Helen West Cannon
Louise Cannon, daughter; Sylvia Cannon, daughter

At least two Le Grand Cannons lived in the United States in the 1950s, an odd coincidence for a name that looks like a Frenchified misspelling of a geographic marvel. One Le Grand wrote novels about the men and women who settled the New England wilderness. The other worked for Commonwealth Edison as the director of power services. He and his family lived at 999.

1989–91
Stephen Ellis Uihlein, Alessandra Branca Uihlein
Alex Uihlein, son; Andrew Uihlein, son
Anna Lucca Uihlein, daughter

1991–95
Richard B. Fizdale
Mara Dana Fizdale

1995–present
Richard B. Fizdale
Suzanne Joy Faber
Melora Sarah Fizdale, daughter
Thomasina Rose Fizdale, daughter

PH

1917–25
Ogden Trevor McClurg

1947–50
William Clarence Tackett (1897–1958)
Vera Pearl Hutchinson Tackett
Pamela Tackett, daughter

In the years leading up to World War II, W. C. Tackett built hundreds of luxury homes in the Chicago suburbs. On May 27, 1939, his construction team completed a home in Lincolnwood that took only five days to build. A spokesman for Tackett claimed they set a new American speed record for building a home.

William Clarence Tackett. (Courtesy of Thomas W. Tackett, his nephew)

Shortly after moving to 999, Osborn and Miriam Andreas separated and divorced. Miriam continued to live in the penthouse. Osborn moved to the south side with his new wife, Margot. Both of them led interesting lives.

A competent painter, Miriam, through her close friend, Gertrude Abercrombie, the self-proclaimed Queen of Bohemian Artists, became regulars on Chicago's jazz scene. They numbered among their friends Dizzy Gillespie, Charlie Parker, Max Roach, Miles Davis and Sarah Vaughan. Gertrude and Miriam were centerpieces at all-night parties. Miriam, a fashion plate, dressed the part of an upscale jazz queen. A friend recalled her wearing a gold brocade dress, a matching jacket with a mink collar and a matching pill-box hat with an elastic chinstrap. She met fledgling writer James Purdy and introduced him to ex-hubby Osborn, who privately published Purdy's first book of short stories, *Don't Call Me By My Right Name*. Purdy went on to enjoy an acclaimed career as a novelist, short-story writer, poet and playwright. British poet, Dame Edith Stillwell, a huge supporter of his work, wrote, "There isn't a single false note, and not a sentence, or a word too much, and not a sentence or a word too little." Gore Vidal called Purdy, "an authentic American genius." Miriam and Osborn inspired four of Purdy's first five books.

Miriam spent her final years in her "chair" at the bar in the Drake Hotel.

Osborn Andreas' career contained elements of Dr. Jekyll and Mr. Hyde without the mayhem until the very end. As the good Dr. Jekyll, he was a literary critic who wrote *Joseph Conrad: A Study in Non-Conformity* and *Henry James and the Expanding Horizon: A Study of the Meaning and Basic Themes of James' Fiction*.

It was as a businessman that the dark Mr. Hyde side of Osborn Andreas emerged.

He was the chairman and chief executive officer of Pentron Electronics, and in 1967 he was federally indicted for price-fixing. Accused of defrauding millions of dollars from investors, a despondent Andreas shot himself twice in the head. The first shot damaged his forehead; the second was fatal.

Price fixing ran in the family. His brother Dwayne Andreas was the chief executive officer of industrial powerhouse Archer Daniels Midland from 1970 to 1997. In 1993 they, too, were accused of price fixing. The 2009 movie *The Informant* starring Matt Damon tells the story of that scandal. Tommy Smothers played Dwyane.

1969-2001
Donald C. Hannah, Susan W. Hannah
Daryl Hannah, daughter
Page Hannah, daughter; Don Hannah, son
(They are the children of Donald C. Hannah and his first wife—also named Susan. They grew up in Long Grove, Illinois, but stayed at 999 when visiting their father.)

Donald C. Hannah had a natural affinity for 999's penthouse with its portholes and panoramic view of the lake. Indeed he was responsible for expanding the bungalow-sized apartment of McClurg's era into a more robust penthouse. He enlarged it in the early 1970s. 990 North Lake Shore Drive was under construction. Hannah persuaded the crane operator at 990 to deliver his construction materials to the roof of 999. Apparently, Hannah remodeled his apartment without a permit from the city.

Hannah inherited the largest tugboat operation on the Great Lakes, Hannah Marine Corp., which he built into a worldwide operation. In 2002, the captains of two of Hannah's tugboats were awarded the American Merchant

Daryl Hannah, shown in costume from the movie Splash, *was never a permanent resident at 999. She did visit her father, Donald Hannah, and slept over as a child.*
(© Douglas Kirkland/Corbis)

Seamanship Trophy for an "extraordinary feat of seafaring" when they answered a mayday call from a 400-foot barge that had escaped its moorings and was floundering wildly in 12-foot waves and gale-force winds on Lake Michigan. The tugs located the barge and towed it back to safety. One of the vessels was named the *Donald C. Hannah*.

Susan W. Hannah, his second wife, was the marketing director of USAuction Inc., a company founded by her husband.

Screen actress Daryl Hannah played a mermaid opposite Tom Hanks in *Splash*, a somersaulting replicant in *Blade Runner* and a one-eyed assassin in Quentin Tarantino's *Kill Bill* films. She dated John F. Kennedy, Jr. Her sister Page Hannah, also an actress, married Lou Adler, a well-known music producer with a star on the Hollywood Walk of Fame. Don Hannah tried acting and appeared in *A Nightmare on Elm Street* as surfer #2. Mostly he worked behind the scenes as a producer, second unit director and video playback operator.

1993–2000
Richard E. Duffy, Sheila C. Duffy

Richard Duffy was a developer who worked on the expansion of McCormick Place (1991–96).

2000–present
William Cheeseman, Linda Cheeseman

"C" UNITS

2C

1915–30
Alexander Smith, Mary Smith

1947
John Dean, Isabel Dean

1947
Preston Tucker
Lucille Tucker Holmes, mother

Preston Tucker had two apartments, 9A and 2C. His mother Lucille lived in Ypsilanti, Michigan but stayed in 2C when she visited Chicago. When Tucker got into financial trouble, he tried to put both apartments in her name. Since his mother didn't live in the building, the board of directors rejected this proposal.

1949–74
Francois Pope, Antoinette Pope

A Frenchman born in Valentigney of parents who really knew how to cook, Francois Pope (1896–1971) immigrated to the United States as a young man. In Chicago he met his wife, Antoinette, an ex-pat from Seneca, Italy. They both loved *haute cuisine* and opened a cooking school in their home on the south side. In the beginning, a lesson cost 75¢. Soon the school outgrew their kitchen and reopened at a variety of different locations in the city as the Antoinette Pope Schools of Fancy Cookery. In 1948, Antoinette published the *Antoinette Pope School Cookbook*, which sold over a million copies. Francois went on television in 1951 with *Creative Cookery*, one of the first cooking shows in the country, and became a pre-Julia Child celebrity chef.

According to their grandson, Robert Pope, they paid $50,000 for their apartment in 1949.

TOP: *Antoinette Pope. Photo signed "To my sweet husband affectionately, Antoinette January 1, 1939."*

RIGHT: *Francois Pope with muskie caught June 21, 1944, Grindstone Lake, Hayward, Wisconsin. Weight: 26-1/2 pounds; Length: 45"; Girth 20".*

(Both photos courtesy of Robert Pope)

1977–81
Melvyn Kushner, Barbara Kushner
Barbara's daughter

1981–83
Dr. William J. McNabb

Dr. William J. McNabb was a dentist.

1983
Dr. Randall Toig, Teri Toig

A graduate of the University of Pittsburgh, Dr. Randall Toig was an obstetrician and gynecologist affiliated with Northwestern Memorial Hospital. Teri Toig was the president and chief executive officer of the Zenner Consulting Group, an attorney search and placement firm based in Chicago. She also founded a firm that provided scholarship assistance to law students. Earlier in her career, she practiced law at Kirkland & Ellis, focusing on corporate and real estate matters. She studied international relations and economics at *L'Institut d'Etudes Politiques de Paris*.

1991-93
Daniel W. Vittum Jr.

1993-99
Thomas B. Haynes

2001-04
Edward Berube

2005-present
Stanley J. Andrie, Barbara A. Andrie

3C

1928
H. L. Baumgarden, Mabel Baumgarden

1947
Helen Jones

1952-57
Dr. Arthur R. Colwell, Jeanne H. Colwell

On June 16, 1950, Northwestern University awarded Dr. Arthur R. Colwell the first Irving S. Cutter professorship in medicine and named him chairman of the department of medicine.

Dr. Arthur J. Colwell, Sr. (Galter Health Sciences Library Special Collections, Feinberg School of Medicine, Chicago)

1958
Harrison J. Bligh, Perle Lund Bligh

On June 10, 1967 North Park College dedicated a ten-foot high statue created by sculptor Egon Weiner, a gift from Harrison J. Bligh, the late manager of a book publishing company. It depicted Christ dressed in long robes with his hands cupped in front of him.

Ten-foot-high statue of Christ named Learn of Me *by Egon Weiner and donated to North Park College with funds provided by Harrison J. Bligh. (Photo by Krista Reynen)*

1962
Gordon C. P. Fletcher, Avis C. Fletcher

1969-79
Alan Stephenson Boyd
Flavil Juanita Townsend Boyd

After leaving the Army Air Force in 1945, Alan S. Boyd returned to college, received his Juris Doctorate from the University of Virginia's School of Law in 1948 and began practicing law in his home state of Florida. In 1959, President Dwight Eisenhower appointed him to the Civil Aeronautics Board. Ike's successor, John F. Kennedy, elevated him to the chairmanship of that board. From that perch, Boyd helped the airline industry standardize rate reductions, encouraged airline service to smaller American cities and fought for airplane designs that met the needs of the physically impaired. President Lyndon B. Johnson made Boyd undersecretary of commerce for transportation and then the 12th member of his cabinet as the nation's first secretary of transportation. Boyd moved to Chicago in 1969 to become the President of the Illinois Central Railroad. Subsequently he was the President of Amtrak and later president of Airbus Industrie. In 1994, he received the prestigious Tony Jannus Award for his contributions to aviation.

Alan Stephenson Boyd, the nation's first Secretary of Transportation, meets with President Lyndon Baines Johnson in the oval office. (The Lyndon Baines Johnson Presidential Library)

1979-1996
Stanley N. Allan, Mary S. Allan

Conceiving, designing, engineering, building and completing a 98-mile rapid transit railway system inside, around and under one of the busiest and most important cities in the world was a public works project comparable to the Great Pyramid of Giza, the Panama Canal and the Golden Gate Bridge. Architect Stanley Allan of Chicago's Harry Weese and Associates was a senior participant in every phase of the creation and development of the Washington, D.C. Metro system (1965–76). It brought public rail transportation not only to the District of Columbia, but to parts of Virginia and Maryland, as well. Allan was the project manager in charge of the realization of this marvel. When the architectural reviews came in, they were triumphant: The "lofty barrel-vaulted volumes" are "magisterial for an American public works project." The effect is "precise, immaculate and colossal." It is "one of the best looking things in the capital." The Metro "restored to civil engineering the visual grandeur and might characteristic of the Great Roman and Victorian engineering feats."

1996-2003
Frederick L. Feldkamp, Judith L. Feldkamp

A graduate of the University of Michigan law school, Fred Feldkamp became a partner at Foley & Lardner, the nation's 15th largest law firm. He was an internationally recognized expert in asset securitization. When he was working in their Chicago office, he was involved in the securitization of Commonwealth Edison's assets following deregulation.

2003
Michael Gallo, Rose Anne Gallo

2011-present
Mark Hausberg, Margaret Hausberg

A Washington D.C. subway station. Stanley Allan oversaw the construction of the D.C. Metro. (©iStock.com/ Zeiss4Me)

4C

1928-30
W. H. Clarke

1930
Florence Addington

1940-90
William B. Requa, Susan Requa
Eloise ReQua (1903-89), daughter
Ailvirlge Stake, maid

The ancestors of William Requa were Huguenots, who fled to England from France in 1681. Eight years later the family began migrating to America. They settled in upstate New York. Two centuries later, William Requa and his younger brother Charles purchased, stored and distributed grain in the Chicago area.

Eloise ReQua saved newspapers, magazines, posters and pamphlets—indeed almost anything that had been printed. The language of origin was irrelevant. In today's parlance, she was a hoarder. She espoused a philosophy to explain her quirkiness. She believed that to understand the peoples of the world it was imperative to understand their history, culture, geography and economy. So she collected everything that loosely fit that brief. That turned out to be a lot of stuff.

With a grant from the Rockefeller Foundation in 1932, Eloise established the Library of International Relations, and became its director librarian. The library collected printed material from around the world, the only repository of information on both sides of almost every issue. At the time of her death in 1989, the library had acquired 300,000 separate volumes of treatises, governmental documents and other literature related to the daily life and commerce of hundreds of countries. Her successor Mickie Voges observed, "The reason this collection is a slice of heaven is because ReQua wasn't a librarian. She didn't start the collection based upon any...pretentious notion of what scholarly publications are. She kept absolutely everything, even press releases." In 1973, Eloise was given the Chicago Medal of Merit, the highest honor Mayor Richard J. Daley could bestow on a private citizen.

1991
Dwight M. Cleveland

Dwight Cleveland, a real estate developer, bought and sold 4C in 92 days without ever living in it. Instead he found a distraction inside the walls of a modest home in Three Oaks, Michigan. It had belonged to the owner of a movie theater who stuffed decades of film posters behind the walls of his home as insulation. Cleveland collected movie posters, an art form he believed was indigenous to America. Curious to peek behind the walls, he bought the home, began to surgically demolish the sheetrock and discovered, among hundreds of rarities, the poster collector's holy grail, a pristine poster created for Busby Berkeley's *Gold Diggers of 1935*. In 2007, he estimated the value of his collection at $3.5 million. He looked for a buyer for years without finding anyone who would meet his price. It was much easier to flip 4C to Mr. and Mrs. Nelson.

Eloise ReQua.
(Chicago History Museum
ICHi-68177)

1991–96
Maurice "Sandy" Nelson Jr., Doris E. Nelson

Sandy Nelson was the head of Inland Steel Industries Inc.'s steel unit from 1991 to 1996, which corresponded almost exactly to his time at 999. Prior to that, he had been the president of ALCOA's sheet and plate division.

1996–99
John C. Halston, Kirsten Halston

John Halston worked for Quiet Light Securities.

1999–00
Robert Stein, Deborah Stein

They owned shares in the building, but never moved into 999.

2000–present
Dr. William R. Panje, Helen S. Panje

5C

1915–30
Frederick Clayton Letts, Marjorie Dodd Letts

1947
Frank H. Linden, Kathleen H. Linden

1953
Dr. Chauncey C. Maher (1898–1970)
Martha Maher

Dr. Maher was a prominent cardiologist in Chicago for 40 years. He had been a member of the Northwestern University Medical School from 1928 until 1965. He was also the chief of staff at Passavant Memorial Hospital and a member of the staff of Cook County Hospital from 1938–47. He served with distinction in World War I, at different times attached to the American and French armies. For his service, the French awarded him the *Croix de Guerre*.

1960
John Paul North, Grace H. North

Dr. Chauncey C. Maher.
(Courtesy of the National Library of Medicine.)

Lawrence O'Connor made an appearance in Sherman Skolnick's 1973 book, *The Secret History of Airplane Sabotage*. Skolnick was an investigative gadfly and author of works that were viewed as either highly paranoid or unflinchingly honest depending on the reader's politics. If Cold War warriors imagined a Communist hiding behind every rock, Skolnick saw a conspiracy in every coincidence. When he was right, he was very right. His dogged investigative work sent Judge Otto Kerner, a former governor of Illinois, to prison.

His discussion of O'Connor begins, "For many years, like clockwork, one Chicagoan went to Washington, D.C. on Monday and came back Friday afternoon on Flight 553 or its equivalent, Lawrence T. O'Connor, Apt. 5-C, 999 North Lake Shore Drive, Chicago, Illinois. On Friday December 8, 1972, he received a call from someone he knows in the White House, telling him not to take Flight 553 but to go instead to a special meeting."

What makes that particular flight on that particular day noteworthy is that it crashed and everybody on board was killed, except for a supposed CIA agent who parachuted to safety, which begs the question, who brings a parachute on a commercial flight? What makes that question even more intriguing is the passenger manifest. Aboard that United flight 553 was James W. Krueger, attorney for the Northern Natural Gas Co., a company former U.S. Attorney General John Mitchell had prosecuted. At this point in American history, Mitchell had just finished running Richard Nixon's campaign for re-election in 1972. But Carl Bernstein and Bob Woodward were about to light the fuse that connected the White House and the campaign to a break-in at the Watergate Office Complex.

According to Skolnick, Krueger boarded the plane with "irreplaceable papers of a sensitive nature," which apparently proved Mitchell had accepted bribes from another gas company to go after Northern Natural Gas. Also traveling on that flight were Michelle Clark, a CBS newswomen working on a Watergate story, and Helen Hunt, the wife of Watergate co-conspirator, E. Howard Hunt. Mrs. Hunt was making noises that she was planning to blow the lid off the scandal if her husband wasn't released from prison. Skolnick claimed that in her carry-on bag, she had $2 million that she had stolen from CREEP, the Committee to Re-Elect the President.

Was the crash a loony but deadly outgrowth of the Watergate cover-up? Was it a conspiracy within a conspiracy, or merely a tragic coincidence? What is certain is that flight 553 never made it to Chicago. Enemies of the White House and everything they carried on board were gone, and Lawrence O'Connor didn't get on the plane. Who called him? With Skolnick behind the story, it's prudent to ask, did the phone call actually happen? The crash certainly did.

Skolnick's Lawrence O'Connor's middle initial was "T." But it was actually an "L" for 999's Lawrence O'Connor. Since Skolnick correctly placed O'Connor in the building, the mistake was either an innocent transcription error or sloppy reportage indicative of Skolnick's episodic indifference to veracity. Lawrence L. O'Connor was an attorney who had been the General Counsel of Sears, Roebuck and Co. and the dean of the DePaul University Law School.

Lawrence L. O'Connor.
(Photographer: Fabian Bachrach.
Special Collections and Archives,
DePaul University Libraries,
Chicago)

1983
J. Alexander Stevens, Jolene Stevens

J. Alexander Stevens became an Exerciser Member of the Chicago Board of Options Exchange when he purchased a full Chicago Board of Trade membership in 1983. In the lore of 999, there is a special place reserved for J. Alexander. He was fond of sunbathing in the nude on his patio, which faced the courtyard, affording those residents who lived on higher floors a view that was not included in the monthly assessment. His public displays were also available to people who lived at 229 and 990 Lake Shore Drive, and 234 East Walton. While indifferent to the visual field of others, J. Alexander was uber-adverse to noise. Jolene and he moved to a quiet village in Switzerland that did not allow cars. In 2006, Mr. and Mrs. Stevens formed Eagle, a market-making business.

1999-present
Joyce Dawson

1928
J. H. Rogers

1940-51
Robert Neil Cowham (1890-1957)
June Provines Cowham (1895-1983)
Neil Cowham, son
Max and Mary Pray, subletters

In 1932, Robert Cowham tried his hand at playwriting, crafting the one-act comedy *The Midnight Ride of Paul Revere*. The play failed to launch him into the stratosphere of legitimate theater, so he switched careers and became a patent adjuster. June began her career as a Chicago journalist. She covered the murder of Bobby Franks and the trial of his killers, Nathan Leopold and Richard Loeb. She accompanied them on their journey to Joliet Penitentiary. The *Chicago Tribune* promoted her to columnist. Using her maiden name Provines as her byline, she wrote the daily column "Front Views and Profiles." She never sacrificed an individual for a line of type. For many years she had a radio show on WGN. Monday through Friday, it could be found at 720 on the dial at 10 p.m. on weekdays.

Before moving into apartment 5B, Max and Mary Pray had sublet the Cowham's apartment.

1955-88
Kenneth M. Wright, Judith Beebe Wright
Emily Muir Wright, daughter

Kenneth Wright married Judith Beebe Atwood in 1959 in Christ Church in Winnetka. His father worked in the coal industry.

1988–90
David W. Frisbee

David W. Frisbee did not invent the Frisbee. He was a vice-president and development officer for Gerald D. Hines Interests.

1991
Robert Stahr Beardsley, Cindy Beardsley

In 1830, an ancestor of Robert Beardsley, Dr. Havilah Beardsley, was the first white settler and landowner of what would become the city of Elkhart, Indiana. Robert Beardsley grew up in Elkhart but moved to Chicago to trade commodities.

1993–present
Jan Zechman

7C

1928–30
Louis A. Rang, Eugenie "Jean" Farrow Rang

1949–79
Marshall Gross Sampsell (1904–1973)
Margaret Carr Sampsell
Miranda Carr Sampsell, daughter
Mary Carr "Niki" Sampsell, daughter
Mr. and Mrs. Louis Skidmore, Jr.

Marshall G. Sampsell was a senior partner at Isham, Lincoln & Beale, one of the city's oldest law firms. He graduated Yale in 1926 and Harvard Law School in 1929. He was a director of R. R. Donnelley & Sons. Margaret Sampsell was one of Chicago's more fashion-forward women. "The tweed was a gray-blue in color, the blue tone heightened by the blouse Mrs. Sampsell was wearing, collar out, as the fashion seems to be these days." Daughter Miranda worked for Marshall Field's in the advertising department, while her sister, Niki, began her career at Tiffany's in Manhattan.

While touring Scandinavia in 1963, the Sampsells let the Skidmores use their apartment. Louis graduated from Yale's school of architecture. His father was the head of architectural design for the World's Fair of 1933.

Margaret Carr Sampsell dusts up the area in front of her fireplace in 7C. (From Chicago Tribune, March 30, 1958 *© 1958 Chicago Tribune. All rights reserved. Used by permission and protected by the Copyright Laws of the United States. The printing, copying, redistribution, or retransmission of this Content without express written permission is prohibited.)*

The coolest letter of recommendation for any prospective tenant of 999 was penned on behalf of Thomas Campbell. It was dated July 23, 1979 and written on stationery with the Supreme Court of the United States embossed on the letterhead.

Gentlemen:
Tom Campbell was employed by me as a clerk for one year ending August 1978. He is a young man of excellent character and with more than enough brains and intelligence to exist comfortably in the practice of law.
Sincerely yours,
Byron White

For those too young to remember, Byron White was a justice on the United States Supreme Court. He also came in second in the 1937 Heisman Trophy voting and was an NFL all-pro tailback for the Pittsburgh Steelers and the Detroit Lions. In his playing days he was known as Whizzer White.

Campbell was valedictorian of Chicago's St. Ignatius College Prep, class of 1969. He received his B.A. and M.A. from the University of Chicago, a J.D. from Harvard Law School (1976) and a Ph.D. in economics from the University of Chicago (1980), where his mentor was Noble Prize winner Milton Friedman. He clerked for Justice White from 1977 to 1978. In 1980 to 1981, he served as a White House Fellow in the offices of the Chief of Staff and Chief Counsel. President Reagan appointed him to the Federal Trade Commission (1981–83). He became a professor at Stanford Law School (1983–88) and served two terms in the U.S. House of Representatives (1988–92) before failing to win the Republican nomination for the U.S. Senate. In 1993, he became a California State Senator. The *California Journal* rated him the best problem solver, the most ethical and the best overall state senator. When Bill Clinton appointed Congressman Norman Mineta to be his Secretary of Commerce, Campbell ran for his empty seat and easily won. This time his stay in the U.S. House of Representatives lasted three terms (1995–2000). He won the Republican nomination for the 2000 U.S. Senate race, but Senator Dianne Feinstein thumped him. Following that defeat he entered private practice as a lawyer and later accepted the position of dean of the Chapman University School of Law. Campbell had not lost his taste for public service and accepted a variety of positions under California Governor Arnold Schwarzenegger.

Thomas J. Campbell clerked for Justice Byron "Whizzer" White of the United States Supreme Court and later became a two-term congressman representing California in the U.S. House of Representatives. (Courtesy of U.S. Government Printing Office)

1981–2003
Milton "Mickey" Lewis, Diane Sabath Lewis

Mickey Lewis became the president of William A. Lewis Clothing Co., a company started by his parents. Milton took it from a store at 47th and Ashland to regional prominence. In radio and television commercials, the William A. Lewis brand was buoyed by the popular slogan "Where the models buy their clothes." This did not mean that models actually shopped there. The bulk of Lewis' customers were recent immigrants to America who bought discount clothing from him.

2005–present
Dr. Tord D. Alden, Carrie Alden
Emersen Alden, daughter
Grae Alden, son

The shopping experience at William A. Lewis.

This dark-blue "little g" wooden yo-yo was made by the Duncan Toys Company in the 1950s. (Smithsonian Institution Collections, National Museum of American History, Behring Center)

8C

1928–40
Mr. and Mrs. Frank Kennicott Reilly

1947
Donald F. Duncan

If all he did were to create the Duncan Parking Meter Company, Donald Duncan would be a notable resident of 999. By 1959, it had manufactured 80% of the world's parking meters. When he founded the Good Humor mobile frozen treats franchise, he established the diversity of his entrepreneurialism. But he earned the bulk of his fame and fortune from the Duncan Yo-Yo, the best-selling and most revered yo-yo of all time. Duncan introduced the looped slip-string, which made it possible to perform advanced tricks and propelled the Genuine Duncan Yo-Yo into the pantheon of children's toys.

1947–63
G. Kenneth Crowell

In the aftermath of World War II, Kenneth Crowell joined the C.I.C. association of Chicago, comprised of former army counter-intelligence officers. While a partner in the Chicago law firm of Crowell and Leibman, he was elected to the board of directors of the International Cellucotton Products Company. He sold his apartment in 1963 when he moved to Neenah, Wisconsin to become an executive vice-president of Kimberly-Clark Corp., the makers of Kleenex.

1963–94
Elizabeth Paepcke

1995–present
Richard Gordon, Elinor Gordon

1913–15
David G. Hamilton

1928–38
Colonel George Tayloe Langhorne (1867–1962)
Mary Waller Langhorne

1946–83
Dr. James K. Stack, Mary S. Stack
James K. Stack, Jr., son; John Stack, son
Christopher Stack, son

Dr. James K. Stack, Sr., an orthopedic surgeon on the staff of the Northwestern University Medical School for 50 years, helped develop the Magnuson-Stack shoulder procedure, designed to reduce shoulder instability. For 30 years, he was also the attending orthopedic surgeon at Cook County Hospital. He served as the chief-of-staff at Passavant Hospital (1955–56). Dr. Stack attended Notre Dame in the 1920s. He played on some of Knute Rockne's most celebrated football teams. Also a track star, he set the school record for the quarter mile. In 1960, his son James, Jr. followed in his fleet footsteps and sped to the fastest 440-yards in Yale University history.

James Stack was a reserve on the 1924 Notre Dame football team, which featured the "Four Horseman," went undefeated and beat Stanford in the Rose Bowl 27-10. (University of Notre Dame Archives GBBY 57G/0261)

1983–89
Stephen Ellis Uihlein, Alessandra Branca Uihlein
Alex Uihlein, son

1991–95
Richard B. Fizdale
Mara Dana Fizdale

1989–91
Martha Ossian Hesse

1995–present
Richard B. Fizdale
Suzanne Joy Faber
Melora Sarah Fizdale, daughter
Thomasina Rose Fizdale, daughter

With one foot in the world of business and the other in government, Martha Hesse's career spanned both worlds with equal skill. After his inauguration, President Ronald Reagan appointed her executive director of the task force on management reform for the U.S. Office of Management and Budget. In 1982, she became Assistant Secretary for Management and Administration for the U.S. Energy Department. Four years later he elevated her to chairman of the U.S. Federal Energy Regulation Commission.

Her business résumé is equally impressive: co-founder and chief operating officer of SEI Information Technology (1969–80); senior vice-president corporate affairs for First Chicago Corporation (1986–89); president and CEO of Hesse Gas Co. (1990–2003); and board member and later chairman of Enbridge Energy Partners (2003–). Hesse also sits on many other corporate boards.

Martha Hesse shaking hands with President Reagan at the Enrico Fermi Award Ceremony at the Department of Energy Conference Room, April 25, 1983. (Ronald Reagan Presidential Library)

CHAPTER SEVENTEEN

Forever Relevant

The passage of time is not kind to objects made by man. To paraphrase Cyndi Lauper, weather changes everything. Temperature and humidity expand and contract wood and metal as if they were alive and breathing. Sunlight discolors and ice displaces surfaces. Pellets of hail chip paint. Rain nestles in crevices. Gravity leads water down a path of least resistance, sometimes to microscopic openings, gateways to interior walls, and a new path is created, essentially the same way the Colorado River sculpted the Grand Canyon. Water and wind reshape what the mason's trowel had once made smooth. Corrosion creeps like an assassin toward all things metallic.

The innards of buildings also bend to the will of time. Screws work their way loose. Switches break. Pipes leak. Boilers cough. Manually operated elevators go electric. Cable TV gets invented. Visual home entertainment morphs into a venture capital infused rush of choices. Three channels become 12 and then a thousand. Videocassettes made Beta obsolete only to be displaced by the DVD, which is in the process of being consumed by video streaming and who knows what else. *I Love Lucy* arrived in a rabbit-eared analogue haze. Tony Soprano ran his crew with high-definition authority. The asocial behavior of *Breaking Bad* looked even more deranged enhanced as it was by the clarity of digital technology. Soon 3D-TV will throw spears at your heart, boomerangs at your head and hand grenades at your feet. It will lift you from your easy chair, hurl you head first into the digestive tract of a black hole and drop you into the first row of a concert given by the greatest rock band that hasn't been born yet. Someday you will watch gap-jawed as a holographic Rhett Butler emerges from a device in your bedroom to carry a panting Scarlett up a staircase you didn't even know you had. Skype, Bluetooth, iTunes, Xbox and their cousins are

drum rolls in the inexorable parade of change.

Weather, obsolescence and technological breakthroughs challenge the board of directors of 999. With every problem comes a philosophic choice. To keep expenses at a minimum should the board defer maintenance, replacing moribund aspects of the building only when they have passed a point of no return? Or should the board address the first sign of decay when the risks are almost nonexistent or wait until something vital snaps, crumbles and dies? Should the board seek a cable TV and Internet service provider whose offerings include a portal to the future or wait until the residents are clamoring for the latest and greatest?

The current board is convinced that the only way to maintain a first-class building is with first-class attention to detail, and that the costliest time to dedicate resources to an issue is when it is too far gone to ignore. Outside engineers are brought in on a regular basis to inspect the building, identify potential cancers and recommend courses of action. When something must be done, there is no cutting corners, no ignoring expert advice and no low bid always wins—the most thoughtful and complete bid prevails. Still, there are unpredictable emergencies. Rather than pulling a succession of unexpected special assessments out of a hat, the board prefers to maintain a substantial reserve whenever possible.

The mansard roof is an example of 999's maintenance principles in action. For nearly a century Chicago's weather attacked its slate panels with the persistence of a medieval siege. Panels were picked off one at a time. Some cracked or faded. Others detached. A few remained pristine. The mansard roof is only visible from the street at a distance. To patch up the roof, slate panels of roughly the same quality and color could have been good enough. But, at 999, good enough is never good enough. To ensure a perfect match, the replacement slate was acquired from

*The current board is convinced
that the only way to maintain
a first-class building is with
first-class attention to detail,
and that the costliest time
to dedicate resources to an issue
is when it is too far gone
to ignore.*

the same quarry in Indiana that produced the original 1912 slate, approved by Marshall, McClurg and Shepard.

The dormers, which protrude from the sloped mansard roof, needed to be painted. A new coat could have been applied on top of layers of old, older and oldest paint. Instead decades of ancient coloration were scraped off the metal frames, revealing three distinct types of metal that had been used in the original construction. Each one had to be prepared and primed differently, the only way fresh paint would properly adhere to the overall surface. A casual observer strolling on the beach could not possibly notice this attention to detail. But for the residents of 999, their home had been returned to its original glory and value was preserved.

During the mansard project, structural engineers inspected the entire roof. They discovered the concrete beneath it did not require any repairs, testimony to the materials and construction practices of E. L. Schneider, Jr. & Son.

In 2002, the board agreed to an extensive riser project. 999's 17 risers carry fresh water up to the apartments and dirty water down to the sewers. After 90 years of commendable service, 11 of them needed to be replaced top to bottom. The other six risers were working well—still are—and didn't need to be replaced at that time. Riser-by-riser, floor-by-floor, apartment-by-apartment, old pipe was removed and new, higher quality pipe took its place. The project lasted 18 months and cost $1.8 million. Intrusive and expensive, yes, but the new risers have a life expectancy of 75 to 100 years. The cost was amortized over decades, allowing future generations to pay for the healthy pipes they will be using then. Recently, that tactic was challenged and a new one adopted. By dipping into the reserve, paying off a portion of the riser debt and refinancing the remaining debt at lower interest rates, the board was able to reduce the monthly assessment for here and now residents.

During the riser project, the lobby was renovated. The carpet was showing its age. Decades of uneven wear and discoloration were replaced with marble. Limestone walls were stripped of generations of paint. Since 1913, staircase railings had been covered with 18 layers of paint, blurring the intricate detailing. They were restored to their original metal. New furniture was installed in the lobby, as were new light fixtures. Vintage photographs taken between 1910 and 1920 depicting life in Chicago during 999's formative years were acquired from the Chicago History Museum and hung in the lobby.

The building's covered driveway is the first impression visitors have of 999. Over the years its base had been nicked and scratched as faint-of-heart drivers navigated its curved and narrow space. The damaged areas were not repaired. They were replaced.

In recent years, all exterior window frames were stripped to bare wood and inspected. Frames that were beyond repair were thrown away and new ones were installed. Everything was repainted. Sewer lines have been replaced, light wells renovated and fire escapes repaired. A favorable bulk rate deal was negotiated with a premier cable television and Internet provider.

A few years ago the Chicago City Council passed a tough new life safety ordinance that applied to every high-rise building in the city. The required work had to begin in 2011 and be completed by 2015. For 999 the scope of the Life Safety project includes new fire rated doors for each apartment, the lobby and the 10th floor. A new damper was placed in the boiler room ductwork. An emergency communication system and smoke detectors were installed in the back stairwells. All fire hose locations will be clearly identified. All windows that lead to fire escapes will be inspected. Those that are not fire-rated will be replaced.

As part of 999's 100th anniversary, the board approved a plan to upgrade the roof deck. Previously, the deck

*999 Lake Shore Drive is not
a fossilized relic preserved in
amber, nor is it exactly the
same building Marshall and
Fox designed. Its external
beauty continues to dazzle.*

consisted of a handful of wrought-iron tables and chairs, a grill and a scattering of plants. The wooden floor was weather damaged. Despite its aesthetic emptiness, the deck was a convivial place to meet neighbors, enjoy outdoor cooking and watch the annual Air Show. The deck deserved to be upgraded.

The roof deck was always 29-feet across at its widest point and 37-feet long at its farthest reach. A committee of 999ers re-imagined it. They created five distinct outdoor spaces that seamlessly flowed from one to another. The entrance was made level; an ankle-twisting set of stairs was eliminated. The masterstroke was adding a cocktail lounge near the entrance with a custom-made stone fire pit and a black granite counter top. A sofa and two chairs provide comfortable seating. The new flooring was constructed of Italian pavers, a theme which was repeated in the outdoor kitchen. The roof deck is clothed in whitewashed cedar. Four steps up from the lounge is the pergola, its space defined by two parallel six-foot-long planters. Between them is a large rectangular table that seats eight. Next comes the dining area with two round tables that seat four people each. The highlights of the kitchen include two outdoor grills from which a cornucopia of foods spring forth, a seven-foot black granite countertop with four barstools, storage space for cooking utensils and cleaning products, a sink and a long hose for watering the plants. Finally a second lounge overlooks the lake. It was designed for relaxation with two lounge chairs, an ottoman and a cocktail table.

Clumps of blue-green North Wind switch grasses reach skyward from rectangular planters on the south wall. In the summertime finely textured yellow flowers emerge to crown the grass. Formally manicured boxwood scrubs, trimmed to be flat on the top and sides, line the pergola. Hydrangeas and clematises gracefully climb up and embrace the trellis, pergola, latticework and walls. The greenery and flora on the deck complement the spectacular views of the lake and provide contrast with the cityscapes that partially surround 999. As of this writing no other building on East Lake Shore Drive has a roof deck.

999's landmark status limits the extent to which the building's exterior may be altered. The Landmark Commission must approve any proposed change beyond routine maintenance. The red brick can never be doused in green paint. A billboard cannot be erected on the roof. Turning the rear courtyard into a swimming pool is a no-no.

But the interiors of the apartments are the dominion of the tenants. The only building rules protect the building's structural integrity. Any interior wall can be moved—or removed—as long as it doesn't hold up the building. Examples of this can be found in the photographs displayed on the next two pages. Those photographs and the ones on the following pages demonstrate different approaches to decorating 999.

999 Lake Shore Drive is not a fossilized relic preserved in amber, nor is it exactly the same building Marshall and Fox designed. Its external beauty continues to dazzle. What one sees is lasting greatness, dipped in the Beaux Arts, commanding the bend on the Drive and the great mass of buildings arrayed behind it: first among equals. What cannot be seen is its heartbeat, strong enough to outlast the next 100 years, or its character—no other vintage building in Chicago has done more to remain forever relevant.

OPPOSITE: The foyer of a B-side apartment seems to be imported from a story spun by Scheherazade.

B-tier living rooms. The photographer stood in almost the exact same spot for both pictures on this page. In the top image, a large painting dominates the wall at the upper left. Below, the wall has been shortened to accommodate an entrance to the kitchen and a view of the lake.

On the right side of the top photo, a wide entranceway leads to a chartreuse room—a library. In the center left of the top picture on page 219, the library is behind French doors and transom-like windows—holdovers from their original installation in 1912–13.

*The oddly cool chartreuse of one apartment and the hot reds
of another in the C-tier (bottom) testify to the lack of a unified
design sensibility. From an infinity of hues, residents pick
whatever brightens their day.*

Four public spaces from different apartments. The one at the top of this page is from a B-unit; the others are located in the A-tier.

Four approaches to decorating the library.

ALL PHOTOS THIS SPREAD SHANE WELCH, CHICAGO

Afterword

riginally *999: A History of Chicago in Ten Stories* was going to be an eight to 16 page brochure. Its purpose was to commemorate the building's 100th anniversary and to serve as a marketing aid to help tenants sell their apartments. An early outline called for a beauty shot of 999's exterior, a page or two of history with an emphasis on Benjamin Marshall and the establishment of his architectural chops, a list of notable residents, a compendium of recent improvements, the differences between co-ops and condos, and as many contemporary photographs of apartments as the remaining space allowed. The final product pretty much turned out to be the initial vision on steroids.

At the beginning, I asked two questions, both of which inflated the size of the book. "Where did the landfill come from?" and "Who lived here?" As the answers revealed themselves, I lost all interest in a puffed up marketing piece. As I began to research the land, the building and its people, I realized that on a small scale I had a history book on my hands. The back-story overflowed with possibilities. At first, I thought it began with Potter Palmer's desire for a frontage road and George Streeter's collision with a sandbar. I was prepared to end it with the murder of John A. Kirk and Streeter's life sentence. It took a few years to understand that the Chicago Fire created the conditions where re-imagining the near north side became a necessity and that the decision by Ogden McClurg and Stuart Shepard to build 999 on Streeter's battlefield actually ended the war. These stories could not be squeezed into a brochure.

When I decided to try to run down *every* person who ever lived at 999, all fidelity to the initial concept went kaput. I no longer cared how long it took to finish the book or if it turned out to be a thousand pages.

Writing *999* was a long slog. Osborn Andreas is a case in point. For nearly two years I went with the assumption that the census taker had written Oscar Andrews on the census form. I couldn't find anything about that guy and around 50 others—needles lost in the haystack of history. The search was as maddening as looking for Mary Smith.

Since the last time I looked, Ancestry.com had created a typed version of every name in the 1940 census. With a click of my mouse, Oscar transformed into Osborn. Andrews became Andreas. I didn't flinch when I learned that Osborn had been indicted for price-fixing and killed himself, presumably to avoid prison or to bury his shame. Would his inclusion add value to 999? Probably not, nor, I reasoned, would it detract from it. He was a flawed man, a professor of literature and a crook, whose wife's story included Dizzy Gillespie and Charlie Parker, a boon to any book. In a shorter format, the Andreas' story would have been thrown out with the trash. Now the couple has a permanent place in 999's historical record. No other vintage apartment building in Chicago has an historical record.

Taking Andreas a step farther, I confess to a great fondness for the tenants whose foibles made them human. There are two exceptions—R. Newton McDowell cheated people out of their homes and Terry Druggan killed for expediency's sake. But what harm did Muriel Rockefeller McCormick bring to anyone with her urn full of ashes? I would take the first Mrs. Dahlberg's eccentricities over a room of bean counters. Does it really matter that Terence O'Brien pretended to be John Kerwin Stewart? Using an alias, he became a valued member of society. Eloise ReQua moves me because she transformed her sad and sedentary hoarding into a resource for historians.

Nor was I bothered that Benjamin Marshall trained to be a tailor and not an architect. He was a brilliant businessman who knew what he liked and commanded a small army of top-flight architects who executed his visions.

999 is a great building. It set the tone for all the other great buildings on East Lake Shore Drive and throughout Streeterville. It remains the best of breed.

When I look back at the roster of 999 residents, I see a broad engagement with the last 150 years of American history. As the creation of 999 unfolded, I was struck by how many of its residents touched history. I imagined a dinner party where Colonel Dickason and George Stuart regaled the guests with their recollections of the Civil War, and Alice Corwith reminisced about her friend Ulysses S. Grant. I would sit near Colonel George Langhorne, who fought in the Spanish American War and was improbably stationed with the Germans in World War I. What stories he could tell! If the memories weren't too painful, the bewilderment and terror in the trenches of the Great War as relived by Addison Stillwell and the ghost of Alexander McKinlock would bring the room to a sympathetic, reverential silence. William Wilms would be encouraged to share the German perspective. Of the many veterans of the Second World War, Dr. Charles Puestow saw almost as much of the fighting as the History Channel, while administering to the twisted flesh of the wounded; seated next to him, David Sciaky, who may have done more to win the war than any other civilian. Terry Druggan would opine on another kind of war—the one between Al Capone and Bugs Moran. His insider information might solve a few murders. For safety's sake, Marjorie Letts would be stationed behind him with her nine iron aimed at his head.

Other guests could pontificate on how shipping, railroading, coal, oil, automobiles, banking, and finance—among other pursuits—contributed to the industrialization and economic growth of America. Elizabeth Paepcke, a napkin in her lap, would deflate overbearing egos as soon they began to strut. John Lee Mahin, Jr., explaining how difficult it was to turn *The Wizard of Oz* into a movie, let

alone a great one, would give everybody a peek behind the Hollywood curtain. John Carpenter would play the piano. Marie Keith would sing. Kitty Simmons would dance.

Of course, you'd all be invited.

One of the most illuminating factoids uncovered while doing research on 999 came from a single document—the building permit. Issued on December 11, 1911, it established the earliest possible start date for construction. Four hundred sixty-two days later, on March 17, 1913, it gives us the exact date when the building was approved for occupancy, and therefore the date of our 100th anniversary. (Later I discovered that at least two families had moved into 999 in 1912. Oh, well.) Unable to have the published book in the hands of current residents on March 17, 2013, I wrote a toast for the occasion and circulated it:

On March 17, 1913, the day 999 Lake Shore Drive was approved for occupancy, the bloodiest conflict in American history had been over for nearly 48 years. A young, rosy-cheeked volunteer in 1860 would be an old man in 1913, but he was plausibly alive. Colonel Livingston T. Dickason was such a soldier. Severely wounded at Shiloh, he is completely paralyzed when he is wheeled into 999 for the first time. What thoughts, past or present, occupy his mind as he passes through our lobby?

I raise my glass to the colonel, our oldest resident.

And to Ralph Shaw, whose family history takes us back even farther to 1776 and the beginning of the American drumbeat. His great-grandfather Hiram—traveling on foot through the Cumberland Gap, deep into the land of indigenous people, the black bear and the slippery elm until he got to Kentucky where he settled—and his son learned to pilot a riverboat, and his grandson how to make hats, so that Ralph, a high-priced, corporate lawyer, could experience the good life at 999;

To the Stuarts—George, Charles, Harold, Harriet and

Elizabeth—whose direct linear ancestors were Kings and Queens;

To Frances Welles Shepard, a few years younger than Colonel Dickason, a daughter of Pennsylvania, and her son Stuart Gore Shepard, one of the men who built 999. How proud he must have been, his hand on her elbow, guiding his mother from room to room, welcoming her to their new home.

To the genuine heroes: Colonel George Langhorne, chasing Pancho Villa's men across the Rio Grande into Mexico, shooting at them from the back seat of his Cadillac; Geoffrey Kent rescuing 60 Jewish children from the Nazi onslaught; and David Sciaky winning World War II with a welding machine;

To the quixotic dreamers: Al Gowen, sailing around the world to discover his wife didn't love him; Muriel Rockefeller McCormick, marrying the ghost of a man she never met and Preston Tucker, inventing the greatest automobile ever and almost going to jail for it;

To Roy and Elizabeth McWilliams, and Livingston and Miriam Fairbank, cakewalking across the dance floors of Paris;

To Colonel Daniel Devore for bringing Dasher and Dancer, Prancer and Vixen, Comet and Cupid, and Donner and Blitzen to Alaska;

To Henry Field, who once parked a camel in his A-side dining room; and Royden Keith who sang and danced his way into the audience's heart;

To Eloise ReQua, a hoarder honored by Chicago for being a hoarder;

To the messier lives: Bror Dahlberg and his wandering wife; Osborn Andreas, both the good and not-so-good sides of him; and R. Newton McDowell, who purchased people's homes for cents on the dollar and blew them up for profit;

To nurse Dollie Chesher, who may have fallen, but could have been pushed;

To Alex Hannah, a traveling salesman who built a hotel for traveling salesmen;

To Ralph Wagner, who, on the best day of his life, beat Jesse Owens, the fastest man on earth, in a sprint;

To William Huey, a champion in one sport, and Marjorie Dodd Letts, a champion in two;

To Adelaide Ryerson, for arranging to have masterpieces by Cézanne, Gauguin, Matisse, Picasso, Seurat, Toulouse-Lautrec and van Gogh donated to the Art Institute;

To John Alden Carpenter, whose music inspired Gershwin;

To Walter and Elizabeth Paepcke, who dreamed of Athens and invented Aspen;

To Henry Glover Hall, our only farmer, and Lola Shepard, our only farmer's daughter;

To the doctors 20; the lawyers 17; the investment bankers 14; the real estate professionals 12; the commercial bankers and manufacturers seven; the lumbermen and public servants five; the ad women, publishers and inventors four; and the architects three;

To Borg, Donnelley, Field, Kraft, McCormick, Pullman (who was also a Pinkerton), Rockefeller, Shedd and Swift, who called 999 Lake Shore Drive home, and who were no better and no worse than the less familiar names in our midst;

And, most especially, to Ogden Trevor McClurg, who discovered Mayan ruins, won the Chicago to Mackinac race three times, published Tarzan of the Apes, hired Benjamin Marshall and gave 999 its address.

And, finally to the three 999ers waiting to be born.

To all of them, to all the others and all of you,

Happy 100th Anniversary.

And to the detractor who said 999 has no pedigree, I say "Bunk!"

Acknowledgements

To get 999 started, some of my neighbors lent me file folders containing a handful of newspaper articles and a few photocopies of pages taken from books and magazines. All of them related to 999. These random, unconnected scrapes had been collected over decades, and represented all of the then known history of 999. As I looked through the various folders, it became clear that a great deal of the information was redundant—a photograph of Benjamin Marshall greeting the Prince of Wales, an article about George Borg's purchase of 999, or a retrospective on Chicago's great apartment buildings.

The most unique artifact—found in only one folder—was a handwritten note dated September 9, 1993 from Stan Allan to future tenants:

"Greetings: These clippings were passed on to us by Eloise ReQua who lived at 999 for over 40 years. She had a strong loyal sense of history regarding the building, which I think we all share, keeping alive and vibrant the architectural legacy created by Ben Marshall 80 some years ago."

And so Miss ReQua, our esteemed resident hoarder, provided the first few glops of library paste incorporated into the foundation of *999: A History of Chicago in Ten Stories*. The neighbors who supplied the remnants of her hoarding were Anne and Steve Deli, Caroline and Bill Freivogel, Nancy and Jim Golding, Lynne and Harvey Golomb, Elinor and Richard Gordon, and Jan Zechman. Had they kept their folders to themselves this book would not have had such a solid jumping off point.

Anne Deli also contributed in another significant way. She pushed for a celebration of 999's 100th anniversary. She proposed a number of concepts that could have been used jointly or separately to leverage our 100th. A new roof deck was one of her many ideas. A marketing brochure and a book were separate items on her menu. At a meeting in Meme and Gary Hopmayer's apartment, I volunteered to write the brochure with Anne. But she dropped out of the project for personal reasons and the brochure turned into an oversized history book.

In the same meeting, we decided to photograph individual apartments and publish the images in a coffee table book. Gary, who is an excellent photographer, recommended a young man he had met at Columbia College—Shane Welch. I hired him and never regretted it. He is a talented young man and an acute observer of people and things. He took almost 3,000 photographs inside apartments and outside 999. We only had room for 20 in the final product, in part because the nature of the book changed from photography-centric to text-driven.

Shane and I appreciated the kindnesses shown to him by the following 999ers who let him photograph their homes—Joyce Dawson, the Delis, the Golombs, Connie and Tom Haynes, the Hopmayers, Brenda and Tom Johnson, Beth and John Jostrand, Helen and Bill Panje, Arlene and Bill Staley, Nancy and Bob Szalay, Penny and John Van Horn, Brenee and David Wilkinson and Suzanne and me.

When I mistakenly thought Shane and I had reached an impasse over a contract for which I sincerely apologize, I brought in Bart Harris, one of Chicago's premier photographers to give us his vision of 999 exteriors. Images from both men enhance the final product.

Deborah Seed introduced me to some people, long dead, who had lived at 999. I called Deborah at her new home in California to get a fix on how many Seeds, Seed spouses and Seed grandchildren lived at 999 during their 39-year stay. After Deborah identified the various Seedlings, I asked if I could read the names of some 999ers about whom I knew nothing other than they lived in the building at roughly the same time as she and Dr. Randy Seed.

Deborah agreed and put Randy and Allison, one of their daughters, on the speakerphone. When I got to Dr. Donald King and his wife Dr. Mary Elizabeth King, Deborah exclaimed, "We were friends. She told me she lived at 999 as a child."

"Do you remember her maiden name?" I asked.

She didn't, but promised to look for it and get back to me. Less than an hour later, she sent an email stating that Mary Elizabeth's maiden name was "Dickason." It rang a bell. A young man whose name I thought was Livingston Dickerson, Jr.—spelled with an "er"—lived at 999 with his mother Elizabeth Walls in the early 1920s. Elizabeth was married to Dr. Frank Walls. I knew nothing substantive about any of them, other than Dr. and Mrs. Walls attended the 1920 Kentucky Derby.

But the moment I searched for Livingston Dickason with an "a," I not only found the boy but also his father,

*Some of the best anecdotes
about the prehistory of 999
and the idiosyncratic life experiences
of a few long-forgotten tenants
were shared with three residents
on a fairly regular basis.*

Livingston Sr., a wounded civil war veteran and our oldest resident.

Deborah also provided recipes from Yvonne Sciaky for cheesecake florrie and chocolate mousse florrie, as well as a concoction from James Wilson Reilly that contained liver sausage and whipped cream. Some day I aim to try it.

I am deeply indebted to Trevor Potter, Bob Pope and Alvin Hulse, three kind strangers I met along the way. Trevor Potter is Ogden Trevor McClurg's grandson. He dove into his late mother's family photo collection and shared some extraordinary images with us. Bob Pope is the grandson of the culinary inclined Antoinette and Francois Pope. He provided a picture of each that brings them to life. Alvin Hulse owns a collection of still photographs from a film project John Mahin, Jr. worked on with Clark Gable. Too bad there weren't any shots of them together.

I would be remiss if I neglected to mention Estelle Hickey, Mary M. Higgins and Bob Epstein, the census enumerators who were assigned to 999 in 1920, 1930 and 1940 respectively. Despite occasional handwriting mysteries, they provided enough clearly delineated names, birthdates and other salient information to help me to discover human identities for most of the residents they interviewed.

Ditto for the folks at Wolin-Levin, especially Marion Fainman and Debra Russo, for opening their 999 files to me.

Thanks to the Aspen Historical Society for providing essential information about Walter and Elizabeth Paepcke, as well as photographs of them. Mirte Mallory gave us access to Ferenc Berko's incredible catalogue of Aspen photographs, documenting its history. He was Mirte's grandfather. Through her good graces, we were able to include relevant images of Arthur Rubenstein, Gary Cooper and Albert Schwietzer.

My good friend, Karen Mozer, who helped design 9A for Suzanne and me, introduced me to John Zukowsky, the founder of the Architectural and Design Department of the Art Institute. John is writing a scholarly book on Benjamin Marshall. John and I swapped stories about Benny. He confirmed my hunch that Marshall was both a rainmaker and the source of brand identity for his firm, but not necessarily its best architect.

To Jane and Didier Lepauw, founders of the Benjamin Marshall Society, who encouraged the book, shared insights about Benjamin Marshall and honored 999 for being the first building on East Lake Shore Drive.

Some of the best anecdotes about the prehistory of 999 and the idiosyncratic life experiences of a few long-forgotten tenants were shared with three residents on a fairly regular basis. Just by listening, Tom Haynes, Tom Johnson and John Van Horn helped me discover the essence of some of the best stories before I committed them to paper.

Their positive reactions and continued encouragement convinced me that the book had potential. John also detailed the building's on-going efforts to keep the physical wellbeing of 999 healthy and relevant. Tom Haynes and John read the book in manuscript form and corrected errors in spelling, punctuation and fact. Each added stories that had previously flown under my radar.

When I struggled to fill in some glaring gaps between the creation of the landfill and the appearance of 999. I hired Elizabeth Blasius, an architectural researcher, whose name was given to me by the Chicago History Museum. She introduced me to the Lake Shore Drive Improvement Association and the document transferring ownership of our property to McClurg and Shepard. She ferreted out the building permit authorizing 999's construction, as well as the periodic comments of the building inspector. She found details about dozens of 999 residents and made the historical record more expressive and complete.

Elizabeth enlisted two friends of hers. Nick Freed turned my commas into semi-colons, my semi-colons into dashes, the occasional period into a question mark, and

There are the three people, who,
more than anybody else made 999
possible—my daughters, Melora and
Thomasina, and my wife, Suzanne.
They granted me the time and space
to build this book fact-by-fact and
sentence-by-sentence.

pointed out that some of my densely constructed paragraphs defied comprehension. Evan Demma created the bibliography. Some day I hope Evan gets to put his name on a book of his own.

Two delightful people, Donald and Tanya Smith provided the map of Kinzie's Addition on page 32 from their remarkable library. In an unbroken line, Donald's lineal descendents have been surveyors in the Boston and Chicago areas since 1810.

Joyce Goldenstern handled the job of developing the index with professionalism and a smile.

When it came time to look for historical photographs to accompany the text, I turned to Krista Reynen, a major contributor to *The Encyclopedia of Chicago*, and David Robson of Ampersand, who had never tried his hand at research, but demonstrated his commitment to the book by jumping in with both feet. He proved invaluable. Krista and David found nearly every vintage photograph in the book. In addition, they unearthed a dozen or so forgotten residents, as well as biographical information about a host of 999ers. We communicated largely by email until we had enough images to call the final product a coffee table book.

David Robson also designed the book. He picked the typeface, the paper stock and the printer, all the while letting me think those were my decisions. I trusted him and did whatever he advised. I love the look he gave to 999. I am proud to have my name associated with his work.

Suzanne Isaacs runs Ampersand, Inc. She agreed to publish 999 before it was finished. She walked this amateur through every step of the publishing process. She forced me to conform to the *Chicago Manual of Style*, seeing through my vain attempt to pretend that I had some idea what it was. She was a thoughtful editor, whose every suggestion made 999 a better book. Most important, Suzie rescued 999 from a manuscript I kept re-writing and turned it into a real book.

Thanks in advance to Chantel Luxem, who wandered in from the Oprah Winfrey Show, to help market 999.

Finally there are the three people, who, more than anybody else made 999 possible—my daughters, Melora and Thomasina, and my wife, Suzanne. They granted me the time and space to build this book fact-by-fact and sentence-by-sentence. The children were toddlers when I went downtown to an office building to earn the money we live on today. They probably can't image that the unshaven lump in a hoodie who wastes whole days watching TV from the most comfortable chair in their home once was a peacock, who found joy working 12 to 20 hour days. What they know of my work ethic is what they saw as I sat in front of my computer screen for hours on end hunting and pecking for something we all could be proud of. I hope they take some of my commitment to never stop working until the job is done with them on their journeys through life. I promised both of them they could help with book. But when push came to shove, I decided high school was more important.

Suzanne was my muse. When I wanted to abandon the project, which was often, she lovingly coaxed me back to reality. I have wanted to write a book ever since I learned to read. Suzanne knew that. She read every draft, even the lousy ones, praising the writing when it was good and shaming me with sarcasm when it stunk. She would puncture the windbag in me and say, "This is crap." I would argue with her. But when she left the room, I would do exactly what she counseled and the bad writing—at least much of it, I hope—hissed away into oblivion.

Never once did I think Suzanne was wrong.

I can never thank her enough.

Selected References

These resources were consulted in telling the stories of families, individuals, places and products associated with 999, to reinforce the commentary and substance of the information. This is not meant to be a complete record, but an indication of the range of data reviewed. Entries are organized under family and individual surnames of those who lived at 999, in alphabetical order, followed by chapters describing other facets of the building and its times. Dates are listed from earliest to latest under each source for each entry. Online References cite date viewed on the Web, when available.

ADDINGTON
Chicago Daily Tribune
February 15, 1916. "Faints at Russian Ballet; Carried Out; Faints Again: Mrs. Keene H. Addington of Lake Forest Overcome at End of the First Part of Spectacle."

August 1, 1917. "Lake Foresters in Gas Masks Come Up for Air: Police Called to Save Populace from Agony."

March 28, 1919. "Lake Forest to Rebuild Town Razed by Foe: Funds Sought to Enable French in Stricken City Harvest Crop."

April 19, 1919. "Lake Forest May Buy Water Company Plant."

February 27, 1927. "Miss Addington Becomes Bride of Otis Hubbard: Spring Note Predominates Casino at Reception."

February 28, 1931. "Sarah S. Wood, J. R. Addington Are Engaged."

October 28, 1951. "Obituary 4."

October 30, 1954. "Miss Boyer to Be Wed to James R. Addington."

Online Resources
Wikimedia Foundation. *Wikipedia.* "Benjamin Electric Manufacturing Company." Accessed March 19, 2013. http://en.wikipedia.org/wiki/Benjamin_Electric_Manufacturing_Company.

Lopat, Rommy. *Findagrave.com.* "Keene Harwood Addington." Accessed March 19, 2013. http://www.findagrave.com/cgi-bin/fg.cgi?page=gr&GRid=27925221.

ALLEN
Online Resource
Skolnik, Kathleen Murphy. *Architecture Week.* "Creating the Washington Metro." Accessed March 19, 2013. http://www.architectureweek.com/2010/1027/culture_1-1.html.

ALLMENDINGER
Chicago Daily Tribune
August 3, 1889. "Tobias Allmendinger's Estate: His Widow and Son the Principal Heirs—Other Court Matters. A Receiver Asked For. Rights of Park Commissioners. Notes The Record."

November 26, 1901. "Wants a Second 'Jeff'; Great Chance for Right Man On the West Side."

ALTGELD
Chicago Daily Tribune
June 22, 1896. "All Altgeld Says."

ANDREAS
Chicago Daily Tribune
August 2, 1961. "Pick Andreas As Chairman of Pentron."

Chicago Tribune
October 5, 1967. "Price-Fixing Figure Found Shot to Death."

Pittsburgh Post-Gazette
March 15, 2009. "James Purdy, Died March 13, 2009; Gay-Themed Works Inspired Outrage, Admiration."

The Wall Street Journal
January 3, 1962. "Pentron Acquires Ballonoff."

October 10, 1962. "Pentron Electronics Sees Sales Up in Fiscal '62: Official Expects Considerably Better Earnings; Holders Approve Ballonoff Acquisition."

October 5, 1967. "Pentron Ex-Chairman Found Shot to Death; Police Call It Suicide: Andreas Was Under Indictment in Stock Case; Chicago Detectives Say He Left Notes, 'Contract.'"

The Washington Post
October 5, 1967. "Stock-Rigging Figure Dies."

Interview
August 24, 2013. "On Miriam Andreas," *An Interview with Holly Siegel.*

Online Resource
Uecker, John. *James Purdy: Memento Mori 1914-2009.* Accessed September 11, 2013. http://jamespurdy.org.

BALDWIN
Bulletin of Yale University.
January 1, 1952. "Obituary Record."

Chicago Daily Tribune
September 11, 1912. "Society and Entertainment: Poole-Baldwin Wedding on Lake Forest Lawn."

Chicago Examiner
September 11, 1912. "Wedding of Lake Forest Society Pair under Arbor of Evergreens."

July 13, 1912. "Stage Love Becomes Real: Miss Helen Poole to Wed."

Special to The New York Times
October 23, 1950. "Abraham R. Baldwin."

BALKE
Chicago Daily Tribune
December 26, 1936. "Julius Balke Dies; Retired Manufacturer."

December 27, 1936. "Obituary 19— No Title."

Chicago Tribune
March 15, 1970. "The 11th Frame."

The New York Times
September 21, 1888. "How Schaefer Will Play."

Sporting Life
February 16 1907. "Balke-Brunswick-Collender Company."

The Washington Post
October 19, 1890. "People in General."

BANCO DI ROMA
Chicago Tribune
March 31, 1972. Michael McGuire, "Announced by Ogilvie: Big Italy Bank to Open Chicago Facility."

March 29, 1973. "Banco di Roma Gets Charter."

The Washington Post
April 3, 1977. James L. Rowe Jr., "Foreign Bankers Settle in Chicago, Reap Big Benefits: Foreign Banks Put Branches in Chicago."

BARTLING
Chicago Daily Tribune
May 14, 1893. "Examining Lake Shore Drive Deal: Investigating Committee from the State Legislature Continues Its Work."

May 16, 1893. "Can't Hold the Land: Lincoln Park Investigations Hear Expert Evidence."

May 20, 1893. "All Favored the Lake Shore Drive: W. J. Campbell Before the Lincoln Park Investigators—E. S. Taylor Testifies."

May 27, 1893. "Thinks It A Benefit: Horatio N. May Before Bartling's Committee—Peter Lauer's Story."

November 3, 1894. "How About Illinois: Legislative Estimates from all Districts in the State."

BAY
Chicago Sun-Times
May 4, 1997. "Julie Beich Bay, 70, Wife of Bays English Muffin Exec."

Chicago Tribune
December 26, 1980. Margaret Sheridan, "Toast of the Town: 2 English Muffins from Chicago Top a Taste Test."

November 15, 1984. Barbara Sullivan, "George Bay Is Not Only An English Muffin Man: He Loves All Good Food."

April 3, 1997. Kenan Heise, "James Bay Sr.; Led English Muffin Firm."

BEARDSLEY
Online Resources
ruthmere.org. *Ruthmere Campus.* "Havilah Beardsley House." http://www.ruthmere. org/index.php?option=com_content&view =article&id=25&Itemid=75.

Taylor, Richard Dean. *American Trek Books.* "History of Elkhart." http://www. richarddeantaylor.com/htm/elkhart.htm.

BENTON
Chicago Tribune
September 23, 1999. Bradley Keoun, "Ralph Wagner; Was Exec at Britannica."

The New York Times
March 19, 1973. Alden Whitman, "William Benton Dies Here at 72; Leader in Politics and Education."

May 4, 1973. "Mrs. William Benton Is Dead."

May 24, 1979. "Louise Benton Wed to Ralph Wagner."

June 13, 1999. "Paid Notice: Deaths Wagner, Louise Hemingway Benton."

September 15, 1999. "Paid Notice: Deaths Wagner, Ralph."

BERTHA
Chicago Daily Tribune
August 13, 1916. "Trading Slumps in Apartments; One Large Deal: $170,000 Sale in Stony Island Avenue Tops Transactions of Week."

May 16, 1919. "Big Theatre in Woodlawn Will Cost $350,000: Land Bought for a Playhouse That Will Seat 3,200."

September 20, 1919. "Pays $177,000 for Two Large Flat Buildings: E. M. Bertha Purchases In Michigan Avenue and Woodlawn."

February 8, 1922. "Sell Gold Coast Flats, $325,000, in Record Time."

February 22, 1922. Al Chase, "$700,000 Paid for Sheridan Pratt Corner."

January 23, 1923. Al Chase, "Pays $200,000 for Apartment on Chestnut St."

The Wall Street Journal
January 9, 1925. "Chicago Exchange Seats Sold."

BLIGH
Online Resources
Fisher, Joy. *USGenWebArchives.* "Cook County, IL Archives History – Farm." October 24, 2007. Accessed March 19, 2013. http://files.usgwarchives.net/il/ cook/directories/farm/1944/ membersh153gms.txt.

Waymarking. *Waymarking.com.* "North Park College Campus, Chicago, IL – Learn of Me – Statues of Religious Figures." Accessed March 19, 2013. http://www.waymarking. com/waymarks/WMCWGF_Learn_of_Me_ North_Park_College_Campus_Chicago_IL.

BORG
Chicago Daily Tribune
December 15, 1928. "Agree to Merge Borg Warner with Disc Co: Report Follows Stock Spurts Here."

February 22, 1960. "George Borg, Auto Clutch Inventor, Dies: Former Borg-Warner Chairman."

The New York Times
February 22, 1960. "George W. Borg, Inventor, Dead; Designer of Auto Clutch Was 71."

Book
1948. Casey, Robert J. *Mr. Clutch: The Story of George William Borg.* Indianapolis: Bobbs-Merrill.

Online Resource
Rock Island Illinois. *Rigov.org.* "Historic Structures. Borg House (George and Florence Borg)." Accessed March 19, 2013. http://www.rigov.org/index. aspx?NID=959.

BORLAND
Chicago Daily Tribune
October 24, 1919. "Financial Notes."

February 1, 1934. Judith Cass, "Betrothal of Miss Beatrice Borland Told: Fiancé is Character in Her Travel Book."

BOWERS
Special to The New York Times
November 1, 1914. "Thomas Bowers Weds Miss Helen: Son of Late Solicitor."

BOYD
Chicago Tribune
April 27, 1967. William Kling, "Boyd Urges Designs to Meet Needs of Handicapped."

September 3, 1975. Leonard Wiener, "Railroad Gets Unfair Shake, Says Boyd."

The New York Times
March 17, 1950. "Thomas Bowers, Lawyer 37 Years: Former Assistant Counsel of Federal Reserve Bank."

February 2, 1967. "Era in Transport Ending, Boyd Says: Secretary Asks Wider Role for U.S. and More Profit."

The Wall Street Journal
January 23, 1969. "Illinois Central Road Names as President Alan Boyd, Former Transport Chief."

February 28, 1972. "Illinois Central Road Gives Boyd New Post of Chief Executive."

Online Resource
Wikimedia Foundation. *Wikipedia.* "Alan Stephenson Boyd." Accessed March 19, 2013. http://en.wikipedia.org/wiki/ Alan_Stephenson_Boyd.

BURTON
Online Resources
Wikimedia Foundation. *Wikipedia.* "Burton Process." Accessed March 19, 2013. http:// en.wikipedia.org/wiki/Burton_process

Wikimedia Foundation. *Wikipedia.* "William Merriam Burton." Accessed March 18, 2013. http://en.wikipedia.org/wiki/ William_Merriam_Burton.

CAIRNS
Chicago Daily Tribune
January 18, 1928. "Miss J. E. Cairns Wins Decree and $1,000 a Month: Wealthy Broker Divides Holdings with Her."

The Wall Street Journal
July 15, 1929. "Open Chicago Office."

CAMPBELL
Online Resource
Wikimedia Foundation. *Wikipedia.* "Tom Campbell (California Politician)." Accessed March 19, 2013. http://en.wikipedia.org/ wiki/Tom_Campbell_(California_politician).

CANNON
Chicago Daily Tribune
June 21, 1952. Judith Cass, "Recorded at Random,"

March 29, 1963. "Obituary 5—No Title."

CARPENTER
Chicago Daily Tribune
February 15, 1912. "Society, Meetings and Entertainments: Smith College Alumnae Will Receive for Leader."

August 4, 1920. "James B. Waller Dies Suddenly; Heart Disease."

January 10, 1933. "Mrs. Waller Borden to Wed J. Carpenter: Report Mrs. Waller Borden and John Alden Carpenter to Wed."

January 31, 1933. "J. A. Carpenter and Mrs. Borden Married in East."

November 18, 1943. Judith Cass, "Chicago Symphony Will Play John Alden Carpenter Work: New Carpenter Symphony Will Be Heard Here."

September 14, 1949. "J. B. Waller Dies; Leader in 43rd Ward."

February 25, 1951. Symphony to Honor John Alden Carpenter this Week: Plays Suite to Celebrate 75th Birthday of Composer."

August 17, 1956. "Ellen Still Can't Support Adlai in Race: Sends Congratulations Before Nomination."

October 24, 1956. "Mrs. Stevenson Drops Plan to Publish 'The Egghead and I.'"

February 28, 1960. Ernest Fuller, "Borden Home, Gold Coast Landmark, Is Being Sold."

Chicago Tribune
July 29, 1972. "Daughter of Prominent Chicago Family: Ellen Borden Stevenson Dies."

The New York Times
January 11, 1933. "Mrs. Ellen Borden Engaged to Marry: Chicago Society Leader Announces Her Troth to John A. Carpenter, Composer."

January 31, 1933. "Mrs. Waller Borden Wed: Becomes Bride of John Alden Carpenter, Composer, In Cambridge."

October 24, 1956. "Time Limit Cooks 'The Egghead and I.'"

Book
1968. Ewen, David. *The World of Twentieth-century Music*. Englewood Cliffs, NJ: Prentice-Hall, 140–45. Print.

Online Resource
Hampson, Thomas. *pbs.org*. "I Hear America Singing: John Alden Carpenter (1876–1951)." Accessed October 2, 2013. http://www.pbs.org/wnet/ihas/composer/carpenter.html.

CHATFIELD-TAYLOR
Chicago Daily Tribune
March 17, 1917. "Mrs. Adele Blow Wayne Chatfield-Taylor."

Chicago Examiner
October 28, 1915. "Mrs. Henry Shepard's Apartment to be Taken by the William Blows."

The New York Times
September 3, 1977. "Adele Chatfield-Taylor, Civic Aide."

Special to The New York Times
November 23, 1967. "Wayne Chatfield-Taylor Dead; Roosevelt and Truman Aide, 73."

CLARKE, T. H.
Chicago Tribune
May 12, 1973. "Rites Today for Clarke of Masonic."

CLARKE, W. E.
Chicago Daily Tribune
April 11, 1929. "Wife Awarded Divorce From Wm. E. Clarke."

September 2, 1946. "Mrs. Holbrook Clarke." (Obituary).

CLEVELAND
Online Resource
Los Angeles Times. *latimes.com*. "24 Frames." Accessed March 20, 2013. http://latimesblogs.latimes.com/movies/2011/09/cinema-history-movie-poster-collector-seeks-buyer-for-archive-rare.html.

CLEVELAND, GROVER
Online Resource
Graff, Henry F. (Consulting Editor). University of Virginia Miller Center. *Millercenter.org*. "Grover Cleveland (1837–1908)." Accessed October 10, 2013. http://millercenter.org/president/cleveland/essays/biography/3.

COLWELL
Chicago Daily Tribune
June 17, 1950. "First Cutter Professorship to Dr. Colwell."

COOPER
Chicago Tribune
July 29, 1900. "Lake Shore Drive Transfer."

April 5, 1920. "Death Takes H. N. Cooper, Long in Realty Business."

Book
1893. *The Biographical Dictionary and Portrait of Representative Men of Chicago*, St. Louis, American Biographical Publishing Company, 675.

CORWITH
Chicago Daily Tribune
June 19, 1898. "John E. Corwith of Galena Dies as He Sleeps in Tacoma. Prominent Illinois Financier, While on His Way to Alaska, Expires in a Western Hotel of Heart Disease."

COWHAM
Chicago Daily Tribune
September 30, 1939. June Provines, "Front Views and Profiles: Coals-to-Newcastle Note."

July 30, 1941. June Provines, "Front Views and Profiles: Shades of the Virile West."

November 29, 1960. Eleanor Page, "Mrs. Robert Neil Cowham Wed."

Online Resource
Library of Congress Copyright Office. *Catalog of Copyright Entries, Volume 5, Number 3*. Accessed March 29, 2013. http://books.google.com/books?id=Yc5DAAAAIAAJ&printsec=frontcover&source=gbs_ge_summary_r&cad=0#v=onepage&q=cowham&f=false

COX
Chicago Daily Tribune
June 22, 1898. "Deep On Made Land: William H. Cox Gives It On Lake Front Property."

Document
December 1908. William H. Cox, "Origin of Title to Lake Front Lands."

December 1908. "The Greatest Conspiracy Ever Conceived," *Chicago Lake Front Lands*.

COXE
Chicago Tribune
December 19, 1988. William B. Crawford, Jr., "For CBOT, 'Progressive' Flag Unfurled."

CROMWELL
Chicago Daily Tribune
February 24, 1949. "Fete Tomorrow Night to Honor New Leader of Chicago C.I.C."

The New York Times
July 29, 1952. "Executive Changes."

The Wall Street Journal
October 1, 1965. "Kimberly-Clark Sees Second Fiscal Half Reserving Profit Drop."

CUDAHY
Chicago Daily Tribune
September 20, 1935. Judith Cass, "Honore White Is Engaged to W. B. Cudahy: Surprise to All but Their Best Friends."

November 24, 1935. Judith Cass, "Honore White Becomes Bride of W. B. Cudahy: Young Couple to Spend Honeymoon in Hawaii."

June 7, 1947. "W. B. Cudahy, 35, Divorces Wife for Desertion."

Palm Beach Post
November 23, 1996. Tim O'Meilia, "William B. Cudahy, Former Mayor, Dies."

Online Resource
Wikimedia Foundation. *Wikipedia*. "Cudahy Packing Company." Accessed October 10, 2013. http://en.wikipedia.org/wiki/Cudahy_Packing_Company.

CUNNINGHAM
Chicago Daily Tribune
October 8, 1912. "Society, Meetings, and Entertainments: Secor Cunningham Will Move to the North Side."

March 15, 1922. "Hold Estate of Stone Doubled by Cunningham."

The New York Times
December 25, 1953. "Mrs. Secor Cunningham."

DAHLBERG
Boston Daily Globe
December 4, 1927. "'Poison Pen' Leads to Suit in Chicago: Wealthy Widow Brings Suit Denying She is Author, Claims Couple Who Feted Princess Accused Her of Ridiculing Them."

March 24, 1932. "Dahlberg Files Suit for Divorce."

February 22, 1954. "Bror G. Dahlberg."

Chicago Daily Tribune
March 24, 1924. "Bror Dahlberg Asks a Divorce for Desertion: Wife Now Living on Isle off Spanish Coast."

November 24, 1931. "Dahlberg Denies He Made $10,000 Present to Davis."

November 25, 1931. "Dahlberg Firm Gives to Both Parties' Funds: U.S. Investigation Finds Celotex Records."

April 24, 1932. "Bror Dahlberg Divorces Wife for Desertion: Lawyers Work on Property Division."

May 26, 1932. "Bror G. Dahlberg and Aids Sued by 2 Stockholders."

June 7, 1932. Jay Allen, "Mrs. Dahlberg Uninterested in Love, Thank You: Balearic Monastery."

February 24, 1933. "Bror Dahlberg Will Settle Bill for Tight Suits."

March 2, 1934. "Former Wife of B. Dahlberg Sees Mate Shot."

May 12 1934. "Bror Dahlberg Faces Court for $41,250 Alimony: Former Wife Will Ask Action on Monday."

June 14, 1934. "Dahlberg Suit Takes A New Turn In Court: Judge Holds up Hearing of Alimony Case."

June 17, 1934. "Dahlberg Brief Claims Wedding to Ex-Wife Void: Denies Validity of Settlement."

September 12, 1934. "Non-suit Stops Genealogy Case of Mrs. Chapin: Historical Society Drops Action for $1,700."

January 7 1938. "Bror Dahlberg Answers Critics of Stock Dealer."

May 2, 1938. "Kidnap and Rob 6 on Drive: Bror Dahlberg Party Loses $20,000 Gems."

July 27, 1938. "Mary A. Chapin, Former Wife of Dahlberg, Dies: Often in Court; Artist Mate in Mexico."

September 20, 1950. Seymour Korman, "Dahlberg Sued Over Custody of Foster Son: Parents Seek to Collect $40,000 Damages."

September 15, 1951. "Bror Dahlberg Sued over Pact on Foster Son."

February 22, 1954. "Bror Dahlberg Dies; Founded Celotex Corp: Developed Product from Sugarcane Waste."

The New York Times
July 31, 1926. "Princess Maria, the King of Spain's Cousin, Arriving Here Alone, Has Baggage Trouble."

March 29, 1927. "Thief at Ritz Robs Mrs. B. G. Dahlberg of $60,000 in Jewels."

March 30, 1927. "Dahlberg Gem Loss Remains a Mystery: Questioning of 20 Persons on Reported Theft at the Ritz Leaves Police in the Dark. Jewels Valued at $72,000. First Figure is Raised as Missing Articles are Listed—Hotel Sure Its Employees Are Innocent."

June 5, 1927. "Lay Widener Crime to Dahlberg Thief: Detectives Believe the Same Person Committed Both Robberies. Checking up Employees, Also Former Occupants of Room 701 at the Ritz—No Clues Found, They Say."

The Wall Street Journal
January 7, 1938. "Dahlberg Answers Banker Critics."

Online Resource
Davis-Montham Aviation Field Register. *dmairfield.com.* "Passenger List." Accessed March 24, 2013. http//:www.dmairfield. com:people:dahlberg_bg:index.html.

DERBY
Chicago Daily Tribune
December 14, 1892. "William M. Derby's Will is Filed: It Disposes of an Estate Valued at Several Million Dollars—Other Testaments."

December 21, 1941. "Miss Coleman Is Married to Ensign Casey."

Chicago Tribune
April 19, 1985. "Falah Campbell Derby."

April 19, 1985. "Obituary 4—No Title."

November 16, 1987. "William Ballard Derby."

DEVORE
Special to the New York Times
January 17, 1934. "Box Party Is Given by Mrs. Roosevelt: She Is Hostess to the Wives of Cabinet Members at Mrs. Townsend's Musicale. Eide Norena Guest Artist. Others Taking Part Are Rene Leroy, Sheridan Russel and Pierre Jamet."

The Washington Post
April 11, 1914. "Army Orders."

November 7, 1920. "Historic Chatham Estate is Sold: Replica of Famous Pitt House in Virginia Bought by D.B. Devore. Property Covers 50 Acres."

The Washington Post, Times Herald
March 13, 1956. "Gen. Devore, 95, Dies; Soldier for 75 Years."

August 2, 1960. John P. MacKenzie, "Mrs. Devore Leaves $10 Million Estate to Help Crippled, Retarded Children."

DICKASON
Chicago Daily Tribune
January 7, 1911. "Dickason House Sold for $100,000: Former Rawson Homestead Said to Have Been Bought by Texas Man. Purchased 54 Acre Tract Plant of Western Bank. Note Conveyed to the American Bank Note Company."

April 16, 1913. "Wills $5,000 to Secretary: L.T. Dickason Leaves Bequest to Miss Ida M. Gibson. Twenty Years in Service. Former Servant in Kenosha Left $50,000 Estate by Employer."

September 8, 1925. "Day's News in Society."

Online Resource
Wick, Sharon. *US Genealogy Express.* "Illinois Genealogy Express – Vermilion Co., IL – Biographies – History 1879." Accessed March 20, 2013. http://www. usgenealogyexpress.com/~il/vermilion/ vermco_biosindx_1879.html.

DICKASON, L. T.
Chicago Daily Tribune
February 8, 1917. "Changes Mind: Young Chicago Society Woman Decides Not to Go Abroad as Red Cross Nurse."

September 6, 1917. "Finally: Anxious Mrs. Dickason Weds Now That Dorothy Is All Settled."

Chicago Examiner
January 30, 1910. "Car Goes 126,000 Miles: L. T. Dickason Claims This Record for Thomas Flyer."

March 10, 1910. "Col. L. T. Dickason Is Stricken in the South."

April 1, 1913. "In the World of Society."

April 16, 1913. "Dickason Leaves $767,000—Two Daughters and Son Named in Will of Chicagoan."

September 17, 1913. "Dickason Leaves Family Millions."

January 30, 1917. "Plans to Join French Cross Despite Betrothal."

February 8, 1917. "Miss Dickason Halts War Trip."

February 11, 1917. "Mrs. Dickason Leases Lake Shore Apartment."

April 26, 1917. "Society Girl Trains For Air Corps."

June 13, 1917. "Her Decision Made."

June 15, 1917. "Janet Miller Is Bride of A. C. Dixon: Wedding Unites Two Well-Known Families; Dorothy Dickason Is Married to Lieutenant Stauffer at Home of Her Mother."

September 6, 1917. "Mrs. L. T. Dickason Weds Dr. Walls."

February 19, 1918. "Mrs. Dickason's Second Wedding Costs Her $50,000."

DODGE
Chicago Daily Tribune
March 14, 1948. "Miami Gay With Parties In Final Month of Season."

Chicago Tribune
March 25, 1973. "Where Do Oscars Come From?"

July 15, 1979. "Oscar, Emmy Pull Out of Illinois."

Los Angeles Times.
March 31, 1985. "Ray E. Dodge; Oscar Manufacturer."

Nation's Business
July 1951. Al Stump, "An Oscar for Everybody."

The New York Times
March 31, 1985. "Ray E. Dodge: [Obituary]."

San Francisco Chronicle
April 1, 1985. "Ray E. Dodge."

Book
1946, "Ray Edgar Dodge," *National Cyclopedia of American Biography.*

Online Resources
Edmonston, Jr., George. *Oregon State Alumni Association.* "Up Close and Personal: OSU's Rich Legacy in Track and Field." Accessed March 20, 2013. http://www.osualum.com/s/359/index. aspx?sid=359&gid=1&pgid=448.

TrackField.Brinkster.net. "Track and Field Statistics – USA Olympic Trials – Men." Accessed March 20, 2013. http://trackfield. brinkster.net/OlympicTrials.asp?TourCode =T&Year=1924&Gender=M&TF=T&P= F&By=Y&Count=.

Auntique & Uncle Tony: Early 20th Century Bookends. "Dodge, Inc." Accessed March 20, 2013. http://antiquebookends.net/dodge. htm.

DONNELLEY
Chicago Daily Tribune
June 27, 1905. "Knight and Donnelley Fail: Big Stock and Grain Commission House in Receiver's Hands. Dull Trade Chief Cause. Receiver Appointed on Petition of Creditors with $16,000 Bill. Members are Well Known. Three Creditors on Petition. Effect on the Exchanges. Firm Organized in 1895. Gossip of Big Profit."

May 27, 1917. "News of Chicago Society: She Will See Programs at Herald-Tribune Artists' Baseball Game Today. Comment War Horrors Told in Letters from Behind the Lines. News of Chicago Society."

February 25, 1925. "Reuben H. Donnelley Dies Suddenly: Heart Attack Causes Death of Publisher; Pioneer in Chicago Business World."

Online Resource
Thorn, John Coutant. *Descendants of William Thorne.* "Ninth Generation." Accessed March 20, 2013. http://thorn. pair.com/williamthorne1/d936.htm.

DRUGGAN
Chicago Daily Tribune
February 26, 1921. "Chief Shuts Up 'Little Bohemia,' Killing Scene."

April 26, 1924. "Oust Druggan From Flat? No, Druggan Says."

October 11, 1924. "U.S. Judge Evans Flays Counsel For Beer Ring: Hits Darrow's Attempt to Save Druggan."

November 2, 1924. "Terry Druggan Again Staves Off Return Here."

November 12, 1924. "Terry Druggan Fashion Show for Jail Birds."

August 29, 1925. "Westbrook Case Investigated by Federal Agent: Up Charges of Favoritism."

August 30, 1925. "U.S. Will Grill Jail Staff Over Druggan Expose: Ousted Official to Be Quizzed Tomorrow."

September 13, 1925. "'Am I In Russia?' Druggan Asks of Justice Lynch: Court Indicates the Trial Won't Be Delayed."

September 17, 1925. "Contempt Trial Faces Sheriff, Druggan, Lake: Aids of Hoffman Also Involved."

September 26, 1925. "Sits Up Druggan Stand: Role of Magnate and of Gangster."

September 26, 1925. "Druggan Agile In Dodging Law As Poor Youth: Beat 3 Cases Before Beer Riches Came."

September 29, 1925. "Foerst Tells Bribe Traffic at County Jail: Druggan Wit Balks Defense Traps."

October 28, 1925. "Terry Druggan Goes Free. Mayhem Case."

January 17, 1926. "Druggan Enemy, With Long Crime Record, Is Slain."

December 11, 1926. "Hoffman Asked Ease For Terry, Woman Asserts: Tells of Phone Talk at Jail Scandal Trial. Women Testifies Hoffman Asked Favors for Lake and Druggan."

January 16, 1927. "Order Arrest of Terry Druggan in Bribe Quiz: Two Others Sought on Contempt Warrants."

August 7, 1928. "Terry Druggan A Track Owner? He Denies It. But His Associate Admits a Share."

November 2, 1929. "U.S. Indicts Three Beer Barons: Druggan, Lake, Capone Caught Tax Frauds—U.S. Acts Against Gang Leaders."

April 24, 1930. "List 28 As 'Public Enemies': Crime Board Asks Exile of Gang Leaders. Police Plan Action to Oust Hoodlums."

November 7, 1930. "Raid Druggan's Hotel Suite: Beer Baron, Too Ill For Court, Is Out On Jaunt—Rouche Seizes Mass of Records."

January 13, 1931. "Druggan Pleads Guilty to Tax Fraud: Awaits Test Case Appeal."

January 15, 1931. "Terry Druggan in Again, Out Again: Jailed by Lyle For Year; Writ Wins Freedom. Burke Grants Bail Pending."

August 4, 1933. Walter Fitzmaurice, "Scandal Puts Terry Druggan in Prison Bed: Scandal Sends Druggan to Bed in Penitentiary—Blonde Woman Friend Is Here, But In Hiding."

July 31, 1934. "U.S. Frees Terry Druggan Quietly; Ex-Beer Baron Vanishes as He Leaves Prison."

October 30, 1938. "Sues Druggan."

March 6, 1954. "Terry Druggan Rites Today; Old Gang Gone."

Daily Boston Globe
November 8, 1930. "Capone Death Plot By Druggan Seen: Beer Baron Is Sought By Chicago Police."

Los Angeles Times
March 6, 1954. "Terry Druggan, Al Capone Aide, Dies Unnoticed."

The Washington Post
August 30, 1925. "Convicts Are Given Nights At Liberty U.S. Officials Say: $20,000 Jackpot."

October 1, 1930. "Gangster Quintet Feels Law's Hand."

Online Resources
Leagle, Inc. *leagle.com.* "United States v. Hoffman, No. 5179, District Court N. D." Accessed November 20, 2013. http://www.leagle.com/decision/192528213F2d269_1181/html.

Lieberman, Michael. *Book Patrol.* "The Biggest Jew in Chicago Part 3." Accessed December 4, 2013. http://www.bookpatrol.net/2010/03/the-biggest-jew-in-chicago-part-3.html.

Touhy, John William. *Rick Porello's American Mafia.* "The Valley Gang." Accessed November 20, 2013. http://www.americanmafia.com.

DUNCAN
Chicago Daily Tribune
July 9, 1953. "Donald Duncan Seeks Divorce; Accuses Wife."

Los Angeles Times
May 17, 1971. David Shaw, "Donald Duncan Dies; Gave Yo-Yo to U.S."

The New York Times
May 16, 1971. "Donald Duncan, 78; Promoter of Yo-Yo and Parking Meter."

The Washington Post
November 10, 1965. "Yo-Yo Firm Bankrupt."

Washington Post, Times Herald
May 17, 1971. Martin Weil, "Donald F. Duncan Sr., 71, Made Millions from Yo-Yo."

Online Resource
Wikimedia Foundation. *Wikipedia.* "Donald F. Duncan, Sr." Accessed March 20, 2013. http://en.wikipedia.org/wiki/Donald_F._Duncan,_Sr.

ELLIOTT
Online Resource
Eichelberger, J. T., Transcriber. *Findagrave.com.* "Dembinski, Klotylda Paula Matuszczak." http://www.findagrave.com/cgi-bin/fg.cgi?page=gr&GRid=82346553.

EVERSZ
Chicago Daily Tribune
July 18, 1922. "Funeral of Dr. Eversz to be Held This Afternoon."

May 24, 1925. "Life Ends: E. H. Eversz of Banking Firm Dies, Aged 53."

The Washington Post
February 7, 1909. "Mrs. Swift-Eversz Sues: Daughter of the Chicago Packer Brings Action for Divorce."

FAIRBANK
Chicago Daily Tribune
March 28, 1903. "Death Comes to N. K. Fairbank: Advanced Age and Stroke of Paralysis Suffered a Year Ago the Cause. Benefactor of Chicago. Gives to Many Charities and Public Enterprises for a Half Century. Starts as Brick Layer's Apprentice. Big Deals on Board of Trade. Aids Public Building Projects."

January 31, 1925. "Musical Fairbanks of Livingston Fairbank Sought-After Affairs."

March 13, 1925. "Fairbank's Heir in Friendly Suit for Home Funds."

January 30, 1927. Camille Haynes, "Chicagoans Prefer Social Joys of Paris to Gay Riviera Whirl."

November 23, 1927. "Mrs. Miriam Fairbank to Give Song Recital."

June 28, 1928. "Miriam Fairbank Makes Debut in London Today."

November 19, 1932. Judith Cass, "Debut Party of Jane Boyce Is Lovely One: Delightful Affair Held at Fairbank Home."

February 26, 1933. May Birkhead, "Mrs. Livingston Fairbank Entertains for John Alden Carpenters."

The New York Times
December 6, 1942. "Mrs. M. P. Fairbank Married in Home: Wedding to Lt. Nelson Levings, U.S.N.R., Performed by Capt. T.B. Thompson of Navy."

Special to The New York Times
July 2, 1934. "Livingston Fairbank: Son of Chicago Financier Was Graduate of Harvard."

Online Resources
Chicago Tribune. *News – November 23, 2000.* "Fairbank." Accessed March 20, 2013. http://articles.chicagotribune.com/2000-11-23/news/0011240365_1_mr-fairbank-island-health-washington.

Duke University Library. *Digital Collections.* "As Mrs. Livingston Fairbank Of Chicago Sees It." Accessed March 20, 2013. http://library.duke.edu/digitalcollections/eaa_P0191/.

Wikimedia Foundation. *Wikipedia.* "N. K. Fairbank." Accessed April 11, 2013. http://en.wikipedia.org/wiki/N._K._Fairbank.

FARWELL
Chicago Daily Tribune
May 13, 1926. "Margaret Willing Becomes Bride of John V. Farwell III."

April 29, 1937. Judith Cass, "Spring Brings Many Changes of Addresses: Ambergs Move After 33 Years in House."

April 26, 1950. "J. V. Farwell Is Accused of Defying Census."

Chicago Tribune
March 20, 1992. Kenan Heise, "John Farwell III, 96; Ran Companies, Banks."

FAY
Boston Daily Globe
January 9, 1916. "Yachts and Yachtsmen: Addison G. Fay's Shawnee. Auxiliary Ketch Fine Addition to C.Y.C. Fleet. C. P. Curtis to Race Valiant."

FELDKAMP
Bond Buyer
September 28, 2000. "Foley & Lardner Moving in on Detroit Public Finance Market."

Business Wire
September 25, 2000. "Foley & Lardner, Nation's 15th Largest Law Firm Opens Detroit Office; Firm Brings Automotive, Intellectual Property, and Labor and Employment Expertise."

FIELD
Boston Globe
February 5, 1953. "Dr. Henry Field to Wed Ex-Hub Girl Lion Tamer."

January 6, 1986. William P. Coughlin, "Anthropologist Henry Field, 83; Found Mankind's Oldest Wheel."

Chicago Daily Tribune
April 17, 1938. Marcia Winn, "Mr. Field is at Home to Men and Animals: Guests Crawl, Fly and Wiggle at a Nice Party. Animals Have a Field Day in Field Apartment."

October 25, 1953. Wilton M. Krogman, "Henry Field on Track of Man."

The Washington Post
September 8, 1928. "Million-Year-Old Skeletons Stir Interest of Scientists: Bones from Babylonian Ruins Described by Henry Field, Young American Curator, Before British Association—Copper Frog Discloses Ancient Art."

Online Resources
Wikimedia Foundation. *Wikipedia.* "Henry Field (anthropologist)." Accessed March 18 & 20, 2013. http://en.wikipedia.org/wiki/Henry_Field_(anthropologist).

Wikimedia Foundation. *Wikipedia.* "Animal Fair (song)." Accessed November 30, 2013. http://en.wikipedia.org/wiki/Animal_Fair_(song).

FITZ-SIMONS
Chicago Daily Tribune
February 3, 1891. "The State Claims the Land: Fitz-Simons & Connel Enjoined from Filling In the North Shore."

FOX
The Washington Post
August 24, 1912. "Army Orders."

GARBE
Chicago Daily Tribune
February 24, 1946. "4th Group of Winning Designs in the *Chicago Tribune* Prize Home Contests: Fourth Group of Prize Winning Homes."

Chicago Sun-Times
October 5, 1988. "Raymond W. Garbe; Pioneered Medical Building Architecture."

January 4, 1989. Neil Steinberg, "Ruth Moore Garbe, 80; Sun-Times Writer Loved Architecture."

Chicago Tribune
January 5, 1989. Kenan Heise, "Ruth Moore Garbe, 80, Author and Ex-Reporter."

The New York Times
May 10, 1931. Edward Alden Jewell, "Panorama of the Week: The Prix de Rome Winners—Various Exhibitions—Gainsborough in Cincinnati."

San Francisco Chronicle
October 5, 1988. "Raymond W. Garbe."

GARY
The Washington Post
November 1, 1906. "Death of Judge Gary: Chicago Jurist Presided at Famous Anarchists' Trial in 1886."

GOWEN
American Magazine
January, 1922. Merle Cromwell, "How Much Money Could You Have Saved Mr. Gowen? What He Didn't Know Cost Him $115,000! Here Is a Chance to Find Out How Much General Information You Have."

Chicago Daily Tribune
January 14, 1922. Jack Myers, "Speejacks in Sydney; Cocoa Milk for Water."

December 30, 1923. "The Cruise of the Speejacks: Photographs Taken by Mr. and Mrs. Albert Y. Gowen, Former Chicagoans, During Their 38,000 Mile Journey Around the World in a 98-Foot Gasoline Yacht."

June 21, 1924. Maureen M'Keernan, "Mrs. Gowen, of Speejacks, Asks Divorce."

The New York Times
December 1, 1922. "Speejacks Is Home; Circled the Globe: Ninety-Eight-Foot Craft Is Welcomed at Miami After a 35,000 Mile Trip. Was Twice Reported Lost. Yacht, Owned by Mr. and Mrs. A. Y. Gowen of Cleveland, Left More Than 14 Months Ago."

Book
1926. Collins, Dale. *Sea-tracks of the Speejacks: Round the World.* Garden City, NY: Doubleday, Front Inside Cover. Print.

Online Resource
Holm, Donald. *The Circumnavigators: Small Boat Voyagers of Modern Times.* "The Circumnavigators Table of Contents." Accessed March 20, 2013. http://www.stexboat.com/books/circumnav/ci_table.htm.

GRAETTINGER
Chicago Tribune
December 28, 1968. Donna Gill, "Transplant Team Feels Fatigue, Joy."

August 15, 1996. Kenan Heise, "Dr. Graettinger, Cardiologist."

November 23, 2008. "Death Notice: Elizabeth Graettinger."

Online Resource
Heise, Kenan, Staff Reporter, Chicago Tribune. *Article. August 15, 1996.* "Dr. John Graettinger, Cardiologist." Accessed March 20, 2013. http://articles.chicagotribune.com/1996-08-15/news/9608150015_1_presbyterian-hospital-luke-s-medical-center-rush-presbyterian-st.

GRAHAM
Chicago Daily Tribune
June 6, 1960. "Obituary 6—No Title."

GREENE
Los Angeles Times
November 20, 1936. "Chicago Jurist Gives Christian Science Lecture."

HAMILTON
The New York Times
February 6, 1915. "David G. Hamilton Dead: Chicago Street Car Magnate Was in His 73rd Year."

June 5, 1933. "Mrs. David G. Hamilton."

HANNAH, A. D.
Chicago Daily Tribune
December 6, 1913. "A. D. Hannah of
Brevoort Dead: Hotel Owner and One of
Founders of Hannah & Hoog Succumbs.
Donor to Charities. Member of Scottish
Societies. Gave Much Anonymously During
Career."

December 25, 1949. Al Chase, "Brevoort,
Old Hotel, Sold to Chicago Group: Planning
$350,000 Remodeling."

Online Resource
Bingham, Stephen D. *Genealogy Trails
History Group.* "Mackinac County, MI
Genealogy & History." Accessed November
20, 2013. http://genealogytrails.com/mich/
mackinac/biohannah.html.

HANNAH, D. C.
Business Wire
June 18, 2002. "Vital Living Appoints
Donald C. Hannah to Board of Directors;
Additionally, Hannah to Chair the
Company Audit Committee."

Chicago Tribune
March 1, 1984. Gary Stern, "Tempo/Arts:
At 23, Daryl Hannah Making A Big Splash
in Hollywood."

December 19, 1985. "James A. Hannah, 92;
Founded Tug, Barge Firm."

March 10, 2002. Mike Esposito, "*Chicago
Tribune* Boating Column."

October 21, 2006. Trevor Jensen, "James A.
Hannah Jr.: Heir to Barge Shipping Fortune.
'World-Class Playboy' Enjoyed High Society
of London, Palm Beach, FLA, Other Posh
Ports."

Fairfield County Business Journal
June 22 1992. "Entrepreneur of the Year:
Donald C. Hannah."

HEMPSTEAD
Online Resource
Jones, Mrs. Egbert, Mrs. Amos Draper,
Mrs. Horace McIntosh. *Directory of the
National Society of the Daughters of the
American Revolution.* "Illinois. Mary C.
Hempstead." Accessed March 28, 2013.
http://books.google.com/books?id=_AktA
AAAMAAJ&pg=PA163&lpg=PA163&d
q=Mary +C.+Hempstead+Directory+of+
the+National+Society+of+the+daughter
s+of+the+american+revolution&source=
bl&ots=oCCkVwlpQX&sig=QiqVPcpc
87FAobaPubNXPOZ1n5k&hl=en&sa=
X&ei=859UUfrpM6KGyAGChttp://
books.google.com/books?id=_AktAAAAM
AAJ&pg=PA163&lpg=PA163&dq=Mary
+C.+Hempstead+Directory+of+the+
National+Society+of+the+daughters+
of+the+ameri can+revolution&source=.

HESSE
Houston Chronicle
August 2, 1986. "Reagan to Nominate Hesse
to FERC."

August 16, 1987. William E. Clayton Jr.,
"FERC Takes New Shape Under Hesse's
Helm."

The New York Times
October 17, 1989. Robert D. Hershey,
Jr., "Business People; U.S. Energy Official
Joining First Chicago."

Online Resource
Jones, Mrs. Egbert, Mrs. Amos Draper,
Mrs. Horace McIntosh. *Directory of
the National Society of the Daughters
of the American Revolution.* "Illinois.
Clara Isabella Green Hesse (Mrs. Charles
Benton)." Accessed March 28, 2013. http://
books.google.com/books?id=_AktAAAA
MAAJ&pg=PA163&lpg=PA163&dq=
Mary +C.+Hempstead+Directory+of+
the+National+Society+of+the+daughters
+of+the+american+revolution&source=
bl&ots=oCCkVwlpQX&sig=QiqVPcpc8
7FAobaPubNXPOZ1n5k &hl=en&sa=
X&ei=859UUfrpM6KGyAGChttp://
books.google.com/books?id=_AktAAAAM
AAJ&pg=PA163&lpg=PA163&dq=Mary
+C.+Hempstead+Directory+of+the+
National+Society+of+the+daughters+of+
the+american+revolution&source=.

PR Newswire
November 12, 2001. "Martha Hesse Joins
Terra's Board of Directors."

HIXON
Online Resource
Munson, Drucilla Kathleen. *Seminar Paper.*
"A Sketch of Gideon Cooley Hixon: La
Crosse Lumberman." http://murphylibrary.
uwlax.edu/digital/seminar/1967/munson.
pdf.

HOPKINS
Railway Age Gazette
August 11, 1916. "Hopkins."

Online Resource
Anonymous. *Printers' Ink Volume 96.*
Accessed April 24, 2013. http://books.
google.com/books?id=cTcyAQAAMA
AJ&printsec=frontcover&dq="printers
'+ink+volume+96"&hl=en&sa=X&ei=
DT94UYaZC4zvqQHItoHgBA&ved=oCD
oQ6AEwAA-v=onepage&q="printers'ink
volume 96"&f=false.

HOWARD
Chicago Daily Tribune
June 21, 1938. "Mayor Kelly Names Louis E.
Golan to Park District."

June 25, 1938. "Hubert Howard, Ex-Dry
Chief in State, Divorced."

October 31, 1940. Barry Howard, "Another
Business Man Enters Race Game—As State
Official."

Los Angeles Times
November 27, 1949. "Munitions Chief
Pledges Master Plan for War."

The New York Times
August 12, 1949. "Policy Chairman Named:
H. E. Howard to Head Defense Department
Board."

November 25, 1949. Austin Steven, "H. E.
Howard, Coal Leader, Named Munitions
Chairman: Truman Gives Long-Vacant Post
to Chicagoan, Head of a Defense Board. H.
E. Howard Gets Munitions Post."

June 22, 1950. "Coal Concern to Expand:
Truax-Traer to Get Stock of Binkley and
Pyramid."

HRON-MANZONI
Chicago Tribune
October 12, 1999. "Carol Berlin Manzoni,
52, Pioneering Woman Lawyer."

Business Wire
November 11, 1999. "Michael G. Hron
Named General Counsel for Telephone and
Data Systems, Inc."

HUEY
Chicago Daily Tribune
October 1, 1915. "Huey Wrests World's
Title from Moore: Chicago Cueist Defeats
Champion in Play for 3 Cushion Honors."

October 17, 1915. J. G. Davis, "Champion
Huey Quits Cue Game After Success."

HUTCHINS
Chicago Daily Tribune
October 2, 1961. "Mitchell, Hutchins Adds
'Inc.' to Name."

JACOBS
Chicago Daily Tribune
May 14, 1941. "Mrs. Whipple Jacobs Gets
Divorce and $700 a Month."

July 18, 1943. "Whipple Jacobs Will Be
Cited on W-G-N Program."

December 31, 1948. "Jacobs Quits Belden
Mfg. for Phelps."

August 20, 1952. "Whipple Jacobs, Phelps
Dodge President, Dies: Headed Belden Firm
in Chicago Till '49."

JUDD
November 14, 1936. "Husband Upheld in
Bid for Half Wife's Estate: Rejects 1/6 Share
Under Will; Gets $500,000."

Online Resource
Elizabeth (ID*****5332). *GenForum.* "Elmer
Judd Marries, 1929." Accessed March 28,
2013. http://genforum.genealogy.com/
judd/messages/2197.html.

KEITH, MRS. E. G.
Chicago Daily Tribune
September 4, 1886. "Edson Keith & Co."

May 4, 1900. "Speaks for a National: Holger
Drachman, Danish Poet and Painter,
Addresses 20th Century Club at Residence
of E. G. Keith."

March 15, 1902. "In the Society World:
Mrs. Meynell to Address Twentieth
Century Club. Next Meeting to Be Held
on Friday at Residence of Mr. and Mrs.
Elbridge G. Keith—Wedding of Miss Persis
Bouton to Mr. Robert McDougal of New
York—Annual Dance of Tau Phi Gamma
Sorority Last Night at the Auditorium,"

July 16, 1903. "This Is My Birthday."

May 18, 1905. "Death Takes E. G. Keith: Fails to Recover from Winter Attack of Pneumonia. Born in Vermont in 1840. Other Lines of Activity."

KEITH, R.
The Billboard
March 2, 1918. "Marie Morrisey, American Contralto."

Chicago Daily Tribune
July 23, 1917. "News of the Stage."

November 29, 1942. "Activities of Chicago Land Women's Clubs."

April 30, 1950. "Spring Lunch of Music Club to End Season."

January 6, 1955. "Royden Keith Dies; Rites to be Tomorrow."

Online Resources
Osterink, Carole. *The Gossips of Rivertown*. "'Nobody Home' Pleased Good-Sized Audience." Accessed March 28, 2013. http://gossipsofrivertown.blogspot.com/2012/06/more-hudson-in-another-era.html.

National Federation of Music Clubs. *Administrative Division #AD 9-1*. "Important Events in the History of the Federation." http://www.nfmc-music.org.

KENT
Chicago Tribune
April 27, 2008. "Death Notice: Geoffrey Kent."

Book
1960. Shirer, William L. *The Rise and Fall of the Third Reich; a History of Nazi Germany*. New York: Simon and Schuster, 721–23. Print.

Online Resources
Chicago Tribune. *News - July 22, 2007*. "Kent, Katharine Mary." Accessed March 28, 2013. http://articles.chicagotribune.com/2007-07-22/news/0707220163_1_chicago-ave- arlington-heights-river-forest.

Chicago Tribune. *News - April 27, 2008*. "Death Notice: Geoffrey Kent." Accessed March 28, 2013. http://articles.chicagotribune.com/2008-04-27/news/0804260678_1_liver-function-clinical-applications-geoffrey-kent.

Northwestern University. *Northwestern Magazine*. "In Memoriam – Geoffrey Kent." Accessed March 28, 2013. http://www.northwestern.edu/magazine.

Mackay, Doug. *Past Forward Heritage Limited*. "The History of a Mystery Train Wreck Solved." Accessed March 28, 2013. http://www.pastforward.ca/perspectives/columns/08_05_16.html.

Kent, Andrew. *Team Athletes to End Alzheimers*. "SPOTLIGHT: Andrew Kent." Accessed March 28, 2013. http://nycmarathonspotlight.blogspot.com/2009/08/spotlight-andrew-kent.html.

Flacker, Edgar. *The Association of Jewish Refugees*. "The Last Kindertransport." Accessed June 7, 2013. http://www.ajr.org.uk/index.cfm/section.journal/issue.Sep01/article=573.

Leverton, Bertha (Editor). *Kindertransport Newsletter, AJR Special Interest Section*. Accessed June 7, 2013. http://www.ajr.org.uk/documents/ktsep06.pdf.

Koschland, Rev. Bernd (Editor). *Kindertransport Newsletter, AJR Special Interest Section*. Accessed June 7, 2013. http://www.ajr.org.uk/content/view.cfm/documents/KT_Newsletter_April_13.pdf.

Gramps 3.2.6-1. *Haapalah/Aliyah Bet*. "SS Bodegraven." Accessed June 7, 2013. http://www.wertheimer.info/family/GRAMPS/Haapalah/plc/8/b/bc3cd9a31b6246992b8.html.

KING
Special to The New Times York
December 31, 1951. Pat Liveright, "Dr. Mary Dickason Engaged to Marry: Affianced."

May 6, 1952. "Dr. Mary E. Dickason to be Married May 31."

KINZIE
Document
1912. "History of Cook County," *Andreas*, Land Purchase.

KIRK
Chicago Daily Tribune
April 2, 1894. "Charles S. Kirk Is In A Dilemma: He Thinks He Is Perhaps After All A Lincoln Park Commissioner."

January 18, 1897. "Charles S. Kirk Is Dead: End Comes Suddenly at the Paxton Hotel in Omaha, Neb."

KOCHS
Chicago Daily Tribune
February 14, 1938. Judith Cass, "Benj. Crawford is Engaged to Omaha Girl: Benj Crawford is Betrothed to Omaha Girl."

June 30, 1957. "'Country Living' on Lake Shore Drive: Lake Puts on a Colorful Show in Apartment's 'Front Yard.'"

October 7, 1962. "Exchange Vows in City."

KRAFT
Chicago Daily Tribune
June 3, 1943. "John H. Kraft New President of Cheese Firm."

KRETZINGER
Chicago Daily Tribune
March 9, 1899. "Sharp Rebuke for Teachers: Mrs. George W. Kretzinger and Dr. Emil G. Hirsch Methods in Vogue in the Public Schools."

November 19, 1930. "Mrs. George W. Kretzinger Funeral to Be Tomorrow."

LAING
Chicago Daily Tribune
December 18, 1903. "She Wakes Too Late: After 27 Years Mrs. Malcolm Finds She Is an Heiress. Money Now Is Missing."

The Washington Post
February 22, 1905. "Daughter Sues Father: Chicago Real Estate Dealer Accused of Larceny of Her Fortune."

LAMBERT
Chicago Daily Tribune
October 10, 1910. "Lambert Tree, Pioneer Lawyer of Chicago, Who Died In New York."

LANGHORNE
Chicago Daily Tribune
May 9, 1933. Judith Cass, "Re-Elect President George Langhorne President of Friends of China: Dr. Laufer Shows Member Through Oriental Galleries of Field Museum after Business Session. Col. Langhorne Is Renamed by China. Friends Tour Oriental Galleries of Museum."

January 26, 1962. "Langhorne, Old Soldier, Is Dead at 94: Colonel Had a Long, Busy Career."

The New York Times
May 9, 1916. "Langhorne Leads Pursuit: Colonel Sibley to Join Him Later and Assume Command."

May 11, 1916. "Forty Bandits Ride into Texas; Make No Raid; Langhorne's Troops Reported across Border."

May 16, 1916. "Langhorne Waits to Attack: His Advance Column Expects Reinforcements Under Sibley."

May 18, 1916. "Our Calvary Kills 5 Bandits, Seizes 2; Rescues Captives: Ringleaders in Glenn Springs Raid Overtaken 135 Miles South of Border. Paine and Deemer Freed. Langhorne's Men Ride Day and Night and 30 Volunteers Make Final Dash. Prisoner Posed as German. Deemer Says Outlaw Told of Order to Protect Germans as Supporters of Brigands."

April 13, 1928. "Col. G. T. Langhorne, Lady Astor's Cousin, Weds Mary Waller of Chicago Near London: Surprise to Chicago Friends. Fought in Two Campaigns."

June 15, 1937. "Lady Astor Arrives to Visit Ill Brother: Member of Parliament Denounces Dictatorships and Reiterates Her Faith in England."

San Francisco Chronicle
May 22, 1916. "Yaqui Band Trails Langhorne's Troopers."

May 23, 1916. "Sibley-Langhorne Expedition Back with Four Captives: 175-Mile Dash Crowned with Success; Bandits Scatter in Hills; Yaquis Follow Langhorne and Sibley. Rides to Prevent Massacre."

Special to The New York Times
March 24, 1915. "Observer Back from War: Major Langhorne Data Will Be Used for Army Reorganization."

February 8, 1916. "Major Langhorne's Recall: His Name Used Fraudulently with Bogus Wireless Dispatches."

Online Resources
Kohout, Martin Donell. *Texas State Historical Society.* "Glenn Springs Raid." Accessed March 28, 2013. http://www.tshaonline.org/handbook/online/articles/jcgdu.

Wikimedia Foundation. *Wikipedia.* "Pancho Villa Expedition." Accessed March 28, 2013. http://en.wikipedia.org/wiki/Pancho_Villa_Expedition.

Rosenberg, Jennifer. *About.com 20th Century History.* "Historical Importance of Pancho Villa." Accessed March 28, 2013. http://history1900s.about.com/cs/panchovilla/p/panchovilla.html.

LEHMANN
Chicago Daily Tribune
November 19, 1918. "Obituary 1— No Title."

January 8, 1922. Al Chase, "Elks Purchase Lehmann Home for $500,000: $3,000,000 Memorial to Be Built on Site."

December 6, 1927. Lane French, "O. W. Lehmann, of Chicago, Starts New Racing Stable."

Special to The New York Times
September 7, 1922. "Horse Show Blues Go to Middle West: O. W. Lehmann's Field Marshal Victor in Featured Class at Rochester."

LENZ
Special to The New York Times
January 19, 1959. "J. Mayo Lenz."

LETTS
Chicago Daily Tribune
September 2, 1917. Joe Davis, "Mrs. Letts Takes Title Second Time: Brilliant Golf Nets 5 and 4 Win Over Miss Rosenthal."

October 6, 1921. "Cecil Leitch Is Beaten One Up by Mrs. F. Letts, Jr."

July 18, 1922. "Mrs. F. C. Letts, Jr. Leads Field of Women Golfers—Employ Women in Place of Striking Railway Shopmen."

The Washington Post
August 26, 1916. "Title to Mrs. Letts in Western Tourney."

Online Resource
Wikimedia Foundation. *Wikipedia.* "Marjorie Dodd." Accessed March 28, 2013. http://en.wikipedia.org/wiki/Marjorie_Dodd.

LEWIS
Chicago Sun-Times
November 17, 2003. Shamus Toomey, "Milton Lewis; Operated Chain of Clothing Store."

Chicago Tribune
November 17, 2003. "Lewis, Milton."

Online Resource
Chicago Tribune. *News - November 17, 2003.* "Milton 'Mickey' Lewis, 89." Accessed March 28, 2013. http://articles.chicagotribune.com/keyword/matthew-lewis

LILL
Maggio, Alice. *Gapersblock.com: Ask the Librarian.* "Lill & Diversey: A Short History of Early Chicago Brewing." Accessed March 28, 2013. http://gapersblock.com/airbags/archives/lill_diversey_a_short_history_of_early_chicago_brewing/.

LINCOLN PARK BOARD OF COMMISSIONERS
Chicago Daily Tribune
February 28, 1886. "The People's Park. The Famous Resort of the North Side the Most Popular in the City."

LIST
Chicago Tribune
May 11, 1983. "Robert Stuart List, 80; Ex-Newspaper Publisher."

LOCHRIDGE
Chicago Daily Tribune
January 4, 1946. "Kraft Files Suit to See if it Can Make Bing Sing: Report He Objects to Selling Cheese."

July 18, 1950. "Obituary 1—No Title."

Book
1998. John Dunning. *On the Air: The Encyclopedia of Old-time Radio.* New York: Oxford UP, 1998. 91–93, 386, 462–463. Print.

LYDON
Chicago Daily Tribune
May 24, 1940. "Mrs. Lydon Dies; Widow of Dock Firm's Founder."

February 16, 1954. Eleanor Page, "Travelers Aid Board Elects Two New Women Members."

Special to The New York Times
November 24, 1963. "Eugene K. Lydon, 60, Led Dredging Firm."

LYONS
Online Resources
Garvey, Gloria. "I Knew A Real Mob Doctor," *Gloria Garvey blog,* September 19, 2012. Accessed March 29, 2013. http://gloriagarvey.com/i-knew-a-real-mob-doctor.

Haskin, W. H., M.D. *The JAMA Network* (Article. November 1925, Vol. 2, No. 5). "American Laryngological, Rhinological and Otological Society: Thirty-First Annual Meeting, May 22–25, 1925, Atlantic City." http://archotol.jamanetwork.com/article.aspx?articleid=539707.

Author Unknown. *The Laryngoscope.* (Article. June 1933, Vol. 43, Issue 6.) "Society Transactions American Laryngological, Rhinological and Otological Society, 39th annual meeting." Accessed March 23, 2013. http://onlinelibrary.wiley.com/doi/10.1002/lary.v43:6/issuetoc.

MADIGAN
Chicago Tribune
August 4, 1992. John Schmeltzer, "Madigan's Plans to Close after Christmas Season."

May 25, 2012. "Death Notice: Joseph Dennis Madigan, Jr."

MAHER
Chicago Tribune
July 3, 1970. "Dr. C. C. Maher Dies at Age 72; Cardiologist: Headed Passavant and Taught at N. U."

MAHIN
Chicago Daily Tribune
December 18, 1903. Defines a Good 'Ad' Man: John Lee Mahin of Chicago Makes Address at Madison. Students of the Commercial Club of University of Wisconsin Told the Qualities Requisite for Success in the New Profession—Business Has Been Raised to High Plane and Holds Out Rewards for Those Who Master it. Good Men Are in Demand."

April 8, 1949. Hedda Hopper, "Looking at Hollywood."

Chicago Examiner
September 30, 1909. "Montezuma Dance Feature of Pageant, Boys in Huguenot and Old English Garb to Sing Through Grounds."

Los Angeles Times
January 21, 1906. "Ad Men Talk Common Sense; Wisdom and Wit Distinguish Annual Coast Session; Mayor of Fresno Tells How He Won Election; Morning Newspaper Pre-eminent Among the People."

The New York Times
November 10, 1930. "John L. Mahin Dies; Advertising Man: Was Nationally Known for Bringing Many Products Before the Public. Began Career as Editor, Entered Advertising Field While on a Chicago Newspaper—Had Written Several Books."

The Advertising Age and Mail Order Journal
February, 1917. "Seeds of Success."

Film Comment
January 1, 1986. Lee Server, "Bright Star."

Online Resource
Wikimedia Foundation. *Wikipedia.* "John Lee Mahin." Accessed March 23, 2013. http://en.wikipedia.org/wiki/John_Lee_Mahin.

MARQUIS
The New York Times
May 5, 1902. "Death of Potter Palmer."

MARSHALL
Chicago Daily Tribune
June 22, 1913. Benjamin H. Marshall, "Apartment More Like Residence: Reform in Chicago Housing Facilities Pointed Out by Architect Marshall. Make Rooms Larger. Ten and Twelve Story Buildings Erected to Accommodate Modern Demands."

November 25, 1923. "Marshall Sues to Break Noted Architect's Firm: Says C. E. Fox Is Unfair in Partnership."

June 20, 1944. "B. H. Marshall, Aged 70, Noted Architect, Dies: Designed Blackstone and Drake Hotels."

Chicago Tribune
January 31, 1971. "Ben Marshall Still Casts Giant Shadow."

February 7, 1971. "The Opulent Style of Marshall."

January 16, 2011. Blair Kamin, "An Unsung Architect Left Lakefront Legacy."

Los Angeles Times
January 1, 1904. "Chicago's Awful Calamity."

Special to The New York Times
December 31, 1903. "Theatre's Architect Talks: Says He Will Never Allow Wood in Another Theatre—Declares There Were Plenty of Exits."

The Washington Post
January 22, 1904. "Architect of the Iroquois: Blind Passage in Which Many Were Killed, Not Intended for Exit."

Books
1992. Miles L. Berger. *They Built Chicago: Entrepreneurs Who Shaped a Great City's Architecture.* Pages 161–170. Chicago: Bonus. Print.

2008. Neil Harris and T. J. Edelstein. *The Chicagoan: A Lost Magazine of the Jazz Age.* Page 230. Chicago: University of Chicago. Print.

2012. Wilbert Jones, Kathleen Willis-Morton and Maureen O'Brien. Bob Dowey (Photography). *Chicago's Gold Coast.* Pages 9–10. Charleston, SC: Arcadia Pub. Print.

MATUSZCZAK
See Elliott.

MAY
Chicago Daily Tribune
October 2, 1898. "Horatio M. May Dies in Germany: Brief Cablegram from His Widow Informs His Business Partner."

MCDURNEY
Chicago Daily Tribune
August 30, 1928. "Mother and New Husband Adopt Her Own Daughter."

MCCLURG
Boston Globe
October 11, 1914. "The McClurg Fall List: Some Excellent Fiction Included in Catalogue. History, Biography, Drama, Poetry and Juveniles Presented."

April 21, 1926. "Ogden T. McClurg Dead in Chicago: Wealthy Sportsman Found Stricken on Road; Had Explored Jungles of Yucatan—Married Brookline Girl."

Chicago Daily Tribune
April 16, 1901. "General A. C. McClurg Dies in Florida: Head of the Publishing House and Veteran Succumbs to Old Malady."

July 29, 1905. "Exodus of Yachts Today: Local Boats to Start on Long Cruises. Much Interest in Races. List of Yachts Entered. First Boats Leave at 3 O'Clock. Power Boats to Race. Put-in Bay Prize Winners. Golf Events for Today. Columbian Knights' Sport."

August 23, 1908. "Yachtswomen Who Sail with the Daring of Men: Woman Who Makes Good Landing. Miss Meacham Heads List. Early Racing Days Recalled. Sailabouts at Delavan Lake. List of Women Sailors at Delavan. Miss Beck Strives for Honors."

December 16, 1910. "Lakeshore Drive Gets New Flats: O. T. McClurg and S. G. Shepard Will Build Eight Story Apartment House. Site Right on the Bend. Action of Buyers Indicates Character of Development in Section Off Oak Street."

August 15, 1913. "New Apartments for Lake Shore: Geo. F. Porter to Erect $500,000 Ten Story Building Near Lincoln Parkway. Big Tract Purchased. B & O Chicago Terminal Sells Last Acres on Milwaukee South of Lawrence."

March 1, 1916. "O. T. McClurg Plans Yachting Honeymoon."

February 18, 1920. Al Chase, "999 Lake Shore Drive 10 Story Apartment Sold."

April 22, 1920. "Ogden McClurg Sues When Rent Goes up to $325."

August 17, 1923. Walter Eckersall, "Culver's Crew Here Today for Tribune Regatta."

April 20, 1926. "Stroke Fells Ogden McClurg: Found in Ditch Beside His Car Near Elmhurst. Ogden T. McClurg Striken Suddenly."

April 26, 1926. Genevieve Forbes Herrick, "Ogden McClurg Dies After Being Stricken in Auto: Publisher's Fatal Illness Laid to Blood Pressure."

Chicago Examiner
December 17, 1910. "Taft Gets $50,000 for Wabash Ave. Property—H. C. Metcalf Acquires Peculiar Lease and Gets Fee Nineteen Years Later."

January 17, 1911. "$500,000 to Be Expended for New Loop Structure—Jacob Franks Leases Property at Fifth Avenue and Randolph for Ninety-Nine Years."

January 22, 1911. "$200,000 Flat Building on Lake Shore Drive Planned."

December 3, 1911. "Two Sheridan Road Residence Sites Sold."

December 7, 1911. "Shore Drive Safe as Fashion's Home."

March 3, 1914. "$400 Front Foot for N. Side Site."

October 1, 1911. "Effort to Maintain Boulevard Prestige."

Chicago Tribune
November 20, 2002. Bill Glauber, "Months after Mackinac, Storm over Skipper Brews."

Los Angeles Times
April 4, 1926. "Lost Cities of Mayans Reveal Old Civilization: Scientists Brave Perils of Tropics in Expedition through Yucatan Where Race of American Aborigines Dwelt Amid Magnificent Palaces and Temples. Mystery of the Mayans."

Portland Press Herald
March 24, 1999. "Eleanor McClurg Hunnewell, Lifelong Summer Resident of Prout's Neck."

Special to The New York Times
June 26, 1912. "McClurg in Divorce Case: Publisher Is Named by Chicago Attorney, Suing His Wife."

January 10, 1926. "Sail to Find Cities Buried in Jungle: Mason-Spiden Expedition, Off to Yucatan, Will Send News to The Times. Will Report by Wireless. Pen and Camera to Picture Later in Detail the Discoveries in Central America."

Afro-American
May 2, 1903. "Late News: The Souls of Black Folks."

Antiques and Arts Weekly
April 2, 1999. "Eleanor M. Hunnewell, 79, Ran Boston's Ellis Show With Spirit and Intelligence."

The Economist
February 21, 1920. "999 Lake Shore Drive. Ogden T. McClurg and Stuart G. Shepard Sell to Undisclosed Buyers Their Ten-Story Apartment House, 999 Lake Shore Drive. Property Valued by Appraisers for the Purchasers at $1,400,000. Oliver & Co. Represented All Parties to the Transaction."

Books
1953. Emmett Dedmon. *Fabulous Chicago.* Page 204. New York: Random House. Print.

1996. Donald L. Miller. *City of the Century: The Epic of Chicago and the Making of America.* Page 518. New York: Simon & Schuster. Print.

Online Resources
Embree, Edwin R., and Yale University. *Directory of the living graduates of Yale University,* issue of 1912. Accessed March 29, 2013. http://www.ebooksread.com/authors-eng/yale-university/directory-of-the-living-graduates-of-yale-university-issue-of-1912-hci/page-27-directory-of-the-living-graduates-of-yale-university-issue-of-1912-hci.shtml.

Prindle, R. E. *ERBzine,* Volume 1456. "Trying To Find A Way Home: A Discussion of Edgar Rice Burroughs' *The Girl from Farris's.*" Accessed March 29, 2013. http://www.erbzine.com/mag14/1456.html.

Connelly, Bob. *Silver Cities of Yucatan: The Mason-Spinden Expedition, a Film by Bob Connelly.* Accessed March 29, 2013. http://www.silvercitiesofyucatan.com.

MCCORMICK
Chicago Daily Tribune
September 12, 1937. Judith Cass, "Miss Bersbach Bride of Young R. H. M'Cormick: Autumn Colors Motif at Winnetka Ceremony."

Chicago Tribune
December 28, 1963. "R. H. McCormick, Civic Leader, Dies at Age 85: Had Wide Ranging Interests."

Online Resource
Heise, Kenan, Tribune Staff Writer. *Chicago Tribune, April 4, 1997.* "Robert Hall McCormick, Helped Develop Landmark." Accessed March 29, 2013. http://articles.chicagotribune.com/1997-04-04/news/9704040140_1_estate-developer-drapes.

MCCOY
Chicago Daily Tribune
February 2, 1919. "Comment: She Is to Wed Canadian Artilleryman. News of Chicago Society. Chicago Society Lacking in Many Social Graces."

July 24, 1919. "Society and Entertainments: Spend Vacations on Wyoming Ranch, Tramping Mountains."

August 28, 1919. "Society and Entertainment: Guests to Be Feted Over Labor Day by Lake Geneva Colony."

July 27, 1922. "Chicago Girl Wed by Minister Who Wed Parents."

The Wall Street Journal
February 8, 1910. "Public Securities Co."

MCDONALD
The New York Times
July 20, 1925. "MacMillan's Radio Thrills the Eskimos: They Talk Over It With Friends Across the Harbor, but Cannot Comprehend It."

Radio Daily—The National Daily Newspaper of Commercial Radio and Television
June 24, 1946. "Water Speedster."

The Washington Post
July 6, 1925. "MacMillan Finds Navy Radio Sets Ineffective."

April 3, 1929. Robert D. Heinl, "McDonald Plans New Arctic Trip: Chicago Radio Man to Accompany McMillan North in June on Allegro—Comes to City in Luxurious Yacht."

Online Resource
The Military Honor Wall. *TogetherWeServed—Connecting US Navy Sailors.* "McDonald, Eugene, Jr. (Gene), LCDR." Accessed April 1, 2013. http://navy.togetherweserved.com/usn/servlet/tws.webapp.WebApp?cmd=ShadowBoxProfile&type=Person&ID=525383.

MCDONOUGH
Chicago Tribune
February 18, 1990. "Lynne Madden to Wed Paul H. McDonough."

The New York Times
September 29, 1985. "W. J. McDonough Weds Suzanne Falk."

The Wall Street Journal
January 28, 1980. "First Chicago Picks William J. McDonough for Top Finance Post."

The Washington Post
February 11, 1945. "Reckless Buying."

September 24, 2005. Carrie Johnson, "McDonough to Step Down as Accounting Board Chief."

Strategic Finance
May 2003. Kathy Williams, "SEC Chooses William McDonough to Head PCAOB."

U.S. Newswire
February 26, 2004. "William J. McDonough to Receive FPA Medal at Financial Services Dinner."

Online Resources
Wikimedia Foundation. *Wikipedia.* "William Joseph McDonough." Accessed April 1, 2013. http://en.wikipedia.org/wiki/William_Joseph_McDonough.

The New York Times. *Article, September 29, 1985.* "W. J. McDonough Weds Suzanne Falk." Accessed April 1, 2013. http://www.nytimes.com/1985/09/29/style/wj-mcdonough-weds-suzanne-falk.html.

Soylent Communications. *NNBD: Tracking the Entire World.* "William J. McDonough." Accessed April 1, 2013. http://www.nndb.com/people/747/000163258/.

MCDOWELL
Online Resource
Author Unknown. *The TNT Story.* "The Story." Accessed April 1, 2013. http://thetntstory.blogspot.com/p/story.html.

MCGILLEN
Chicago Daily Tribune
March 2, 1924. "John McGillen, Long Leader of Democrats, Dies: Served in the Council for Eight Years."

MCINTOSH
Chicago Daily Tribune
July 24, 1916. "Society and Entertainment: Lake Forest Plays Bridge in French."

January 10, 1919. "Society and Entertainment: News of Society."

MCKINLOCK
Boston Globe
January 18, 1923. "Harvard Given New Dormitory: Memorial for George A. McKinlock, Jr, War Hero. Pres. Lowell in Annual Report Says More Are Needed. Thinks Students Should Enter at Earlier Age."

Chicago Daily Tribune
September 10, 1931. "Miss Muriel McCormick to Be Bride Today."

February 26, 1933. "Mrs. George McKinlock Stages Palm Beach Garden Club Show: Surpassing Beauty, Characterized by Vivid and Gay Coloring, Marks Display of Flowers; President of Club Honored at Buffet Luncheon. Mrs. McKinlock Runs Palm Beach's Garden Club Show."

December 17, 1936. "G. A. McKinlock Dies Suddenly at Winter Home: Heart Attack Follows Cold in Florida."

Palm Beach Post
October 30, 2006. Eliot Kleinberg. "The Ghost Bride Muriel McCormick's Haunted Life."

Special to The New York Times
December 17, 1936. "Article 9—No Title."

Book
2010. Celia Hilliard. *The Prime Mover: Charles L. Hutchinson and the Making of the Art Institute of Chicago.* Page 80. Chicago, IL: Art Institute of Chicago. Print.

Online Resource
Northwestern University. *Feinberg School of Medicine.* "McKinlock Campus Poster Now Hangs in Galter Library." Accessed April 1, 2013. http://www.feinberg.northwestern.edu/news/2005/2005C-October/poster.html.

MCWILLIAMS
Chicago Daily Tribune
February 26, 1913. "Cube Gowns Worn at Freak Party: Roy McWilliamses' Compliment to John A. Carpenter's Apartment Takes Palm for Originality. New Art Marks Event. 'Futurist' Enthusiast Drapes Apartment with Splashes of Color."

April 21, 1916. "Mrs. Carpenter Registering Persuasiveness."

September 28, 1919. "News of Chicago Society: Comment Evanston Brides and One Who Goes to...."

May 18, 1957. "Leaves Bulk of Million to Two He Reared: Roy McWilliams Will Is Filed Here."

Online Resource
The Art Institute of Chicago. *Catalogue of an Exhibition of Paintings and Pastels by Wm. Penhallow Henderson.* Accessed April 1, 2013. http://www.artic.edu/sites/default/files/libraries/pubs/1913/AIC1913WPHndrsn_comb.pdf

MOLONEY
Chicago Daily Tribune
February 21, 1894. "Mr. Moloney Smells A Land Grab."

March 15, 1894. "Moloney's Injunction Was To Restrain Further Prosecution Of The Work On Lake Shore Drive."

April 12, 1894. "He Vetoes The Drive: Atty. Gen. Moloney to Fight the South Lake Shore Project."

April 13, 1894. "The Suit Proposed By AG Moloney To Restrain The Further Construction Of LSD."

April 13, 1894. "Docks On The Drive."

April 14, 1894. "Moloney Willing to be Convinced."

April 15, 1894. "Will Sue Park Board: Gen FitzSimmons Serves Notice on President Waller."

April 27, 1894. "To Rescue The Lake."

April 30, 1894. "Ropes In Uncle Sam: May Be Made Defendant In The Lake Shore Drive Case."

May 5, 1894. "Property Owners Fight Back Against Moloney."

May 10, 1894. "Make A Forced Moved: Lake Shore Property Owners Act On Moloney's Threats."

May 23, 1894. "Would Stop Work On The Drive."

November 28, 1894. "Could Start Here."

November 28, 1894. "Moloney Thinks The Law Is Illegal: Suit Against North Shore Property Owners Begun."

November 29, 1894. "In The Hearings Samuel S. Greeley Pointed Out Surroundings."

November 29, 1894. "Value Note In Point: North Shore Property Owners Win Their Contention."

December 1, 1894. "Many Piers On Shore."

December 14, 1894. "Arguing The North Shore Case."

December 15, 1894. "Moloney Makes Closing Argument."

January 31, 1895. "May Push The Drive: Judge Windes Dismisses Moloney's North Shore Suit."

June 23, 1895. "Can't Make The Park: Attorney General Moloney To Stop All Lake Filling."

June 18, 1896. "Events Of A City Day: Lake Shore Drive To Be Extended South To Ohio Street."

June 4, 1900. "Illinois Will Oppose Ratio: Adlai E. Stevenson Is Chosen By the Delegation For Vice President."

The Northeastern Reporter
November 27, 1896. "The Northeastern Reporter," *West Publishing Company*.

Online Resource
Bienen, Leigh. *Northwestern University School of Law.* "Moloney, Maurice T." Accessed October 10, 2013. http://florencekelley.northwestern.edu/legal/lawyers/mauricetmoloney/.

MUNNS
Chicago Daily Tribune
July 5, 1950. Judith Cass, "John J. Munns and Daughter to Go Around World by Air."

May 4, 1952. Judith Cass, "Faurot-Munns Wedding Held on North Shore: Couple Leave for Europe after Ceremony."

NELSON
The Wall Street Journal
March 27, 1996. "Inland Steel's Nelson to Retire as President of Steel Subsidiary."

Metal Center News
December 2001. Corinna C. Petry, "Service Center Executive of the Year: Sandy Nelson of EMJ."

NICHOLS
Special to The New York Times
April 2, 1922. "Child of Armour Family Dead."

O'CONNOR
Chicago Tribune
February 3, 1971. "People."

Online Resource
Skolnick, Sherman. *The Secret History of Airplane Sabotage.* Sherman Skolnick's Report, August 6, 2001. Accessed April 1, 2013. http://www.skolnicksreport.com/shistory.html.

OGDEN
Online Resource
Designslinger. *Designslinger Blog*, July 9, 2009. "Ogden: The Story of a School, a House, and a Trust." Accessed October 16, 2013. http://designslinger.com/2009/07/09/ogden-the-story-of-a-school-a-house-and-a-trust.aspx.

OLIVER
Chicago Daily Tribune
December 24, 1911. "Oliver Elected President of Chicago Realty Board: Reports of Retiring Officers Show the Organization Has Gained in Its Membership."

June 22, 1913. Frederick S. Oliver, "Looks to Change in Loop Realty: Frederick Oliver Says Conservative Investors Will Start Next Boom. Cites New York Facts. Asserts Owners Here Want Seven to Ten Per Cent Instead of Usual Three."

February 18, 1920. Al Chase, "999 Lake Shore Drive 10 Story Apartment Sold."

October 3, 1920. Al Chase, "Real Estate News: Co-Op Flat Idea Sweeps Along the Gold Coast. 3 More Big Apartments to Be Tenant-Owned."

March 30, 1924. Al Chase, "'999, Residence of Fashionable,' Changes Hands. Sold for $1,500,000; to Become 'Co-op.'"

April 10, 1931. "Frederick Oliver, Realty Operator, Is Seriously Ill."

Legal Document
September 11, 2012. "Certificate of Authenticity," 1923 *Print. Frederick S. Oliver Chicago Real Estate Land.*

PAEPCKE
Chicago Daily Tribune
June 26, 1949. John Evans, "Aspen Fete to Pay Honor to Goethe Genius."

Chicago Tribune
January 28, 2001. "Aspen, The Town Chicago Built."

Denver Post
June 16, 1994. "'Grande Dame of Aspen' Dies; Paepcke's Vision Helped Mining Town Blossom."

The New York Times
May 15, 1960. Robert Alden, "Advertising: Image of Good Taste Created: Late W. P. Paepcke of Container Corp. Charted Course 'Great Ideas Series' Linked Philosophy and Original Art."

January 1, 1995. Ted Conover, "Lives Well Lived: Elizabeth Paepcke; Eve in the Garden of Aspen."

Special to The New York Times
April 14, 1960. "Walter Paepcke, Art Patron, Dies: Developer of Aspen, Colo. as Cultural Center Was head of Container Corporation."

Boxboard Containers International
1999. Christine Lyall, "Walter Paepcke."

Book
1991. Sally Barlow-Perez. *A History of Aspen.* Pages 41–42, 46–47, 49–63, 68, 71, 80, 85, 89–90, 97–191. Aspen, CO: WHO. Print.

PALMER
Chicago Daily Tribune
April 9, 1882. "Residence On The Lake Shore Drive."

August 20, 1882. "Potter Palmer's New House."

November 26, 1893. "Future Name Of Lake Shore Drive: Mr. Palmer Would Probably Again Object To a Change."

May 22, 1898. "Recent Realty Sales and Leases: Potter Palmer's Purchase of Lake Shore Drive Property."

May 5, 1902. "Career of Potter Palmer: For Fifty Years a Leader in the Growth and Development of Chicago. Builder of State Street. Comes of Colonial Stock."

May 6, 1902. "Last Rites For Potter Palmer."

May 30, 1913. "Block's Effort at Squatting on Mrs. Potter Palmer's Land: Adrian C. Honore, Brother, Has Police Drive Away Workmen Who Begin Unloading Material at Night."

Chicago Tribune
November 30, 1969. "When Potter Was King and Bertha Was Queen."

March 31, 1985. "Lost Lake Shore Drive: Mourning An Era; Mansions Of Rich and Famous Yield To Giant Condos."

The New York Times
May 5, 1902. "Death Of Potter Palmer— Chicago Millionaire Unexpectedly Passes Away In His Home."

Special to The New York Times
July 26, 1902. "Potter Palmer's Estate: Inventory Filed In Probate Court Shows He Was Worth $7,896,195.36."

Books

1953. Emmett Dedmon. *Fabulous Chicago*. Pages 129–130. New York: Random House. Print.

1995. Karen Sawislak. *Smoldering City: Chicagoans and the Great Fire, 1871–1874*. Page 223. Chicago: University of Chicago. Print.

2009. Sally Sexton Kalmbach. *Jewel of the Gold Coast: Mrs. Potter Palmer's Chicago*. Pages 11, 15, 24, 25, 30, 32, 39, 41, 42, 60–62, 81–84, 91–93. Chicago, IL: Ampersand, Inc. Print.

2011. Robert P. Ledermann, *State Street: One Brick at a Time*. Pages 23, 32. Charleston, SC: History. Print.

Online Resource

Palmer House, a Hilton Hotel. *Website*. "About Our Hotel." Accessed October 16, 2013. http://palmerhousehiltonhotel.com/about-our-hotel/.

PARDRIDGE

Chicago Daily Tribune
April 18, 1896. "Ed Pardridge Dead: Famous Chicago Bear Speculator Passes Away Quietly."

PARKER

Chicago Daily Tribune
December 18, 1913. Keene Gardiner, "Parker at Head of C.A.A. Ticket: Railroad Official Nominated for President of Cherry Circle Club. Election Date Jan. 20. George B. Walker, Harold Dyreforth, and Fred H. Rawson on Regular Slate."

February 7, 1919. "Nurse Missing on Daily Walk on Shore Drive: Police Search North Side; Employer Fears Tragedy."

February 11, 1919. "Business Men Cited in Case of Missing Nurse: New Angles Develop in Effort to Solve Mystery."

February 14, 1919. "Nurse Tired of Job at Parkers; Maybe Just Quit: Chauffeur Gives New Sidelight on the Chesher Case."

January 7, 1920. "Obituary 1—No Title."

PEABODY

Chicago Daily Tribune
February 13, 1909. Francis S. Peabody to Wed; On Way East For Ceremony: Takes Train for New York."

February 14, 1909. F. S. Peabody Will Wed Today: Mum, However, Regarding Plans for Ceremony in New York."

August 28, 1922. "Peabody Falls Dead at Hunt: Coal Magnate's Body Found Beside Horse; Long a Power in Politics."

The New York Times
August 22, 1922. "F. S. Peabody Found Dead on Hunting Field: Wealthy Coal Mine Owner Stricken at Meet on His Estate Near Chicago."

Online Resource

Wikimedia Foundation. *Wikipedia*. "Francis S. Peabody." Accessed October 2, 2013. http://en.wikipedia.org/wiki/Francis_S._Peabody.

PIKE

The New York Times
April 27, 1941. "Charles Pike Dies; Leader."

POPE

Chicago Daily Tribune
October 10, 1958. "Mrs. Columbus Discovers Francois Pope Spaghetti Sauce."

June 12, 1960. "Francois Pope: French Chef in a Business Suit."

May 27, 1993. Jean Marie Brownson, "Chicago's Chef Antoinette Pope's Schools and Books Led Generations of Men and Women into the Regimen of the Kitchen."

Online Resources

Hevrdejs, Judy. *The Stew Blog, August 5, 2009.* "Before Julia Child, There Was Antoinette Pope." Accessed April 2, 2013. http://leisureblogs.chicagotribune.com/thestew/2009/08/before-julia-child-there-was-antoinette-pope.html.

Heise, Kenan. *Chicago Tribune Article, May 1, 1993.* "Cookbook Author Antoinette Pope, 97." Accessed April 2, 2013. http://articles.chicagotribune.com/1993-05-01/news/9305010035_1_mrs-pope-measurement-culinary.

PRAY

Chicago Daily Tribune
February 20, 1955. Judith Cass, "Fashions and Fancy."

January 17, 1956. Judith Cass, "Being a Musical's 'Angel' Profitable, Mrs. Pray Finds."

The Wall Street Journal
July 17, 1948. "Max Pray No. 1 State, Benedum Field Wildcat Shows No Oil on Test."

Online Resources

Palm Beach Daily News. *Article, April 10, 1969.* "Max Pray Dies in Local Hospital." Accessed April 2, 2013. http://news.google.com/newspapers?nid=1961&dat=19690410&id=rxIuAAAAIBAJ&sjid=F5cFAAAAIBAJ&pg=5809,1256548.

investmentsinenergy.com. *Pray 1 Kranzler Oil and Gas Investment.* "Max Pray." Accessed April 2, 2013. http://www.investmentsinenergy.com/max-pray-pray-1-kranzler-oil-and-gas-investment/.

PROVINES

Chicago Daily Tribune
July 29, 1934. "June Provines' Readers Follow Her On Air Show."

PRUSSING

Chicago Daily Tribune
July 14, 1936. "E. E. Prussing, 81, Dies; Ex-Lawyer and Author Here: Stricken in West; Wrote Illinois Trust Law."

PUESTOW

Chicago Daily Tribune
August 8, 1937. "Doctors Have a Day as Winning Yacht Racers: Take Chicago Y. C.'s Star and R Events."

Chicago Tribune
May 27, 1966. Stephanie Fuller, "Friends to Honor Dr. Puestow."

February 11, 1973. "Doctor C. B. Puestow of Henrotin Dies at 71."

The New York Times
February 12, 1973. "Doctor Charles B. Puestow, A Surgeon and Educator."

PULLMAN

Chicago Daily Tribune
July 26, 1921. "Gives Up Her Usual Trip East for Lure of Chicago's Summer."

July 2, 1925. "Fashionable Throng Sees Madeleine Childs Become Mrs. Pullman."

January 29, 1933. "List $2,322,000 Securities Left by Mrs. Pullman: Owned No Real Estate, Inventory Shows."

Chicago Tribune
November 23, 1988. Kenan Heise, "William Pullman, 87, Set Up Botanic Garden."

Special to The New York Times
June 10, 1932. "Mrs. W. C. Pullman: Widow of Pullman Company Official Was Chicago Social Leader."

RANG

Chicago Daily Tribune
September 23, 1922. "Mrs. Fifi Rang Given $15,000 Alimony in Cash: Payment Ends Five Year Feud with Broker."

January 20, 1928. "Louis A. Rang Estate Valued at $1,300,000: Board of Trade Member Wills All to Wife."

RANSOM

Online Resource

Visual Arts at Eckerd College. *Website*. "A Brief History of the Art Department: 1961–65." Accessed April 2, 2013. http://www.eckerd.edu/academics/visualarts/history/index.php.

RATHBONE

Chicago Daily Tribune
October 24, 1948. Claudia Cassidy, "Two Fine Character Actors, Rathbone and Ferrer, Open Here Tomorrow: They Star in 'The Heiress' and 'Whistle.'"

November 21, 1948. "Stars of the 'The Heiress.'"

Los Angeles Times
December 20, 1944. "Vacs to Sponsor Christmas Parties for Wounded Vets."

December 19, 1948. "Rathbone Due Here in 'Heiress.'"

REED

Chicago Daily Tribune
July 21, 1914. "Society and Entertainment: Mrs. K. C. Reed Coming to Chicago."

REILLY

Chicago Daily Tribune
May 26, 1932. "Frank K. Reilly, Book Publisher, Is Found Dead: Heart Trouble, Depression Blamed for Suicide."

REILLY/CUNEO
Chicago Daily Tribune
September 18, 1942. "Frank Cuneo, 80, Pioneer Produce Merchant, Dies: Italian-American Leader for Many Years."

Chicago Tribune
December 17, 2001. "Reilly."

August 20, 2004. "De Angelis, Madeline Reilly."

Online Resource
SortedByBirthdate.com. "Persons Born 6 May 1918." Accessed April 2, 2013. http://ssdmf.info/by_birthdate/19180506.html.

REQUA
Chicago Daily Tribune
April 28, 1940. Eve Cousin, "Pan-American Tea Given by World Library."

Chicago Tribune
October 11, 1973. Eleanor Page, "There's Merit to This Medal—and Irony Too."

September 29, 1989. Kenan Heise, "Eloise ReQua: Founded Foreign Relations Library."

October 11, 1994. Anthony DeBartolo, "Consular Ball a Colorful Salute to Pack Rat's Legacy."

Special to The New York Times
December 22, 1938. "Charles H. ReQua: Chicago Grain Merchant Once a Board of Trade Director."

RIGALI
Chicago Daily Tribune
February 27, 1936. "John E. Rigali, Sacred Statue Dealer, Is Dead."

April 9, 1950. Betty Jane Merrill, "Company Makes Church Art for Distant Places: Chicago Created Statues Found Abroad."

Chicago Tribune
December 23, 1963. "Obituary 1—No Title."

Online Resource
Matland, Richard E. *Harvard International Review, May 1, 2010.* "Richard E. Matland Articles." Accessed April 2, 2013. http://hir.harvard.edu/article-authors/richard-e-matland.

ROGERS
The New York Times
January 11, 1887. "Judge Rogers Drops Dead: A Popular Chicago Magistrate's Sudden Death."

ROSE
Chicago Daily Tribune
November 15, 1925. "Wife Sues for Divorce from Landon C. Rose: Charges Banker Deserted Her in 1923."

Special to The New York Times
December 21, 1931. "Landon C. Rose Dies; A Chicago Banker: President of the North Avenue State Bank; Victim of a Cerebral Hemorrhage; Was in Banking 38 Years; Began in a House Founded by His Family—Was a Member of Several Chicago Clubs."

Online Resource
Currey, Josiah Seymour. *Chicago: its history and its builders, a century of marvelous growth (Volume 4).* Accessed April 2, 2013. http://books.google.com/books?id=WJUU AAAAYAAJ&pg=PA445&lpg=PA445& dq=landon+cabell+rose+president+of+th e+colonial+trust&source=bl&ots=h2Oou NbL_z&sig=oOZVDuyUtZ6kIFK1TBm8j b4ttLs&hl=en&sa=X&ei=w2JbUZ2lE6fp 2QXGmoCIAQ&sqi=2&ved=oCC8Q6AE wAQ - http://books.google.com/books?id= WJUUAAAAYAAJ&pg=PA445&lpg=P A445&dq=.

RUSSELL
Chicago Daily Tribune
December 11, 1940. "Edward Russell, Former Broker, Kills Self at 83: Ends Life With Gun; Body Found in Apartment."

RYERSON
Chicago Daily Tribune
March 2, 1905. "In the Society World."

November 9, 1949. Eleanor Page, "New Gallery Is Opened by Antiquarians."

March 8, 1961. "Funeral Rites Saturday for Dr. Ryerson: Former President of Orthopedic Group."

Chicago Tribune
October 17, 1966. "Services Are Set for Mrs. Ryerson, 85."

January 15, 1968. "Ryerson Gift Sets Up N. U. Surgery Chair."

SAMPSELL
Chicago Daily Tribune
April 26, 1942. Judith Cass, "Fashions as I See Them."

Chicago Tribune
June 11, 1963. Genevieve Maher, "Leave Home to Newcomers: Sampsells to Go to Europe."

December 18, 1967. Eleanor Page, "Toasts Greet Sampsell Announcement."

Special to The New York Times
June 20, 1973. "Marshall G. Sampsell."

SCIAKY
Chicago Daily Tribune
August 24, 1942. Cecil Le Boy, "Frenchmen Aid Allies Toward Air Supremacy Thru Welding."

Chicago Tribune
August 4, 1996. "Maurice Sciaky."

Online Resource
Chicago Tribune. *News, December 15, 2006.* "Sciaky, Yvonne." Accessed April 2, 2013. http://articles.chicagotribune.com/2006-12-15/news/0612150088_1_yvette-wallace-marcel-proust.

SCOTT
Chicago Daily Tribune
February 10, 1939. "George E. Scott Leaves $850,000 to Nine Relatives."

Special to The New York Times
January 13, 1939. "George E. Scott, Steel Firm Head: President of Foundries in Chicago Since 1929 Dies of Heart Attack."

SEAMAN
Chicago Daily Tribune
January 28, 1925. "$10,000 Coat Is Stolen at Party; Suspect Guest at Home of Mrs. Countiss."

May 12, 1936. "George Seaman, Paper Company President, Dies."

June 24, 1936. Judith Cass, "Mary Seaman and W. L. Folds Wed; Surprise: Three Day Courtship Leads to Marriage."

SEED
The Atlanta Journal
January 8, 1998. "Would-Be Human Cloner Is 'Brilliant,' 'A Little Crazy.' If Anyone Can Do It, It's Eccentric Physicist Richard Seed, Friends and Admirers Say."

Boston Globe
September 6, 1980. Arthur J. Snider, "New Technique May Help Women Who Are Infertile."

Online Resource
Wikimedia Foundation. *Wikipedia.* "Richard Seed." Accessed April 2, 2013. http://en.wikipedia.org/wiki/Richard_Seed.

SENGSTACK
Online Resources
Town Topics. *Obituaries, January 2, 2008.* "David K. Sengstack." Accessed April 3, 2013. http://www.towntopics.com/jan0208/obits.html.

Music Together, LLC. *Our History.* "Happy Birthday, Music Together." Accessed April 3, 2013. http://www.musictogether.com/ourhistory.

SHAW
Chicago Daily Tribune
May 4, 1949. "Ralph M. Shaw, Loop Law Firm Member, Dies."

Online Resources
Ancestry.com. "Ralph Martin Shaw (1869–1949)." Accessed April 3, 2013. http://freepages.genealogy.rootsweb.ancestry.com/~sunnyann/shawralphmartin-869.html.

Ancestry.com. "Shaw—Hiram Shaw, Hatter of Lexington, Fayette Co., KY." Accessed April 3, 2013. http://freepages.genealogy.rootsweb.ancestry.com/~sunnyann/shaw.html.

SHELDON
Book
1916. *The National Encyclopedia of American Biography.* James T. White & Company.

SHEPARD
Chicago Daily Tribune
March 15, 1898. "Affairs of Various Clubs: Chicago Chapter, D.A.R., Gives A Reception for Mrs. H. M. Shepard—Other Meetings."

October 17, 1904. "Death Comes to Judge Shepard: Cook County Jurist of the Appellate Court Ill During Half Year."

July 30, 1914. "Society Happenings and About Chicago."

November 28, 1917. "Stuart Shepard Named War Risk Bureau Counsel: McAdoo Selects Senior Member of 'Tribune' Law Department."

August 28, 1919. "Society and Entertainment: Guests to Be Feted Over Labor Day by Lake Geneva Colony."

The Investment Dealers' Digest
May 20, 2009. Joshua Hamerman, "Kirkland's Law: Kirkland & Ellis Has Made Some High Profile Hires of Late, Bulking up its M&A and Restructuring Practices."

The New York Times
February 18, 1897. "To Build A Colonial Hall: A Scheme for the Daughters of the American Revolution."

SIMMONS
Chicago Daily Tribune
March 10, 1909. "Relatives To Act In Fenner Case?"

Laguna Beach
May 24, 2012. "A Laguna Beach Dancer: The Story Of Kitty Simmons."

SLADE
Chicago Daily Tribune
December 21, 1945. "Highland Park Party to Seek Togs for Vets."

March 10, 1949. Robert Cromie, "Assign 'Thrift' A Meaning that Webster Missed: It Can Be Anything if Sold in This Shop."

SNEAD
The New York Times
October 25, 1959. Robert E. Bedingfield, "Personality: A Trucker Woos Competition: Snead Seeks a Tie-In With Other Modes of Transportation."

January 4, 1961. "Snead Is Back in Trucking Field as Head of Chicago Express, Inc."

SNYDER
Chicago Daily Tribune
August 31, 1950. "Wheaton to Put School Building Plan to Voters: Decide on $20,000 Program Sept. 9."

September 14, 1950. "Wheaton School Board Defers Action on Four Resignations."

STACK
Chicago Daily Tribune
June 22, 1955. "Name Dr. J. K. Stack New President of Passavant's Staff."

June 7, 1960. "Jim Stack Races to Yale Track Honors."

Chicago Tribune
June 10, 1983. Kenan Heise, "Obituaries: Dr. J. K. Stack; Orthopedic Surgeon."

Book
1977. Richard M. Cohen, Jordan A. Deutsch, and David S. Neft. *The Notre Dame Football Scrapbook*. Pages 50–52. Indianapolis: Bobbs-Merrill. Print.

STEWART
Chicago Daily Tribune
July 27, 1916. "John K. Stewart Leaves 2 Wills for $5,000,000: Illinois Admits One Document and New York Another to Probate."

November 16, 1921. "Records Show 'Skeleton' of J. K. Stewart."

Special to The New York Times
November 19, 1921. "A John K. Stewart Double: New England Town Sees Parallel Case in Another Terence O'Brien."

December 6, 1921. "Says J. K. Stewart Really Was O'Brien."

Online Resource
Wikimedia Foundation. *Wikipedia*. "John K. Stewart." Accessed November 9, 2013. http://en.wikipedia.org/wiki/John_K._Stewart.

STOCKTON
Chicago Daily Tribune
January 29, 1892. "New Lincoln Park Commissioners: W. C. Gondy, H. N. Stockton, Christopher Strassheim."

STREETER
Boston Daily Globe
November 15, 1915. "Streeter Taken After a Battle: Chicago Police Storm Captain's Oasis. Fifty Shots Exchanged and One Woman Is Wounded. Illegal Liquor Selling on Sunday Charged."

Chicago Daily Tribune
November 7, 1891. "He Is A Modern Crusoe: Capt. Streeter Monarch of Lakeshore Property Worth $500,000."

March 10, 1897. "Lamoreux on Two Sides: Commissioner Reverses Himself on North Shore Land."

May 7, 1899. "Put Streeter to Rout: Forces of District of Lake Michigan Arrested."

July 13, 1900. "Streeter Sells to the Police: Thirty Patrolmen Are Purchasers of 'Lots' in His 'District of Lake Michigan.'"

October 11, 1900. "Streeter Army on Trial: Lake Front Invaders Face Conspiracy Charges."

September 1, 1901. "A Quiet Day in the Life of Captain George Wellington Streeter: H. Gent's Parlor."

February 12, 1902. "District Battles Ends in Murder. Streeter and Three Retainers Locked Up at Police Station on the Charge of Homicide."

March 31, 1902. "To Weigh Streeter's Charge: North Shore Property-Owners Accused of Murder Will Appear in Court on Wednesday."

July 10, 1902. "Clash in Streeter Trial: 'Captain Shakes Fists in Gen. Fitz-Simons' Face."

August 8, 1909. "Unprepared for War, Chicago Fate Trembles in the Balance: The Shore Line Is Open and Cap. Streeter Only 60 Miles Away."

August 15, 1909. "'Deestrick of Lake Michgant' Still Waiting for Capt. Streeter. Boundaries of Cap's Claim. Nothing Doing in Building."

September 13, 1910. "Cap'n Streeter Back 'By Cracky.'"

January 31, 1911. "'Deestrict' Lots Are Sold. Warden of Michigan City Penitentiary Appears In $100,000 Deal with 'Cap' Streeter."

February 6, 1911. "Captain Streeter's Case. Matter Is Found Still Subject to Judicial Inquiry as to Whether Public's Right Has Been Conserved."

December 27, 1911. "'Cap'n' Streeter Found in 'Deestrict': Builds Wagons."

May 4, 1915. "Captain Streeter, Musket Ready, Guards Domain: Police Hurried to Scene As Rival Claimant Fences Up Disputed Land."

November 10, 1915. Henry M. Hyde, "'Twas a Famous Victory Foes of the 'Cap'n' Won: His Army Invading 'Deestrict' Where He Held Election Taken by One Man. Makes a Fortune Off Lots."

November 11, 1915. Henry M. Hyde, "Syndicate Once Tried to 'Grab' Streeter Domain: Scrippers' Scandal Recalled; U.S. Official Quit Under Fire. Almost Got a Patent."

November 12, 1915. Henry M. Hyde, "New Claimant to 'Made' Land Appears in Suit: Shore Ground Between Illinois and Erie Streets in Dispute Like Streeterville. On Squatter's Right Basis."

February 24, 1918. "Court Decision Ousts Streeter From 'Deestrict': Pinckney Calls the Capn's Title Forgery; Old Man to Fight."

August 18, 1929. "Streeter's Claim Mouldering in Grave; Name Marches On: Deestrick Dead, Streeter's Name Goes On— Only Accomplishment of 35 Year Battle."

July 8, 1931. "Title Company Wins, Points in Streeter Case."

October 19, 1936. "Ma Streeter Dead; Squatter of Gold Coast: Widow of Cap'n, Claimant to Millions, Penniless."

September 5, 1937. "Year Real Estate War: Picturesque Squatter's Futile Fight—The 40 Year Streeterville War—An Old Squatter's Futile Fight For Property."

The Chicago Defender
December 23, 1911. "Captain Streeter's Land Sold Again: 'Deestrict' Goes Under Hammer for Second Time in Ten Years to Satisfy a Judgment of $10,000 in Favor of Attorney W. G. Anderson—Brings $2,525."

January 23, 1914. "Attorney W.G. Anderson Wings A Notable Decision: Judge Foell, of the Superior Court, Sustains Attorney Anderson's Demurrer to Streeter's Son's Bill for Injunction. Injunction Will Now Be Dissolved and Sheriff's Deeds Issued to Purchasers."

Chicago Examiner
August 1, 1909. "Streeter Sails On Warship To Raise Flag Over Deestrict."

July 20, 1910. "Capt. Streeter to Storm 'Pirates Warship On Wheels Of Terror.'"

August 19, 1910. "Streeter To Attack Enemy Today."

November 12, 1915. "Spy Pilfers Something Dark In Streeterville."

November 15, 1915. "Deestrict Captured, Streeter Wounded."

November 15, 1915. "Fortifications Of Streeterville Demolished."

September 30, 1916. "Deestrict Colony May Lose Votes."

April 5, 1918. "Well, He's In Again!"

Chicago History
Fall, 1976. K.C. Tessendorf, "Captain Streeter's District of Lake Michigan."

Chicago Tribune
May 5, 1981. Michael L. Millenson, "Streeter Legacy Thriving."

December 18, 1988. June Sawyers, "A Fighter To The End Was Old Cap'n Streeter."

February 27, 1997. "July 11, 1886. A Truly Colorful Captain of His Destiny Series: *Chicago Tribune* 150 Years. Events That Shaped Chicago."

May 8, 2007. "Streeterville Quite a Bit Ritzier Than Streeter Was."

Los Angeles Times
December 22, 1918. "The Story of 'Cap' Streeter. Famous Chicago Squatter Once More Evicted; Latest Epoch in a Long and Picturesque Career; Captain's Home Wrecked and Wreckage Burned."

July 17, 1924. "Ma Streeter Will Fight: Organizes Billion-Dollar Corporation for Battle to Obtain 200 Acres in Chicago."

The New York Times
December 4, 1892. "Capt. Streeter In Luck. A Shipwreck Caused Him to Blossom Out as a Capitalist."

May 27, 1900. "Chicago Has Real War: 300 Armed Policemen Sent to Capture Streeter's Force. Squatter's Followers Backed by Gatling Guns Were Entrenched on State Land, but Surrendered."

May 27, 1924. "Ma Streeter Fights for Chicago Lands: Takes Up Battle of Shooting Cap'n and Sues 1,500 Persons for $100,000,000."

San Francisco Chronicle
October 17, 1915. "Squatter's Fight Began Years Ago: Captain George Wellington Streeter Has Long Resisted the Chicago Authorities—Gained Much Sympathy—Present Trouble Over Lake 'District' Recalls Early Battle Over Water Front."

South Bend Tribune
April 12, 2001. "Riverboat History Maker, Researcher, Discovers Area 'Rogue' in Captain Streeter."

The Washington Post
August 12, 1895. "Clumsy Effort at Forgery: An Attempt to Obtain Chicago Lake Front Land. An Old Land Patent Issued by Martin Van Buren Was Forged and Grover Cleveland's Name Inserted as President in 1837."

December 4, 1902. "Streeter Found Guilty. 'Governor of District of Lake Michigan' and Comrades Are Convicted."

November 15, 1904. "Capt. Streeter Set Free. Famous Chicago Squatter Escapes State's Prison on Technicality."

November 17, 1915. "Streeter District 'Dry': Bondsman for Chicago 'Squatter' Soon Settles the Matter. Aged Captain, His Wife and Fourteen Others in Court After Being Taken in Raid in 'District.'"

May 27, 1924. "Ma Streeter Asks $100,000,000 in Suit."

October 19, 1936. "Ma Streeter Dies in Chicago, Destitute, Alone: Helped Husband Fight for $350,000,000 Gold Coast Property"

Book
2011. Wayne Klatt. *King of the Gold Coast: Cap'n Streeter, the Millionaires, and the Story of Lake Shore Drive*. Charleston, SC: History. Print.

Online Resources
The Day Book. *Chicago, December 13, 1916.* "Witness Accuses Chicago Title & Trust Co. of Conspiring Against Streeter." Accessed April 24, 2013. *chroniclingamerica. loc.gov/lccn/sn83045487/1916-11-17/.../ seq-4/.*

Wikimedia Foundation. *Wikipedia.* "George Streeter." Accessed April 24, 2013. http:// en.wikipedia.org/wiki/George_Streeter.

Chicago Public Library. *Streeterville Collection.* "Historical Note: Streeterville Archival Collections." Accessed April 24, 2013. http://www.chipublib.org/ cplbooksmovies/cplarchive/archivalcoll/ str.php.

STILLWELL
Chicago Daily Tribune
March 2, 1914. "Society and Entertainment. World the Field for Chicago Honeymooners."

December 28, 1922. "Heiress Granted Divorce; Refuses to Take Alimony. Says Addison Stillwell Deserted Family."

September 16, 1923. "Stillwell Weds Mrs. Pearsons: Divorce-Marriage Chain Involves 3 Couples."

July 17, 1928. "Mrs. Stillwell Seeks Divorce from Broker."

Special to The New York Times
July 17, 1928. "Sues Addison Stillwell: Wife Seeks Divorce in Chicago from New York Broker."

STUART
Chicago Daily Tribune
November 10, 1934. Phillip Kinsley, "Mundelein Aids Harold Stuart in Insull Trial: Cardinal Testifies to War Service."

June 12, 1935. "Jury Is Chosen to Try Insull for Last Time: Lawyers to Make Opening Statements Today."

September 29, 1943. Judith Cass, "George Stuart to Be Feted on 100th Birthday."

November 20, 1943. "George Stuart Dies at 100; Civil War Vet and Retired Broker."

April 4, 1953. Phillip Hampson, "The Road to Success—A Sketch of Harold L. Stuart, Head of Halsey, Stuart & Co."

The New York Times
July 1, 1966. "Harold L. Stuart, Financier, 84, Dies: Headed Halsey, Stuart & Co., Chicago Investment House."

Special to The New York Times
May 3, 1933. "17 Are Arraigned in Insull Charges: H. L. Stuart, Stanley Field, Samuel Insull Jr. and Others Attack the Indictments. Formal Pleas Deferred. Validity of the Law on Mail Fraud Challenged in Corporation Securities Company Case."

November 9, 1934. "Insull Associate Upheld by Dawes: Former Vice President Testifies To 'High Reputation' of Harold L. Stuart. Accounting is Defended. F. K. Shrader Says in Chicago That Corporation Securities Followed Usual Practice."

The Washington Post
June 15, 1935. "Insull Triumph in Court Again Kills All Cases: U.S. Stops Prosecution When Judge Rules Out Bankruptcy Charge."

Book
1962. Forrest McDonald. *Insull*. Pages 39, 42–43, 95, 131–132, 149–161, 204, 220, 229–230, 247–249, 275, 325, 335. Chicago: University of Chicago. Print.

SWIFT
Chicago Daily Tribune
September 23, 1924. "E. F. Swift, Jr., Sued by Wife, 'Incompatible.'"

June 8, 1932. "$1,500,000 Left to Charity by E. F. Swift Will: Most of Remainder Goes to His Family."

Chicago Tribune
January 13, 1965. "E. F. Swift, Jr. Estate Valued at $4.2 Million."

TACKETT
Chicago Daily Tribune
August 14, 1938. "Tackett May Build Seventy More Homes in Mount Prospect."

May 28, 1939. "Builds House in Five Days; Uses No Short Cuts: Tackett Breaks National Record."

April 3, 1938. Al Chase, "Suburbs Build Homes Faster Than Chicago—200 New Units Planned: W.C. Tackett Will Build 48 More Houses. Fourteen Are Scheduled for Lincolnshire."

May 5, 1940. "Chicago Residential Builder Plans Town Houses in "Meekerville": Tackett Buys Sheridan Road Sites for Nine Homes; Will Cost Up to $27,500."

TOIG
Online Resources
BlockShopper South Florida. *Blockshopper News Service, July 13, 2009.* "Corporate Lawyer, OB/GYN Get 4BD in Jupiter, South Florida." Accessed April 3, 2013. http://southflorida.blockshopper.com/news/story/1300028307-Corporate_lawyer_OB_GYN_get_4BD_in_Jupiter.

Northwestern University Feinberg School of Medicine. *Faculty Profile Search.* "Randall M Toig, M.D." Accessed April 3, 2013. https://fsmweb.northwestern.edu/faculty/facultyprofile.cfm?xid=13562.

TRAYNER
Chicago Daily Tribune
July 24, 1906. "Chicagoans Wed in West: Miss Elizabeth Sanders Bride of Charles J. Trayner. Wedding Justice Office. Surprise to Groom's Parents."

April 27, 1908. "Obituary 2—No Title."

June 10, 1946. James Segreti, "Harness Racing Officials See a Boom in Wagers."

December 21, 1952. James Segreti, "3 Chicago Trot Tracks Get 172 Racing Nights: Season to Open April 15 at Maywood."

April 6, 1956. Lucy Key Miller, "Front Views & Profiles: Sport of Kings."

June 20, 1956. "Obituary 2—No Title."

Chicago Tribune
February 10, 1978. "Obituary 4—No Title."

TUCKER
Chicago Daily Tribune
November 1, 1946. "Tucker Takes Plant Fight to White House: Tucker Takes Plant Dispute to White House—Expect Announcement on Decision Today."

June 4, 1948. "Tucker Auto Power Drive Details Told."

October 29, 1948. "Sources of Auto's Design Disclosed by Preston Tucker."

October 6, 1949. Thomas Furlong, "U.S. Accuses Tucker: Firm Cash Misused: Prosecutor Bares Weird Deals. U.S. Denounces Act of Tucker as Trial Opens, Kerner Charges Fraud in Use of Funds."

Los Angeles Times
January 23, 1950. "Jury Acquits Tucker, Car Promoter: Seven Associates Also Found Innocent Of Criminal Action."

The New York Times
December 27, 1956. "Preston Tucker, Car Maker, Dies: Designer of Rear-Engined Torpedo Auto—After War Went Bankrupt in 1949; Leased Huge Plant. Acquitted of Fraud."

Orlando Sentinel
August 3, 2000. "Tucker-ed Out? 'Car of Tomorrow' Stills Draws Crowd Today; Preston Tucker Produced Only 51 of His Rear Engine Luxury Cars, but Enthusiasts Help His Dream Live on."

Special to The New York Times
October 28, 1949. "Racecar Designs Held Not Tucker's: Widow, Son of Harry Miller, Noted Auto Builder, Say He Was Only 'Contact Man.'"

Toronto Star
March 28, 1987. Bill Vance, "Preston Tucker's Great Car Hounded by Trouble."

August 13, 1994. Bill Vance, "Preston Tucker Promised Moon to Public."

The Wall Street Journal
June 15, 1948. "Preston Tucker Say SEC Is Investigating His Automobile Firm: Insists He Doesn't Know Reason: Hopes New Car Will Be Priced at $2,485 for Chicago."

Online Resource
Wikimedia Foundation. *Wikipedia.* "Preston Tucker." Accessed April 3, 2013. http://en.wikipedia.org/wiki/Preston_Tucker.

UPHAM
Boston Daily Globe
February 16, 1925. "F.W. Upham Dies At Palm Beach."

Los Angeles Times
February 16, 1925. "Republicans Lose Prominent Leader: F. W. Upham, Republican Leader Dies."

Special to The New York Times
August 7, 1921. "Mrs. Upham Under Knife."

VITTUM
Chicago Tribune
May 17, 2009. "Death Notice: Daniel W. Vittum, Jr."

WALKER
Online Resources
Hennessey, LeRoy. *Bench and Bar of Illinois, 1920.* Accessed April 3, 2013. http://www.ebooksread.com/authors-eng/leroy-hennessey/bench-and-bar-of-illinois-1920-ala/page-23-bench-and-bar-of-illinois-1920-ala.shtml.

Piola, Erica. *Beyond the Reading Room: The Library Company of Philadelphia Blog.* "Revisiting the Past, October 10, 2010." Accessed April 3, 2013. http://librarycompany.blogspot.com/2012_10_01_archive.html.

WELLS
See Dickason.

WHITAKER
Special to The New York Times
November 4, 1961. "Clem Whitaker, Sr. Dead at 62; Directed 85 Political Campaigns."

Online Resources
Wikimedia Foundation. *Wikipedia.* "Whitaker and Baxter." Accessed April 3, 2013. http://en.wikipedia.org/wiki/Whitaker_and_Baxter.

Catapano, Terry, et al. SNAC: *The Social Networks and Archival Context Project.* "Whitaker & Baxter Campaigns, Inc." Accessed April 3, 2013. http://socialarchive.iath.virginia.edu/xtf/view?docId=whitaker-baxter-campaigns-inc-cr.xml.

WILLETT
Chicago Daily Tribune
June 11, 1931. "Walter Willett Dead; Head of Bus Company."

Chicago Tribune
May 11, 1963. "H. L. Willett, Trucker, Civic Leader, Dies: Led Family Freight Firm Many Years."

Book
Encyclopedia of Biography, University of Wisconsin.

Online Resource
Curry, J. Seymour. *Chicago: its history and its builders, a century of marvelous growth (Volume 5).* Accessed April 3, 2013. http://www.ebooksread.com/authors-eng/j-seymour-josiah-seymour-currey/chicago-its-history-and-its-builders-a-century-of-marvelous-growth-volume-5-rru/page-29-chicago-its-history-and-its-builders-a-century-of-marvelous-growth-volume-5-rru.shtml.

WILMS
Chicago Daily Tribune
April 29, 1904. "In the Society World.: Miss Adeline Thomas Married to R. B. Watter, Baltimore. Ceremony Takes Place at Home of the Bride—Wedding of Miss Marry Taylor and Edmond Herzog—Engagement of Miss Lydia of Glencoe to William Wilms of Chicago Is Announced—Miss Cora Hill of Evanston Is a Bride."

October 18, 1917. "Veil Torn from Von Reiswitz Spy Payments: Used Rich Friend to Camouflage His Transactions."

February 23, 1933. Judith Cass, "Costume Fete Is Given for Paula Wilms: Will Be Bride Today of Malcolm Henderson."

May 13, 1934. "Holds Rites for Wm. Wilms, Stone Company Chairman."

Chicago Examiner
October 1917. "Wilms Avers Hindu Plot Was Paid For By Reiswitz."

Los Angeles Times
October 18, 1917. "Chicago Man German Tool. Wilms Financial Agent for Hindu Revolt Leader; Gave Kaiser's Consul Check for Forty Thousand; Another Witness Hired to Foment Trouble in Siam."

WINTERBOTHAM
Chicago Daily Tribune
February 21, 1888. "New Lincoln Park Commissioner: Gov. Oglesby Appoints A Successor to Col. James A. Sexton."

April 14, 1888. "Oglesby Tree In Lincoln Park."

February 1, 1892. "End of A Hero's Life: Sketch of Lieut. Col. John Russell Winterbotham."

March 3, 1892. "To Divide $825,000: John Russell Winterbotham's Estate Probated."

June 18, 1955. "Joseph Winterbotham Art Treasure Left to Institute."

Special to The New York Times
January 9, 1938. "Mrs. John R. Winterbotham."

WRIGHT
Chicago Daily Tribune
April 5, 1959. Judith Cass, "Miss Judith Beebe Atwood Bride of Kenneth Wright."

Chicago Tribune
August 29, 2000. "Wright."

ZINZOW
Chicago Daily Defender
November 16, 1965. "Women Voters Set College Program."

February 14, 1966. "Women Voters in On-Campus Program Series."

Chicago Tribune
November 18, 1965. "Program for Voters Planned."

GENERAL SOURCES

General History of Chicago
Chicago Daily News
March 8, 1935. "Local Oddities."

Chicago Daily Tribune
January 26, 1947. "Tenants Purchasing Apartments."

Chicago Sun Times
October 9, 1981. Jack Hafferkamp, "The Cooperative Lifestyle."

Chicago Tribune
November 6, 1983. David Ibata, "World of Co-Ops: Lots of Opulence— and Easy to Sell."

April 11, 1986. Anne Little, "Apartments with a View to Gracious Living—Architects Innovated High-Rises for the Rich and America Followed."

The New York Times
February 18, 1996. Robert Sharoff, "Luxury Conversions in a Chicago Enclave—Lake Shore Drive Becomes Condo and Rental a Co-Op."

Apartment and Condominium News
August 1985, "East Lake Shore Drive: A Landmark Decision," Pages 5–9.

Chicago Today
January 15, 1973. "Richest Block in Chicago—E. Lakeshore Drive—High Class."

1984. Commission on Chicago Historical and Architectural Landmarks. *East Lake Shore Drive District: Preliminary Summary of Information.* Pages 1–10.

Books
1917. A.J. Pardridge & Harold Bradley. *Directory to Apartments of the Better Class: Along the North Side of Chicago.* Chicago, IL.

1958. Herman Kogan, and Lloyd Wendt. *Chicago: A Pictorial History.* New York: E. P. Dutton. Print.

1969. Harold M. Mayer, Richard C. Wade, Glen E. Holt, and Gerald F. Pyle. *Chicago: Growth of a Metropolis.* Chicago, IL: University of Chicago. Print.

1975. David Lowe. *Lost Chicago.* Boston, MA: Houghton Mifflin. Print.

1982. Heise, Kenan and Michael Edgerton. *Chicago, Center for Enterprise: An Illustrated History.* Woodland Hills, CA: Windsor Publications. Print.

1983. Emmett Dedmon. *Fabulous Chicago: A Great City's History and People.* New York: Atheneum. Print.

2000. Miller, Ross. *The Great Chicago Fire.* Urbana: University of Illinois. Print.

2010. Hilliard, Celia. *The Prime Mover: Charles L. Hutchinson and the Making of the Art Institute of Chicago.* Chicago, IL: Art Institute of Chicago. Print.

2012. Wilbert Jones, Kathleen Willis-Morton, Maureen O'Brien, and Bob Dowey. *Chicago's Gold Coast.* Charleston, SC: Arcadia Pub. Print.

2013. Tom Dyja. *The Third Coast: When Chicago Built the American Dream.* New York: The Penguin Press. Print.

Online Resources
Wikimedia Foundation. *Wikipedia.* "Land Trust." Accessed April 11, 2013. http://en.wikipedia.org/wiki/Land_trust.

Chicago History Museum. *The Electronic Encyclopedia of Chicago.* "Rand McNally & Co.'s New Street Number Guide Map of Chicago, 1910." Accessed April 11, 2013. http://www.encyclopedia.chicagohistory.org/pages/10451.html.

Pre-999 Era
June 11, 1899. "Protest Against the Suggested Pier as a Blemish to Lake Shore Drive: Residents Say It Would Give Them an Inland Street. Breakwater in the Lake. Run by 'Sandsuckers.'"

September 16, 1900. "Chicago Real Estate: Proposed Lake Shore Drive Apartment Building Plan Under Consideration to Erect a New Central Church and Music Hall on the Mason Property in Washington Street— State Frontage Appraisal—Lloyd J. Smith Secures a Second Mortgage of $10,000 on Family Homestead in Sheridan Road."

October 20, 1907. "The Romances of the Famous Lake Shore Drive: Death on Story's Every Page."

May 8, 1910. Mary Isabel Brush, "When Fashion Meets the Shore Line in Chicago."

October 29, 1911. "Prominent Families Favor Apartments; Lake Shore Drive Scene of 'Flat' Building."

Other Periodicals
Town and Country
June 17, 1905. Milton Marks, "Chicago's Lake Shore Drive."

999 Era
Chicago Daily Tribune
August 21, 1904. "Injuries Cause Veteran's Death."

July 14, 1907. "Real Estate Transaction 1— No Title."

June 3, 1911. "Real Estate Transaction 1— No Title."

October 7, 1911. "More New Flats are Being Built. $150,000 Structure Planned Fifty-First Street and Champlain Avenue. Another on Woodlawn."

October 10, 1911. "Gunther Sells State St. Site: Premises at 438–440 Bring $7,300 a Front Foot; Price $180,000. $500,000 Flats Planned. Orrin J. Holbrook Will Erect 10 Story Building on Lake Shore Drive."

November 5, 1911. "Real Estate Transaction 2—No Title."

December 11, 1911. "Boulevards Save 'Colony' of Rich. Eleven Blocks Worth $10,000 on North Side Projected from Business Inroads. Land Owned by 43 Men. Lake Shore Drive Improvement Association Plans Beautifying Project."

August 15, 1913. "New Apartments for Lake Shore: Geo F. Porter to Erect $500,000 Ten Story Building Near Lincoln Parkway."

December 16, 1913. Henry M. Hyde, "No Romance Here? Watch Lake Front on Starry Night: Benches Filled with Couples Discussing Certain Phases of Feminist Movement."

April 9, 1914. "David B. Lyman Dies Suddenly: Former Head of Chicago Title and Trust Company Stricken in Loop Store. Funeral on Saturday. Services to Be Held at Emanuel Episcopal Church, La Grange."

July 24, 1915. "Fight on Taxes Organized on Lake Shore Drive: Association Contends Values are Too High. Against $10 for Link. Will Appeal to the Board."

December 31, 1915. "1915 Ranks Next to 1911 in City's Building Work: Second Biggest Year in History of Chicago Despite Labor Troubles."

November 28, 1916. "F. A. Hardy Buys Tower Building for $1,600,000: Loop Skyscraper and Ground Included in Big Real Estate Deal."

February 18, 1920. Al Chase, "999 Lake Shore Drive 10 Story Apartment Sold."

November 22, 1923. Genevieve Forbes, "Small's Road Bonds Politics, Women Told: 'Pay as You Go Plan' Outlined at Convention."

April 17, 1926. Al Chase, "Pay $1,333 Per Front Foot on East Erie St."

April 27, 1934. "Classified Ad 4— No Title."

February 5, 1937. "999 Lakeshore Foreclosure Suit Is Filed."

June 23, 1944. Al Chase, "999 Lake Shore Dr. Building Is Sold to Borg for $300,000."

January 18, 1947. Frank E. Siudzinski, "999 Lake Shore Goes Co-Op Again. Tenants Acquire Building for $550,000, Buy Stock."

January 19, 1947. "Tenants to Buy Apartments at 999 Lakeshore."

January 26, 1947. Al Chase, "Purchase Offer on Drake Tower Reported Near: Proponents Say 90 Pct. Of Tenants Agree."

April 6, 1952. Jospeh Egelhof, "Drama Cloaks Chicago Real Estate Deals. Colorful Since Early Days."

April 12, 1964. "Our Town: Lake Shore Drive—A Good Address But Extremely Odd One."

Chicago Sun Times
November 12, 1946. Adeline Fitzgerald, "At the Moment—New Co-Op Policy for 999 Lake Shore Dr. Holds Little Hope for Apartment Hunters."

January 18, 1980. "Right at Lake, 999 Building Classy Co-Op."

Chicago Tribune
January 17, 1985. John McCarron, "Lake Shore Drive Plan Gets Polite 'No': from Page 1 Landmark."

March 31, 1985. Ron Grossman, "Lost Lake Shore Drive: Mourning an Era: Mansions of Rich Famous Yield to Giant Condos."

April 11, 1986. Anne Little, "Apartments with a View to Gracious Living: Architects Innovated High-Rises for the Rich, and America Followed."

July 15, 1990. Margaret Carroll, "Chicago's Debt. Art Institute Owes Much to 1890s Patrons."

The New York Times
November 17, 1891. "The Thin Crust at Chicago."

Unidentified Newspaper
March 11, 1958. "Old 999—On the Way Home."

Other Periodical
May 29, 2013. "Lake Shore Drive Residents Unite." Lake Shore Drive Improvement Association.

Online Resource
About.com. *US Economy*. "Stock Market Crash Of 1929." Accessed April 11, 2013. http://useconomy.about.com/od/glossary/g/Stock-Market-Crash-of-1929.htm.

Books
1953. Emmett Dedmont. *Fabulous Chicago*. New York: Random House. Print.

1973. Condit, Carl W. *Chicago*. Chicago: University of Chicago. Print.

History of Lake Shore Drive
Chicago Daily Tribune
January 24, 1892. "Lake Shore Drive Assured. An Improvement Which Will Practically Create $12,000,000 Worth."

July 26, 1892. "It Can Extend East: What Operations Along the North Shore Are Proving. Chicago Not Limited in Growth of Territory to the North, West and South— Making Land on the Lake Front."

July 20, 1893. "Take Steps to Widen Pine Street: Lincoln Park Commissioners Establish Main Entrance to Sheridan Drive."

July 21, 1893. "To Extend the Lake Shore Drive."

September 17, 1872. "Going to Help Themselves.: Highly Important Meeting of the North Side Improvement Association."

September 12, 1875. "The Lake Shore Drive."

January 24, 1890. "The Lake Shore Drive Extension.: Archbishop Feehan's Suit to Restrain the Park Commissioners on Trial."

Online Resources
Chrucky, Serhii. *Forgotten Chicago*. "Lake Shore Drive Redux." Accessed April 11, 2013. http://forgottenchicago.com/articles/lake-shore-drive-redux/.

Miscellaneous
Chicago Dock, Canal Firm
Chicago Daily Tribune
February 10, 1957. Ernest Fuller, "Dock, Canal Firm Nearing Centennial: Lincoln Had Part in Founding."

Northside Land Association
Chicago Daily Tribune
July 31, 1892. "North Side Residence Purchases.: Gilt-Edged Property Secured for Improvement with Fine Structures."

Northwestern Law Review
2013. *Northwestern University Law Review* Northwestern University School of Law. 107: 3.

Pine Street Land Association
Chicago Examiner
October 8, 1901. "Effort to Maintain Boulevard Prestige."

SOURCES FOR IMAGES
(page number follows)

Chicago in 1862 (29)
Guyer, I. D. *History of Chicago; its Commercial and Manufacturing Interests and Industry; Together with Sketches of Manufacturers and Men Who Have Most Contributed to its Prosperity and Advancement, With Glances at Some of the Best Hotels, Also the Principal Railroads which Enter Chicago.* Chicago: Church, Goodman & Cushing. 1862.

Map (31)
Robinson's Atlas of the City of Chicago, Volume 3, Plate 11. 1886.

Map (32)
"Kinzie's Addition to Chicago" is copied from unique archives of Greeley-Howard-Norlin & Smith, established in Chicago in 1854, c/o Donald Smith, Land Surveyor. © 2014 Greeley-Howard-Norlin & Smith.

Map (33)
Bretz, J. H. *Geology of the Chicago Region: Part I—General: State of Illinois,* Geological Survey Division, Bulletin 65, Part I, Figure 30. 1939-40.

George Wellington Streeter (44)
Ballard, Everett Guy. *Captain Streeter, Pioneer.* Chicago. Emery Publishing Service. 1914.

Streeter Repairing the Reutan (45)
Ballard, Everett Guy. *Captain Streeter, Pioneer.* Chicago. Emery Publishing Service. 1914.

The Reutan (46)
Ballard, Everett Guy. *Captain Streeter, Pioneer.* Chicago. Emery Publishing Service. 1914.

Garbage Wagons in Streeterville (47)
Report of the submerged and shore lands legislative investigating committee, made in pursuance of the statute, to the governor of the state of Illinois and the forty-seventh General assembly of Illinois. Volume 2. 1911.

Map (49)
Atlas of Chicago published by Rascher. Volume 1. Sheet #21. 1891.

Maurice T. Maloney (55)
The Journal of the American-Irish Historical Society. Volume 16. 1917.

Henry Bartling (55)
Babeuf, J. *The Portraiture of the 39th General Assembly, Illinois, Containing Portraits of Members and All Desirable Information Regarding Same.* 1895.

Charles Fitz-Simons (58)
Memorials of Deceased Companions of the Commandery of the State of Illinois, Military Order of the Loyal Legion of the United States from July 1, 1901 to December 31, 1911. Volume 2. 1912.

Silas W. Lamoreaux (59)
The Stark County Democrat. Page 3. Canton, OH. April 01, 1897.

Map (60)
Northeastern Reporter. Volume 45, Page 832. West Publishing Company. 1897.

Streeterville in 1910 (61)
Report of the Submerged and Shore Lands Legislative Investigating Committee, Made in Pursuance of the Statute, to the Governor of the State of Illinois and the Forty-Seventh General Assembly of Illinois. Volume 2. 1911.

McGillan (73)
French, Charles. Editor. *Biographical History of the American Irish in Chicago.* Chicago. American Biographical Publishing Co. 1897.

Henry Martyn Shepard (76)
Stiels, Henry R. *The History and Genealogies of Ancient Windsor, Connecticut.* Hartford, Connecticut. Press of the Case. Lockwood & Brainard Company. 1892.

Benjamin Marshall (77)
Currey, Josiah Seymour. *Chicago: Its History and Its Builders, a Century of Marvelous Growth.* Volume 5. Chicago. S. J. Clarke Publishing Company. 1912.

Floorplan 999 (80)
Pardridge, Albert J. and Harold Bradley. Compilers. *Directory to Apartments of the Better Class on the North Side of Chicago,* 1917.

George Wellington Streeter (82)
Ballard, Everett Guy. *Captain Streeter, Pioneer.* Chicago. Emery Publishing Service. 1914.

Pokagon (82)
Buechner, Cecilia Bain. *The Pokagons.* Indiana Historical Society Publications. Vol. 10, No. 5. 1933.

Frederick Oliver Cartoon (90)
McEvoy, J. P. "Live Wires in Their Line in Cartoon and Rhyme." *Chicago Evening Post.,* 1923.

George Borg (91)
Casey, Robert J. *Mr. Clutch: the Story of George William Borg.* Indianapolis. The Bobbs-Merrill Co. 1948.

Secor Cunningham (97)
Portraits and Biographies of the Fire Underwriters of the City of Chicago. Chicago. Chas. T. Rothermel & Co. 1897.

David Hamilton (98)
The Biographical Dictionary and Portrait Gallery of Representative Men of Chicago and the World's Columbian Exposition. Chicago. American Biographical Publishing Company. Page 541. 1892.

James C. Hutchins (99)
McEvoy, J. P. "Live Wires in Their Line in Cartoon and Rhyme." *Chicago Evening Post.* 1923.

Mahin Ad (101)
Mahin's Magazine. Volume 3. Page 186. April–May, 1904.

Mason Spinden Expedition (102)
Mason, Gregory and Herbert Joseph Spinden. *The Silver Cities of Yucatan.* G. P. Putnam's Sons. 1927.

Livingston T. Dickason (104)
The National Tribune. Page 8. Washington D.C. June 18, 1908.

Frances Welles Shepard (107)
Scott, Rose Moss. *Daughters of the American Revolution.* 1929.

Ralph Martin Shaw (114)
Hennessey, LeRoy. Editor. *Bench and Bar of Illinois.* 1920.

Speejaks and the Gowens (116-117)
Collins, Dale. *Sea-Tracks of the Speejacks Round the World.* Garden City, New York. Doubleday, Page & Company. 1923.

Mrs. Livingston Fairbank (133)
Good Housekeeping. Volume 80, Number 6, June 1925.

Al Capone (134)
Chicago Gang Wars in Pictures. X Marks the Spot.

Borg Images (139-140)
Casey, Robert J. *Mr. Clutch: The Story of George William Borg.* Indianapolis. The Bobbs-Merrill Co. 1948.

Keith (143)
Spaeth, Sigmund Gottfried. Editor. *Who is Who in Music: Biographical Reviews, Pictorial and Other Features of Interest to and Concerning Persons in the World of Music.* Chicago. Berghan Pub. Co. 1927.

Balke (143)
Spink, Al. *Spink Sport Stories.* Volume 2. 1921.

William Wilms (156)
American Lumberman Magazine. Chicago, Illinois. January 20, 1906.

Edward Russell Perry (163)
"Notable Men of Chicago and Their City." *Chicago Daily Journal,* 1910.

Bentons (178)
Wisdom. Volume 3. Number 30. June 1959.

William B. Huey (188)
McEvoy, J. P. "Live Wires in Their Line in Cartoon and Rhyme." *Chicago Evening Post.,* 1923.

Index

Page references in *italic* indicate photographs or illustrations.

Abercrombie, Gertrude, 199
Acheson, Dean, 195
A. C. McClurg & Company, 75
Adams, Ansel, 155
Adams, Samuel, 114
Addington, Florence LaVictorie, 148–49, 205
Addington, James, 148–49
Addington, Keene Harwood, *148*, 148–49
Adler, Lou, 200
Adler, Mortimer, 152
Aetna blasting caps, 98
Aetna Explosives Company, 98
Airbus Indstrie, 203
Albert Lasker's Lord & Thomas, 178
ALCOA, 206
Alden, Carrie, 211
Alden, Emersen, 211
Alden, Grae, 211
Alden, Tord D., 211
Alger, Russell A., 108
Allan, Mary S., 204
Allan, Stanley N., 204
Allis Chalmers, 72
Allmendinger, Minnie, 55
Allmendinger, Tobias, 43, 72
American Cancer Society, 197
American District Telegraph Company, 119
American Fire of Philadelphia, 97
American Medical Association, 175, 177
American National Bank, 167
American Red Cross, 106, 159
American Steel Foundries, 159
Amphenol Electronics, 140
Amtrak, 203
Anderson (Mr.), 94
Anderson, Arthur, 127
Anderson, Fannie, 127
Anderson, Ida, 99
Anderson, Mable, 136, 179
Anderson, Paul J., 187
Andreas, Dwayne, 199
Andreas, Margot, 199
Andreas, Miriam Bomberger, 199
Andreas, Osborn, 199, 225, 227
Andrew, Elizabeth, 146
Andrew, Henry, 146
Andrews Sisters, 138
Andrie, Barbara A., 202
Andrie, Stanley J., 202
Annovazzi, Maria Louisa, 172
Annovazzi, Sergio, 172
Anthon, W. R., 5
Antoinette Pope School Cookbook, 201
Antoinette Pope Schools of Fancy Cookery, 201
Archer Daniels Midland, 199

Arlington Jockey Club, 195
Armstrong, B. J., 16
Army and Navy Club, 144
Army Corps of Engineers, 51
Art Institute of Chicago, 56, *111*, *111*, 113, 119, *123*, 227
Aspen Center for Environmental Studies, 154
Aspen Center for Physics, 154
Aspen Institute for Humanistic Studies, 154
Aspen Music Festival, 154
Aspen Program on World Economy, 154
Aspen Skiing Company, 153
Atchison, Marion, 159
Atchison, Topeka and Santa Fe railroad, 98
Avery, Samuel, 65
Axelrod, David, 175

Baasek, Inga, 157
Baker, Skinny, 138
Baldwin, Abraham Rosecrans, 95
Baldwin, Helen Poole, 95
Baldwin family, 11, 95
Balke, Julius, Jr., 142, 143, *143*
Barnes, Harriet, 127
Barrow, J. T., 135
Bartling, Henry, 53, 54–61, *55*
Bauer, Margaret Z., 167, 187
Bauer, Marshall, 187
Bauer family, 94
Baum, Frank L., 146
Baumgarden, H. L., 139, 202
Baumgarden, Mabel, 139, 192, 202
Bay, Beich, 174
Bay, James N., 174
Bayer, Herbert, *152*
Bays English Muffin Corporation, 174
Beardsley, Cindy, 209
Beardsley, Robert Stahr, 209
Beck, Julia, 115
Beck, Marshall, 139, *139*
Becker, Hermoine, 156
Becker, Paul, 156
Beebe, Anne, *125*
Behring, Tillie, 99
Belden Manufacturing Co., 163
Bell, Joshua, 154
Bellow, Saul, 155
Bell Telephone Company, 119
Benjamin, Reuben, 149
Benjamin Electric Company, 149
Benson, Marie, 112
Benton, Louise H., *178*, 178–79
Benton, William, *178*, 178–79
Benton and Bowles, 178
Bernhardt, Sarah, 38
Bernstein, Carl, 207
Bertha, Agnes Hanes, 162
Bertha, Edward M., 162
Bertha, Edward M., Jr., 162
Berube, Edward, 202

B. F. Goodrich Rubber Company, 73
Bias, Harriet, 107
Black, Hugo, 154
Blackmun, Harry, 154
Blake, Shaw & Company, 77
Bligh, Harrison J., 203
Bligh, Perle Lund, 203
Bliss, Cornelius, 63
Blixt, Alice, 111
Bloomington Limestone Company, 157
Bognar, Gabriella S., 149
Bolger, Ray, 100
Boork, Anne, 149
Borden, Ellen, 170
Borden, John, 76, 169
Borden, Mary Elizabeth, 169, 170
Borden, William, 53
Borden Dairy, 170
Borg, Carl W., *139*, 139
Borg, Effie, 139
Borg, George W., *91*, 92, 109, 139–41, 148, 166, 198, 227
Borg, George W., Jr., 139
Borgana, 140, *141*
Borg and Beck clutch, 139, *140*
Borg & Beck, 139, *140*
Borglura, 140
Borg-Warner Corporation, 92, 109, 139
Borland, Beatrice, 149
Borland, Beatrice "Belle" McCullough, 149
Borland, Belle, 149
Borland, Chauncey Blair, Jr., 149
Borland, Chauncey "Charles" Blair, 149
Borland Manufacturing, 149
Bowen, Clymer S., *125*
Bowers, Lloyd W., 112
Bowers, Louise Hellen, 112
Bowers, Thomas W., 112
Bowles, Chester, 178–79
Boyce, Jane, 132
Boyd, Alan Stephenson, 203, *203*
Boyd, Flavil Juanita Townsend, 203
Boys Clubs of America, 159
Bradley, Harold, 80
Bradley, W. H., 35
Bradt, Samuel F., 73
Brevoort Hotel, 99, *99*
Brewster & Co.
  See Edward L. Brewster & Co
Bricking, Rudolph, 127
Bridges, Jeff, 180
Britten, Benjamin, 154
Brooks, Springer (Mr. and Mrs.), 94, 97
Brown, C. W., 126
Brown, Frank Townley (Mrs.), 137
Brown, Sarah E., 175
Brunen, May, 111

Brunswick (billard and bowling equipment), 143
Bureau of Charities, 118
Burger, Warren, 154
Burgess, A. H., 26
Burke, Billie, 100
Burroughs, Edgar Rice, 75, 94, 97
Burton, Francis E., 58–59
Burton, William M., 14, 113, *113*
Burton family, 115
Bush, George H. W., 154
Bush, George W., 154
Byram, Frank, 162
Byram, Mary, 162
Byrd, R. E., *158*

Cadillac touring car, 15, 145, *145*
Cagney, James, 135, *135*
Cairns, Anna M. (daughter), 142
Cairns, Anna May (mother), 142, 192
Cairns, James E., 142
Calhoun, John B.., 34
California Chamber of Commerce, 176
Camel Company, 111
Campaigns, Inc., 175–77
Campbell, Suzanne M., 210
Campbell, Thomas J., 210, *210*
Cannier, Caroline, 99
Cannon, Helen West, 198
Cannon, Le Grand, 198
Cannon, Louise, 198
Cannon, Sylvia, 198
Capone, Albert Francis "Sonny," 149
Capone, Alphonse, *134*, 134–35, 149, 195, 226
Carlson, Anne, 114
Carlson, Emma, 94, 97
Carpenter, Alice, *125*
Carpenter, Ellen Waller, 169
Carpenter, George Herriman, 169
Carpenter, John Alden, 105, 132, 169, 169–70, 226, 227
Carpenter, Rue Winterbotham, 13, 105, 106, 111, 169
Carroll, J. F., 78
Carson Pirie Scott & Co., 157
Carter, Jimmy, 154
Cartier-Bresson, Henri, 154–55
Cawley, Agnes, 114
Celotex (bagasse-based insulation), 136
Celotex Corporation, 136, 138
Central Electric Company, 119
Central Trust Company, 110
Chalmers, William J., 72, 73
Chambers, Nellie, 94, 102, 179
Chapin, Huntley, 137–38
Chapman, Oscar, 195
Chase, Al, 89
Chatfield-Taylor, Adele Blow, 107, *107*
Chatfield-Taylor, Wayne, 107

Cheeseman, Linda, 299
Cheeseman, William, 299
Chesher, Dollie, 106, *106*, 227
Chicago, Indiana and Southern
    Railroad, 107
Chicago American, 134, 135, 178
Chicago Bible Society, 118
Chicago Board of Education, 118
Chicago Board of Options
    Exchange, 208
Chicago Crime Commission, 149
Chicago Cubs, 38
Chicago Daily News, 86, 103
Chicago Daily Tribune, 73, 76.
    See also Chicago Tribune
Chicago Dock and Canal, 30, 55
Chicago Edison Company, 128
Chicago Elevated Railways, 128
Chicago Evening Post, 90, 99, 188
Chicago Examiner, 47, 70, 78, 95,
    96, 105, 109, 110
Chicago Flexible Shaft, 109
Chicago Great Western Railway,
    114
Chicago Historical Society, 56,
    108, *108*
Chicago Junction Railway, 114
Chicago Latin School, 75
Chicago Public Library, 26
Chicago Radio Laboratory, 158
Chicago Railway Company, 111
Chicago Realty Board, 89
Chicago Sun-Times, 86, 92, 164
Chicago Symphany Orchestra,
    169, 172, 191
Chicago Telephone Company, 73
Chicago Telephone Supply
    Company, 177
Chicago Title and Trust, 53, 59,
    69, 73, 83, 118
Chicago Today, 178
Chicago Tribune, 26, 36, 53, 57,
    59, 72, 86, 89, 132, 174, 187,
    192, 208
Chicago Zoological Society, 138
Child, Julia, 16
Children of the Kindertransport
    sculpture, 171, *171*
Children's Memorial Hospital, 56,
    94, 97
Childs, C. Frederick (Mrs.), *125*
Childs, Claire, *125*
Childs, L. Newell, *125*
Christie, Mary L. Russell, 163
Churchill, Winston, 19
Citizen's Committee for Passage of
    the Gun Responsibility Bill, 178
Civil Aeronautics Board, 203
Clancy, Katherine, 114
Clark, Mary, 136
Clark, Michelle, 207
Clark, Thomas J., 109
Clarke, Bertha Holbrook, 142
Clarke, Thelma I., 195
Clarke, T. Howard, 195
Clarke, W. H., 205
Clarke, William E., 142
Clemens, Eva, 115
Clemens, Howard, 115
Clemens, Margetta, 115
Clemens, Myrtle, 115
Clemens, Ralph, 115

Clemens, Thomas, 115, 188
Cleveland, Dwight M., 205
Cleveland, Grover, 47, 54
Clinton, Bill, 154, 210
Cole Brothers Circus, 161
Colonial Trust & Savings, 110
Colwell, Arthur R., 202, *202*
Colwell, Jeanne H., 202
Commission on Chicago
    Landmarks, 20
Commonwealth Edison Co., 72,
    128, 198, 204
Conlon, Arthur, 109
Conlon, Michael, 109
Connecticut Mutual Life
    Insurance Company, 38
Consolidated Crushed Stone
    Corporation, 193
Consolidated Freightways, 171
Container Corporation of
    America, 152
Conway, R. C., 135
Cook, Estella, 142
Cook, Esther, 142
Cook, John P., 142
Cook, Mary G., 142, 173
Cook, W. C., 142, 173
Cook County Hospital, 206, 212
Cooper, Gary, *152*
Cooper, Henry N., 43, 57, 59, 66,
    68, 72, 73
Coppola, Francis Ford, 180
Corwith, Alice Rebecca
    Hughlett, 111, 226
Corwith, John E., 111
Corwith family, 115
Coughlin, Bessie, 115
Cousins, Norman, 155
Cowham, June Provines, 208
Cowham, Neil, 208
Cowham, Robert Neil, 208
Cowham family, 166
Cox, William H., 47, 59, 63
Coxe, Alexander Brown, 196
Coxe, Colleen, 196
Coxe, Owen, 196
Coyle, E. A., 142, 195
Coyle, Violet, 142, 195
Cramer, Ervin, 191
Creedon, Nellie, 107
Cregier, Dewitt C., 73
Crosby, Bing, 16, 164, *164*
Crowell, G. Kenneth, 212
Crowell and Leibman, 212
Cudahy, William, B., 166, 167, *167*
Culver, B. F., 34
Cuneo, Frank, Jr., 173
Cuneo, Frank, Sr., 173
Cuneo Press, 173
Cunningham, Althea Stone,
    94, 97
Cunningham, Secor, Jr., 94, 97
Cunningham, William Wood
    "Secor," 94, 97, *97*
Cunningham family, 115
Curtis, Diane, 163
Curtis, Doris Russell, 163
Curtis, Theodore, 163
C. W. Canby & Co., 96, *96*

Dahlberg, Alma Lee, 136, 179
Dahlberg, Bror Gustave, 136, *136*,
    138, 179, 227
Dahlberg, Gilda Krieger Lichtle,
    136, 138, 179
Dahlberg, Mary Alexander,
    136–38, *137*, 179
Dahlberg family, 94
Dale Bakery, 77
Damon, Matt, 199
Damon Runyon Cancer Fund, 138
Daprato Brothers Company, 170,
    170
Darrow, Clarence, 135
Daughters of the American
    Revolution, 107, 111
Davis, Bette, *186*, 187
Davis, Miles, 199
Dawson, Joyce, 208
D'Cruz Tharsus D'Cruz,
    Matrona, 187
Dean, Isabel, 299
Dean, John, 299
Decker, H. H., 89
Dedmon, Emmett, 86
Deemer, Jesse, 145
de Gaulle, Charles, 16, 190
Deli, Anne, 173
Deli, Steven, 173
Dennehy, Marion Warner, *125*
Dennehy, Thomas C., Jr., *125*
DePaul University, 207
Derby, Falah Campbell, 190
Derby, William Ballard, 190
Devore, Daniel B., 115, 227
Devore, Helen G., 115
Diaghivlev, Serge, 169
Dick, Edison, *125*
Dickason, Dorothy, 95–97, *96*, 179
Dickason, Elizabeth Gilbert
    Barber, 95–96, 179
Dickason, Katherine Hogg
    Maxwell, 124, 179, 196
Dickason, Livingston Thomas, 95,
    96, 226
Dickason, Livingston Thomas, Jr.,
    95, 124, 179, 196
Dickason, Mary Elizabeth, 124,
    179
Dickason family, 11, 94, 95, 115
Disraeli, Benjamin, 26
Dockery, Margaret, 94, 102, 179
Dodd, Leander J., 89
Dodge, Ada Williams Ince, 186
Dodge, Ray Edgar, *186*, 186–87
Dodge family, 186
Dodge Trophy, 187
Doig, Margaret Stuart, 127
Donnelley, Eleanor, 113
Donnelley, Laura Belle Thorne,
    113
Donnelley, Reuben Hamilton, 113,
    113, 227
Donnelley & Sons.
    See R. R. Donnelley & Sons
Douglas, Emily Taft, 176
Douglas, Helen Gahagan, 176, 177
Douglas, Melvyn, 177
Douglas, Stephen A., 72
Douglas Aircraft, 189
Dreiser, Theodore, 75
Dreyer, E.S., 51

Druggan, Terry, *134*, 134–35, 180,
    225, 226
Dubois, W. E. B., 74, 75
Dubussy, Claude, 132
Duffy, Richard E., 299
Duffy, Sheila C., 299
Duncan, Donald F., 211
Duncan Parking Meter Company,
    211
Duncan Toys Company, 211, *211*
Duncan yoyo, 211, *211*
Dy-Dee Wash, Inc., 114

Eagle, 208
Early, Stephen, *195*
Edison, Thomas, 16, 72
Edison, Thomas Alva, 127–28
Edward L. Brewster & Co, 163
Edwards, Betty, 142
Edwards, B. H., 142, 197
Edwards, B. H., Jr., 142
Edwards, Estella, 197
Edwards, Helen K., 167
Edwards, Marion, 142
Egg McMuffin, 174
Ehlenz, Daniel J., 182–83
Eiger family, 73
Eisenhower, Dwight, 17, 138, 170,
    177, 203
Elizabeth I (queen of England), 127
Elizabeth II (queen of England),
    19, 149
Eller, Morris, 135
Elliott, D. K., 197
Elliott, Kathryn, 162
Elliott, Marion, 197
Elliott, William A., 162
Ellis, Howard, 76
Ellis Memorial Antiques Show,
    104
Elman, Mischa, 169
E. L. Schneider, Jr., & Son, 73, 215
Emmanuel, Rahm, 16
Enbridge Energy Partners, 213
Encyclopedia Britannica, 178
English muffins, 174, *174*
Eversz, Barbara, 97
Eversz, Ernest H., 97
Eversz, Ethel Wood, 97

Faber, Suzanne Joy, 198, 213
Fairbank, Livingston, Jr., 132, 227
Fairbank, Livingston III, 132
Fairbank, Miriam Patterson, 132,
    132, *133*, 227
Fairbank, Nathaniel Kellogg, 47,
    48, 55
Fairbank, N. Kellogg, 132
Fair Store, 126
Fantus, Bernard, 168
Farwell, Joan, 157
Farwell, John V., 48, *48*, 55, 157
Farwell, John V. III, 157
Farwell, John V. IV, 157
Farwell, Margaret Willing, 157
Faubus, Orville, 17
Fay, Addison G., 98
Fay, A. Orville, 98
Fay, Emily W., 98
Fay, Martha, 98
Fay, R. Arshman, 98
Federal Land Office, 12

Federal Reserve Bank of New York, 172
Federal Trade Commission, 210
Feehan, Patrick Augustine (bishop), 40
Feinstein, Dianne, 210
Feldkamp, Frederick L., 204
Feldkamp, Judith L., 204
Fermi, Enrico, 155
Field, Eugene, 75
Field, Henry, 160, 160–61, 227
Field, Marshall, 38, 53, 160
Field, Placidia White Knowlton, 160
Field Museum of Natural History, 160, 160–61
Fireman's Fire of York, 97
First Chicago Corporation, 172, 213
First National Bank of Chicago, 172
FirstService Residential, 15, 94, 166
Fischer, Dr., 156
FitzFlaad, Alan, 127
Fitz-Simons, Charles, 43, 51, 53, 54, 55, 57, 58, 69
Fitz-Simons and Connell, 51
Fizdale, Mara Dana, 198, 213
Fizdale, Melora Sarah, 198, 213
Fizdale, Richard B., 198, 213
Fizdale, Thomasina Rose, 198, 213
Fleming, Renée, 154
Fletcher, Avis C., 203
Flowers, Inez W., 149
Flowers, Joseph C., 149
Folds, William, 136
Foley & Lardner, 204
Foote, Cone and Belding, 178
Force, William, 68
Forest, Henry, 135
Fox, Agnes, 162
Fox, Charles Eli, 10, 73, 79
Fox, Helen Heyl, 162
Fox, Milo Pitcher, 162
Frances Clark Library, 174
Frank, Dora M., 150
Franks, Bobby, 208
Freed, Adelaide Josie Beauregart, 196
Freed, Lawrence, 196
Freivogel, Caroline, 188
Freivogel, William, 188
Friedman, Milton, 210
Friends of China, 144
Frisbe, David W., 209
Fugard and Knapp, 19
Fuller, Buckminister, 155
Fuller, Melville, 76
Fuson, Richard, 149

Gable, Clark, 100
Gabor, Eva, 138
Gabreez, Lewis, 94, 187
Gabricle, Mario A., 172
Galena and Chicago Union railroad, 29
Galena National Bank, 111
Gallo, Michael, 204
Gallo, Rose Anne, 204
Garbe, Raymond, 162
Garbe, Ruth Moore, 162

Garfield, James A., 118
Garland, Judy, 100
Gary, Joseph E., 50, 51
Gaynor, Janet, 100
Geithner, Tim, 172
General Electric, 119
General Mortgage Investments, Inc., 92
George W. Borg Corporation, 139–40
Gerde, Elsie, 162
Gerde, Erick, 162
Gerde, Lillian, 162
Gibson, Charles Dana, 144
Gibson, Irene, 144, 144
Gibson, Irma, 144
Giles, Hartwell, 148
Giles, Nora, 148
Gillespie, Dizzy, 199, 225
Girl from Farris's, The (Burroughs), 97
Glass, Philip, 154
Gleason, Mary, 111
Goethe, Johann Wolfgang von, 153
Goetz, Frances, 146, 147
Golding, Andrew, 168
Golding, James L., 168
Golding, Nancy, 168
Golding, Phillip, 168
Golomb, Adam, 190
Golomb, Harvey M., 190
Golomb, Lynn R., 190
Golomb, Sara, 190
Good Humor frozen treats, 211
Goodrich Company.
    See B. F. Goodrich Rubber Company
Gordon, C. P. Fletcher, 203
Gordon, Elinor, 212
Gordon, Richard, 212
Gorman, Anna, 114
Gowen, Albert Younglove, 116–18, 117, 227
Gowen, Jeanne Bouchet Lyle, 116–18, 117
Grable, Betty, 138
Graceland Cemetery, 56
Graettinger, Elizabeth "Betty," 191
Graettinger, John S., 191
Graham, Edna F. Freeman (Hellwig), 192
Graham, John G., Jr., 192
Grant, Frederick, 76
Grant, Ida, 76
Grant, Ulysses S., 111, 226
Great Lakes Dredge and Dock Company, 187
Great Lakes Mortgage Corporation, 92
Great Lakes Paper Company, 136
Greeley, Samuel Sewell, 32
Greene, Samuel, 167
Greene, Viola Pryor, 167
Greenwald, Herb, 173
Griffin, Abby H., 174
Griffin, Jeremiah, 174
Griffin, Leona "Lee" E., 174
Griggs & Co.
    See S. C. Griggs & Co.
Grimm, Richard H., 168

Griscom, Ludlow, 104
Gross, Samuel, 53
Guenzel, Louis, 73
Guzik, "Greasy Thumb," 135

Hagan, Ruth, 190
Haley, Jack, 100
Hall, Henry Glover, 118, 227
Halsey, Stuart & Co., 127, 130, 131
Halston, John C., 206
Halston, Kirsten, 206
Hamilton, Bruce P., 98
Hamilton, David G., 98, 98, 123, 212
Hamilton, Margaret, 100
Hamilton, Mary, 123
Hamilton, Mary Jane Kendall, 98
Hanks, Tom, 199
Hannah, Alexander D., 99, 227
Hannah, Catherine Grady, 99
Hannah, Daryl, 199, 199–200
Hannah, Don, 199–200
Hannah, Donald C., 102, 199–200
Hannah, Page, 199–200
Hannah, Susan H., 199–200
Hannah family, 115
Hannah & Hogg, 99
Hannah Marine Corp., 199
Hardy, Francis A., 73
Harlan, John Marshall, 154
Harlow, Jean, 100, 135
Harriman, Arvell, 195
Harris, James, 119
Harrison, Benjamin, 54
Harrison, Carter, 72
Harry Weese and Associates, 204
Hart, Frances, 126
Harvey, Byron (Mrs.), 161
"Hassel," 134, 135
Hausberg, Margaret, 204
Hausberg, Mark, 204
Hawthorne, Nathaniel, 143
Hayes, William, 66
Haynes, Antonia, 174
Haynes, Connie Hsu, 174
Haynes, Thomas, 174, 202
Healy, George, 73
Healy, George P. A., 56, 56
Healy, Louisa, 66
Healy, Marquette (Mr. and Mrs.), 118
Healy family, 76
Heehn, Carrie, 69
Heidelmeier, Max, 65
Heisman Trophy, 187
Hemming, Rudolph, 118
Hemming, Yvonne, 118
Hempstead, Mary, 15, 111
Henderson, William Penhallow, 105–6
Henrotin Hospital, 136, 197
Henry VIII (king of England), 127
Hepburn, Katherine, 100
Hermann, Marie, 156
Hesse, Martha Ossian, 213, 213
Hesse Gas Company, 213
Higgins, Mary, 149
Higginson, Harriet, 161
Hill, Alice, 188
Hill, Arthur, 110
Hill, John D., 188

Hill, John D., Jr., 188
Hill, Lillian, 119
Hillside Shopping Center, 195
Hines, Gerald D., 209
Hines Veterans Hospital, 197
Hitchcock, Alfred, 51
Hixon, Blanche Kelleher, 99
Hixon, George Cooley, 99
Hixon, Gideon Cooley, 99
Hixon family, 115
Hoeldtke, Henry "Klondike," 68
Hoffman, Malvina, 160
Hogg, David, 99
Hogg, Frank, 116–17
Holbrook, Orrin J., 73
Holden, Hale, Jr., 125
Holt, Cutting & Sidley, 112
Home for the Friendless, 56, 118
Honeyman, Marian Stewart, 109, 109
Honeyman, Robert B., 109
Honnegger, Arthur, 132
Honoré, Adrian C., 73
Hoover, Herbert, 19
Hopkins, Anna F., 111
Hopkins, Farley, 111
Hopkins, James McHenry, Jr., 111
Hopkins, James McHenry, Sr., 111
Hopkins family, 115
Hopmayer, Gary Stephen, 192
Hopmayer, Marlene (Meme) Esther, 192
Hotz, Lila, 107
Hotz, Robert S. (Mrs.), 107
Howard, Arlene, 174
Howard, Helen M. Bishop, 195
Howard, Hubert E., 195, 195
Hron, Michael E., 197
Hubbard, Elisha Dyer, 122
Huey, Catherine, 188
Huey, William B., 188, 188, 227
Huey Company, 188
Hughes, Langston, 169
Hulbert, Horace, 55
Hunnewell, James F., 104
Hunt, E. Howard, 207
Hunt, George, 50
Hunt, Helen, 207
Hussein, King, 19
Hutchins, Agnes, 99
Hutchins, James C., 99, 99
Hutchins, James C., Jr., 99
Hutchins, John M., 99
Hutchins, Robert Maynard, 152
Hutchins family, 115
Hutyara, Betty, 149

Illinois Central Railroad, 12, 106, 203
Illinois Masonic Medical Center, 195
Illinois Racing Commission, 195
Illinois Surgical Society, 197
Ingraham, Jay, 116
Inland Steel Industries, 206
Insull, Samuel, 72, 127–28, 130–31, 163
Insull, Samuel, Jr., 125
International Cellucotton Products Company, 212
International Harvester, 29, 173

Interstate Commerce
Commission, 171
Iroquois Theatre, 77–78
Isham, Helen, *125*
Isham, Lincoln & Beale, 209
Italian Chamber of Commerce,
173

Jacobek, Christine L., 194
Jacobs, Whipple, 163
James (king of England and
Scotland), 127
James, Henry, 190
Jenkins, Anna, 127
John D. and Catherine T.
MacArthur Foundation, 183
Johns, Jasper, 154
Johnson, Anna, 116
Johnson, Brenda, 174
Johnson, Christina, 142
Johnson, Craig, 136, 138, 179
Johnson, Emma, 114, 123
Johnson, Lyndon B., 203, *203*
Johnson, Mildred, 99
Johnson, Peter J., 58–59
Johnson, Selma, 123
Johnson, Thomas P., Jr., 174
Jones, Addington, Ames &
Siebold, 149
Jones, Helen, 202
Jostrand, Beth, 179
Jostrand, John, 179
Judd, Elmer M., Jr., 146
Judd, Eugenie "Jean" Farrow, 146
J. Walter Thompson Company,
164–65

Kaltenmark, Nelly, 150
Karatz, Abe, 182
Katria, Johanna, 124
Kearney, Joseph D., 69
Keith, Elbridge Gallet, 118
Keith, Harriet G., 118
Keith, Marie M., 169, 226
Keith, Royden James, 169, 227
Keith Brothers Company, 118
Kennan, George, 154
Kennedy, John F., 203
Kennedy, John F., Jr., 199
Kent, Geoffrey, 171, 227
Kent, Katharine Mary Ruscoe,
171
Kerner, Otto, 182, 183, 207
Ketting, E. Ogden, *125*
Kimberly-Clark Corp., 212
King, Carl H., 118
King, Donald West, 124, 196
King, Marjorie, 118
King, Mary Elizabeth Dickason,
196
Kinney, Eugene McDonald
"Skipper," 158
Kinsella, Audon, 95, 124, 179
Kinzie, John, 29
Kinzie, Robert, 29
Kirby, William T., 182, 183
Kirk, Charles S., 58
Kirk, John A., 66, 68, 225
Kirkland, Weymouth, 76
Kirkland & Ellis, 194, 201
Kirk's American Family Flakes,
147

Kiser, J. W., 143, 167
Kissinger, Henry, 154
Knapp, Elisabeth, 104
Knight, Donnelley & Co, 113
Knight, Goodwin, 177
Koch, Teresa, 150
Kochs, Herbert W., 193
Kochs, Judith Ann, 193
Kohn, Gershon.
See Kent, Geoffrey
Kraft, John H., 162, *162*, 227
Kraft, June, 162
Kraft Cheese, 162
Kretzinger, George Wilson, Jr.,
142, 175
Kretzinger, Louise, 142, 175
Kroc, Ray, 174
Krueger, James W., 207
Kushner, Barbara, 201
Kushner, Melvyn, 17, 201

La Chance, Leander H., 109
LaFollette, Harvery M., 63
LaFollette, Robert, 63
LaFollette Coal, Iron and Railway
Company, 63
Lahr, Bert, 100
Laing, Cuthbert, 55
Lake, Frank, *134*, 134–35
Lake, William, 142
Lake Forest Water Company, 148
Lake Shore Building Company,
73, 89
Lake Shore Drive Improvement
Association, 73
Lake Shore Drive Land
Association, 72
Lake Shore Drive project, 35–36,
43, 50–53, 54–59, 60, 69
Lamarr, Hedy, 138
Lamoreaux, Silas W., 47, 59, *59*, 63
Land, Signe, 149
Landis, Kenesaw Mountain, 156
Lange, Dorothea, 155
Langhorne, George Tayloe
(colonel), 15, 144–45, *145*, 161,
212, 226, 227
Langhorne, Mary Waller, 144, 212
Langhorne, Nancy Witcher (Lady
Astor), 144
Larson, Amanda, 163
LaSalle National Bank, 157
LaSalle Theater Company, 108
Lauenstein, Albert N., 139
Lauenstein, Augusta, 139
Laughlin, Mary, 161
Laughlin, Nellie, 106
Lawton, Frederick, 195
Leahy, David, 166, 167
Learn of Me (statue), 203
Leavitt, Elaine E., 188
Lee, John H. S., 73
Legal Aid Society, 56
Lehmann, Ernst, 126
Lehmann, Otto W., 126
Lehmann, Otto W.(Mrs.), 126
Lehrer, Jim, 191
Leitch, Cecilia, 112
Leiter, Levi Z., 38
Lenz, Jacob Mayo, 177
Lenz, Mary, 177

Lenz Manufacturing Company,
177
Leopold, Nathan, 208
Letts, Frederick Clayton, 112,
148, 206
Letts, Marjorie Dodd, 112, *112*,
148, 206, 226, 227
Letts family, 115
Lewis, Diane Sabath, 211
Lewis, Jack, 116
Lewis, Milton "Mickey," 211
Lewis Clothing Co.
See William A. Lewis Clothing
Co.
Library of International Relations,
205
Lichtenstein, Roy, 154
Liecht, N. E., 54
Lill, William, 34, 34–36
Lill and Diversey (brewery), 30
Lincoln, Abraham, 72, 98
Lincoln, Robert Todd, 20, 53
Lincoln Park Board of
Commissioners, 36, 41, 43, 50,
51, 53, 54–55, 57, 59, 61
Lindberg, Emiy, 111
Lindbergh, Charles, 19
Linden, Frank H., 206
Linden, Kathleen H., 206
List, Claire, 178
List, Robert Stuart, 178, *178*
Live Stock National Bank, 114
Livingston, Phillip, 132
Lochridge, Florence Sturges,
164–65
Lochridge, Willard Fiske, 164–65
Loeb, Richard, 208
Lopakta, Anna, 106
Los Angeles Times, 100
Lourdenadin, Sir Morgan, 187
Lourdenadin family, 94
Lowden, Harriet, *125*
Luce, Clare Boothe, 155
Lundin, Elaine, 124
Lydon, Eugene K., 187
Lydon, Natalie C., 187
Lydon, William, 187
Lydon family, 94
Lyman, David B., Jr., 73
Lyons, Alice (daughter), 149, 190
Lyons, Alice (mother), 149
Lyons, Horace R., 149, *149*, 190
Lyons, Jeanette Jennings Gartz,
149, *149*

MacArthur, Douglas, 16, 162
MacArthur Foundation.
See John D. and Catherine T.
MacArthur Foundation
Madigan, Carol M., 194
Madigan, Joseph D., Jr., 194
Madigan's department story, 194,
194
Maher, Chauncey C., 206, *206*
Maher, Martha, 206
Mahin, John Lee, 15, 100, 226
Mahin, John Lee, Jr., 15, 100, *100*
Mahin, Julia Graham Snitzler, 100
Mahin, Margaret, 100
Mahin, Marian, 100
Mahin Advertising Agency, 100,
101

Mahoney, Joseph C., *131*
Manaster, Ina F., 197
Manaster, Murray L., 197
Manzoni, Carol, 197
Marble and Wilson, 77
March, Frederick, 100
Marcus, John, 138
Marie de Bourbon, 137
Marquis, Anna, 102
Marquis, Emily C., 102
Marquis, George Paull, 102
Marquis famiy, 115
Marshall, Benjamin H., 9, 10, 12,
13, 19, 72, 73, 76–83, *77*, 225, 227
Marshall, Caleb Howard, 77
Marshall, Celia F. Le Baillie, 10, 77
Marshall, Thurgood, 154
Marshall and Fox, 10, 19, 72, 73,
76, 79, 79–81, 82–83, 87–88
Marshall Field's, 209
Mary, Queen of Scots, 16, 127, *127*
Mason, Gregory, 104
Mathews, Walter, 115
Matuszczak, Klotylda, 162
Mavroudis, Constantine, 179
Mavroudis, Martha, 179
Maxwell, Katherine Hall, 95
May, Horatio N., 53, 54–55
Mayo Clinic, 197
Maywood Park Trotting
Association, 190
McAdams, Spike, *183*
McBurney, Cassius Clay, 146
McBurney, Geraldine, 146
McCarthy, Joseph, 179
McCarthy, Margaret, 114
McClurg, Alexander C., 75, 76
McClurg, Barbara Ogden, 94, 102,
104, *104*, 179
McClurg, Eleanor Wheeler, 94,
102, 104, *104*, 179
McClurg, Gertruce D. Schwarz,
94, 102–4, *103*, *104*, 179
McClurg, Marian Gordon Ewen,
102
McClurg, Ogden Trevor, 12, 70,
72, 73, 74, 75–76, 79, 86, 89, 94,
97, 102, 102–4, *103*, 124, 159,
179, 198, 225, 227
McClurg & Company.
See A. C. McClurg &
Company
McClurg family, 115
McCormick, Clarence, *195*
McCormick, Cyrus Hall, 29, 30,
34, 43, 53, 121, 173, 227
McCormick, Harold, 53, 86, 121,
121
McCormick, Leander, 173
McCormick, Muriel Rockefeller,
15, 119, 121, *121*, 132, 225, 227
McCormick, Robert Hall III, 173
McCormick, Robert R., 76
McCormick family, 20, 55, 122
McCormick Place, 299
McCormick Reaper Company,
173
McCoy, Homer W., 104
McCoy, Jessie O., 104
McCoy family, 115
McCreery, Jessica, 55

McDonald, Eugene Francis "E. F.", 158, 158–59
McDonald, Forrest, 130
McDonald, Inez Riddle, 158
McDonald, Jean Marianne, 158
McDonough, Lynne Madden, 172
McDonough, Paul H., 172
McDonough, Suzanne Clarke, 172
McDonough, William J., 172, 172
McDowell, R. Newton, 193, 225, 227
McEvoy, J. P., 90, 99, 188
McGillen, John, 72, 73
McGurn, Jack, 135
McIlvaine, John, 125
McIlvaine, Peggy, 125
McIntosh, Callas, 114
McIntosh, Donald, 114
McIntosh, Harry Milne, 114
McIntosh, Marjorie, 114
McIntosh family, 115
McKee, William, 63
McKinley, William, 63, 108
McKinlock, George Alexander, Jr., 119, 120, 121
McKinlock, George Alexander, Sr., 119, 119, 226
McKinlock, Marion Wallace Rappelye, 119, 119, 122
McLean, Margaret, 94, 102, 179
McLucas, Barbara Lyneis, 191
McLucas, Donald, 191
McManners, Billy, 68
McMillan, Donald, 159
McNabb, William J., 201
McNamara, Billy, 67
McNeill, A. C., 55
McNeill, B. G., 55
McWilliams, Elizabeth, 105–6, 227
McWilliams, Roy, 105, 105–6, 106, 227
Meakes, J.R., 171
Medill, Joseph, 26, 28
Melbye, Serena, 168
Melbye, Sverre, 168
Melbye, Victoria, 168
Merrill, Thomas W., 69
Mesta, Pearl, 192
Metropolitan Life Insurance, 92, 148
Metropolitan National Bank, 118
Michigan Avenue Trust Company, 110
Mies van der Rohe, Ludwig, 155, 173, 173
Milhaud, Darius, 132
Mill, John Stuart, 26
Miller, Bill, 179
Miller, Fred, 150
Miller, Harry, 181
Milstein, Nathan, 153
Mineta, Norman, 210
Mitchell, John, 207
Mitchell, Louise, 125
Model D-6 motor (Scripps), 98
Moloney, Maurice Thomas, 53, 54–61, 55
Monteux, Pierre, 132
Montez, Reymundo, 191
Montgomery Ward & Co, 113
Moore, Catherine, 95, 124, 179
Moore, George, 188

Moran, "Bugs," 135, 226
Moran, Linda, 127
More, M. M., 159
Morgan, J. P., 128, 130, 131, 163
Morton, Joy, 72
Morton, Mary, 176
Mosher, C. D., 50
Moyers, Bill, 155
Mullarkey, Margaret, 150
Mulvihill, Edward, 134–35
Mulvihill, Edward (Mrs.), 134–35
Mundelein, Cardinal, 131
Muni, Paul, 100
Munns, Gertrude, 192
Munns, Harriet Hollingshead, 192
Munns, John James, 192
Murchie, Guy, Jr., 161
Murphy, Margaret, 95, 124, 179
Muzak, 178

Nabisco, 77
National Builders Bank, 157
National Federation of Music Clubs, 143
National Institute of Social Science, 138
National Residency Matching Program, 191
National Society of Colonial Dames of America, 123
National Women's Democratic Club, 107
NATO, 195
Naughton, Mary, 142
Navistar, 173
Nehru, Jawaharlal, 19
Neidlinger, Eleanor, 193
Neidlinger, Harriet M., 193
Neidlinger, Phillip S., 193
Neidlinger, Phyliss, 193
Nelson, Doris E., 206
Nelson, Gust, 139
Nelson, Maurice "Sandy," Jr., 206
Nelson, Oscar, 186, 187
Newberry, Walter L., 56
Newberry Library, 55, 56
New York Central Railroad, 107
New York Times, 145
Nichols, Herman Armour, 126
Nichols, Lynette Craven, 126
Nichols, Marie Louise, 126
Nicks, Dorothy, 188
Niebuhr, Reinhold, 154
Niles, William, 64, 66
999 Lake Shore Drive Building Company, 89
Nitze, Paul, 152
Nixon, Richard, 177, 177, 207
Noble Network of Charter Schools, 194
Nordfeldt, Bror Julius Olsson, 105, 105
North, Grace H., 206
North, John Paul, 206
Northern Natural Gas Co., 207
Northern Trust Bank, 190
Northern Trust Company, 53
North Side Improvement Association, 34–36
North Side Land Association, 51, 53

Northwestern Memorial Hospital, 201
Northwestern University, 119, 120, 120, 123, 195, 206, 212
Northwestern University Settlement Association, 194
Nowan, Elsie, 99
N. W. Halsey & Co., 127

Obama, Barack, 16, 19
O'Brien, Terence. See Stewart, John Kerwin (a.k.a. Terence O'Brien)
O'Connor, Lawrence L., 207, 207
Ogden, Mahlon D., 26
Ogden, Sheldon & Co., 50, 55
Ogden, William B., 26, 29, 30, 34, 36, 43, 55, 61, 75
Ogilvie, Richard, 172
Oliver, Francis, 126, 132
Oliver, Frederick Stanley, 89, 90, 126, 126, 188
Oliver Company, 89
O'Malley, James, 68
O'Neal, Allie, 162
Oregonian, The, 176
Ortega y Gasset, José, 154
Oscar trophy, 186, 187
Osmond, Adele, 191
Osmond, Rob, 191
Owens, Jesse, 227

Packard Touring Car, 82
Paepcke, Anina, 150
Paepcke, Antonia, 150
Paepcke, Elizabeth Nitze, 15, 150–55, 151, 153, 154, 167, 174, 179, 212, 226, 227
Paepcke, Herman, 150, 152, 156
Paepcke, Paula, 150
Paepcke, Walter, 150, 150–55, 152, 153, 174, 227
Paepcke-Leicht Lumber Co., 156
Paine Webber, 99
Palmer, Bertha, 38, 38, 40–41, 43, 53, 56, 73
Palmer, Potter, 37–43 37, 53, 55, 102, 110, 225
Palmer family, 20
Palmer House Hotel, 38, 39, 40
Panje, Helen S., 206
Panje, William R., 206
Pardridge, Ed, 58, 59
Pardridge, Albert J., 80
Park, Mary, 125
Parker, Charlie, 199, 225
Parker, Clarence Farleigh, 106
Parker, Harriet Crangle, 106
Parker family, 115
Parkinson, Elizabeth D., 146, 174
Passavant Memorial Hospital, 206, 212
Patterson, William, 153
Patton, George, 145
Payne, Monroe, 145
Peabody, Francis Stuyvesant, 108, 108, 124
Peabody, Marian Bryant, 108, 108
Peabody Coal Company, 108, 110
Peabody Fairbanks investment bank, 107

Peabody Museum of Anthropology and Ethnology, 160
Peason, Matilda, 124
Pentron Electronics, 199
Percival, Franklin, 135
Perlman, Itzhak, 154
Perrette, Clarisse, 196
Pfeifer, Friedl, 152, 153
Phelps Dodge, 163
Piatigorsky, Gregor, 154
Pike, Charles Burrall, 108, 108
Pike, Frances Alger, 108
Pine Street Land Association, 51, 53, 57, 59
Pinkerton, Allan, 125, 227
Pokagon, Charles, 63–64
Pokagon, Simon (chief of Potawatomi), 62, 63
Pope, Antoinette, 201, 201
Pope, Francois, 201, 201
Pope, Robert, 201
Potter, Charles S., 104
Potter, Trevor, 81, 94
Powell, Catherine, 111
Powers, Tom, 135
P. Palmer and Company, 37
Pray, Mary Sherlock, 192, 192, 208
Pray, Max L., 192, 208
Presbyterian Hospital, 191
Princess Electric Iron, 109
Procter & Gamble Company, 147
Prohibition Enforcement for Illinois, 195
Proust, Marcel, 190
Prussing, Florence Whiting Bourne, 174
Prussing, Rudolph, 174
Public Enemy, The, 135, 135
Puestow, Charles B., 197, 197, 226
Puestow, Lorraine Knowles, 197
Pullman, George, 38, 125, 227
Pullman, Madeleine Childs, 125, 125
Pullman, Margaret Allen, 125
Pullman, William A., 125, 125
Pullman, William Allan Pinkerton, 125
Pullman, William C., 125
Pullman Company, 125
Pullman family, 16
Purdy, James, 199

Quiding, Merie, 139
Quiet Light Securities, 206

Rang, Eugenie "Jean" Farrow, 146, 209
Rang, Fifi Schultz, 146
Rang, Louise A., 146, 209
Ransom, Christina L., 196, 196
Ransom, Woodbury, Jr., 196, 196
Rascher Company, 48
Rathbone, Basil, 136, 138, 138, 179
Rauschenberg, Robert, 154
Ravel, Maurice, 132
Ready, John J., 163
Reagan, Ronald, 177, 210, 213, 213
Red Cross Canteen, 119
Red Cross Motor Corps, 104
Reed, Helen Shedd, 112, 227
Reed, Kersey Coates, 112

Reed, Mary C., 112
Reilly, Annette May Cunco, 173
Reilly, Carlin Walker, 146
Reilly, Frank Kennicott, 146, 211
Reilly, Frank Kennicott (Mrs.), 211
Reilly, James Wilson, 15, 173
Reilly, Madeleine, 173
Reilly, Meric, 173
Reilly & Lee, 146
Reis, Allison Seed, 168
Reis, Mike, 168
Reiswitz, Kurt von, 106
Reliance of Philadelphia, 97
Remus, George, 138
Reproduction and Fertility Clinic, 168
Requa, Charles, 205
ReQua, Eloise, 15, 205, 205, 225, 227
Requa, Susan, 205
Requa, William, 16, 205
Riedmayer, Anne, 167
Rigali, Helen Houlahan, 170
Rigali, John Emil, Jr., 170
Roach, Max, 199
Robbins, Lewis, 161
Roberts, George, Jr., 125
Robertson, Richard, 125
Robert the Bruce, 127
Robson, David, 164
Rockefeller, Edith, 53, 121, 227
Rockefeller, John D., 121
Rockefeller family, 20
Roephenack, Leona, 150
Rogers, Burney, 116–17
Rogers, J. E., 146
Rogers, J. H., 208
Rollander, Jennie, 99
Roosevelt, Eleanor, 176
Roosevelt, Franklin, 160, 176, 193
Roosevelt, Theodore, 130, 130, 159
Rose, Landon Cabell, 110
Rose, Louise Grout, 110
Rose & Co., 110
Ross & Hardies, 197
Rostand, Edmond, 53
Rothesay, Duke of, 127
Rove, Karl, 175
Roxbury Latin School, 75
Royden, James Keith, 142, 143
Royden, Marie Morrisey, 142–43, 143
R. R. Donnelley & Sons, 113, 209
Rubinstein, Arthur, 154
Ruscoe, A. A., 171
Russell, Brewster & Co., 163
Russell, Ed, 128
Russell, Edward Perry, 163, 163
Ryan Car Company, 111
Ryerson, Adelaide Hamilton, 98, 123, 227
Ryerson, Edwin, 98, 123

Salerno-Sonnenberg, Nadja, 154
Salter, Leslie E., 131
Sampsell, Margaret Carr, 209, 209
Sampsell, Marshall Gross, 209
Sampsell, Mary "Niki," 209
Sampsell, Miranda Carr, 209
Sand, George, 137
Sandburg, Carl, 15–16
Sandquist, Anna, 109

Sanitary Scale Company, 157
Sawyer, Charles, 195
S. C. Griggs & Co., 75
Schleh, Helen F., 150
Schneider, E. L., 78
Schneider Jr. & Son.
    See E. L. Schneider Jr. & Son
Schock, Bigford and Company, 26
Schroeppel, Margaret, 157
Schwarzenegger, Arnold, 210
Schweitzer, Albert, 16, 152, 154
Sciaky, David, 16, 189, 189–90, 226, 227
Sciaky, Mario, 189
Sciaky, Maurice, 189
Sciaky, Sam, 189
Sciaky, Yvonne, 189, 189–90
Sciaky family, 166
Sciaky welder, 189
Scott, Edith Wells, 94, 187
Scott, George Eaton, 159
Scott, John, 58
Screenwriter's Guild, 100
Scripps Motor Company, 98, 98
Seaman, Adelaide M. Herzberg, 136
Seaman, George Milton, 136, 192
Seaman, Margaret, 136
Seaman, Mary, 136
Seaman Paper Company, 136
Sears, Roebuck and Company, 149, 178, 207
Sebush, Mary, 102
Seed, Deborah, 168
Seed, Deeda, 168
Seed, Jennifer, 168
Seed, Lindon, 168
Seed, Randolph W., 168
Seed, Richard, 168
Seed, Vanessa, 168
SEI Information Technology, 213
Selfridge, Harry, 53
Sengstack, David K., 174
Seurat, Georges, 123, 123
Shaw, Hiram, 114, 226
Shaw, Louise "Lola" Shepard, 114, 124, 227
Shaw, Nathaniel, 114
Shaw, Ralph Martin, 114, 114, 226
Shaw, Ralph Martin, Jr., 114
Shaw, Thomas, 114
Shaw family, 115
Shawnee III, 98
Shedd, John G., 112, 227
Sheldon, Henry I., 43, 50, 53
Shepard, Frances Welles, 107, 107, 227
Shepard, Henry Martyn, 76, 76, 107, 124
Shepard, Louise M., 124
Shepard, Perry M., 107
Shepard, Stuart Gore, 12, 70, 72, 73, 76, 79, 89, 107, 225, 227
Shepard family, 115
Sherlock Holmes, 138, 138
Sherman, William Tecumsch, 75
Shore, Dinah, 138
Sibley, Frederick, 145
Sidley & Austin, 197
Simmons, Kate W. "Kitty" Pope, 108, 226

Simmons, Russell Mix "Manny," 108
Sinclaire, Upton, 177
Sisto, Vittorio, 172
Skidmore, Louis, Jr., 209
Skidmore, Louis, Jr. (Mrs.), 209
Skolnick, Sherman, 207
Slade, Alma L., 159
Slade, Samuel, 159
Slatkin, Leonard, 154
Smith, Alexander, 109, 299
Smith, Anita, 125
Smith, Mary, 109, 148, 225, 299
Smith family, 115
Smithsonian/Folkways Records, 174
Smothers, Tommy, 199
Snead, Jack, 16
Snead, Jack L. S., Jr., 171
Snead, Kathryn W., 171
Snyder, George W. K., 167, 193
Snyder, John, 195
Snyder, Mildred Swift, 193
Sons of the American Revolution, 110
Spalding, Albert, 38
Spector, David P., 190
Spector, Lorraine, 190
Spender, Stephen, 154
Spinden, Herbert, 104
Stack, Christopher, 212
Stack, James K., Jr., 212
Stack, James K., Sr., 212, 212
Stack, John, 212
Stack, Mary, 212
Stake, Ailvirlge, 205
Staley, Arlene D., 197
Staley, William D., 197
Standard Oil, 117
Standard Oil of California, 143
Standard Oil of Indiana, 14, 113
Stauffer, Walter Henry, 96–97
Stavinsky, Igor, 154
Steelman, John R., 195
Stein, Deborah, 206
Stein, Robert, 206
Stelle, John M., 195
Stephens, Mary, 114
Stern, Isaac, 155
Stevens, J. Alexander, 208
Stevens, John Paul, 154
Stevens, Jolene, 208
Stevenson, Adlai Ewing, 54, 108
Stevenson, Adlai III, 170
Stewart, Alexander, 115
Stewart, Jeanne, 109
Stewart, John Kerwin (a.k.a. Terence O'Brien), 109, 225
Stewart, Julia Pearl Butler, 109
Stewart, Phillip B., 193
Stewart, Wilhelmina H., 193
Stewart-Warner Speedometer Corporation, 109
Stillwell, Addison E., 124, 226
Stillwell, Addison H., 124, 124
Stillwell, Edith, 199
Stillwell, May Henderson, 124
Stillwell, May Peabody, 124
Stillwell Lumber, 124
St. Luke's Hospital, 56, 123
Stock, Frederick, 169
Stockton, Richard, 53

Stone, Grace, 99
Stoody, Clyde A., 162
Straus & Co.
    See S. W. Straus & Co.
Straw, H. Foster, 106
Straw, Virginia Parker, 106
Streeter, Elma, 67, 68, 69, 83
Streeter, George Wellington, 22, 43, 44, 45, 45–48, 58, 59, 61, 62, 63–70, 64, 67, 68, 70, 71, 83, 83, 126, 225
Streeter, Maria Mulholland, 45–48, 67, 68
Streeter, Miss R. D., 69
Stuart, Charles, 127, 130, 226
Stuart, Elizabeth Barnes, 127, 131, 227
Stuart, George, 127, 163, 191, 226
Stuart, Harold Leonard, 127–31, 129, 226
Stuart, Harriet Barnes, 127, 131, 226
Stuart family, 15
Stumpel, Mary, 163
Sudbury Star, 171
Sudler & Company, 92, 94, 166
Suito, Segunda, 162
Sullivan, Marie, 194
Sullivan, Stephen, 194
Sullivan, Wesley, 194
Sunbeam, 109
Suzuki Method, 174
Swanson, Agnes, 112
Swanson, Rita, 94, 97
Swift, Edward Foster "E. F.", Jr., 159, 227
Swift, Gustavus, 97, 159
Swift, Kathryn Thompson Matlier, 159
Swift, Ruth May, 97
Swift & Company, 159
Swift family, 16
Swing, David, 53
S. W. Straus & Co., 89
Symington, Stuart, 195
Szalay, Nancy K., 172
Szalay, Robert N., 172

Tackett, Pamela, 198
Tackett, Vera Pearl Hutchinson, 198
Tackett, William Clarence, 198, 198
Taft, Robert A., 112
Tarzan of the Apes (Burroughs), 74, 75, 227
Taylor, E. S., 55
Taylor, Martin, 109
Telephone and Data System, Inc., 197
Tenak Products Company, 95
Tennyson, Alfred Lord, 26
Thatcher, Margaret, 16, 155
Thibodeaux, Carrie, 195
Thibodeaux, Harold, 195
Thompson, Charles Donald (Mr. and Mrs.), 112
Thompson, Jim, 16
Thompson, J. Walter.
    See J. Walter Thompson Company
Thompson, Laura, 125

Thompson, William Hale, 83
Thorne, James Ward (Mrs.), 113
Thyes, Matilda, 104
Tiffany's, 209
Tillet, Gladey, 176
Time-Warner, 174
Tobin, Maurice, 195
Toig, Randall, 201
Toig, Teri, 201
Torrio, Johnny, 134
Toulmin, Harry Aubrey, Jr., 182
Toulouse-Lautrec, Henri de, 123, 123, 227
Townsend, Charles D., 114
Townsend, Mary H., 114
Townsend family, 113
Toynbee, Arnold, 154
Tracy, Spencer, 100
Traveler's Aid, 187
Trayner, Charles J., 110, 190
Trayner, Elizabeth, 110
Trayner, John, 110
Trayner, Owen, Jr., 190
Trayner, Owen R., Sr., 110, 190
Trayner, Veronica, 190
Tree, Lambert, 51
Tremont Hotel, 66
Trilling, Lionel, 155
Truman, Harry, 177, 178, 195
Tucker, John, 180
Tucker, Lucille Tucker Holmes, 299
Tucker, Mary Lee, 180
Tucker, Noble, 180
Tucker, Preston, 180, 180–85, 183, 227, 299
Tucker, Preston, Jr., 180
Tucker, Shirley, 180
Tucker, Vera, 180
Tucker 48, 180, 180, 185
Tucker automobile, 180–83, 180–85, 185
Tucker Corporation, 181, 181–85
Tucker family, 94
Tucker: The Man and the Dream, 180
Tucker Torpedo, 180
Tully, Margaret, 114
Turnbull, Joseph, 183
Turner, Lana, 138
Tyler, Louise T., 114
Tyler, Theodore, 114

Uihlein, Alessandra Branca, 198, 213
Uihlein, Alex, 198, 213
Uihlein, Andrew, 198
Uihlein, Anna Lucca, 198
Uihlein, Stephen Ellis, 198, 213
UNESCO, 178
Union Stockyards, 104
Union Stock Yards & Transit Company, 114
United Charities of Chicago, 56
United Nations War Relief, 107
United States Pipe and Foundry Company, 114
University of Chicago, 98, 178, 196
University of Illinois, 195
Upham, Frederick W., 110, 110
Upham, Helen Hall, 110

USAuction Inc., 199
U.S. Department of Defense Munitions Board, 195
U.S. Energy Department, 213
U.S. Energy Regulation Commission, 213
U.S. Office of Management and Budget, 213
Valliant, R. D., 193
Vanderbilt family, 128
Van Diver, Lewis H., 58
van Gogh, Vincent, 111, 111, 227
Van Horn, John, 191
Van Horn, Penelope, 191
Varese, Edgar, 132
Vaughan, Sarah, 199
Verlaine, Paul, 169
Victor Emmanuel (king), 173
Victoria (queen), 26, 28
Vidal, Gore, 199
Vieregg, Carilane Newman, 191
Vieregg, R. Todd, 191
Villa, Pancho, 16, 144, 144–45, 227
Villard, Henry, 128
Visiting Nurse Association, 104
Vittum, Daniel W., Jr., 194, 202
Vogel, Charles, 48
Voges, Mickie, 205
Volcker, Paul, 172
Von Bernsdorff, Johann Heinrich, 156, 157
Von Reiswitz, Kurt, 156, 157

Wagner, Ralph C., 178, 178, 179, 227
Walker, Bertrand, 107
Walker, Ida Fleetwood Drew, 107
Walker, Marie Antoinette, 114
Waller, James Breckenridge, 169
Waller, J. B., Jr., 169
Wall family, 94
Walls, Elizabeth Dickason, 124, 179
Walls, Francis X., 95, 124, 179
Walsh, Delia, 136
Walska, Ganna, 121, 122, 132
Warhol, Andy, 154
Warner Brothers, 178
Warner Instrument Company, 109
Warren, Earl, 177
War Risk Insurance Bureau, 89
Washburn Company, 107
Washington, George, 169
Washington D.C. Metro, 204, 204
Watkins, William A. P., 125
Wayne, "Mad" Anthony, 114
Weber, Alma, 162
Weiner, Egon, 203
Wells, Orson, 121
Westbrook, Wesley, 135
Western Grocery, 112
Westinghouse Electric Supply Company, 142
Westminister Abbey, 149
Wheeler, Eleanor, 75
Whitaker, Clement Sherman, 175, 175–77
Whitaker, Leone Baxter, 175, 175–77
White, Bryon, 210
White, Jack, 135
Whitehouse, Francis M., 74

Whiting, Francis, 104
Widermann, Johanna, 155, 195
Wilder, Thornton, 154
Wilhelm II (kaiser), 156
Wilkinson, Brence, 168
Wilkinson, David, 168
Willett, Alvin T., 146
Willett, Charmain, 146
Willett, Florence Collins, 15, 146
Willett, Helen, 146
Willett, Walter D., 16, 146, 168
Willett bus, 146, 146
Willett Company, 146
William A. Lewis Clothing Co., 211, 211
Williams, Nanny, 110
Wilms, Herman, 156
Wilms, Lydia Paepcke, 156, 173
Wilms, Paula, 156, 157
Wilms, William, 156, 156–57, 173, 226
Wilson, John P., 104
Wilson, June, 104
Wilson, Woodrow, 108, 149
Winchell, Walter, 138
Windes, Thomas G., 58, 59, 61
Winston, Payne, Strawn and Shaw, 114
Winston & Meagher, 114
Winterbotham, Amelia A., 13, 111
Winterbotham, John Russell, 111
Winterbotham, Joseph, 111
Winterbotham, Joseph, Jr., 111
Winterbotham, Katherine, 111
Winterbotham family, 115
Wizard of Oz, The, 16, 100, 100, 146, 226
Wolin-Levin, Inc., 15, 94, 166
Wood, Ernest, 97
Wood, Leonard (general), 144
Wood, Robert E. (general), 149, 178
Wood, Sarah, 149
Woodward, Bob, 207
Woodward, Ray, 106
Worthy, John, 53, 54
Wren, Christopher, 115
Wright, Emily Muir, 208
Wright, Frank Lloyd, 99
Wright, Judith Beebe, 208
Wright, Kenneth M., 208

Yeltsin, Boris, 154
Yoyo (Duncan Toys Company), 211, 211

Zechman, Jan, 209
Zenith Radio Corporation, 158
Zenith short wave radio, 159
Zenith TV set, 158
Zenner Consulting Group, 201
Ziegfield, Florenz, 82, 82
Ziegfield Follies, 82
Zinzow, Dorothy M., 168
Zinzow, John R., 168
Zorn, Anders, 43, 56

About the Author

R ichard "Rick" Fizdale has entered the fourth stage of his life. Growing up on the north side of Chicago an inch above the poverty line, he found refuge in reading and talking. As an eightyear-old, he walked five blocks to grammar school with other boys and girls, all of whom were younger than Rick and lived in the same vermin infested tenement. To keep the others from wandering off, Rick made up a story about pirates that began in September and ended in June. Thankfully, the long-winded serial tale has been lost to memory.

As an angry young man, Rick drifted into the hippie haze and anti-war protests of the 1960s. He wasn't a leader. Like Forrest Gump, he was just there. On a heady day in May 1967, he met various illuminati of the counter culture—Allen Ginsberg, Phil Ochs, Paul Krassner, Timothy Leary and Jerry Rubin at Abbie and Anita Hoffman's apartment in Greenwich Village. That night he was introduced to Leonard Bernstein backstage at Lincoln Center. His writing career almost began the next morning when Rick started to outline a series of stories about going nowhere, doing nothing and stumbling into history. The project died in the fall of 1967 after the March on the Pentagon. For the entire day, Rick was a few yards behind Norman Mailer. What Mailer saw, he also saw. When Rick read Mailer's account of the protest, *Armies of the Night*, he was struck by the iron grip of Mailer's memory and his ripened ability to describe what Rick knew was uncannily accurate. Intimidated by the work of a literary bully, Rick gave up writing. During the street theater of the 1968 Democratic Convention, he made the unwilling acquaintance of various members of the Chicago Police, the Red Squad and the FBI. A friendly cop suggested that he get a job. Thus began the third phase of his life.

On the first working day of 1969, he went to work as

BART HARRIS, CHICAGO

the lowest paid copywriter for the Leo Burnett Company, a large global advertising agency. When he retired on the last working day of 2000, he had been its chairman of the board, chief executive officer and chief creative officer. During Rick's time at the helm, Leo Burnett handled some of the world's largest clients—McDonald's, Coca-Cola, P&G, Kellogg's, General Motors, Philip Morris, United Airlines, Nestlé, Kraft, Hallmark and Allstate.

Stage four overlapped three. It commenced when Rick moved to Chicago's East Lake Shore Drive in the late 1980s. He purchased two apartments in 999 in 1991. Having fallen in love with the building, with time on his hands and an itch he had never scratched, he agreed to author its history as part of a celebration of its 100th anniversary.

ABOUT THE TYPE

*The book is set in LTC Kennerley, originally designed
by Frederic W. Goudy in 1911 for the American Type Founders.
It was named after publisher Mitchell Kennerley.*

*"999" on the jacket front and initial capitals throughout the book
are set in Goudy Old Style BT, also originally designed by Goudy,
a seminal figure in American design.*

*In the late nineteenth century, Goudy worked
at the A. C. McClurg publishing house, where he learned about design
and type from George Millard, who ran the Saint and Sinners Corner
in the bookstore owned by Ogden Trevor McClurg's father.*